Science

Has science disposed of God?

John Blanchard

EP Books (Evangelical Press), 1st Floor Venture House, 6 Silver Court, Watchmead, Welwyn Garden City, UK, AL7 1TS
sales@epbooks.org   www.epbooks.org

In the USA, EP Books are distributed by JPL Books, 3741 Linden Ave. S.E., Wyoming, MI 49548
Office:877-683-6935
order@jplbooks.com   www.jplbooks.com

This book is based on material from *Has Science Got Rid of God?* by John Blanchard, first published 2004.

British Library Cataloguing in Publication Data available

ISBN 978-1-78397-167-1

Contents

Preface

Science and belief in God are two of the most pervasive influences the world has ever known and they affect virtually every person now living on our planet. Use an internet search engine to search 'science' or 'religion' or 'science and religion': you will have millions of sites crammed with facts and figures, claims and counter-claims, ideas and opinions.

For many people, combining the science with belief in God is precisely the problem, as they are often held to be diametrically opposed to each other. One writer began a book on the subject with the words: 'The divorce between science and religion is one of the most significant aspects of our modern philosophical scene.' There are times when this 'divorce' expresses itself in a kind of 'cold war', with both sides ignoring each other. At other times the 'hot war' spills across the media, sometimes sparked by such things as a new scientific discovery, an exciting archaeological 'find', a medical breakthrough that raises moral or ethical issues, or the educational establishment's way of teaching about the origins of the world or of the human race.

The idea that science and belief in God are in conflict has had a long shelf life, dating at least from the last third of the nineteenth century, but does it have any solid basis? Are we forced to take one side or the other? Must we accept that they will always be at loggerheads? Is there no case for saying that each has a valid part to play in our understanding of reality and in our daily experience?

If you are looking for a comprehensive examination of these questions that delves into every nook and cranny of scientific discovery and expounds the depths of religious thought over the centuries you will obviously need to look elsewhere — including those millions of internet pages! The book you are holding is nothing more than a basic outline of the fundamental issues involved, yet I believe it points to there being a clear and convincing answer to the question the subtitle asks.

John Blanchard
Banstead
Surrey
July 2016

1 Fine-tuning the question

Let me come clean. I am neither a scientist nor the son of a scientist. This may seem an unpromising start, but half a century of fascination with the subject, fuelled by countless hours of reading, discussion and note-taking, to say nothing of access to a cascade of information on the internet, provides more than enough expert information and analysis to offer a straightforward resolution to the conflict indicated in the book's subtitle.

First things first: what is 'science'? Science seeks to discover, observe and understand the principles and laws that govern the natural world. It is not static, but dynamic; not a product, but a process; not an entity, but an enterprise. It is 'work in progress', an honest, open-ended, ongoing, objective, painstaking pursuit of reliable knowledge about our world and everything in it. It addresses an endless stream of questions, using what we now call 'the scientific method' — observation, the formulation of hypotheses that fit the data, the examination of other possibilities, and repeated experiments (that can either succeed or fail). When scientists have jumped through all those hoops they can reasonably claim to have established a scientific theory. To put all of this more simply, science is the ongoing process of learning things about the natural world. We shall use this as a working definition from now on.

In dealing with 'God' we must begin by defining 'religion'. The *Oxford Dictionary of English* defines it as 'the belief in and worship of a superhuman controlling power, especially a personal God or gods', and scientist Sir John Houghton notes that religion has always been a universal phenomenon: 'There is general evidence that most human beings, from whatever part of the world and from the earliest times, have exhibited a fundamental belief in a divine being or beings, and in some sort of spiritual world.' Religion comes in all shapes and sizes and its claims range from the amusing to the amazing.

The big five

These days it is fashionable to lump all religions together and to say that they all amount to the same thing but as we can easily show, the idea that all religions are equally valid paths to ultimate spiritual reality falls apart at the seams as soon as we try to pick it up.

Consider the five main religions:

Hinduism, which dates back at least as far as 3,000 B.C., has a bewildering assortment of religious and philosophical ideas is said to accommodate no fewer than thirty-three million gods.

Buddhism is based on the teachings of Siddhartha Gautama, who was born about 563 B.C. Some modern Buddhists worship him, along with many other gods borrowed from Hinduism, but traditional Buddhism does not have a personal god.

Islam is the youngest and second largest of the world's major religions. Its teachings are enshrined in the Qur'an, made up of visions said to have been received by Muhammad, who was born in the Arabian city of Mecca at some time between A.D. 570-580. Like Buddha, Muhammad made no claim to divinity. Islam's deity is Allah, an austere and remote figure unaffected by people's actions and attitudes and 'not personally knowable'.

Judaism's teaching is derived from the Bible's Old Testament but is centred on the Torah. This consists of writings based on the first five books of the Bible. Judaism stresses the uniqueness and transcendence of

God, but not his intimate interaction with humankind.

Christianity takes the entire Bible to be 'the living and enduring word of God'. There are variations within Christianity, but I will take the time here to outline Christianity as the Bible reveals it. This reveals God as the sovereign creator of all reality outside of himself, including time and space. God did not create because he had to, but because he chose to. Nothing in creation needs any justification beyond the fact that in his infinite wisdom God willed it to be, and in his infinite power brought it into being. God is not merely a cosmic force or 'higher power', but is both personal and eternally self-existent. He exists as a Trinity of distinguishable persons, identified in the Bible as the Father, the Son and the Holy Spirit. He is perfect in all his ways, unchangeable and abounding in love.

He is the sole and sovereign ruler over all that he has made: He sustains the entire created order and governs the natural world, the spiritual world, international affairs, earthly authorities and the lives of individual human beings: he 'works out everything in conformity with the purpose of his will'. Ultimately, the final destiny of every human being is in his hands and he will 'judge the world with justice'.

God's relationship with humankind is centred in the fact that about 2,000 years ago he broke into history in the person of Jesus Christ, who assumed humanity while retaining his deity. His virgin birth, perfect life and voluntary death in the place of others were all hallmarks of his deity, confirmed by his resurrection from the dead, which showed him to be 'the true God', who promises the forgiveness of sins and eternal life to all who put their trust in him.

Even on the basis of this sketchy overview, it is perfectly obvious that all religions are not the same. Even an entrenched atheist like Bertrand Russell noted, 'It is evident as a matter of logic that, since they disagree, not more than one of them can be true,' while the *Daily Telegraph's* Janet Daley fine-tuned the point: 'You cannot defend all faiths — at least not at the same time — because each has beliefs that render those of the others false.'

Nor is there any mileage in the trendy idea that a given religion may be 'true for one person but not for another'. As a one writer said, 'To say "All roads lead to God" is as illogical as saying that a bus ride to the shops is much the same as taking a trip to the moon on a space shuttle. The route, mode of transport and destination are all completely different!'

Although some of what is to follow is true of the relationship between science and all religious faiths, I am writing as a committed Christian, convinced intellectually, emotionally and experientially that the entire Bible is 'God-breathed', an inerrant revelation of God's nature and will.

2 Scientism: the godless god

Now that we have nailed down our definitions, we can tackle the issue head-on: is science, the ongoing, open-ended search for truth in the natural world, really in conflict with the God revealed in the Bible? Some have said that science has disposed of any need for God and they further affirm that the scientific view is the only valid one, a view for which it is not difficult to find an eloquent spokesman. Peter Atkins is a very highly qualified scientist, and also a passionate and eloquent atheist who claims that science has now obliterated God. In the course of a debate at Oxford University in 1998 he said, 'I am on the brink of understanding everything and I commend you to use your brains, because your brains are the most wonderful

instruments in the universe, and through
you will see that you can do without God. '
necessity for God *because science can explain*
Four years later he described religions as 'qu ___ ways
of disguising ignorance, propagating wishful thinking
and exercising power over the ignorant and weak',
then targeted Christianity in particular, accusing it of
propagating 'manifest nonsense that is totally
incompatible with our scientific understanding of the
world'.

This is rousing language — but it is not science!
Instead, it is *scientism*, also known as materialism,
which uses much of science's terminology, but has few
of its virtues. Far from being part of science,
materialism is a philosophy about science. It says that
all of reality can be explained without the need to go
beyond the material or natural, and that only natural
(as opposed to supernatural or spiritual) laws and
forces are at work in the world. More concisely put,
this says that everything in the world can be reduced
to matter and chance.

The agenda

As we shall see in a later chapter, modern science can
be said to date from the time when scientists who
believed in God as the creator of the universe began to
lean heavily on the scientific method in investigating
natural causes. Scientism has turned the whole process
on its head by rejecting God altogether, claiming that

only natural causes exist and that they do so independently. Materialism has a powerful grip on contemporary society, especially in mainstream educational circles.

Recent surveys in the United States seem to confirm this. While about 90% of those polled said they believed in God, only about 40% of scientists said so, while among members of the prestigious U.S. National Academy of Sciences (the 'top brass' of the country's scientists) the figure dropped to less than 10%. Just as importantly, the group of scientists most responsible for presenting 'science' to the wider community is dominated by people who have explicitly adopted atheism and a materialistic philosophy of life.

Nobody provides a better example of this than Peter Atkins. After the September 11 terrorist attacks the British government moved to introduce a law aimed at preventing 'incitement to religious hatred'. In response, Peter Atkins wrote a letter in which he railed against religion as denying the power of the human intellect, encouraging laziness as a mode of argument, being deceitful in offering benefits in the afterlife, blighting individual freedom and encouraging violence. His two opening sentences revealed the aim that lay behind the assault: '*This letter is intended to be an incitement to religious hatred*. I believe it is not yet a crime to encourage people to despise religion and almost all it stands for, but as time is running out for freedom of expression, I thought it appropriate to try and save the world from itself before it is too late.'

This confirms materialism's agenda, which is to free mankind from all forms of religious belief: firstly, because religion insists that there is a spiritual world beyond nature; and, secondly, because in the materialist's eyes religion is irrational, depending on nothing more than faith at best and superstition at worst, something that developed during a primitive stage in the evolution of the human species.

Richard Dawkins, perhaps Britain's best-known atheist, makes no bones about this. In a television interview he expressed his annoyance that some people 'spend enormous amounts of time learning church teachings' because 'to me, religion is very largely an enemy of truth'. Elsewhere, he famously attacked religion as 'a virus of the mind' and called religious faith 'stupefied superstition'.

As far as the Christian faith is concerned, attacking it as mere superstition is misplaced. What we need to grasp here is that materialists are driven, not by the kind of facts they demand in their science, but by their world-view. Wherever the evidence seems to point, they refuse to go beyond physics to metaphysics.

It would be difficult for anyone to be more up-front about this than Professor Richard Lewontin: 'Our willingness to accept scientific claims that are against common sense is the key to an understanding of the real struggle between science and the supernatural.

We take the side of science *in spite* of the patent absurdities of some of its constructs, *in spite* of its failure to fulfil many of its extravagant promises of health and life, *in spite* of the tolerance of the scientific community for just-so stories, *because we have a prior commitment to materialism.* ... Moreover that materialism is absolute for *we cannot allow a Divine foot in the door*.'

Stephen Barr underlines the importance of this as we try to answer the question being posed in this book: 'What many take to be a conflict between religion and science is really something else. It is a conflict between religion and materialism. Materialism regards itself as scientific, and indeed is often called 'scientific materialism', even by its opponents, *but it has no legitimate claim to be part of science*.'

Questions

If materialism is true it raises a raft of questions to which it can produce no answers:

- If there is no absolute beyond the existence of matter, how can there be a transcendent truth that tells us this is the case?

- If human beings are nothing more than accidental items in a universal mass of matter — Atkins says that humankind is 'just a bit of slime on a planet' —

how can a person have individual value or personal worth?

- If matter is all there is, what possible meaning can we give to concepts such as good, evil, morality, justice, truth, love, beauty, desire, or hope?

- How does the materialist explain creativity in the worlds of music, drama, art — or science, for that matter?

- If human beings are purely material, where can we find a source for imagination or belief?

- If a human being is just a mass of matter, how or why does he or she remember the past, evaluate the present and anticipate the future?

These are no more than examples of the questions materialism has to face because it refuses to recognize an important distinction — namely, that while science is a tool which man can use with amazing effectiveness in many areas, there are many other areas beyond its reach. We shall develop this in the next chapter, but we should no more expect science to answer every question we can ask than we should use a pea-shooter to launch a space probe, or a pickaxe to do brain surgery.

Men or machines?

The questions we have posed so far are more than awkward for materialists, but these are not the only ones they have to face. This is because materialism goes hand in glove with determinism, which says that everything we do is conditioned by heredity and environment. The link is obvious: if there is no God, or other transcendent reality, all we have is a closed, mechanistic universe, with humankind as one of its 'working parts'. Nobody seriously denies that some chemical, psychological and sociological factors affect the way people think and act, but this falls a long way short of determinism, which says that *all* our decisions are the inevitable result of materialistic factors over which we have no control.

As human beings, we are not only aware of sensations, we reflect on them. We engage in complex reasoning and lateral thinking; we evaluate data, develop ideas, exercise imagination and make decisions. Yet Peter Atkins insists that '... at the deepest level, decisions are adjustments of the dispositions in the molecules inside large numbers of cells in the brain.' Richard Dawkins takes the same line and argues that love is 'a product of highly complicated equipment of some sort, nervous equipment or computing equipment of some sort'. But is this an adequate explanation of the powerful emotions and life-changing experiences we associate with the word 'love'? Materialists lean heavily on this kind of thinking, but another scientist easily pointed out its radical and fatal flaw: 'If we are nothing but atoms and molecules organized in a particular way through the chance processes of evolution, then love, beauty, good and evil, free will, reason itself — indeed all that makes us human and raises us above the rest of the created order — lose their objectivity. Why should I love my neighbour, or go out of my way to help him? Rather, why should I not get everything I can for myself, trampling on whoever gets in my way?'

Materialistic determinism cannot possibly be squared with moral, responsible human living. The difference between human beings and machines is not just relative, but absolute.

True science is honest, open-ended, reasonable and humble. Scientism is exactly the opposite. It is pseudo-science, and not only arrogant, irrational and illogical, but cruel, robbing us of any basis for dignity, meaning, purpose or hope. As Peter Atkins openly admits, 'Everything is driven by motiveless, purposeless decay.'

Unbelieving believers

In the course of a visit to South Africa a few years ago, I was invited to take part in a radio programme produced in Cape Town. For days beforehand the programme was trailed as 'Believer versus Unbeliever'. The one-hour show began with the presenter (an atheist) introducing me as the believer and himself as the unbeliever, but in my opening comments I questioned the whole premise of the programme and insisted that he, too, was a believer. He strongly challenged this, but I pointed out, 'I gladly admit that I am a believer — I believe in the existence of God. But you are a believer too — you believe in the non-existence of God. What I would like you to share with the listeners is the evidence on which you base your faith in God's non-existence.' He was completely at a loss what to say. This was hardly surprising, because one would need to possess all the evidence available in the universe before one could be sure that there is none pointing to God's existence.

People can choose *what* to believe, but not *whether* to believe, as faith is built into the whole business of being human. As one writer put it, 'Those who characterize themselves as "unbelievers" do not believe in nothing. On the contrary, they often have a very definite set of beliefs, which may be held just as passionately as so-called "believers" hold to the tenets of their faith.' We shall pursue this in a later chapter, but the point needs to be made here because it holes scientism below the waterline. Science makes much of the verification principle, which says that in order to be accepted as true a theory must be capable of verification or falsification. But if this is the case, how can we prove scientifically that the only reality is that which can be proved scientifically? Scientism says, 'What you see is what you get' — *but how can we know this?* When scientism says that only what can be known and proved by science is rational and true it is being *irrational*, because the claim itself cannot be proved scientifically! To say that 'Seeing is believing' is hardly good enough. For the materialist to claim that nothing else is possible, he needs more backing than the statement that there is nothing else that he can see. As someone has said, 'What could be more inconsistent than to limit one's system to observable phenomena, and then make pronouncements about the non-observable?' For scientism to say that God does not exist it has to abandon the rules by which it operates when making its own claims.

Scientism has been called 'dangerously seductive propaganda', but the Bible goes further than that. All truth ultimately has its source in God, who created all reality outside of himself and sustains all that he created. In the person of his Son, Jesus Christ, he told Pontius Pilate, 'Everyone who is of the truth listens to my voice.' To elevate any purely human idea to the same level is nothing less than idolatry.

3 Reality check: science and its limits

It is usually accepted that in its modern form science dates from about the early part of the seventeenth century. The breakthrough was led by a remarkable English courtier, politician, philosopher and scientist Sir Francis Bacon. Born in 1561, he put forward a new idea which became known as the inductive method, stressing the importance of observation and experiment. Bacon saw himself as the inventor of a method of kindling a light in nature 'that would eventually disclose and bring to light all that is most hidden and secret in the universe'. The torch that Bacon and others lit has been blazing ever since and nobody can seriously deny that science and its daughter, technology, are revolutionizing our lives in ways that would have been beyond belief a hundred years ago. In 1899, Charles H. Duell, a Commissioner of the US Office of Patents, claimed, 'Everything that can be invented has been invented.' In 1943 IBM's Chairman Thomas Watson said, 'I think there is a world market for maybe five computers'! In 1949 an article in *Popular Scientist* suggested that computers might eventually weigh as little as 1.5 tons! There is more computing power in today's average smart phone than there was on the spacecraft that in 1969 put the first man on the moon.

Science and technology are filling our lives with a constant flow of gadgets, devices and equipment aimed at making our lives longer, fuller, easier and more enjoyable. Had I lived in the seventeenth century I would have played golf with a more-or-less round leather pouch stuffed with a hatful of boiled feathers. The ball I use today has an intertwined molecular construction combining zinc diacrylate and high density rubber. In heavy rain, a seventeenth-century golfer would have got soaking wet (and possibly caught fatal pneumonia). Today, I am protected by a Teflon-coated rain suit with a hydrophilic laminate outer layer, a capillary-style membrane and a technical mesh dropline (whatever that means!), the whole technological triumph weighing less than 700 grams.

Bryan Appleyard writes, 'This unarguable and spectacular effectiveness is the ace up science's sleeve ... You are dissatisfied with the quality and convenience of music in your home? Here is a compact disc player. You wish to avoid smallpox? Here is an injection. You wish to go to the moon? Here is a rocket. You are hungry? Here is how to grow more food. You are too fat? Here is how to lose weight. You feel bad? Here is a pill, feel better. No problem, says science.'

There is a pointer here to the reason that many people think science and religion have become divorced. As we shall see in a later chapter, the scientific method was built on a God-centred view of nature, but influential movers and shakers began to pull away from this idea and to suggest that God might be superfluous. Today, increased knowledge of the physical universe and phenomenal achievements in technology have tended to accelerate the movement. Who needs God when we can transplant human organs, manipulate genes and produce an endless conveyor belt of 'wonder drugs' to control or eliminate diseases that proved fatal a few years ago?

Descriptions, corrections, dissension

There are at least four reasons why science can never be a replacement for God.

1 The scientific description of something is not the only one

If you were visiting me and I were to say, 'I am going to infuse *Camellia sinensis* leaves in a liquid compound of oxygen and hydrogen,' you might wonder what I meant, but this is a scientific way of stating, 'I am going to make the tea.' If I were to say to my wife, 'Let us juxtapose our orbicular muscles and have a reciprocal transmission of carbon dioxide and microbes,' I would expect a puzzled frown, but if I made the same suggestion in non-scientific language — 'I would like to kiss you' — I would hope to get a more encouraging response! If you invited me to watch somebody rubbing the entrails of a dead sheep with the hairs of a dead horse you would meet with a decidedly cool reception, but if you were to phrase the same invitation differently and ask me to join you in listening to a violin solo I might want to check my diary. By the same token, to say that a piano concerto is nothing more than black blobs and lines on sheets of paper is hardly to tell the whole story!

2 Scientific statements are not set in concrete

The history of science has numerous examples of scientific 'facts' that have later been abandoned in the light of subsequent discoveries. Some of these will be mentioned later in this book.

3 Scientific statements about a given subject are often contradictory or imprecise

Cosmologists are constantly at loggerheads with one another over whether the universe had a time-related beginning and whether it will end in a 'Big Crunch' or a 'Big Bounce'. Some scientists believe in general relativity; others in spatial particle theory. There is great disagreement over the exact nature of electrons and other subatomic particles.A newspaper review of a book on evolution concluded, 'Modern Darwinian evolutionists are among the bitterest of squabblers,' while the biochemist Malcolm Dixon makes the important point that '... there are more disagreements and apparent contradictions within science itself than there are between science and religion.'

Nor can any one branch of science give us a full or strictly accurate picture, as a classic modern fable illustrates. The story goes that a social scientist, a biologist and a physicist went on a hiking holiday to Scotland. Seeing a sheep on a hillside, the social scientist called out, 'Look, the sheep in Scotland are black.' The biologist replied, 'No, you are jumping to conclusions. What you mean is, "In Scotland some sheep are black."' 'Not at all', the physicist protested, 'All we can say from what we have seen is that in Scotland there is at least one sheep, at least one side of which is black'!

4 Vast swathes of knowledge are beyond the reach of science

Richard Dawkins claimed, 'I think science really has fulfilled the need that religion did in the past, of explaining things, explaining why we are here, what is the origin of life, where did the world come from, what life is all about,' and 'Religion is no longer a serious candidate in the field of explanation. It is completely superseded by science.' Yet these fanfares are out of tune with accepted facts, beginning with those relating to the existence and nature of the universe.

Square one

Science is unable to tell us why the universe came into being

In some ancient cultures it was believed that Earth sat fixed in the centre of a static and eternal arrangement of heavenly bodies, with others spread evenly throughout an infinite universe. In the next chapter we shall look at one successful challenge to this idea. Another came in 1915 when Albert Einstein published his general theory of relativity, which unexpectedly predicted that cosmic space expands. In 1929 the American astronomer Edwin Hubble discovered the expansion of the universe experimentally, while later work by other scientists took this a significant step further, arguing that, if the universe was expanding, at some point in the past all its matter must have been packed closely together into an infinitesimally small point called a 'singularity'. This idea produced the first version of what is now universally known as the 'Big Bang theory', which says that the universe had a definite starting-point — now usually put at around fourteen billion years ago.

The theory has gained such momentum that in a newspaper poll nearly forty per cent of those interviewed said they believed in a Big Bang 'that produced the raw material of today's universe'. However, in an article accompanying the result of the poll, readers were reminded that Big Bang was 'just a theory' and added, 'It might be right, but scientists bicker about it all the time ... It might be that the Big Bang will turn out to be a small flop.' Be that as it may, it leaves some much more interesting questions unanswered: Where did the original 'singularity' come from? What do we mean by 'original'? How did it get its energy? When did time begin? What came before 'time zero'? For a modern physicist to tell us, 'Our universe is simply one of those things which happen from time to time,' leaves us none the wiser.

The universally accepted First and Second Laws of Thermodynamics say that the cosmos could not have been self-generated. There has to have been a moment when energy, matter, time and space came into existence. If an eternal, infinite, transcendent and omnipotent God is ruled out, where can science turn to explain the origin of these, when it cannot go any further back than the moment at which the laws on which it leans began to operate? Edgar Andrews pinpoints the problem: 'No matter how close to the instant of origin one may be able to press the scientific model of the cosmos, it remains impossible for such an explanation to be applied at or before the time zero point. Thus it follows that *science, even at its most speculative, must stop short of offering any explanation or even description of the actual event of origin.*'

Hard-core materialists use all kinds of ideas to skate around this. Peter Atkins latches on to what has become known as the quantum fluctuation hypothesis, in which, to quote him in *Creation Revisited*, 'space-time generates its own dust in the process of its own assembly'. Whatever Atkins had in mind, an article in *New Scientist* — a journal not at all known for its sympathy with Christian thought — neatly exposes the weakness of the whole idea: 'First there was nothing, then there is something ... a quantum flutter, a tremor of uncertainty ... and before you know it they have pulled a hundred billion galaxies out of their quantum hats.'

Even those who profess to understand quantum mechanics reach a point at which the laws of physics break down and they are faced with the need to explain where energy and matter came from in the first place, why a Big Bang should ever have happened

— and why there should be something rather than nothing. As Stephen Hawking notes, 'Although science may solve the problem of how the universe began, it cannot answer the question: why does the universe bother to exist? I don't know the answer to that.'

Science is unable to explain why there are scientific or natural laws, or why they are so consistent and dependable

Science works because scientists assume the validity, consistency and dependability of the laws of physics, yet there is no scientific explanation of *why* these laws exist, where they come from, or why they operate as they do. There is more to the world than physics can ever explain or express, and science has no idea how energy came to be distributed in such a way that our universe is cosmos, not chaos. Edgar Andrews says: 'If we ask science why the laws are such as they are, and not otherwise, if we ask why the law of gravity is an inverse square law with respect to distance, science can do nothing but shrug its mathematical shoulders and reply, "That question lies outside my terms of reference."' When Peter Atkins tells us that, for all its staggering immensity, diversity and interlocking order, the entire universe is 'an elaborate and engaging rearrangement of nothing', he is hardly making a helpful contribution to the subject.

Science cannot explain why the universe is so amazingly fine-tuned to support intelligent life on our planet

For Earth to function as it does in sustaining life, there needs to be an extremely complex and exact arrangement of terrestrial and extra-terrestrial elements. To give some of the best-known examples, the size of Earth, its rotational speed, the tilt of its axis relative to the plane of its orbit, its distance from the sun and its land/water ratio all have to be correct. We need light, but not too much ultra-violet; heat, but not too much. We need the earth's magnetic field to shield us from cosmic rays, atmosphere over our heads to shield us from meteorites and a screen of rock under our feet to prevent us from being incinerated. Atheist J. L. Mackie, admitted 'It is ... surprising that the elements of this unique set-up are just right for life when they might easily have been wrong.'

He is hardly exaggerating. In recent years science has assembled a complex mass of evidence to support the so-called 'anthropic principle', which says that the universe is fine-tuned to support intelligent life on our planet. This includes the relationship between the relative strengths of the four fundamental forces of nature (gravity, electromagnetism, the strong nuclear force and the weak nuclear force), the mass ratio of the proton and the neutron, two of the three subatomic particles that form the atom and the slight excess of matter over antimatter. It has been said that had the excess of matter over antimatter been different by about one particle per ten billion our life-sustaining world would never have come into being. Had there been equal amounts there would have been 'a vast annihilation event' leaving 'only very few particles of matter and antimatter in scattered, isolated remnants'. In addition, the way in which the critical density of the universe affects the gravitational attraction between cosmic structures had to be meticulously accurate. Even accepting today's most popular theory about origins, Stephen Hawking nevertheless says, 'If the rate of expansion one second after the Big Bang had been smaller *by even one part in a hundred thousand million million*, the universe would have recollapsed before it ever reached its present size.' The balance between the effects of expansion and contraction is so precise that one scientist likened it to aiming at a target an inch wide on the other side of the observable universe and hitting the mark.

Carbon and oxygen are essential for life, yet the structure of the carbon atom depends on such narrow tolerances that even the slightest deviation would have made life impossible. Commenting on the precise energy levels required, Astronomer Royal Sir Martin Rees and science writer John Gribbin concluded, 'This combination of coincidences, just right for resonance in carbon-12, just wrong in oxygen-16, is indeed remarkable. *There is no better evidence to support the argument that the universe has been designed for our benefit — tailor-made for man.'* Rees and Gribbin both reject the idea of a personal Creator, but when the world-renowned astronomer Sir Fred Hoyle grasped the implications of what they found he confessed, 'Nothing has shaken my atheism as much as this discovery.' Stephen Hawking goes even further and says, 'It would be very difficult to explain why the universe should have begun in just this way, *except as the act of a God who intended to create beings just like us.'*

Life and living

Science cannot explain why as human beings we are persons and not merely objects

Science can tell us amazing things about human physical structure, all expressed as mind-boggling statistics, yet they give us no explanation as to why we are more than physical phenomena. In February 2001 the international Human Genome Project published its long-awaited report spelling out the three billion letters that make up the human genome. Physician James Le Fanu said that this 'impressive achievement' was also 'devastating news for science, and in particular for those who, for the past 20 years, have regularly promised us that once the genome is cracked, all that is currently obscure will be made clear'. After pointing out the extent of the information shortfall, he went on, 'The holy grail, the dream that science would soon tell us something significant about what it means to be human, has slipped through our hands — and we are no wiser than before. *The human genome ... can tell us absolutely nothing about the really important things in life.'*

Physicist and Nobel laureate Stephen Weinberg says that human life is 'a more-or-less farcical outcome of a chain of accidents'; Richard Dawkins calls us 'robot vehicles'; and Fred Hoyle claims that we are 'no more than ingenious machines that have evolved as strange by-products in an odd corner of the universe' — yet none of these atheistic assertions can explain our *humanity*: our self-consciousness, our ability to remember the past, evaluate the present and contemplate the future, our sense of dignity and worth, and our innate aesthetic appreciation. Even an entrenched evolutionist like Michael Ruse admits, 'Nothing even yet scratches at an explanation of how a transformed ape could produce the magnificence of Beethoven's *Choral Symphony*.'

Science can tell us nothing about why the mind exists and functions as it does

Peter Atkins called human brains 'the most wonderful instruments in the universe'. Elsewhere he claimed that, at the deepest level, '... decisions are adjustments of the dispositions of the molecules inside large numbers of cells within the brain.' But to dismiss the thinking process in this way is sheer 'nothing-buttery' and gives rise to a host of tremendously important questions. If the brain was programmed by chance, how do we know that it will come up with the truth more often than randomly generated letters will produce meaningful ideas? If human thinking is nothing but complex chemistry, nerve impulses and the firing of synapses, how can we ever say that any given thought — even the thought that this is the case — is rational or true? If what we treat as rational thinking is nothing but 'molecular adjustment', how can we expect it to produce any premise, theory or conclusion on which we can rely? How can we get rationality from non-rational nature? Would we trust a computer print-out if we knew that the instructions in the machine had been programmed by random, non-rational forces? How can we explain our openness to truth? G. K. Chesterton wrote, '[The Materialist] cannot explain why anything should go right, even observation and deduction, why good logic should not be as misleading as bad logic, if they are both movements in the brain of a bewildered ape.' Geneticist (and atheist) J. B. S. Haldane developed this even further: 'If my mental processes are determined wholly by the motions in my brain, I have no reason to suppose that my beliefs are true ... and hence I have no reason for supposing my brain to be composed of atoms.'

Science rightly leans heavily on rational thinking, but to say with Francis Crick that 'our minds can be explained by the interaction of nerve cells and molecules' gets us no further. Biochemist Arthur Peacocke gives us the simple truth of the matter: 'Science can investigate all the physical aspects of the brain, but there is still something about the mind — and therefore about who you really are — *that it cannot get at.*

Science can add nothing to the inner quality of life

We have already seen some of the many ways in which science and technology can radically affect our lives in terms of things like health, comfort and communication, but these leave the inner qualities of life itself untouched. Sir John Houghton later assessed the results of a session on the theme 'Quality of Life' at a major international meeting of scientists: 'Although we could largely agree on those factors which ideally make up quality of life, as scientists we could say virtually nothing (and there was considerable debate on the issue) about how to achieve it in practice. In particular, how could we overcome the inherent selfishness, greed and other undesirable characteristics shown by human beings? The problems can be described by science, as can the factors which may exacerbate them, *but science cannot solve them.*

Science cannot define or explain ethical principles

Recent years have seen great advances in socio-biology, behavioural science and related subjects, yet science has been unable to explain the principles involved in human behaviour. It can say nothing about love, justice, freedom, beauty, goodness, joy or peace. Every sane person acknowledges the existence and authority of the conscience; as long ago as the first century B.C. a Roman author wrote, 'Even where there is no law, there is conscience.' Yet science cannot explain what it is, or why it operates as it does. Richard Dawkins claimed to have 'an ordinary citizen's view of goodness ... all the right emotions against injustice' and 'a strongly developed sense of good', but he conceded that '... as a biologist I haven't a very well worked-out story where that comes from.' He went on to suggest that 'good' was 'just something that emerged', but this hardly qualifies as an explanation. Nor does the claim by two other modern scientists that '... ethics, as we understand it, is an illusion fobbed off on us by our genes.' It might be argued that evolution could promote certain instincts, but this falls a long way short of explaining a consistent moral order.

It is impossible to jump from atoms to ethics and from molecules to morality. If we are merely genetically programmed machines, where can we find a consistent basis for moral values? William Provine, one-time Professor of Biological Sciences at Cornell University, said that 'giving up the idea of God is great for a rational mind' and made no bones about our position once God is ruled out: 'No inherent moral or ethical laws exist, nor are there any absolute guiding principles for human society. The universe cares nothing for us and we have no ultimate meaning in life.' This is a recipe for moral and social chaos, and science is unable to lift a finger to help us. It offers no moral guidance or values to govern our lives. Science cannot even tell us how to distinguish between right and wrong, nor why we should choose one rather than the other. J. B. S. Haldane said bluntly, 'Science can't give an answer to the question, "Why should I be good?"', while the atheistic journalist Natasha Walter admitted on BBC Television's *Soul of Britain*, 'I don't think any scientist would say that it was for science to say what is ethically right to do.'

Science is not able to answer life's deepest questions

Steve Jones, an avowed materialist, freely admits this in his book *The Language of the Genes*: 'Science cannot answer the questions that philosophers — or children — ask: why are we here, what is the point of being alive, how ought we to behave? Genetics has almost nothing to say about what makes us more than machines driven by biology, about what makes us human. These questions may be interesting, but scientists are no more qualified to comment on them than is anyone else.' The eminent psychiatrist Paul Tournier came to the same conclusion: 'Everybody today is searching for an answer to those problems to which science pays no attention, the problem of their destiny, the mystery of evil, the question of death.'

These are among the most fundamental questions we could ever ask — and in response, science can only shrug its shoulders and pass them elsewhere.

The ultimate issue

Some years ago, *Encyclopaedia Britannica* published a set of fifty-four volumes pulling together the writings of many eminent thinkers on the most important ideas that men have studied and investigated over the centuries. The topics chosen included law, science, philosophy and history, but the longest essay of all was on the subject of God. Addressing the question as to why this should be the case, co-editor Mortimer Adler wrote, 'More consequences for thought and action follow from the affirmation or denial of God than from answering any other question.' Adler was obviously right, yet science is unable to decide the issue, or even to address the question.

We need not deal with *scientism* here. As we saw in the last chapter, it is not even open to the suggestion that God might exist — it 'cannot allow a Divine foot in the door' — but to approach the subject having already decided the answer to the question hardly qualifies as being honest, let alone reasonable. Our concern is with true science, which depends on the use of repeatable observations or experiments with consistent results *not manipulated in any way by the world-view of those making or conducting them*. Science is uncovering an amazing amount of fascinating information about the wonder and vastness of God's creation and the ways in which natural laws function, yet there are three obvious reasons why molecular biologist Andrew Miller is right to say, 'It is certainly not a scientific matter to decide whether or not there is a God.'

The God revealed in the Bible has no physical or material dimensions or characteristics

In other words, he has none of the properties belonging to matter. In the Bible's own words, 'God is spirit'; that is to say, he has no 'parts'. He is simple, as opposed to complex; indivisible as well as invisible. This means that while science can examine creation it cannot examine the Creator.

God transcends the realm in which science operates

A second and related reason why science is unable to disprove God's existence is that, although he permeates every nook and cranny of the universe, he is uniquely transcendent — over, above and beyond time, space and all finite reality. God cannot be 'reached', however sophisticated the technology. He is distinct and separate from the entire universe and everything in it, and can no more be confined to space than he can be measured by time. He is essentially 'other' than creation, so outside of all reality that is open to scientific investigation. The Bible records God as saying:

> For my thoughts are not your thoughts,
> neither are your ways my ways, declares the Lord.
> For as the heavens are higher than the earth,
> so are my ways higher than your ways
> and my thoughts than your thoughts.
> (Isaiah 55:8-9)

It is impossible for any scientist operating entirely within the natural world to make any discovery in the realm of the supernatural. In Michael Poole's words, 'You cannot measure the beauty of a sunset with a multimeter. Neither is it any use asking science whether there is a God. Science is the study of the physical world. *Questions about God are outside its terms of reference.'*

It is impossible to prove a universal negative

For someone to prove the non-existence of God would mean that person being in possession of every single fact in all of reality. God is clearly a possible fact and to say that science is able to rule him out of existence flies in the face of common sense. Peter Atkins told the atheist (and strangely named!) *Free Inquiry Magazine*, 'Science is progressively advancing toward complete knowledge, leaving religions bobbing in its wake,' but to suggest that 'complete knowledge' is attainable is naïve, while the rest of the sentence is nonsense.

Nothing that has been written in this chapter is to be taken as a criticism of science. As we saw in the opening paragraphs, science is a success story, and growing more successful every day. It is an exciting, elevating exercise in which we can take great pleasure and from which we can derive great benefit. We should thank God for scientists — even those who deny his existence — but we do not honour science by ignoring its intrinsic limitations and pretending that it can explain everything.

4 Evolution: proof or prejudice?

In the supposed war between science and Christianity over the last 400 years the names of two men, an Italian and an Englishman, have often been used as heavy artillery by those on the side of science. The first name is now reduced to little more than a distant echo, and for our present purposes the issue in which he was involved can be dealt with very briefly; the second is still being heard loud and clear whenever science and religion are said to come into conflict.

The Italian

Galileo was born in Pisa in 1564. He earned a reputation as a philosopher and physicist, but his contribution to science and religion was as an astronomer — some have even suggested that he was 'the father of astronomy'. Ancient Greek philosophers such as Aristotle and Plato taught that Earth sat fixed at the centre of the entire universe, with all the other heavenly bodies circling around it. This idea was not seriously questioned for another 1,400 years, when the Polish astronomer and mathematician Nicolaus Copernicus shocked the world by insisting that, within an even vaster universe, the *sun* was at the centre of a massive planetary system of which Earth was merely a part.

Enter Galileo. Using a state-of-the-art telescope he had built, Galileo decided that Copernicus was right, and in his *Dialogue of the Two Great Systems of the Universe*, published in 1616, declared that Earth rotates on its own axis and revolves around the sun. This got him into serious trouble with the (Roman Catholic) Church, which believed it had a monopoly on all truth and accused him of contradicting what the Bible taught. Although Galileo protested that the Bible was intended 'to teach us how one goes to heaven, not how heaven goes' and that 'Two truths cannot contradict each other,' the church turned up the heat. One Dominican Father preached that 'Geometry is of the devil' and that 'Mathematics should be banished as the author of all heresies' — and was promptly promoted! Other religious leaders said that Galileo's ideas upset 'the whole basis of theology', including God's plan of salvation. The case became entangled with a variety of unsavoury religious politics and in 1633 Galileo was hauled before the notorious Inquisition, which had been set up to deal with heretics. Publication of all his works was banned and only his poor health caused his death sentence to be commuted to imprisonment for life.

These are the bare bones of a story some people still use as a trigger for the idea that science has disposed of God. The argument runs like this: *the church refused to accept scientific progress, but Galileo was right. Science beat Christianity hands down and has been a superior source of truth ever since.* However, to draw this conclusion is to play fast and loose with the facts. Firstly, Galileo's argument was not so much with the church as with seventeenth-century science as a whole. The simple fact is that many scientists opposed Galileo. Secondly, even after he had come to his scientific conclusions, Galileo had no dispute with the Bible or the existence of God. Thirdly, to decide that God is non-existent because seventeenth-century theologians wrongly claimed that the Bible endorsed a faulty scientific model dreamed up by ancient Greek philosophers is neither good science nor good sense.

The Englishman

In 2002, BBC Television ran a survey to find 'the greatest Briton of them all'. Nominees included William Shakespeare, Sir Winston Churchill, Sir Isaac Newton, Oliver Cromwell and Queen Elizabeth I, but television journalist Andrew Marr had no doubts as to how the voting should go: 'In all its history Britain has only one world-changer. His name is Charles Darwin.' Before the poll was held, Richard Dawkins wrote that Darwin ranked alongside Newton and Shakespeare as 'Britain's greatest gift to the world' and that '... his guiding genius hovers over all of modern history.'

Their hero had a stuttering start to his adult life. After failing to make the grade as a medical student, and doing poorly when he switched to classics and mathematics, he eventually graduated from Cambridge with a B.A. in theology. His father had hoped that Charles would enter the Church of England ministry, but the young man had no stomach for this and was more or less at a loose end when in 1831, in spite of having had no relevant training, he was offered a place as a naturalist on the survey ship *HMS Beagle*, about to set sail on a five-year expedition.

Prior to joining the *Beagle*, Darwin seems to have gone along with the almost universally accepted belief that, as Creator of the entire universe, God had brought into being all the world's different living species, with independent characteristics suited to their environment. But as the journey went on, Darwin increasingly questioned the fixity of species and eventually became convinced that entirely new species could arise by natural descent from pre-existing ones. For over twenty-five years after *Beagle* returned to England he worked on the manuscript of what would have been a massive volume on the subject. This never saw the light of day, but in 1859, concerned by news that the British naturalist and biologist Alfred Wallace was about to go into print along similar lines, he rushed out a condensed version of his notes under the title *The Origin of Species by Means of Natural Selection or the Preservation of Favoured Species*, now usually referred to as *The Origin of Species* or simply *Origin*. Early indications gave no inkling that it was to be anything other than a collection of interesting ideas by an amateur naturalist. The *Daily News* thought that Darwin was merely repeating what had been said by the Scottish publisher and natural philosopher Robert Chambers in a book published fifteen years earlier and already in its eleventh edition. The editor of the prestigious *Quarterly Review* suggested that if Darwin wanted to become famous he should abandon *Origin* and write a book on pigeons! Even his publisher, John Murray, an amateur geologist, had serious doubts about whether to go ahead with it because he considered Darwin's main theory 'as absurd as though one should contemplate a fruitful union between a poker and a rabbit'.

One of the book's most highly qualified critics was Adam Sedgwick, Professor of Geology at Cambridge, and one of the founders of geology as a science in England. In a letter to Darwin he wrote, 'I have read your book with more pain than pleasure. Parts of it I admired greatly, parts I laughed at till my sides were almost sore; other parts I read with absolute sorrow because I think them utterly false and grievously mischievous.'

A bombshell

The doubters were soon sidelined and within twenty years the book's major thesis, although since described as nothing more than 'a highly speculative hypothesis', had become all the rage. No other theory about life on earth has done more to affect the way people think about themselves and their relationship to other people and to the world around them. Julian Huxley called it 'the most powerful and most comprehensive idea that has ever arisen on earth'. In the definitive modern biography of Darwin, James Moore writes, 'More than any modern thinker — even Freud or Marx — (Darwin) ... has transformed the way we see ourselves on this planet.' Darwinism in one form or another has become a total philosophy which claims to explain the origin and development of everything in the world.

Ironically, the word most often used in employing Darwin's theory as a weapon against God does not even appear in the first edition of *Origin*. That word is 'evolution'. On the face of it, there is nothing about the idea of evolution that should have caused even a tremor in religious, philosophical or scientific circles. It was already widely accepted that great variations occurred *within* existing species and families by perfectly natural processes. Although Darwin called this model (micro-evolution) his 'special theory', it added little or nothing to what was already known and accepted. What turned his book into a bombshell was what is now called his 'general theory' — *macro-evolution*.

Put very simply, macro-evolution says that all the world's life-forms are linked seamlessly together in a natural process of evolution, one species arising from another by spontaneous, random, natural means, without any external power or direction, in an unbroken chain going right back to a single spark of life that appeared on our planet at some point in prehistory. As one researcher makes clear: 'The idea that life on earth originated from a single-celled organism and then progressed onwards and upwards in ever-increasing complexity to culminate in man himself is what the theory of evolution is all about.' In *Origin*, man was not in fact included in the model, but in *The Descent of Man*, published in 1871, Darwin bit the bullet and wrote, 'The main conclusion arrived at ... is that *man is descended from some less highly organized form*.' To underline his point he added that humankind has survived 'not according to some ordered plan but as a result of chance operating among countless creatures by nature's unlimited tendency towards variation'.

The entire package is now taken for granted by countless millions of people and a great deal of modern academic thought is governed by the assumption that all living phenomena have to be seen in evolutionary terms. Professor Ernst Mayr wrote, 'Since Darwin, every knowing person agrees man descended from the apes. Today, there is no such thing as the theory of evolution. It is the fact of evolution.' Richard Dawkins endorses this verdict: 'It is absolutely safe to say that if you meet somebody who does not believe in evolution, that person is ignorant, stupid or insane (or wicked, but I'd rather not consider that).'

In our time, Darwin's idea dominates the entire philosophical, scientific and cultural landscape, yet one of its greatest and most radical effects is religious. In *Origin*, Darwin made a few token allusions to God, but Adam Sedgwick saw past these and anticipated where the book was leading: 'From first to last it is a dish of rank materialism cleverly cooked and served up … and why is this done? For no other solid reason, I am sure, except to make us independent of a Creator.' Marking the centenary of the first publication of *Origin*, Sir Julian Huxley said, 'Darwin's real achievement was to remove the whole idea of God as the Creator of organisms from the sphere of rational discussion.'

In recent times, the same point has often been made by those who have studied Darwin's work. On the last day of 1999, *TIME* Magazine made this dramatic assessment: 'Charles Darwin didn't want to murder God. But he did.'

From zoo to you?

These impressive-sounding claims need to be faced, as so much hinges on their truth or falsehood. As we have seen, the Darwinian model of evolution, taking in all living organisms, begins with the first spark of life, but we shall try to unpack it 'from the outside in', beginning with human beings. How *did* we become what we are? The idea that our immediate ancestors were apelike mammals is now so commonly held that it is generally taken for granted.

Nobody seriously denies that apes and humans share some physical characteristics, and have similar DNA, but that is a long way from proving a direct link between the two species. There is a huge gap between similarities and direct relationship. Haemoglobin, the molecule that carries oxygen in red blood cells, is to be found not only in humans but also in earthworms, starfish, molluscs, in some insects and plants, and even in certain bacteria. Does this mean that they, too, are our immediate ancestors? Some of the data in this field are more confusing than confirming. When scientists examined the haemoglobin of crocodiles, vipers and chickens, they found that the crocodiles were more closely linked to the chickens than to their fellow reptiles, while in another test an identical protein was found on the cell wall of both camels and nurse sharks. The model that sees *Homo sapiens* as evolution's crowning glory is often backed up by diagrams and drawings showing how we emerged from a succession of stooped, hairy creatures. These artists' impressions are often brilliantly done and superficially persuasive, but they are largely the result of guesswork based on evolutionary assumptions, and time and again their message has been discredited by scientific discoveries. This has been especially true in the field of palaeontology, the study of fossils, which has blown huge holes in the 'monkey to man' scenario. Here are just five of many well-known examples that can be cited:

1. In 1857, quarrymen found a partial skeleton in a cave near Düsseldorf in Germany. The bones seemed to be human, but when similar remains were found in Europe, Africa and Asia they were given the common name Neanderthal and said to be pre-human. Artists and others got to work and produced semi-erect, barrel-chested models with short legs, massive eyebrow ridges and strong lower jaws. The complete package was then presented as evidence of a link between humans and some primitive intermediate creature. However, the idea was dealt a fatal blow when a Neanderthal skeleton, buried in a relatively modern suit of armour, was found in a tomb in Poland in 1908. Today, DNA evidence indicates that Neanderthal was 'a card-carrying member of the human family' after all, and

a recent book suggests, 'If a Neanderthal were dressed in jeans and a T-shirt, and went to a ball game, you and I would probably not notice him or her.' The idea that Neanderthal is a 'missing link' has since been quietly dropped from textbooks.

2. In 1912, Charles Dawson, an amateur fossil hunter, took a collection of bones, teeth and primitive instruments to a friend at the British Museum, claiming to have found them in a gravel pit near Piltdown, in Sussex. Scientists declared the remains to be 500,000 years old and the so-called Piltdown Man was touted as 'the sensational missing link', the three scientists responsible for promoting him receiving knighthoods for their work. But in 1953 their hero was proved to be a hoax, consisting of a human skull, the lower jaw of an orang-utan and the teeth of a chimpanzee.

3. In 1922, a single tooth unearthed in Nebraska was enthusiastically claimed to be from an early type of Pithecanthropoid (apelike man) who lived between 1.7 and 5.5 million years ago. The *Illustrated London News* published a double-page feature trumpeting Nebraska Man as a vital link in the 'monkey to man' chain, but six years later it was discovered that the tooth had come from a peccary, a pig-like wild animal. The Nebraska Man claim now shares the peccary's state of extinction, but together they are a good illustration of the comment made by Professor Bolton Davidheiser of Johns Hopkins University:

'The non-scientific public has great faith in what a palaeontologist can do with a single bone.'

4. In 1959, the palaeontologist Louis Leakey and his wife Mary exhumed an interesting skull in East Africa. Dubbed 'Nutcracker Man' because of its huge jaw, it was first dated at 1.75 million years, making it by far the oldest hominoid fossil ever found, but this claim was torpedoed when further bones found *lower down* were dated at only just over 10,000 years. Leakey eventually withdrew his extravagant claim and conceded that his find was one of many *Australopithecus africanus*, now believed to be extinct African apes.

5. In 1974 the American anthropologist Donald Johanson found a tiny skeleton in the Great Rift Valley, Ethiopia. Nicknamed 'Lucy', it was dated at three million years and became a sensation when announced at the Nobel Symposium on Early Man in 1978. Lucy was hailed as the first ape to walk upright and an undoubted link between apes and humans, but in a question-and-answer session at the University of Missouri in 1996, Johanson admitted that the knee joint cited as proof that Lucy walked upright had been found more than two miles away and 200 feet lower in the strata! Richard Leakey, Director of Kenya's National Museum, decided that '... the evidence for the alleged transformation from ape to man is extremely unconvincing,' and that '... it is overwhelmingly

likely that Lucy was no more than a variety of pygmy chimpanzee.' Johanson eventually withdrew his original claim and concluded that Lucy was not related to humans after all.

These are just some of the high-profile cases put forward as evidence that *Homo sapiens* evolved from apelike ancestors, yet, along with hundreds of other attempts, they have failed to make the case. Dr D. V. Ager, President of the British Geological Association, makes this important point: 'It must be significant that nearly all the evolutionary stories I learned as a student have now been debunked ... The point emerges that, if we examine the fossil record in detail, whether at the level of order or of species, we find — over and over again — not gradual evolution, but the sudden explosion of one group at the expense of another.'

Human evolution from apelike ancestors is so loudly and persistently taught that it has become a given in society at large. Virtually every radio and television programme dealing with the natural sciences assumes it to be true, and anyone raising a voice against it is likely to be treated as an eccentric, to say the least. Yet any protester has good company among authorities in the field. The distinguished palaeoanthropologist David Pilbeam, Professor of Anthropology at Harvard University, candidly admits, 'Perhaps generations of students of human evolution, including myself, have been flailing about in the dark

... our database is too sparse, too slippery, for it to be able to mould our theories. Rather, the theories are more statements about us and (our) ideology than about the past.' Elsewhere, he is even more specific: 'There is no clear-cut and inexorable pathway from ape to man.'

In all of this, we need to recognize that the issue is not the fossils themselves, but their interpretation. The hard-core evolutionist puts his theory before the facts and goes to the fossil record governed by his theory and looking to have it confirmed by what he finds. A spokesman for the American Association for the Advancement of Science went so far as to say that 100 million fossils, identified and dated, 'constitute 100 million facts that prove evolution beyond any doubt whatsoever'. The problem with this statement is that the fossil record has been assessed *on the assumption that macro-evolution is an established fact.* But this is a clear example of circular reasoning, leading one professor of anthropology to say, 'The problem with a lot of anthropologists is that they want so much to find a hominid that any scrap of bone becomes a hominid bone.' If we keep to the facts, palaeontology tells us that whenever we discover human fossils — and thousands have been found — they are already fully human, with no signs of transition from a more primitive creature. After many years of research in this particular field, the distinguished anatomist Lord Zuckerman, former

Chief Scientific Adviser to the UK government, concluded that '... if man evolved from an apelike creature, he did so without leaving a trace of that evolution in the fossil record.' There are no apes in human history.

Quite apart from what the fossil evidence tells us, those who insist that we *did* descend from apelike ancestors run headlong into a barrage of questions. If we are only the products of blind, mindless chance, how can we claim to have greater dignity than snakes or seaweed, vegetation or viruses? Why are we inescapably self-conscious? Why should we imagine that our lives have any meaning or purpose? Why do we long for significance? What motivates our goals and aspirations? How can we claim greater rights than buffalo or bacteria? Why do we insist on living within some kind of moral framework, even if we occasionally tweak it to our personal advantage? If we are nothing more than shrink-wrapped bags of biological elements governed by the laws of physics, how do we account for the existence and authority of conscience? Why do we know that there is a radical difference between good and evil? How did we acquire a sense of humour, or an interest in aesthetics? Why do we seem to have an eradicable spiritual dimension? Why do we think (more often than we care to admit) about death? Is there an evolutionary answer to these questions — some biological or chemical accident that can explain their existence?

The break between man and all other material reality is vast. We have no evolutionary ancestors.

Fatal flaws

The general theory of evolution says that we are the latest product of a 'Great Chain of Being', with non-living matter, then protozoans (microscopic, single-cell organisms), metazoan invertebrates (multi-celled organisms without a backbone or spinal column), vertebrate fish, amphibians, reptiles, birds, furry quadrupeds and apes forming our 'family tree'. There is no space here to look at each of these in turn, but there are at least five factors that reveal huge flaws in this widely accepted scenario.

1 The missing links

The first is the fact that, just as in the case of the 'monkey-to-man' idea, *the 'missing links' are still missing*! Concerned about the absence of intermediate links between species, Darwin admitted that this was 'the most obvious and serious objection that could be urged against [his] theory', but decided that this could be explained by 'the extreme imperfection of the geological record'. We are now in a very different position, with a vastly greater number of fossils at our disposal, yet the curator at a major US museum said, 'The situation hasn't changed much. The record of evolution is still surprisingly jerky and, ironically, *we now have even fewer examples of evolutionary transition than we had in Darwin's time ... Darwin's problem has not been alleviated.'* Stephen J. Gould has no hesitation in saying that the extreme rarity of transitional forms in the fossil record 'persists as the trade secret of palaeontology'. Niles Eldridge confirms the conspiracy: 'We palaeontologists have said that the history of life supports ... (the story of gradual adaptive change) ... *all the while knowing that it does not.'* Since the evidence from palaeontology is the only one that claims to present proof of the history of evolution, rather than its results and mechanisms, these admissions are particularly important, as Darwin had hoped that the discovery of further fossils would reveal the missing links needed to confirm his theory.

2 'Typing errors'

The second flaw concerns the mechanism said to drive evolution. Darwin leaned heavily on what he called 'natural selection', which originally said that organisms prey on each other in order to survive and at the same time develop new characteristics in order to cope with their environment. When these characteristics become permanent features, a new species emerges in what Darwin called 'progress towards perfection'. This leads to the concept of 'the survival of the fittest', a phrase Darwin adapted from someone else and included from the sixth edition of *Origin* onwards.

But by the 1930s it had become obvious to biologists that natural selection alone could never produce organic macro-evolution. It might provide a good model for changes *within* species and families, but not for the creation of new ones. Macro-evolution needed a new ingredient; biologists proposed the 'synthetic theory', so called because it merged classical Darwinism and modern genetic ideas. The theory centred on the genes and proposed that if over an immense amount of time these underwent radical, inheritable changes — mutations — nature could use those most suitable for future development, leading eventually to the creation of new orders of animals. *No such transformations have ever been observed.* Instead, they are inferred on the basis of the circular argument that this is how new orders arise according to evolutionary theory.

Nevertheless, this new model, under the general name of neo-Darwinianism, has so completely taken over that Sylvia Baker, a respected writer in the field, goes so far as to say that 'The modern theory of evolution ... stands or falls on this question of mutation.'

If this is the case, the theory is very unsteady on its feet! In the first place, natural mutations occur *extremely rarely*, something like once in every ten million duplications of a DNA molecule. Even a staunch evolutionist like Sir Julian Huxley says that the odds against favourable mutations occurring in one strain through pure chance are so long that it would take three large-format volumes of about 500 pages to print them out. No wonder he adds, 'No one would bet on anything so improbable happening.'

Secondly, 999 out of every 1,000 mutations are *harmful*, weakening or destroying the organism concerned, rather than creating the advantageous changes needed for evolution. In fact, organisms from bacteria to humans have DNA mismatch repair systems consisting of more than a dozen separate proteins which scan the genome (the entire complement of genetic material in an individual set of chromosomes) for 'mistakes' (mutations) or damage induced by environmental factors, and either repair them or target the cell to be removed. Such mechanisms have no means of being selective and will act with equal efficiency to nullify both harmful and the much rarer 'useful' mutations. It seems curious that a process so critical to evolution should generate largely deleterious changes and then be subject to a complex biological preventative mechanism.

Noting that a mutation is a random change in a molecular message (DNA), medical professor Magnus Verbrugge likens it to a typing error and adds, 'Typing errors rarely improve the quality of a written message; if too many occur, they may even destroy the message contained in it.'

Phillip Johnson uses another illustration to make the same point: 'To suppose that such a random event could reconstruct even a single complex organ like a liver or kidney is about as reasonable as to suppose that an improved watch can be designed by throwing an old one against a wall.'

Thirdly, the *time needed* for mutations to trigger a new species is simply not available. Biologist Rémy Chauvin says, 'Since those forms of animal life which mutate very rapidly have remained the same during tens of millions of generations, *mutations could not be considered the motor of evolution.*' Significantly, he goes on, 'This is a matter of good sense, but given the strength of prejudice within science as everywhere else, good sense loses its case in court.'

Biochemist Ernest Chain is equally dismissive: 'To postulate that the development and survival of the fittest is entirely a consequence of chance mutations seems to me a hypothesis based on no evidence and irreconcilable with the facts. These classical evolutionary theories are a gross over-simplification of an immensely complex and intricate mass of facts, and it amazes me that they are swallowed so uncritically and readily, and for such a long time, by so many scientists, without a murmur of protest.'

3 Incomplete means useless

A third flaw in the macro-evolution model is that any new, functional organ has to be a complete, operating entity before it can be of any benefit to the organism concerned. This clashes head-on with evolution's claim that mutation takes place in tiny increments over a vast amount of time. The human eye provides a good illustration. It comes with automatic aiming, focusing and aperture adjustment and its tiny retina has 130 million receptor cells, 124 million of which are rod-shaped and differentiate between light and darkness, and six million of which are cone-shaped and can identify up to eight million variations of colour. Is it possible that all of these features came into being by means of the genetic equivalent of typing errors over millions of years? Those who insist that this is the case (and Darwin did, in spite of admitting that for natural selection to form the eye was 'absurd in the highest possible degree') have surely missed the point that a partial eye is useless. Five per cent of an eye would not give five per cent vision — it would give none. What is more, even if all the physical components of an eye were in place, they would achieve nothing unless they were precisely 'wired' to an amazing complex of nerve cells in the brain. Small wonder that someone has suggested, 'Examination of the eye is a cure for atheism.'

4 Irreducible complexity

A fourth flaw is linked to the third and has to do with irreducible complexity. Darwin once wrote, 'If it could be demonstrated that any complex organ existed which could not possibly have been formed by numerous, successive, slight modifications, *my theory*

would absolutely break down. But I can find no such case.'
He said this knowing nothing of the marvels revealed
by modern microbiology. To Darwin and his
contemporaries the biological cell was nothing more
than a mysterious 'blob' of protoplasm, which they had
no instruments to examine in detail. Microbiology has
now opened this 'black box' of ignorance and revealed
a world of staggering complexity; we know, for
example that even relatively simple bacteria cells can
synthesize up to 6,000 compounds at a rate of a
million reactions per second.

In his best-seller *Darwin's Black Box*, Michael Behe
goes significantly further and identifies numerous
examples of irreducible complexity that could not
possibly have evolved. As Behe explains, something is
irreducibly complex 'if it's composed of several parts
and each part is absolutely necessary for the structure
to function'. As a brilliant example he cites blood-
clotting, which involves a very complex, intricately
woven system consisting of a score of independent
protein parts. He shows that in the case of an invasive
event (a cut) a protein which is found only on the
outside of cells not in contact with the blood is
brought into the bloodstream locally and triggers off
an ordered cascade of events, involving twenty-eight
separate proteins and enzymes, which results in
localized clotting and the sealing of the wound.

The all-important point about the whole process,
which Behe describes in great detail, is that the

cascade is formed in a specific way with a defined number of known interacting molecules. In other words, it is an irreducibly complex system, precisely the kind of thing Darwin admitted would destroy his whole evolutionary system. If natural selection is to produce a fully functioning, irreducibly complex system, it has to do it all at once. Yet Behe says that even a tiny part of such a system coming together by genetic mutation 'would not be expected to happen even if the universe's ten-billion year life were compressed into a single second and relived every second for ten billion years'.

5 The Cambrian conundrum

A fifth flaw is that evolutionism has no answer to the so-called Cambrian Explosion. Over the last 150 years or so, most scientists have revised the supposed age of our planet from a few thousand years to about 4.5 billion years. Using this time-scale, it has been found that an absence of evidence for life-forms prior to 600 million years ago suddenly gives way to a huge number of fossils representing nearly every group of organisms alive today and *without any sign of evolutionary ancestors*. To make matters worse for evolutionists, fossils of highly complex life-forms far outnumber those of the simplest ones and include those representing every one of the major invertebrates. Using their own time-frame, evolutionists estimate that such complex creatures would have required at least 1.5 billion years to evolve, yet there is no pre-Cambrian evidence in support of any such evolution having taken place. As even Richard Dawkins admits, 'It is as though they were just planted there, without any evolutionary history.'

These are among the most damaging blows to the macro-evolution hypothesis. Mathematician and physicist Wolfgang Smith summed up their significance: 'We are told dogmatically that evolution is an established fact; but we are never told who established it, and by what means. We are told, often enough, that the doctrine is founded upon evidence … but we are left entirely in the dark on the crucial question wherein, precisely, this evidence consists.' Later he added, 'If by evolution we mean macro-evolution … it can be said with the utmost rigour that the doctrine is totally bereft of scientific sanction … there exists today not a shred of *bona fide* scientific evidence in support of the thesis that macro-evolution transformations have ever occurred.'

Dr Marcel P. Schutzenberger, was equally dismissive. In *Mathematical Challenges to the neo-Darwinian Theory of Evolution*, he concluded that the probability of evolution based on mutation and natural selection was 'not conceivable' because there is 'no chance … to see this mechanism appear spontaneously and, if it did, even less for it to remain… We believe there is a considerable gap in the neo-Darwinian Theory of evolution, and we believe this gap to be of such a nature that it cannot be bridged with the current conception of biology.'

When some 150 of the world's leading evolutionary theorists met at the University of Chicago for a conference 'to consider the mechanisms that underlie the origin of species' their report stated, 'The central question of the Chicago conference was whether the mechanisms underlying micro-evolution can be extrapolated to explain the phenomena of macro-evolution … the answer can be given as a clear, "No".'

One other point needs to be made, which is that macro-evolution claims to explain the present characteristics of living things, *whatever those characteristics may be*, but it is incapable of giving us a fundamental explanation of how these characteristics came about. R. E. D. Clark makes the point like this: 'Evolutionary explanations are almost entirely of the after-the-event kind. The camel has a hump and this like everything else is due to natural selection which we are told offers "a scientific rational mechanistic explanation". Maybe, but if the camel had no hump, the explanation would be the same. The cat has a tail and natural selection tells us why. But if puss had no tail, natural selection would explain that too. If an animal has a feature which seems to confer no obvious advantage, we are told that it must have an advantage or it would not be there. If difficulties are raised we are told that the advantage lies in some other factor with which the first is genetically linked and *oligogenes* are invented for the purpose... If a feature which would be useful to an animal is *not* there, then of course natural selection explains this too. And so on, whatever the facts to be explained... Nevertheless (this) does not get us very far. After all, natural selection also determines which cars remain on the roads after a lapse of time and which disappear, but this does not tell us how the models are manufactured.'

The first spark

As we track backwards through the evolutionary model we inevitably arrive at the point at which we need to find an explanation for the origin of life itself. To become a starting-point for an ongoing evolutionary process, such a life-form would need to store genetic information, process energy and replicate — three things that non-living systems are incapable of doing. The obvious problem is therefore how to get life started; those who rule God out of the equation have turned to the only alternative — spontaneous generation.

As Darwin wrestled with the problem he fantasized about 'some warm little pond, with all sorts of ammonia and phosphoric salts, light, heat, electricity, etc. present', in which 'a protein compound was chemically formed ready to undergo still more complex changes'. Since then, numerous experiments have been carried out to see if life could have been spontaneously generated in some kind of primordial 'soup', but at best these have been able to produce nothing more than a few basic amino-acids, the building blocks of proteins. Yet even an unlimited supply of proteins would not come close to producing a living cell.

In *The Intelligent Universe*, Sir Fred Hoyle makes the point like this: 'If there were a basic principle of matter which somehow drove organic systems toward life, its existence should easily be demonstrable in the laboratory. One could, for instance, take a swimming bath to represent the primordial soup. Fill it with any chemicals of a non-biological nature you please. Pump any gases over it, or through it, you please, and shine any kind of radiation on it that takes your fancy. Let the experiment proceed for a year and see how many of those 2,000 enzymes [the 'worker' proteins found in living cells] have appeared in the bath. I will give the answer, and so save the time and trouble and expense of actually doing the experiment. You would find nothing at all except perhaps for a tarry sludge composed of amino-acids and other simple organic chemicals. How can I be so confident of this statement? Well, if it were otherwise, the experiment would long since have been done and would be well-known and famous throughout the world. The cost of it would be trivial compared to the cost of landing a man on the Moon ... in short, there is not a shred of objective evidence to support the hypothesis that life began in an organic soup here on the Earth.'

This is hardly surprising when one considers the massive difference between life and non-life and the creative capacity that the most primitive of cells would have needed to survive and reproduce.

Sir Julian Huxley, who claimed that evolution ran all the way 'from cosmic star-dust to human society', thought, 'There is every reason to believe that living matter developed automatically out of non-living matter in certain peculiar conditions of earth's early history', but far from having 'every reason', we have none. We have no evidence that the random flow of energy through chemical 'soup' can lead to the staggering complexity of even the simplest living organism and no knowledge of any mechanism by which this could have been accomplished.

Hard-line evolutionists often say that the problem could be solved by factoring in a sufficient amount of time. As one scientist claimed, 'Time is the hero of the plot. Given enough time, anything can happen — the impossible becomes probable, the improbable becomes certain.' But this escape route turns out to be a dead end. Writing in *Nature* magazine, Frank Salisbury discussed the odds against the spontaneous production of a single gene. He asked his readers to imagine one hundred million trillion planets, each with an ocean two kilometres deep and fairly rich in gene-sized DNA fragments, which reproduce one million times per second, with a mutation occurring at each reproduction. Under such favourable conditions,

Salisbury calculated that it would take trillions of universes to have much chance of producing a single gene in four billion years — even if 10^{100} different DNA molecules could serve the same gene function!

The problem of explaining the origin of life became even greater in 1953 when the British biophysicist Francis Crick and his colleague James Watson discovered the now famous double-helical structure of DNA. Although it is a relatively simple molecule, with just four basic components, it governs all biological reproduction and the transmission of all inherited characteristics. The problem for the evolutionist is that, although DNA does this by *processing* an immense amount of genetic information, it does not *produce* it: 'The DNA molecule is the medium; it's not the message.' This means that macro-evolution has to explain not only the origin of matter, but the independent origin of information, *without intelligence being a part of the equation*. The chemical instructions for the construction of a complete human being exist in every fertilized human egg, and a single chromosome may contain information equivalent to 500 million words. At 400 words to a page, it would take nearly 5,000 books of 230 pages to record it all — and a library of about 250,000 such books to store all the information secreted in the forty-six chromosomes in a single fertilized human egg. As if this were not amazing enough, all this information is encoded in a 'language' that has only four 'letters' and whose dictionary contains only sixty-four three-letter words. Where does this staggering mass of information come from? There is no known law of physics that could spontaneously create information and no example of information arising as the result of a mindless natural process. As our common experience tells us that information always has an intelligent source, it is hardly surprising to find Stephen Grocott concluding, 'I am afraid that as a scientist I simply cannot say strongly enough that spontaneous generation of life is a chemical nonsense and, therefore, I am left with no alternative but to believe that life was created.'

Yet evolutionists continue to search for this most elusive of 'missing links', encouraged by knowing that living and non-living molecules are made up of exactly the same atoms (oxygen, hydrogen, carbon, sulphur and the like) and that under the right conditions small molecules can be made to combine to form larger and more complex ones. What eludes science is how, even given countless millions of years, simple, non-living molecules could have accidentally combined to produce those carrying the first spark of life.

Out of nothing?

This has necessarily been a long chapter, but one last point needs to be squeezed in: where did material reality come from in the first place? We have tracked evolutionism back to an updated version of Darwin's 'warm little pond' — but where did the 'pond' come from? It is impossible to run any scientific programme that will show us how the universe began, but there seem to be just three possibilities: it is eternal; it was self-created; or it was brought into existence by a transcendent reality.

As far as the first possibility is concerned, Einstein's general theory of relativity, the First and Second Laws of Thermodynamics and numerous astronomical observations all point to a universe that is not eternal and static, but to one that had a definite beginning and is changing over time.

The second possibility, that the universe is self-created, also collides with the Laws of Thermodynamics. In the simplest language possible, the First Law says that no new energy or matter can come into being, and none can be annihilated; applied in simple terms the Second Law says that the universe is like a clock that has been wound up and is now running down, becoming more and more randomized (disorganized) in the process.

This leaves just one alternative — that the universe was brought into being by a reality beyond it and greater than it. When there is no natural explanation for the existence of such a reality, should we not look for another one? Isaac Newton was convinced that the cosmos 'could only proceed from the counsel and dominion of an intelligent and powerful Being', and Edgar Andrews calls this argument 'as close to a proof for the existence of God as is possible'. It has been said that in order to have the universe as we know it, five basic things are needed — space, energy, matter, time and intelligence. All five concepts are contained in the Bible's opening words: 'In the beginning God created the heavens and the earth.' Small wonder that C. S. Lewis said he had never come across any philosophical theory about origins that was 'a radical improvement' on these words.

5 Faith and facts

Present people with the words 'faith', 'science', 'facts' and 'religion', and ask them to arrange these in matching pairs, and many would have no hesitation in linking 'science' with 'facts' and 'religion' with 'faith'. Some have done this with passion. Biologist T. H. Huxley, who invented the word 'agnostic' and became known as 'Darwin's Bulldog' because of his passionate promotion of Darwinism, once wrote that faith was no longer in contact with facts of any kind. Richard Dawkins said, 'Faith is the great cop-out, the great excuse to avoid the need to think and evaluate evidence ... faith is not allowed to justify itself by argument.' On another occasion he put it still more clearly: 'I think that a case can be made that faith is one of the world's great evils, comparable to the smallpox virus, but harder to eradicate. Faith, being belief that isn't based on evidence, is the principal vice of any religion.'

Science: the faith factor

We hardly need to spend time proving that facts are the raw materials that fuel all science. They are the elements that science discovers and studies, then uses to make further progress in the endless search for truth in the natural world. The point we need to discuss is whether science is a discipline involving faith. In his speech quoted above, Richard Dawkins went on to say that, in his view, 'Science is free of the main vice of religion, which is faith.' However, there are highly qualified scientists who would say that this combines a wrong presumption (that faith is a vice) and a wrong conclusion (that science has none of it). Harold Urey, a Nobel prize winner, was committed to a materialistic world-view that had no place for God, yet he admitted, 'All of us who study the origin of life find that the more we look into it, the more we feel it is too complex to have evolved anywhere. We all believe *as an article of faith* that life evolved from dead matter on this planet.' Philosopher Marjorie Grene, a distinguished historian of science, wrote, 'It is as *a religion of science* that Darwinism chiefly held, and holds man's minds ... [It is] preached by its adherents with religious fervour.'

As we saw in chapter 2, nobody is a 'non-believer'. The position of scientists who claim to have no faith in the God revealed in the Bible (or in any other god, for that matter) is not one that is devoid of faith, but one governed by the very principle they claim to despise. Atheists may claim that their view of the universe's origin, existence and nature is exclusively based on scientific facts, but the truth is that they lean heavily on the principle of faith. As we can easily show, every scientist acts on basic assumptions that cannot be logically or scientifically proved.

Assumptions

In the first place, scientists obviously assume *the reality and integrity of their own existence*. In the seventeenth century mathematician René Descartes was deeply concerned that established belief systems were being challenged by new scientific discoveries. In an attempt to hold them together, he tried to bring certainty into philosophy by setting aside everything that could possibly be doubted in order to find something that was beyond all doubt. It was one thing for science to claim that we should rely on our senses — but how could we know that they were reliable? After a great deal of tortuous mental wrestling he coined the phrase for which he is now most famous: '*Cogito, ergo sum*' ('I think, therefore I am'). Descartes used his doubts to confirm that he must exist as a thinking, doubting being. He was eventually to push his ideas so far that he became known as one of the fathers of modern rationalism, which says that reason alone is the primary source of all human knowledge and is sufficient to solve all the problems of man's nature and destiny. It is not difficult to dismantle this, but no scientist will make any progress at all until he or she accepts Descartes' most famous dictum.

In the second place, scientists assume that *the universe exists as an objective, independent reality outside of themselves*. This is so fundamental that without it science would not merely grind to a halt; it could never get started in the first place.

Thirdly, scientists assume that *nature is uniform* — that what we have around us is cosmos, not chaos. We have seen only a microscopic part of all natural reality, and have only done so for a tiny amount of time, but we assume that the reality around us is regular in its behaviour, so that we can record its details and work on understanding something of what it means. If we did not assume that processes and patterns in nature were universally consistent, we could never be sure that the laws of nature would work the same way tomorrow as they do today. Yet there is no logical reason why they should. The fact that the sun has risen every day of your life is no logical guarantee that it will rise tomorrow.

Science can only proceed at all on the assumption that the world is orderly and predictable. If the law of gravity suddenly went into reverse so that apples shaken loose by the wind fell upwards instead of downwards, not only scientists would find life difficult and revise the way they act! Paul Davies has no hesitation in conceding what this means: 'You have to accept as an act of faith that there is an existing order in nature that is intelligible to us. That is a huge act of faith.'

Fourthly, scientists in every discipline assume that *their senses enable them to discover accurate data about nature and to communicate true information to others*. In other words, they trust that their senses are telling them the truth because they are in some way 'logged on' to the world around them.

Fifthly, scientists assume t*he law of cause and effect*. The entire scientific enterprise is built on the premise that within an ordered world effects must be related to causes. Scientists have an inbuilt conviction that every event can be explained as the product of some previous event.

Sixthly, scientists believe that *things they can see give clues to things they cannot see*. Del Ratzsch gives an obvious example: 'We cannot directly see atoms and other such micro-entities, yet most scientists are confident of their existence on the basis of large-scale things that human eyes can see — cloud-chamber tracks and so forth. On the other end of the scale are phenomena that scientists are confident about but which are simply too big for humans to see. Scientists talk confidently about the large-scale structure of the universe and about the long-term history or future of the universe. We cannot directly follow such processes on our small temporal and spatial scale of observation, but what we can see is taken as evidence for such processes.'

These six fundamental assumptions knock huge holes in the Dawkins dogma that science is free from the 'vice' of faith. Without faith (in the sense of assuming things that cannot be logically proven) science would never get off the ground. All scientists are deeply committed to the principle of faith: they assume their own integrity, the existence of the world as an objective reality, the uniformity of nature, the dependability of their senses, the law of cause and effect and the existence of reality beyond their physical sight. To put it simply, every scientist exercises faith while searching for facts.

Interestingly, all of these assumptions fit perfectly into a biblical, theistic world-view. The first two are perfectly covered by the statement that God 'made heaven and earth and sea and everything in them'. A biblical view of nature, with God as its Creator, offers a credible explanation of the third assumption, which concerns balance and elegance of natural law. As one theologian puts it, 'The reason science is possible is that we live in a law-ordered cosmos which God has created.' The biblical claim that there is a common Creator of both material and mind goes hand in glove with the fourth assumption, that our senses enable us to 'log on' to the world around us. The fifth, an elegant link between cause and effect, is what we would expect from a Creator whose own character is orderly and consistent. Finally, an amazing cosmos, most of which is beyond the limits of our physical vision, is entirely consistent with its being the work of a transcendent Creator whose greatness 'no one can fathom' and whose ways are 'beyond tracing out'.

At the end of the day, science of any kind is a discipline essentially based on faith. Without the assumption of order in the universe, science could never get started, let alone come to any solid conclusions about anything.

Scientists who accept the truth of these assumptions, but who reject the idea that they are signs of science pointing beyond itself to a transcendent God, run headlong into a thicket of even greater mysteries. The atheist must, of necessity, believe that matter without mind created reason and logic. Matter without intelligence created understanding and comprehension. Matter without morals created complex ethical codes and legal systems. Matter without conscience created a sense of right and wrong. Matter without emotion created skills and art, music, drama, architecture, comedy, literature and dance. Matter without design created in humankind an insatiable hunger for meaning and purpose.

Basis of faith

Nothing I have written in this chapter (or in the rest of the book) is meant to suggest that there are not superb and even world-class scientists who are atheists or agnostics. In addition, there are doubtless equally distinguished scientists who are Jews, Muslims, Hindus or Buddhists, or who subscribe to one of a multitude of other faith systems. Our focus here is on mainstream Christianity and the relationship between facts and faith.

When concentrating on science, we noted that it was fuelled by facts and that the point at issue was whether faith was involved. In concentrating on Christianity, we can obviously turn the coin over and take the issue of faith for granted. The question we need to tackle is whether biblical faith can be justified on any factual basis.

We can get right to the heart of the matter by looking at what is seen by many people to be one of Christianity's greatest weaknesses, the biblical accounts of miracles. The eighteenth-century Scottish thinker David Hume was so sceptical on the subject that he felt the only genuine miracle was that people believed in miracles at all! Yet whatever reason might be advanced for rejecting the possibility of miracles, it is impossible to reject them on *scientific* grounds. As one scientist has said, 'The question of miracles is not primarily scientific, but *theological*. Science simply tells us that these events are against normal expectation. We knew this from the start. *Science cannot exclude the possibility that, on particular occasions, God does particular, unprecedented things.* After all, he is the ordainer of the laws of nature, not someone who is subject to them.'

The laws of nature are merely our assessment of how God normally causes things to happen. But he is not subject to those laws and is at perfect liberty to suspend or change them on a local or more widespread basis whenever and for whatever reason he chooses; nor would his doing so violate any known law. If in the course of setting the table for a meal my wife dropped a knife it would normally fall to the ground, but if I was quick-fingered enough to catch it before it hit the floor I would not be breaking any law of physics, merely intervening. If this is true at a purely human level, it is certainly true at a divine level, and science is unable to prove that such a thing never happens. In a letter to *The Times*, thirteen prominent scientists, most of them university professors, clinically closed this particular door: 'It is not logically valid to use science as an argument against miracles. To believe that miracles cannot happen is as much an act of faith as to believe that they can happen ... miracles are unprecedented events. Whatever the current fashions in philosophy or the revelations of opinion polls may suggest, *it is important to affirm that science ... can have nothing to say on the subject.*'

The only sensible way to tackle the issue is to do so openly and honestly. For anyone to reject miracles not on strictly scientific grounds but because they clash with his or her world-view is to evade the issue instead of examining it. The right approach is to look at the data with an open mind, ask the right questions, examine all the evidence as closely as possible, and then come to a clear conclusion as to where it points. This approach should begin by accepting that if God is personal and wants to communicate with us, it is at least possible that from time to time he might choose to do so in unusual or even unique ways. Ruling God out from the start is to feed false criteria into the whole business; to deny miracles because they are beyond human explanation is both arrogant and foolish. The only way to know whether miracles *can* occur is to see whether any *have* occurred. The Bible gives us a perfect opportunity to pursue the point.

A test case

In the course of an address at the University of Cape Town I was heckled by a militant atheist and after the meeting I had a long discussion with him about the existence of God. Needing to leave for another engagement, I asked him one last question: 'What do you think of Jesus?' His immediate reply was, 'I don't know — but I do realize that everything hinges on whether he rose again from the dead.' He was absolutely right! Christianity stands or falls by this one event, because it pins all the others in place. The Bible says that in rising from the dead Jesus was 'declared with power to be the Son of God' and an amplified version of the original Greek text brings out the force of what is being said: '(He was) openly designated the Son of God in power — in a striking, triumphant and miraculous manner.' In simple terms, the resurrection is said to be a declaration of his deity.

The background can be sketched in very quickly. After being betrayed by Judas Iscariot and tortured by his captors, Jesus was shuttled from one show trial to another, before being put to death by crucifixion just outside Jerusalem. A wealthy follower obtained permission to remove the body and bury it in his own private tomb, carved out of a rock in a nearby garden. There were several witnesses to the burial. Because of the controversy surrounding the trial and execution of Jesus, a detachment of soldiers was posted at the tomb and the Roman governor's official seal was attached to a huge rock placed over the entrance.

Three days later there was the first-century equivalent of a modern media frenzy: *the body was missing*! This was confirmed by at least five people who visited the site on the day the story broke — and nobody ever contradicted their testimony. An empty tomb falls a long way short of proof that Jesus had come back from the dead, but soon afterwards (and for the rest of their lives) his followers openly preached that he had. All the authorities had to do to prove them lunatics or liars was to open the tomb for public inspection, and the fact that they did no such thing is hugely significant. Theologian Paul Althaus rightly said, 'The resurrection proclamation could not have been maintained in Jerusalem for a single day, for a single hour, if the emptiness of the tomb had not been established as a fact for all concerned.'

Some objections answered

Sceptics have always recognized the significance of the resurrection, and over the centuries have come up with a barrage of alternative explanations for the missing body. Here are some of them:

Jesus never died. The so-called 'swoon theory' was popularized in the eighteenth century, but it is a non-starter. Even before his crucifixion, Jesus had been viciously beaten and scourged, while on the cross his body was ripped open by a soldier's spear for the express purpose of confirming his death. At no time during his body's removal and burial did any of its handlers detect the slightest sign of life. Yet the swoon theory asks us to believe that in the stone-cold tomb Jesus came out of a coma, wriggled his way out of tightly-wound grave-clothes layered with sticky, hardening embalming material weighing seventy-five pounds, pushed aside the massive rock lying across the tomb, overcame an armed guard of Roman soldiers, went back into the city stark naked (or clutching some of the grave-clothes) and then convinced his friends, not that he had had a near-death experience, but that he had actually died, then overcome death for ever.

The first visitors all went to the wrong tomb. This idea was first suggested in 1907, but it should have died at birth. Two of these visitors had not only been present at the burial but had even noticed 'how his body was laid in it' — and in any case, would the owner of the tomb he had originally chosen for himself have forgotten where it was?

The body was stolen by a person or persons unknown. This scenario is devoid of evidence, opportunity or motive. As Sir Norman Anderson wryly says, 'A Jew of that period could scarcely be suspected of stealing bodies on behalf of anatomical research.'

The Roman authorities stole the body. They would obviously have had the best opportunity, but no conceivable motive. Their whole purpose in posting an armed guard was *to keep the body where it was.*

The Jewish authorities removed the body. They shared the Roman authorities' interest in keeping the body secure for four days (taking it beyond the 'third day', when Jesus had prophesied that he would rise again) but why should their custody be thought any more secure than that of the Romans, which was backed up by armed force? When Jesus' followers began preaching that Jesus was alive again they were arrested, flogged, imprisoned and assassinated — all totally unnecessary if the Jewish authorities had produced the body.

Jesus' disciples removed the body. This story did the rounds at the time, but we are told that it was deliberately invented by the Jewish authorities to discredit the disciples. Besides, how would a few terrified followers have been able to overcome the Roman guards? Why would they risk their own lives by breaking the governor's official seal? Why move a body already in the safe keeping of one of their own number? Why is there no record of their ever being charged with grave robbery? Why put their lives on the line by preaching that they had seen Jesus alive, when they had his body hidden somewhere? They might have risked their lives for something they imagined, but not for something they had invented.

Charles Colson, one of United States President Richard Nixon's advisers at the time of the Watergate scandal that ended his presidency in the 1970s, tells how, within a month, three of those involved in the notorious burglary had gone to the Department of Justice to turn state evidence. Commenting on this some time later Colson wrote, 'In my Watergate experience I saw the inability of men — powerful, highly motivated professionals — to hold together a conspiracy based on a lie ... Yet Christ's followers maintained to their grim deaths by execution that they had in fact seen Jesus Christ raised from the dead. There was no conspiracy ... Men and women do not give up their comfort — and certainly not their lives — for what they know to be a lie.'

Sir Norman Anderson claims that the disciples' transformation from cowardice to courage is 'far and away the strongest circumstantial evidence for the resurrection'.

There is more...

But we can go beyond circumstantial evidence. There are six independent written testimonies, three of them by eyewitnesses, of Jesus having appeared alive after his dead body had been in the tomb for three days. These record eleven separate appearances over a period of forty days, with over 500 people present on one particular occasion. Sceptics suggest that these reports can be written off as hallucinations, but the appearances fail to conform to any of the known laws relating to the subject. There is no evidence that any of the witnesses were neurotic or psychotic, and Jesus rarely appeared in places where he and his followers had spent time together. What is more, resurrection was the last thing his followers expected. They were utterly demoralized and quite certain that Jesus was dead and buried. His resurrection came as a shock to them, rather than as wish-fulfilment; several did not believe it when they were first told and others were alarmed.

Some 2,000 years on, those claiming to be Christians form the largest religious group the world has ever known, and its origin is to be found, not in its style of worship, nor in any particular stance on social issues, nor in a new line of moral philosophy, but in one single event: *the resurrection of Jesus from the dead.* D. James Kennedy said, 'The Grand Canyon wasn't caused by an Indian dragging a stick, and the Christian Church wasn't created by a myth.'

Others have added more formal endorsements. Just one example: Lord Darling, who served as Lord Chief Justice of England, concluded, 'There exists such overwhelming evidence, positive and negative, that no intelligent jury in the world could fail to bring in a verdict that the resurrection story is true.'

Implications

There are far-reaching implications here, both negative and positive.

If Christ did not rise

If Jesus did not rise from the dead, he himself was either deluded or dishonest (as he said that he would rise) and the early disciples were a rabble of blasphemous deceivers. What is more, all the Christian martyrs down the centuries (and there have been millions of them) have spilt their blood for something that never happened; Christian reformers of society have been motivated by a pack of lies; every Christian church building is a monument to a myth; every service held in them is a pointless farce; and Easter Day commemorates a non-event.

But if he did...

The positive implications are even greater. Jesus clearly stated that God is the Creator of all other reality. He specifically underlined the Old Testament's pivotal creed that God is uniquely and peerlessly sovereign over all of his creation. He fully endorsed the integrity and divine authority of the Old Testament. He confirmed the historicity of events recorded there, including those most often questioned by sceptics. He underlined the God-given authority of the Old Testament prophets. He uniquely claimed to be the fulfilment of all the prophecies about a coming Messiah. He repeatedly taught that every person who ever lived would be morally and spiritually accountable to God on a coming day of final judgement.

This helps to make another tremendously important point, which is that any discussion about the integrity, accuracy, inerrancy or authority of the Bible is directly tied in to the resurrection of Jesus from the dead. His resurrection confirms his deity; his deity guarantees the truth of his teaching; and his teaching establishes Scripture as being 'the living and enduring word of God'. The linkage is clear.

T. H. Huxley's statement that faith is no longer in contact with facts of any kind is worse than threadbare, and for Richard Dawkins to claim that science is free of the 'vice' of faith is to replace reality with rhetoric. True science and true biblical religion both involve faith as well as facts, and they are not antagonists, but allies, combining to give us a true picture of reality.

Albert Einstein used a vivid metaphor in saying: 'A legitimate conflict between science and religion cannot exist. Science without religion is lame; religion without science is blind.'

6 Lazy fatheads?

Peter Atkins drew a distinction between what he called a rational (scientific) and an irrational (religious) search for truth and claimed that the latter led the 'false-footed' to 'sink into the feigned comfort of fraudulent expectations and self-deception masquerading as an understanding'. In an article he warmed to his subject: 'Science respects the power of the human intellect; religion belittles it ... Science is progressively advancing toward complete knowledge, leaving religions bobbing about in its wake ... Religion is armchair speculation well fitted to adipose brains.' He called religion 'outmoded and ridiculous' and claimed that it was 'not possible to believe in gods and be a true scientist'. This hardly leaves us in any doubt as to where he is coming from, and in a review of *Darwin's Black Box* he sharpened his attack by calling

God 'this incompetent figment of impoverished imaginations'.

These are serious accusations, and if Atkins is right the only sensible way to search for truth is to reject any idea of God and concentrate on an approach driven by scientific rationalism — *but is he right*? Peter Atkins still holds to his core claim: 'You can clearly be a scientist and have religious beliefs. But I don't think you can be a real scientist in the deepest sense of the word.'

This seems totally at odds with the fact that the study of the relationship between science and theology is one of the fastest-growing academic areas in the world, with organizations of scientists committed to belief in God flourishing on an unprecedented scale. In the United States, the American Scientific Affiliation has some 1,500 members drawn from most of the nation's fifty states and some forty other countries. Also based in the United States, the Creation Research Society, committed to a biblical world-view, has an international membership, with all its voting members having at least one earned postgraduate degree in a recognized area of science. In Britain, over 4,000 doctors are members of the Christian Medical Fellowship, which also has 800 student members and active links with some sixty similar organizations worldwide. Also based in Britain, Christians in Science has over 1,000 members, including several distinguished senior scientists. Over

150 Ph.D. scientists and 300 other scientists with masters' degrees are members of the Korea Association of Creation Research, whose aim is 'to see science return to its rightful, God-glorifying position'. Listing the many like-minded organizations flourishing on all five continents, whose members are committed believers in specialized fields from astronomy to zoology, would take up too much space in a book of this size, but their sheer numbers and quality would seem to be *prima facie* evidence against Peter Atkins's claim that it is impossible to be 'a true scientist' (or 'a real scientist') and believe in God.

History says...

His claim also sits awkwardly with any honest examination of the rise of modern science. Although the term 'scientist' was not used until 1834, concepts such as the argument from design (i.e., the universe shows evidence of design, so there must be a Designer) go back thousands of years. The Bible lays down some very clear principles here. To quote just one example, an Old Testament writer addresses God in these words:

> Of old you laid the foundation of the earth,
> and the heavens are the work of your hands.
> They will perish, but you will remain;
> they will all wear out like a garment.
> You will change them like a robe, and they will
> pass away,

> but you are the same, and your years have no
> end. (Psalm 102:25-27)

Science as we now know it came into existence in the
sixteenth and seventeenth centuries, and it did so in a
God-centred culture, driven by the biblical conviction
that nature has a divine and eternal Creator upon
whom it is totally dependent. This was vastly different
from a pagan world-view, with its exotic assortment of
deities, including the sun, moon and stars, who were
themselves part of the material universe. As one
historian pointed out, the biblical picture shows us
that '... in total contradiction to pagan religion, nature
is not a deity to be feared and worshipped, but a work
of God to be admired, studied and managed.'

U.S. News & World Report called Dr John
Baumgardner 'the world's pre-eminent expert in the
design of computer models for geophysical
convection'. His three-dimensional computer model
for Earth's interior is recognized as the most capable
computer model of its type in the world and NASA
sees it as cutting-edge science in the field. In an
interview Dr Baumgardner said, 'I believe science as
we know it is a product of the Christian world-view. It
was only in the Christian world that science was
developed and I believe could have developed. For
example, in the Buddhist or Hindu world-view this
physical reality is more or less regarded as an illusion
and not representing ultimate reality. Of course,
Christians don't regard this world as eternal, but

nevertheless it's real. Science has flowed from a Christian understanding of God, and a Christian understanding of the natural world.'

Convictions like these fuelled the explosive launch of modern science. When the Royal Society, which claims to be the oldest learned society still in existence, came into being in 1660, its founders dedicated their work 'to the glory of God'. The manifesto of the British Association for the Advancement of Science, drawn up in 1865 and signed by 617 scientists, including many with outstanding credentials, expressed unambiguous belief in the truth and authority of the Bible and its harmony with natural sciences. These are two outstanding illustrations of the world-view that dominated the thrust of scientific thinking at that time. As Henry Morris says, 'The most discerning historians and philosophers of science have recognized that the very existence of modern science had its origins in a culture at least nominally committed to a biblical basis, and at a time in history marked by a great return to biblical faith.'

Hall of fame

Over the three-and-a-half centuries since then, countless scientists, over the complete range of scientific disciplines, have been committed to a world-view that sees an orderly universe obeying dependable laws put in place by a transcendent Creator who has revealed himself in the pages of the Bible.

Many of these people have made enormous and sometimes seminal contributions to their particular disciplines. Names and numbers are not in themselves any criteria of truth, nor should we rely on an accumulation of honours to prove a point, but there are sufficient examples to make nonsense of the claim that religion belittles the intellect. Science has seen so many God-fearing trailblazers that the problem is not knowing where to start, but when to stop. What follows is mainly a historical survey, but the status of the scientists concerned and the enduring quality of their work are beyond dispute. Taken together, the evidence makes it crystal clear that the very origins of modern scientific thinking were provided by men of faith who had a mindset that has largely been lost by many people currently involved in science. We shall take eleven of these giants as representatives of them all.

As we saw in chapter 3, the philosopher, scientist and politician *Francis Bacon* (1561-1626) made an enormous contribution to science with his development of the inductive method, stressing the importance of observation and experiment. Bacon saw not the slightest conflict between the Bible and natural science: 'There are two books laid before us to study, to prevent our falling into error; first, the volume of the Scriptures, which reveal the will of God;

then the volume of the Creatures, which expresses his power.' This conviction stayed with him throughout his extraordinary career and towards the end of his life he wrote, 'Let no man think or maintain that a man can search too far or be too well studied in the book of God's word or in the book of God's works.' In view of later developments, it is ironic that Charles Darwin reproduced these words on the flyleaf of *Origin*!

The scientist *Johannes Kepler* (1571-1630) is best remembered for discovering the three laws of planetary motion that now bear his name. Kepler saw all his work as a fulfilment of his Christian duty. He famously said that he was only 'thinking God's thoughts after him', and prayed, 'I give you thanks, Creator and God, that you have given me this joy in your creation, and I rejoice in the works of your hands.' He once wrote, 'Since we astronomers are the priests of the highest God in regard to the books of nature, it befits us to be thoughtful, not of the glory of our minds, but rather, above all else, the glory of God.'

The mathematician, philosopher and scientist *Blaise Pascal* (1623-1662) can fairly be called a genius. His Christian faith was his dominant passion, leading him to write, 'Not only do we know God through Jesus Christ alone, but we do not even know ourselves except through Jesus Christ.' He saw bringing glory to God as the sole purpose of all his life and work. Shortly before he died he prayed, 'Grant that I may conform to thy will, just as I am, that, sick as I am, I may glorify thee in my suffering.'

Chemist *Robert Boyle's* (1627-1691) best-known legacy was Boyle's Law, which establishes the relationship between the pressure, temperature and volume of a mass of gas. Above all, Boyle was a committed Christian. He was so concerned to know and understand the Bible that in a single year he taught himself four languages in order to help him do so. He devoted time, energy — and a considerable amount of money — to having the Bible translated and distributed into Irish, Turkish and several native American languages. Far from finding that the Bible's teaching clashed with his scientific discoveries, he repeatedly claimed 'the truth of the history of the Scriptures' and once wrote that 'the seeming contradictions betwixt Divinity and true philosophy' were few 'and the real ones none at all'. Described on his tombstone as 'the father of chemistry', and one of the founders of the Royal Society, Boyle saw no contradiction between his science and his Christian faith. In his last message to the society he urged his fellow scientists, 'Remember to give glory to the one who authored nature.'

One of Boyle's contemporaries was the naturalist, philosopher and theologian *John Ray* (1627-1705), the greatest authority of his day in both botany and zoology. Ray was ordained as a Church of England minister as well as being inducted into the Royal

Society in recognition of his outstanding scientific work. He saw no clash between the two positions. Late in life he wrote two major theological books. The first of these made his personal convictions clear: 'There is for a free man no occupation more worthy and delightful than to contemplate the beauteous works of nature and honour the infinite wisdom and goodness of God.'

The mathematician and philosopher *Sir Isaac Newton* (1642-1727) is generally recognized as one of the greatest scientists who ever lived. A devout Bible student, he said, 'We account the Scriptures of God to be the most sublime philosophy. I find more sure marks of authenticity in the Bible than in any profane history whatsoever.' He also wrote, 'Without all doubt this world ... could arise from nothing but the perfectly free will of God.'

The scientist *Carolus Linneaus* (1707-1778). He has become known as the father of biological taxonomy. Linneaus was a firm believer in special creation and the fixity of species and his works teem with references to God. He once wrote, 'One is completely stunned by the incredible resourcefulness of the Creator ... I followed his footsteps over nature's field and saw everywhere an eternal wisdom and power, an inscrutable perfection.'

Moving on ...

Chemist and physicist *Michael Faraday* (1791-1867) stands as a giant in his field, and today two basic units, one in electrolysis (the faraday) and one in electrostatics (the farad), are named in his honour. Although a towering force in his fields of expertise, Faraday's strong Christian faith was reflected in his humility and he declined both a knighthood and the presidency of the Royal Society, feeling that these were inappropriate honours for a follower of Christ. He preached regularly in his church and subscribed wholeheartedly to its basis of faith, which included the statement: 'The Bible, and it alone, with nothing added to it, nor taken away from it by man, is the sole and sufficient guide for each individual, at all times and in all circumstances.' It is said that in reply to someone who asked him on his deathbed what his speculations were, Faraday testified to his faith in God by replying, 'Speculations? I have none. I am relying on certainties.'

Physicist *James Joule* (1818-1889) was afflicted with a spinal disorder from his early days. In 1849 the Royal Society elected him a member and later honoured him with the Copley Medal, its oldest and highest award. He was twice elected President of the British Association for the Advancement of Science. His work formed the basis of the First Law of Thermodynamics, which states that energy can neither be created nor destroyed, though it can be changed from one form to another, and has been described as 'one of the most important generalizations in the history of science'. Joule made it clear that his appetite for scientific knowledge was fuelled by his faith: 'After the knowledge of, and obedience to, the will of God, the next aim must be to know something of his attributes of wisdom, power and goodness as evidenced by his handiwork. It is evident that an acquaintance with natural laws means no less than an acquaintance with the mind of God therein expressed.' Elsewhere he wrote, 'The phenomena of nature, whether mechanical, chemical, or vital, consist almost entirely in a continual conversion ... into another. Thus it is that order is maintained in the universe. Nothing is deranged, nothing ever lost, but the entire machinery, complicated as it is, works smoothly and harmoniously ... the whole being governed by the sovereign will of God.'

Physicist *William Thomson* (1824-1907) was an astonishing achiever by any standard. Knighted in 1866, Thomson published 661 papers on scientific subjects and patented seventy inventions. Awarded twenty-one honorary doctorates, he was said to have been entitled to more letters after his name than any other man in the British Commonwealth. He joined the Royal Society in 1851, won its Royal Medal in 1856 and its Copley Medal in 1883, and was its President from 1889-1895. He also served as President of the

British Association for the Advancement of Science and three times as President of the Royal Edinburgh Society.

In all of his theoretical and practical work Thomson remained a convinced and articulate Christian. He believed that the coherence of nature and Scripture could be established with 'sober, scientific certainty' and saw God as 'maintaining and sustaining his creation through the exercise of his will'. Although Charles Darwin branded him 'an odious spectre', his convictions remained crystal clear: 'Overwhelmingly strong proofs of intelligence and design lie around us'; 'I believe that the more thoroughly science is studied, the further does it take us from anything comparable to atheism'; 'The atheistic idea is so nonsensical that I can't put it into words.'

The last in our sample of pioneering giants is scientist *James Clerk Maxwell* (1831-1879), now generally recognized as the father of modern physics. Albert Einstein said that Maxwell had introduced a new scientific epoch and that his electromagnetic theory was 'the most profound and most fruitful that physics has experienced since the time of Newton'. Maxwell's faith in God lay behind all his work; he once wrote, 'I have looked into most philosophical systems and I have seen not one that will work without a God.' He was noted for his extemporaneous prayers, at least one of which has been preserved: 'Teach us to study the works of thy hands, that we may subdue the earth to our use and strengthen our reason for thy service.'

Far from our having had to scrape the barrel to find these examples, they are no more than a small sample of a much larger 'hall of fame'.

Each one of the men listed was an outstanding scientist who believed that the entire universe is the creative work of God, that the Bible is the Word of God and that there was no contradiction between his scientific knowledge and Christian convictions. Then what do we make of Peter Atkins's claim that science is incompatible with belief in God? Is he suggesting that none of these outstanding men meets his criteria for being 'a true scientist'? The only alternative seems to be the assertion that, although their science was excellent, they mysteriously lost touch with reality as soon as they turned to religion. Nor does his statement that religion is 'armchair speculation well suited to adipose brains' find any sensible traction in these testimonies. Dictionaries define 'adipose' as 'fat', 'fatty', or 'used for the storage of fat'. As size is obviously not the issue, the only other clue we have is the phrase 'armchair speculation', which seems to hint at lazy or careless thinking. Is he really saying that these giants were lazy fatheads? Granting Atkins all the licence his words will allow, his statements seem to stem from prejudiced rhetoric rather than from principled reasoning.

Update

The position today is essentially no different. All over the world there are outstanding scientists who are men of God as well as men of science. Two modern thinkers have gone even further: 'A significant number of scientists, historians of science and philosophers of science see more scientific evidence now for a personal creator and designer than was available fifty years ago. In the light of this evidence, it is false and naïve to claim that modern science has made belief in the supernatural unreasonable.' We shall allow two outstanding scientists, in very different disciplines, to speak for all of them.

Raymond Jones is a distinguished agricultural scientist. A Fellow of the Australian Institute of Agricultural Science, the Australian Academy of Technological Science and Engineering and the Tropical Grasslands Society of Australia, he has published about 140 research papers and has been honoured with the Urrbrae Award and the CSIRO Gold Medal for Research Excellence. In his early years Jones was a staunch evolutionist, but while at university his beliefs were shaken by the fact that he could not find evidence for the multitudes of intermediate forms which should exist if evolution were true. Asked in an interview whether evolution had great practical value, Jones replied, 'In my experience, I've never seen that. Many scientists might speculate in their papers about how a certain result relates to evolution, but I don't see that it's the driving force that enables breakthroughs, or that it features much in most scientists' work. Is having an evolutionary paradigm more enabling of research? I don't think so. In fact, believing in an almighty God, rather than chance, behind everything could be more of a driving force for your scientific work. It gives you confidence that something will be found when you search, because behind it all is a mind greater than your own.'

Francis Collins trained as a physical chemist, then went to medical school and became a physician. An expert in the genetics of human disease, he was part of the team that identified the genes defective in cystic fibrosis, Huntington's disease and neurofibromatosis. He says that in his early twenties he was 'a pretty obnoxious atheist', but at twenty-seven he became a convinced and committed Christian, largely through the writings of C. S. Lewis.

In the course of an interview, Collins said, 'I think it's critical that we have a meaningful dialogue between people of faith and people involved in science, and ideally it would be nice if some of those were the same people. I see no reason why that can't be the case. In fact, as a scientist, the religious aspects of my life, I believe, add additional meaning to what I do in science.' Asked to elaborate, he replied, 'For me, as a person of faith, that moment of discovery has an additional dimension. It's appreciating something, realizing something, knowing something that until then no human had known — but God knew it. There is an intricacy and elegance in the nature of biology, particularly when it comes to the information-carrying capacity of DNA, which is rather awesome. There is a sense in which those moments of discovery also become moments of worship, moments of appreciation, of the incredible intricacies and beauty of biology, of the world, of life — and therefore an appreciation of God as the Creator.' Elsewhere, he wrote, 'Of all choices, atheism requires the greatest faith, as it demands that one's limited store of human knowledge is sufficient to exclude the possibility of God.'

7 Beyond science

Professor David Horrobin, who died in 2003, has been described as 'one of the most original minds of his generation'. As the author or editor of numerous books and a contributor to more than 800 publications, we can fairly call David Horrobin a truly outstanding scientist. His appearance here stems from a book he wrote in 1969: its title was *Science is God*.

At first glance, this title seems to answer the question, 'Has Science disposed of God?', with an emphatic 'Yes' — but as the following quotations will show, Horrobin took a very different tack:

Science is the modern god... Twentieth-century scientists ... make the wildest claims on behalf of their god ... and bewildered twentieth-century common men have a crude faith in their god which they do not care to have questioned too closely.

Ultimately the psychologist, the psychiatrist, the sociologist must each confess that his work must be prefaced by 'I believe' and not by 'I have proved scientifically'.

Far from saying that science had usurped God, Horrobin was underlining the message of the American scientist Anthony Standen's best-seller *Science is a Sacred Cow*, published in 1950. In simple terms, he was saying that modern man has wrongly elevated science from a discipline to a deity, whose authority is absolute and before whom all other claims to truth must submit.

A recap

This is where we came in. As one scientist says, soon after he became a Christian he concluded that '... the great divide between the Christian faith and scientific knowledge is a mirage promoted by a few noisy people.' This may be the case, but the 'noisy people' are the ones who are being heard the most. The issue of origins provides a good example.

The current 'official' story is one of a universe existing and developing by an ongoing succession of mindless events, those who maintain that a transcendent God is the creator and sustainer of it all are often marginalized or ridiculed.

Science now has such a high profile (and brilliant track record) that in public debate religion is often derided or dismissed, reflecting Peter Atkins's claim that science can explain everything. This 'cool' dismissal of religion is ignited by Richard Dawkins, who calls a biblical belief system 'ignominious, contemptible and retarded'. However, in chapter 2 we drew the distinction between science and *scientism* and showed that the latter is logically unsustainable, as it is only by abandoning the very rules by which it justifies its own existence that it can claim that God does not exist.

When we examined true science in chapter 3 we found that 'Science says ...' is not to be equated with 'The fact is ...' A scientific description of an entity or event is not the only valid one; scientific claims have often been modified or replaced; and scientists of equal merit are sometimes at loggerheads over important ideas or theories. Even more tellingly, we saw that vast areas of knowledge are beyond the reach of science, making its aims much shorter than its claims. For all its brilliant achievements, science is unable to tell us why the universe came into being, why there are consistent and dependable natural laws, why fundamental physical constants are so fine-tuned as to support intelligent life on our planet, why we are persons and not merely animate objects, or why the mind functions as it does. Science is incapable of giving us an inner quality of life, or of defining or explaining ethical principles. It is unable to tell us anything about the purpose of life, or our destiny after death. These are sobering shortcomings. To pick up on just one of them, questions of meaning and value are outside the limits of science, yet without a concept of meaning how can science be justified? What is more, science is unable to prove that God does not exist, firstly because he is spiritual and not material, secondly because he is by definition beyond the comprehension of finite minds, and thirdly because it is impossible to prove a universal negative.

In chapter 4 we concentrated on the theory of macro-evolution, which for many people has become the weapon of choice in attacking God. Relentlessly promoted in educational circles and in the media, the idea has become so pervasive that Sir Julian Huxley called it 'the most powerful and the most comprehensive idea that has ever arisen on earth'. Yet in a single chapter we were able to show that it fell far short of being provable. There is no solid evidence of intermediate life forms between any of the major groupings — *Homo sapiens*, apelike quadrupeds, birds, reptiles, amphibians, vertebrate fish, metazoan invertebrates and microscopic single-cell organisms. In spite of Herculean efforts to find them, the missing links are all missing! Nor is there a shred of objective evidence to show that life arose on our planet as the result of an accidental collision of inert elements in some kind of chemical soup.

Leaning on the 'synthetic theory' that, given an immense amount of time, mutations could pave the way for natural selection to create new orders of animals has proved just as futile, especially since the discovery of DNA, with its staggering 'cargo' of genetic information. As there is no natural law or physical process by which information can be generated or increased, macro-evolution is stuck at the starting-gate.

Biophysicist Dr Lee Spetner is adamant: 'The neo-Darwinians would like us to believe that large evolutionary changes can result from a series of small events if there are enough of them. But if these events all lose information they can't be the steps in the kind of evolution [the neo-Darwinian theory] is supposed to explain, no matter how many mutations there are. Whoever thinks macro-evolution can be made by mutations that lose information is like the merchant who lost a little money on every sale but thought he could make it up on volume.'

The 'information by accident' idea disintegrates as soon as we touch it. If the information in the human genetic code is something that evolved as the result of an unimaginable amount of genetic damage, why should it mean anything to us? If our brains tell us they are merely the products of blind chemical actions and reactions, how can we know that even this message is the truth?

Chapter 5 established that true scientists are men and women of faith, necessarily committed to belief in their own existence, the objective and independent reality of the universe, the uniformity of nature, the integrity of their own senses, the law of cause and effect and the existence of invisible reality. It also showed that all of these assumptions fit perfectly into a biblical world-view, with God at its centre. Finally, it showed that far from being a vague amalgamation of religious ideas, Christianity is firmly rooted in verifiable history.

This was endorsed in chapter 6, in which we confirmed that there was no dichotomy between scientific knowledge and faith in God. Today, thousands of other scientists, many of them with outstanding credentials, give the same testimony, something that came home to me very strikingly when I preached at a normal Sunday morning church service in which the congregation of 300 included over thirty scientists with earned doctorates in disciplines ranging from medicine to microbiology and from pharmacy to physics.

From nothing to nowhere?

Godless science not only has the fatal flaws we have revisited here; it also comes with some very disheartening baggage.

In 1995 Peter Atkins wrote an article which was published in the *Independent* with the title, 'A desolate place to look for answers', and the sub-title, 'The meaning of life in our universe is not as perplexing as it is depressing.' The article concluded like this: 'Where did it come from? From nothing. Where is it going? To oblivion. How is it getting there? By purposeless decay into chaos. And the cosmic purpose? I leave you to draw your own conclusions.'

Bertrand Russell filled out the bleak scenario that materialism offers: 'Brief and powerless is man's life; on him and on all his race the slow, sure doom falls, pitiless and dark. Blind to good and evil, reckless of destruction, omnipotent matter rolls on its relentless way; for man, condemned today to lose his dearest, tomorrow himself to pass through the gates of darkness.'

In *The Selfish Gene*, Richard Dawkins maintains that essentially '... we are survival machines — robot vehicles blindly programmed to preserve the selfish molecules known as genes.' I have always felt that this idea must be desolating to anyone without offspring, and atheist Steve Pinker responds to it with hollow humour: 'Well into my procreating years I am, so far, voluntarily childless, having squandered my biological resources reading and writing, doing research, helping out friends and students, and jogging in circles, ignoring the solemn imperative to spread my genes. By Darwinian standards I am a horrible mistake, a pathetic loser ... But I am happy to be that way, and if my genes don't like it, they can jump in the lake.' Richard Dawkins says that the publisher of a foreign translation of *The Selfish Gene* was so shattered by its cold, bleak message that he could not sleep for three nights. Atheism's creed is clear and cruel: we began as a fluke, we live as a farce and we end as fertilizer.

There is an alternative …

Good news

The idea that science has somehow disposed of God is nineteenth-century folklore masquerading as twenty-first-century fact. Nor is God playing hide and seek with us. In his typically quirky way, the American film producer Woody Allen complained, 'If God would only speak to me — just once. If he would only cough. If I could just see a miracle. If I could see a burning bush or the seas part. Or my Uncle Sasha pick up the check.' Elsewhere he mused, 'If only God would give me some clear sign! Like making a large deposit in my name at a Swiss bank.' One has to smile at Allen's wit, but on this extremely serious issue he misses the point that God *has* spoken and revealed himself to us in at least three dramatic ways.

1 God has revealed himself in creation

As we have seen, atheistic science has no explanation for the existence of the universe, whereas the Bible declares, 'The heavens declare the glory of God, and the sky above proclaims his handiwork.' (Psalm 19:1) This tells us not only that God is distinct from all creation, but that creation is a stupendous signpost to his existence and it reflects the Bible's own insistence that in the wonders of the natural world God has revealed 'his eternal power and divine nature'. Dr Arthur Compton, a Nobel Prize winner, expressed his own convictions very clearly: 'For myself, faith begins with a realization that a supreme intelligence brought the universe into being and created man. It is not difficult for me to have this faith, for it is incontrovertible that where there is a plan there is intelligence. Theoretical physicist Michio Kaku, one of the world's most respected scientists and a developer of the revolutionary String Theory, says, 'To me it is clear that we exist in a plan which is governed by rules that were created, shaped by a universal intelligence and not by chance.' He adds that the very purpose of physics is to find an equation…which will allow us to read the mind of God.' An orderly, unfolding universe testifies to the truth of the most majestic statement ever uttered — "In the beginning God."'

2 God has revealed himself in the Bible

In spite of 2,000 years of investigation, persecution, criticism and cynicism, the Bible remains intact and unscarred. Time and again sceptics have questioned its historical accuracy, only to have further research prove them wrong; not a single one of its hundreds of prophecies has been shown to be false; it sets the highest moral standards known to man and, although written by over forty authors over a period of some

1,500 years, its amazing unity is unequalled in literature of any kind. Sir Isaac Newton was hardly exaggerating when he called it 'a rock from which all the hammers of criticism have never chipped a single fragment'. Quite simply, there is no human explanation for the Bible. In every way that we can test it, it lives up to its claim to be 'the living and enduring word of God'.

The Bible not only tells us of God's existence, but also reveals many of his attributes. He is *transcendently self-existent*, 'the eternal God' who is 'from everlasting to everlasting', above and beyond time, space and all other reality. He is *immutable* and with him 'there is no variation or shadow due to change' and he is never moulded or manipulated by circumstances or experience. He is actively *omnipotent* and 'works out everything in conformity with the purpose of his will'. He is *omniscient* — 'perfect in knowledge' — so that he never has to learn, discover or remember anything. He is utterly *holy*; he cannot 'look on evil' and '... in him there is no darkness at all.' God's holiness is the sum of all excellence and the combination of all the attributes which constitute perfection of character.

Finally, 'God is *love*.' Love is of his very essence, and its depth and breadth are utterly beyond our limited human understanding. This does not mean that he is a 'soft touch', or some kind of celestial sugar-daddy, indulgently lavishing his benevolence on all and sundry in a way that is indifferent to their beliefs and behaviour. Although the Bible speaks of his 'unfailing kindness' and 'wonderful love', it also shows that this love is focused on his purpose to bring people into an eternal relationship with himself.

3 God has revealed himself in Jesus Christ

We saw in chapter 3 that 'God is spirit' and the Bible specifically says, 'No one has ever seen God.' Yet it also says that Jesus Christ 'has made him known'. The phrase 'made him known' is based on the Greek verb *exegéomai*, which means 'to bring out into the open'. In the person of Jesus we have an accessible revelation of the very nature and character of God. In the Bible's amazing words, 'For in him all the fullness of God was pleased to dwell.' He was as fully man as if he were not God, and as fully God as if he were not man. As one writer says: 'God has taken the attributes of his being — his love, his mercy, his holiness, his justice, his power — and has translated them into a form that men can understand, believe and respond to ... The climax of God's revelation of himself is the person of Jesus Christ. In him the ultimate and the unconditional are wed to the transient and the conditioned in such a way that a human being can respond with his or her own personality.'

The Saviour

Yet the Bible makes it clear that, as well as giving us in human flesh and form a revelation of his nature, God had another specific reason for coming into the world in this way: 'For God so loved the world, that he gave his only Son, that whoever believes in him should not perish but have eternal life.'

Elsewhere we are told that Jesus 'came into the world to save sinners'. He did not come as a statesman, a politician, a philosopher, a financial adviser, a psychiatrist or a doctor, but in order to save us from the appalling consequences of our inbuilt rejection of God and his ways.

Jesus came on a rescue mission — at the cost of his own life. The Bible says that '... all have sinned and fall short of the glory of God,' and that '... the wages of sin is death.' Sin separates us from God, not only in this life but in the life to come: 'Nothing impure will ever enter (heaven).' This means that, left to ourselves, we are guilty, lost and helpless, yet 'God shows his love for us in that while we were still sinners, Christ died for us.' In his dreadful death by crucifixion the sinless Jesus took the place of sinners, becoming as accountable for their sins as if he had been responsible for them. God is unutterably holy and cannot leave any sin unpunished, so that when Jesus took the place of sinners he had to bear in full the penalty their sins deserved. On the cross Jesus was exposed to the full extent of God's wrath against the sinners he represented and the sins they had committed.

The only completely innocent person in all of human history voluntarily took upon himself the physical and spiritual death penalty that sin deserves and God demands. Nothing was held back, and in bearing the penalty for the sins of others Jesus had such an appalling sense of separation from his Father that he cried out, 'My God, my God, why have you forsaken me?' We may never be able to know all that this meant; we are faced with a mystery. What we do know is that in the death of his Son, God 'shows his love for us'. One of the early Christians wrote of 'the Son of God, who loved me and gave himself for me'; another stated, 'For Christ also suffered once for sins, the righteous for the unrighteous, that he might bring us to God'; while yet another added, 'By this we know love, that he laid down his life for us.'

But the most gruesome day in human history was followed soon afterwards by the most glorious, when the resurrection of Jesus from the dead infallibly confirmed that his sacrifice had accomplished its intention. As we saw in chapter 5, accepting that Jesus rose from the dead is not a leap in the dark. It is based on an immovable mass of incontrovertible evidence, what the Bible calls 'many convincing proofs'. This is the very heart of the Christian gospel; it is the best news anyone has ever heard.

Believing and believing

When speaking to audiences about the nature of Christian faith I have often made use of the following formula. Dealing specifically with what Christian faith involves, I have said something like this: 'I believe in a cold bath before breakfast every morning. I don't just mean in the height of summer, but all the year round, even when the temperature is below zero and icicles are hanging from the guttering. I believe there is no better way to start the day than by getting smartly out of bed, running a cold bath and jumping straight in.' This has always produced a corporate wince from the audience — followed by a sudden burst of laughter as soon as I have added, 'But I have never had one!'

We have reached that point in this book, and to press the point home I am going to write these final few pages in the second personal singular. Nowhere have I tried to *prove* that God exists, because proving such a thing deductively is impossible. Instead, I have tried to show that the evidence, including the most recent scientific discoveries, *points in that direction*, and that millions of people over thousands of years (including countless scientists with outstanding credentials) have become convinced that this is the case. As you come towards the end of the book, you may have joined them. You may have read the first page as an atheist, an agnostic, or a sceptic of some kind. Now you have come to see the force of the accumulated evidence and to accept that '... there is but one God, the Father, from whom all things came ...'

So far, so good — but this falls a long way short of the faith the Bible requires of us. To believe in God can obviously not mean *less* than giving intellectual assent to propositional truth; the Bible makes the obvious point that '... anyone who comes to him must believe that he exists.' But another New Testament writer makes it equally clear that acknowledging God's existence is not enough: 'You believe that there is one God. Good! Even the demons believe that — and shudder.' The Bible gives us clear examples of this. When two demon-possessed men met Jesus, they cried out, 'What do you want with us, Son of God?' On another occasion an evil spirit possessing a man shouted, 'What do you want with us, Jesus of Nazareth? Have you come to destroy us? I know who you are — the Holy One of God!' These outbursts dramatically underline the point. Faith that consists merely of giving mental assent to certain facts leaves the person concerned knowing the truth but not changed by it. In direct contrast, biblical faith enables a Christian to say, 'Therefore, since we have been justified through faith, *we have peace with God* through our Lord Jesus Christ.'

The key to understanding the difference between 'head faith' and 'heart faith' is to realize that 'heart faith' means responding to a living person, not to a logical proposition. C. S. Lewis put his finger on the spot: 'To believe that God — at least *this* God — exists is to believe that you as a person now stand in the presence of God as a Person... You are no longer faced with an argument which demands your assent, but with a Person who demands your confidence.'

There is a sense in which God is beyond our knowing — and we can certainly never know him purely through our own powers of reasoning. God is not part of his creation and he is not known in the way we know things he has made. Biblical belief in God is vitally different from belief in a scientific hypothesis. Even if we stack up all the evidence pointing to God's existence, we are a long way from experiencing a personal relationship with him, just as we can know a great deal *about* other people without actually *knowing* them.

We can take this further and say that demanding evidence before believing in God (in the style of Woody Allen) is to be condemned, not commended. It is a sign of human arrogance, compounded by the fact that part of us *wants* science to be in conflict with God.

The Bible says that God's revelation of himself in creation alone is sufficient to leave us 'without excuse' if we deny his existence. Strictly speaking, nobody is an atheist. All rational human beings have programmed into their constitutions an inner awareness of deity, a knowledge at some level of their thinking that God exists. Even Jean-Paul Sartre admitted, 'Everything in me calls for God.' All of share this, yet by nature we suppress this instinct, distort its message — and fatally deceive ourselves. As a result, there is a sense in which at one and the same time we both know God and do not know him. True, biblical faith is the solution to this dilemma.

The turning point

In biblical terms, believing in God involves *turning* and *trusting* — and the second aspect is impossible without the first. The Bible's word for turning is 'repentance', which calls for a revolution in heart, mind and will — and God 'commands all people everywhere to repent'. It means ending your rebellion against God and abandoning your self-centred independence. It means acknowledging that God has the prior claim on your life and recognizing that your primary goal should be to bring glory to him through your wholehearted obedience. It means setting your heart on living the kind of life that reflects his purity, love and grace.

As we have already seen, when the Bible speaks of believing it means something far more than the cold acceptance of facts. It means trusting. God promises the forgiveness of sins, eternal life and his own presence and power to enable you to live a God-centred life — but there must first be a wholehearted response to Jesus Christ. He is 'able to save completely those who come to God through him' — but you must come, acknowledging your need of a Saviour from the power and penalty of your sin and casting yourself upon him, trusting him to do for you something that is beyond the reach not only of science, but of sincerity, respectability or religion.

This is exactly what becoming a true Christian involves — abandoning all trust in your own knowledge, merits and achievements and staking your destiny on Jesus Christ, trusting him as your Saviour and submitting to him as your Lord. To do this is not to reject or abandon reason or scientific principles, but to go beyond both and to join millions of others who, over thousands of years, have found God to be true to his word, and whose search for greater truth than science could ever uncover has led them to a life-transforming relationship with their Creator. The Bible's promise could not be clearer:

> ... if you seek (wisdom) like silver
> and search for it as for hidden treasures,
> then you will understand the fear of the Lord
> and find the knowledge of God.
> (Proverbs 2:4-5)

MANCHESTER
UNITED

RUINED MY WIFE

MANCHESTER
UNITED

RUINED MY WIFE

(A FAN FOR ALL REASONS)

DAVID BLATT

© David Blatt 2008

The right of David Blatt to be identified as the author of this work has been asserted by him in accordance with sections 77 and 78 of the Copyright, Designs and Patents Act, 1988.

Know The Score Books Limited

118 Alcester Road Studley, Warwickshire, B80 7NT
Tel: 01527 454482
Fax: 01527 452183
info@knowthescorebooks.com
www.knowthescorebooks.com

A CIP catalogue record is available for this book from the British Library

ISBN: 978-1-905449-81-1

Cover design by Paul W
Photographs by David Blatt
Edited by Andy Searle and David Blatt
Back cover illustration by Jasmine Blatt

Mixed Sources
Product group from well-managed forests and other controlled sources
www.fsc.org Cert no. TT-COC-2082
© 1996 Forest Stewardship Council
FSC

Printed and bound in Great Britain by Cromwell Press, Trowbridge, Wiltshire

REDICATION

This book is dedicated to the women in my life: My two beautiful daughters, Melanie and Jasmine, my delightful granddaughter, Lilyella, and my incredible wife, Hélène, who's had to put up with far more than any woman has a right to expect – and bloody right too!

U-NI-TED! U-NI-TED! U-NI-TED!...

"Ow. She's just read this and she's hit me again."

ACKNOWLEDGEMENTS

FIRST and foremost I would like to thank me, without whom this book would not have been possible. I have known me all my life and I can say without fear of contraception that I wouldn't have been anyone else. Not that anyone else would want to be me.

I would also like to thank the following:

My family (I've got to, otherwise I won't be let back into the house). My wife, Hélène, and two daughters, Melanie and Jasmine, for putting up with my Red rants from the moment they knew I existed.

Barney Chilton, editor of Red News, the original Manchester United fanzine which recently celebrated its 100th issue, whose continual encouragement of me to publish and be dammed. (which I probably will be).

Rick Mayston, from the leaning tower of Tottenham, carrying the burden of the biggest chips in football, without whose knowledge and contacts you wouldn't be reading this.

Andy Searle for believing in the project from the beginning and Simon Lowe of *Know The Score* books for picking up the mantle.

The achievements and sacrifices of Sir Matt Busby and Sir Alex Ferguson, two of the greatest human beings I have ever met, without whose visions for Manchester United I would be but an empty shell, forever circumventing the globe in search of the Meaning of Life.

And finally, the fans, players, staff, stadium, jobsworths, meat & potato pies, Pink, in fact everything that makes up the Power and the Glory that is Manchester United. I have been blessed. I have been truly blessed and I thank MUFC from the bottom of my heart and my wallet.

CONTENTS

FOREWORD
by Sir Alex Ferguson

IT NEVER SURPRISES me when I read of Manchester United supporters' great passion for the Club. Quite a few have put their experiences down in print and it's quite enthralling to follow their path in life with Manchester United.

I met David at my first AGM some seventeen and half years ago. To be honest I thought he was a bit of a hippy with his long flowing locks and moustache, but it didn't hide his love for Manchester United, as I found out in my many meetings and conversations with him over the years. Then all of a sudden he went missing and I wondered where the blazes he had gone, but one day there he was on a flight in France and our debates and chats were revived again.

Although out of sight, he had not lost his passion for the Club, as I am sure you will discover when you read his book. It is a great account of how a football club can engulf your whole life, how your family are sacrificed in the process and how every facet of the day to day existence of Manchester United creates such an emotional response.

As you will find out, following Manchester United is a journey of life's ups and downs. It is not all glory, think of the twenty six years without a Championship – how must the fans have felt – and think of those final moments in Barcelona and you will feel the whole gamut of emotions.

Good luck to David and his family and enjoy the read.

INT-RED-UCTION

I'VE KNOWN HÉLÈNE ever since the first time I met her. She was French at the time and remains so even to this day, which explains quite a lot.

When we first started going out she thought my obsession with Manchester United was "quaint", "cute", a little strange, but then I was English. You see the French consider football as just another leisure activity. OK, OK, stop laughing. Yeah, I know, that's what I call really strange. As the days, weeks, months and years went by she began to realise that my passion for "Le Foot" wouldn't diminish as my passion for her grew. An equation that she hadn't learnt at school presented itself: namely that a man could love both a woman and his football team. Not a concept they are familiar with across "La Manche".

She could have gone either way. I had visions of us crisscrossing this sceptered isle of ours, sharing United's triumphs and disasters together as the years rolled by. Then what could be more romantic than whisking her away for a surprise mid-week break in Europe. From stylish hotspots such as Turin, Milan, Rome, Madrid, Barcelona, Munich and Athens to cosy hideaways such as Florence, Monaco, Montpelier, Gothenberg, Lotz and Wrexham.

She went the wrong way. She took the path of the devil, but he wasn't Red. She went over to the 'other side'. She now detests football with the same intensity I love it. I walk the eternal diplomatic tightrope. When I fall, if the various crews don't get me, my wife will.

But the truth has to be told. Manchester United have taken me to higher highs and lower lows than anything else on this planet, including sex. This may, of course, tell you more about me than the relative merits, or otherwise, of football or sex.

In an ideal world, of course, I'd like to OD on both, but lack of funds and looks put paid to those fantasies. Now be honest. There must be thousands of you out there who feel the same way about your football team, whether you've been blessed by supporting Eric's Disciples on Earth or one of the myriad of pale imitations that proliferate this unique planet of ours. It's illogical I know, but either way you'll understand where I'm coming from. My wife claims I'm not "normal". I'm sad, warped, shallow and should 'get a life'. Perhaps she's right, but if what I've experienced over these last fifty years is anything to go by, I never want to be cured.

I belong to the biggest and best family on Earth, The Red Army. ("Red Army! Red Army! Red Army!") See, there I go again. Can't stop. From the moment I discovered the Manchester United (London & District) Supporters Club at the spotty age of fourteen I was hooked. How could copping a feel with girls compete with getting up at 5.00am on a Saturday morning to travel by coach along the M1/A5/M6 and back, or the world's largest and longest registered orgasm recorded on May 29th 1968, May 26th 1999 and May 22nd 2008 which repeated itself with a vengeance precisely at 01.15 on May 22nd 2008.

What follows is not a complete and exhaustive account of my years following United at home, away and in Europe (you've had enough sleep already) but a rambling prose which I hope captures the highs and lows that every fan of every club goes through, with the exceptions, of course, of May 26th 1999. Millions of you watched on TV, but as Peter Sellers once remarked, "Being There" was the only place to be. And thousands and thousands of United fans will have experienced the most intense orgasms unknown to man.

So lie back, kick out your jams brothers and sisters and let
the fun begin...

1

"O" – MY VERY FIRST TIME

I WAS BORN ON 17th June 1949 at the Middlesex Hospital, Mortimer Street in Central London. I was zero at the time – but not for long. I began life with my parents in boring suburbia, South Woodford to be exact. In 1956 we owned our first television set, a black & white Ferguson. (If you're looking for omens, go no further. Spooky!) It wasn't long before my mother came out with a line that only mothers could ever come out with.

"If you sit in front of the television all day, you'll end up with square eyes. "

Now, hang on a minute here. With the value of hindsight let's examine that statement. In 1956 television programs only came on at something like 3.45pm in the afternoon, then finished abruptly at 6.00pm so as not to temp the little lady of the house from her duties for the 2.4 family. Resumption at 7.30pm consisted of programs that no seven year old would be remotely interested in anyway.

Square eyes. I don't think so.

Didn't parents get away with murder in those days? Still, at the impressionable age of seven you believed everything your parents told you. I didn't want to succumb to this new disease that doctors had yet to find a cure for, so it fell to my Dad to find a solution.

So what was the "answer"? You've guessed it – football.

Now this is quite interesting because my Dad didn't actually like football. Poor man. He paid lip service to Aston Villa, but only because, as a seargent, he was posted to an Italian prisoner-of-war camp in Aston, Birmingham during World War Two. Some of the local sqaddies followed

'The Villa' and I suspect it was more a case of joining in so as to be accepted than some dark, recessed longing for the claret & blues. Also, for no apparent reason, he chose a boy from my class, Stephen Moy, to accompany us to our very first football match. Why Stephen Moy you ask? Beats me. He wasn't even a friend of mine at the time, just a kid in my class at Oakdale County Primary School in South Woodford. In fact, if the truth be told, he was a bit "ruff" and not the sort of boy Mum would normally let me play with.

He dropped all his "aitches" yet had the most beautiful handwriting. (Did I tell you I was impressionable?). A strange package indeed. So, what was our first match? Leyton Orient V Brighton & Hove Albion in the old Second Division of course.

You see, The "O's" were my nearest league team, so it was logical they would be the first team I actually saw live. But I want you to know that I didn't go all the way. Not on a first date. It was OK I suppose. It was cold and everyone seemed bigger than me. I remember one team played in royal blue and one team played in orange. Orange! Mmmmm, nice. So that was the team I supported that day. It was only as we came out of Brisbane Road that I overheard a conversation that lead me to the conclusion that I had mistakenly supported Brighton & Hove Albion in their away colours. Still, no lasting psychological damage was done – the game ended 2-2.

For the next two years my Dad took me to the Bermondsey Triangle of First Division clubs, namely Arsenal, Tottenham and West Ham. At these larger grounds the weather was colder, people were taller and I saw even less. So as you can see. Lots of dates. The odd kiss, but I never went all the way.

Then one night at Highbury it all changed. Even walking to the stadium I could feel the electricity in the air. I began to tingle. Inside the ground I entered a new dimension. WOW! The noise, the atmosphere. And when the teams came out – that ROAR. This was foreplay above and beyond anything I had ever experienced before.

"What team's that, Dad?

"Why, that's Manchester United, son."

"Well Dad, that's the team for me."

At last – penetration. That all encompassing feeling when you know everything has finally come together. That spark that had been missing suddenly exploded in front of me, inside me and all around me. I was in love. This really was the first day of the rest of my life.

The speed, the skill, the sea-saw of scoring and emotion.

I actually saw some of it between mens' heads, shoulders and backs.

To this day I can look anyone in the eye and say, "I saw Duncan Edwards play." Yet I can't recall which one of our players he was. I was 8 years old for Chrissakes! Only years later would the terrible significance of that match truly hit me. However, one thing I can say to you is that all the discussions since time/football began, as to who was/is the greatest ever player would be rendered redundant if you had seen Duncan Edwards in action, had heard what his United/England colleagues have said and written about him, and if the power(s) that be hadn't taken him so prematurely from us.

He had the power, grace, balance, beauty, character and talent to be considered the greatest of them all.

That first time experience set me up for the roller coaster ride that is Manchester United. Even though I wavered when we were Tampered with so horrendously in May 2004 I'm still very much in love.

So, how was it for you?

2

FROM BOY TO MANCHESTER

FROM NERD TO know-how in one easy step.

Up until the spring of 1967 my life on this planet had been largely uneventful. 18 years old and still a virgin but frequently practicing for the big day – or night.

Living in the London suburb that time forgot, Ilford, I felt that the world was passing me by. Certainly girls were. Fortunately fate was to take a hand in the most unlikely shape of my long-lost cousin, Michael Krazney, who revealed the awesome power behind the combined forces of Aladdin's Cave and Doctor Who's Tardis that lurked in the form of the Manchester United (London & District) Supporters Club, run, Mother Teresa like, by the wonderful Mrs Stewart.

David Blaine, David Copperfield, even the gross Paul Daniels would not have been able to work out how a teenager on little more than pocket money could travel from London to Manchester and back, AND get a ticket to see pre-Eric's Disciples on Earth. But the Manchester United (London & District) Supporters Club could. And so on that momentous day in the spring of 1967 I got up at 05.00am without waking up Andrew, my younger brother, otherwise I would have been slapped by my Dad. I left the house an hour later armed with my brand new leather-look plastic United sports bag overflowing with United scarf, sandwiches and a flask of piping hot Heinz tomato soup. (The word "cool" hadn't yet entered Ilford vocabulary)

The tube journey from Gants Hill to Charing Cross seemed to take an age. "What if I miss the coach?" I thought as excitement and knots grew in my stomach that I usually associated with the magazines under my bed. Eventually yours truly was hovering on the pavement outside Charing Cross tube station, Embankment entrance. Gradually other red clothed members of the same tribe as me congregated in twos and threes. I remember being taken aback by the complete spectrum of ages around me. I thought I would only be surrounded by guys my own age but there were children with their Dads and men even older than my grandfather.

And there were girls.

That was something I hadn't bargained for. Conflict of interest? No, not really, 'cos fortunately they were both dogs.

"Is it a bird?"

"Is it a plane?"

No, it was the coach rising like a phoenix that was to take us to Old Trafford, centre of the planet. At 08.00 I clambered on board, unaware of any system or pecking order, and sat down in the middle next to a short, fair haired kid with more acne than me. It was his first time too. We started chatting nervously, neither one of us wanting to appear like away-day virgins. (By the end of the season he had developed, swan like, into a fully fledged Hoolie, attaching himself to one of the "cockney crews", whilst I took the cul-de-sac route to nerdum. Just thought you'd like to know.)

At 10.30am we stopped for half an hour at Watford Gap services on the M1. If the Manchester United (London & District) Supporters Club was Aladdin's Cave, then Watford Gap was the London Dungeon in disguise. Congealed, tepid and rock 'ard – and they were just the one hundred year old Hell's Grannies serving behind the counter! For a cocooned youth from the suburbs this was an eye and bottom opener. Dogburgers sped in from one orifice only to extract themselves with aplomb from the opposing orifice moments later, leaving little or nothing for my stomach to work with. I got back on the coach an older, weaker and wiser young man. A little while later someone came round with tickets for the game, which incidentally was against Leicester City. Not yet wise to the layout of the ground, my new chum and I chose tickets for the Edwards stand.

So, in pre-video 1967, what does a coach full of die hard Reds do on the A5 northbound towards Brownhills, and beyond? Play Bingo, of course. With the effervescent Danny Swanson as Master of Ceremonies, this was to become a regular Saturday ritual until the joys of independent motoring took over a decade later. Finally we were traversing the A56 through Altringham and towards heaven on Earth. Suddenly there was air of expectancy as we passed the world famous "George Best" boutique, a full season behind Carnaby Street but, what the heck! How we cheered. How the two, cool looking sales assistants took the piss.

Groups of Reds started to get off at various pubs along the road before the coach finally pulled into the special car park. As I disembarked I remember taking in a deep breath.

"Manchester air. I was made for this place."

Eighteen years and I'd finally arrived home. I can't explain the emotion. Tears filled my eyes so I avoided peoples' gaze. This was not the time or place, in front of fellow worshipers, nutters and fanatics to appear soft, but inside I was welling up. A meat and potato pie for 12p became my staple pre-match meal for years until I discovered the Chinese shop next to Lou Macari's fish & chip shop that did Indian curries (?) I shuffled down the Warwick Road, my senses filled with noises and smells. I bought a genuine fake Manchester United scarf from one of the stalls then just stood in the front car park breathing it all in. I queued for hours to enter the Souvenir Shop but had no money left to purchase anything. Around 2.00pm I made my way into the stadium and up flights of stairs before emerging into glorious sunlight and viewing the green, green grass of home. More welling up ensued.

As I took my seat half way up near the half way line I saw and heard the most wondrous thing. Down away to my left the Stretford End was in full voice. I immediately realised I was in the wrong place. Why didn't anybody tell me when I bought my ticket on the coach? Naïve or wot? I was finally in the stadium of my dreams and yet I was out of it, you know wot I mean? I looked around me. Ordinary people. No, this must never happen again. I want to go mental. I want to lose it. Never had the feeling been so strong or felt so right. Whilst the girls in our school doted on the Beatles, we related to the Rolling Stones. They had an edge. They were unsafe, and best of all – your parents hated them. The Stretford End – the only place to be.

Finally, with the ground full to bursting, a roar went up and the two teams came out onto the pitch. I was shivering. I was shaking. And there were no dirty magazines in sight. The match passed so quickly, yet in just one game I learned what every United fan has come to accept for generations. If there is an easy way or a hard way to win a game, United nearly always choose the latter. A brilliant 52 victory of breathtaking football, including a double by the King, Denis Law, the 5th being a glorious chip over the world's greatest goalkeeper, Gordon Banks. Sandwiched between, literally, was a brave goal by David Herd, as two Leicester players sandwiched him and broke his leg. Bastards. He was never to play regularly for the Reds again. How was I to know I was witnessing his last proper game? Manchester United. Glory and angst. Wasn't it ever thus?

The journey home was a blur of images swirling round my head. I desperately tried to learn the songs I had heard that day, so that when I eventually emerged from Gants Hill underground station at 1.00am on Sunday morning I was able to sing them at the top of my voice all the way home. Judging by the number of lights that came on as I passed, I felt pretty sure I was impressing the local neighbourhood.

Life now was just beginning.

3

SCARF ACE

WHAT A DIFFERENCE a year makes. When my parents first discovered my intent, at the age of seventeen, to spend almost every Saturday getting up at five o'clock in the morning in order to experience the delights of the M1-A5-M6 by coach to Manchester, they were not amused. But for the first time in my life I disobeyed orders. I had found my vocation and no earthly intervention was going to change my behaviour pattern.

Over the following twelve months my resolve gradually dissolved theirs, so much so that my mother must have resigned herself to the inevitable with a, "If you can't beat 'em, knit 'em."

On the morning of the penultimate game of the 1967/68 season I was preparing for our last home game against Newcastle United. Manchester City, who had overhauled us in the championship race, were due to play Tottenham Hotspur in London. As I left home at 06.15 I had an extra weapon in my armoury. My mum had knitted me a brand new red & white scarf.

She must have endured hours of anguish and doubt as to the value of her contribution to my newly formed religious fervour. By presenting me with a 'one-off' special from her knitting conveyor belt, she was re-enforcing my commitment to the Red cause. I was left in no doubt as to the sacrifice she had made, both mentally and physically, in the creation of the said scarf, and woe betide me if anything should happen to it.

That was a rather heavy thing to lay on me at the time.

Shit. I was only eighteen years old and it was only a bloody scarf. I didn't need the weight of Damocles hanging over my head.

So there I was, walking towards the tube station, resplendent in red jacket with "MAN UTD" painted in white emulsion paint on the back, white trousers, white United T-shirt with red crest and completing the ensemble, my new red & white scarf. In addition I was carrying my portable radio/record player. I was the Fonz of the

'Back Seat Boot Boys'. In my mind I was cool. I was oblivious to the outside world.

I was early in arriving at Charing Cross underground station for our fleet of eight o' clock coaches but a number of Cockney Reds were already assembled on the pavement. We had a small, tasty crew at that time. I wasn't considered 'ard enough to join their ranks so just nodded in their direction and waited for my lot to turn up.

The London branch's set off point on the Embankment was well known in football circles, and occasionally away fans with a fixture in London would make an early morning excursion along the banks of the Thames to inform us of their presence. At around a quarter to eight we heard this deep, thundering roar and looking up we saw a large herd of about three hundred City fans coming towards us slowly but surely. We numbered about one hundred, enough to fill two coaches. With women and children first, we bunched together and with the assistance of improved acoustics provided by the underground overhang, produced an impressive sonic response that temporarily halted the City masses. (And never forget, City are a "masses" club) With timing that paid homage to the climaxes in old westerns, the cavalry appeared triumphantly over the horizon in the form of our two coaches. They glided to a stop, forming a physical barrier between them and us. We got on the coaches in full voice, extracting the Michael out of the light blue hordes. I put my things on the back corner seat (in one short year I had risen to become a 'Back Seat Boy'. Impressed, huh?) and, together with some of our rougher elements, got off the bus again to taunt the City fans. I was in mid taunt when someone shouted from on my coach.

"Dave! They've opened the back door of the coach and taken your scarf."

"AAAAAAAHHHHHHHHhhhhhhhh!"

My mum's scarf. Not my mum's scarf. Anything but my mum's scarf! I saw red. (Quite appropriate considering the circumstances) Before I thought about what I was doing I rushed straight for the middle of the City mob and demanded my scarf back.

Mistake.

They formed a giant circle around me and three of them came forward. One of them had my scarf attached to one of his epaulets.

"Strange." I thought. "He's got a number of different teams' scarves around his person, yet he looks like a City fan.

Why would he want have mine?"

Oh the innocence of (this) youth.

Then I realised my predicament. United fan 1 City fans 300, and growing, or so it seemed to me. I tried to buy some time.

"What d'yer take my scarf for? (I still didn't get it, see)

There were some collective smirks as three leaders edged forward. Then one of them threw a punch which hit me on the cheek. It wasn't very good though and, more important than anything else, I stayed on my feet. The other two then came forward and I expected the worse when a miracle of biblical proportions was performed, and like the parting of the Red Sea their ranks split in two and one of the women who ran the Manchester United London & District Supporters Club came striding up to us.

I forget what she said but it was mighty effective because the guy who had nicked my scarf meekly handed it over, muttering under his breath. I looked up and our small, tasty crew had now gathered behind her. Although completely outnumbering us, the City Zulu hordes had been dispelled by a woman. (No, not me, the vision from the front seats).

As I returned to the coach an almighty cheer went up. My stock had risen faster than a virgin in a knocking shop. The Cockney Crew took me temporarily to their collective bosom. I'm sure to this day, tales are told of the meek young fan that roared Red defiance at the City dragon. What these fables fail to mention is that I was more in fear of my mum's reprisals than anything those light blue losers could have inflicted on me.

Sitting on the coach I basked in my new found hero status. To all and sundry I had proved I was Red to the core, only I knew it was surrounded by the brown of my underpants.

4

KEYSTONE COCKNEY REDS

HOW FAR CAN YOU GO? Do you know your own limits? Have you been to the other side and back, and lived to tell the tale?

I have and this is my story.

In nineteen hundred and sixty cough cough (I've forgotten the exact year) three Red mates and I made our way north from littleold London town to the centre of the Earth, Manchester, for a night league game against Everton. Journeys like these were made possible as I was the first amongst my Cockney Red mates to own a car. A twenty second hand Mini with sprayed on tinted windows that looked cool for five minutes, but less and less so as each 400 mile round trip accompanied with dogburgers, Watneys Red Barrel Party 7, sweat and B.O. took its toll. The tint began to peel off as a result of turgid, humid heat created by four nerdy looking, acne and angst ridden male bodies. (You've come to the wrong place if it's top shelf turn-on prose your after).

The rain had been falling intermitedly on the five hour journey north but we thought nothing of it as we negotiated the rush hour after hour traffic and the (in)famous A5 through Brownhills. (However it's amazing to realise that over 30 years later, my drive from London to Manchester for the Tottenham game took SIX hours, even with the benefit of a seamless 170 miles of M1/M6. That's progress I suppose.)

An entertaining game ended 2-0 to the Reds, despite the continual downpour throughout the second half. As we made our dripping way back to my car I mentally prepared myself for the return drive, confident as always that GOOD United winning adrenaline would triumph over EVIL sleep inducing numbness brought on by mile upon mile of pitch black motorway. Once partially disrobed of soggy garments I turned on the engine. So far so good. Then I turned on the windscreen wipers. So far so bad. Nothing. Click, click...nothing Tap, tap...nothing Bang, bang, bang, bang...nothing. Swear, swear, swear, swear...nothing

Right. Decision time. To quote the yet to be formed Clash... "Should I stay or should I go now?" The Moody Blues answered in time honoured fashion...... "Go Now".

So off we did go. At a snails pace at first along the A56. "Not bad". I can do this." I thought, as I made out blurred versions of everything about me. My mates were naturally concerned. In fact, if I recall they were actually questioning the parenthood of both my car and myself using the long forgotten Anglo Saxon vernacular. Forty five minutes later, at around 11.00 pm, I turned onto the southbound carriage-way of the M6 motorway.

I quickly devised what I thought would be a foolproof system. You see, by this time the only colours breaking up the solid blackness all around us were wobbly red blobs and wobbly white blobs. I figured that wobbly red blobs were vehicles going my way and wobbly white blobs were vehicles going the other way, so as long as the wobbly red blobs were in front of me and the wobbly white blobs to my right I'd be all right. Right?

Well, I seriously undestimated the effect concentration would have on my... errr ...concentration. Matchstick eyelids developed within the hour.

God, I needed a break, but I wasn't going to tell my mates that I wasn't Superman. Anyway, they'd fallen asleep so I put into operation foolproof system number two. Whenever the wobbly red blobs disappeared on a long, straight stretch of highway I would close my eyes and count to ten. OUT LOUD. You see, by counting 1 to 10, OUT LOUD, I could actually hear myself and, therefore, not unwittingly fall asleep. Your impressed, aren't you? I can tell.

Finally we arrived at the Stafford turn off for the A5. Road lights and speed changes offered partial relief to the lead weights dangling from my eyes. By 1.30 am we were back on the M1 Highway To Hell at Rugby. Edgar Allen Poe blackness descended to test me once more. God, my eyes hurt.

"Only 90 minutes, only 90 minutes, only 90 minutes..."

I'd changed my name to Mantra United. Foolproof system number two was reactivated, only this time I became aware of a worrying side effect. When I closed my eyes at "1", there was Keystone Cockney Reds nothing on the road, yet when I reached "10" and opened them again, a bloody great lorry would appear out of nowhere and dominate my windscreen. Driving. Bloody Hell.

As predictable as an England batting collapse, between Newport Pagnell and Toddington the inevitable happened. Dusty Springfield had once sung – "I close my eyes and count to 10", only this time it didn't go according to plan. I closed my eyes for the umpteenth time and started to count. The next thing I knew I heard my mate, Hairy, shout "DAVE!!!"

I opened my eyes only to find that I was driving at 80 mph and at 45° up the grass verge by the side of the motorway. Keystone Cops eat your hearts out. I didn't fall asleep again. Brown trousers and mad mates made sure of that.

OK. All together now. "We only sleep when we're winning"...

5

REAL MADRID GOT AWAY

COMING AS NO surprise to any United fans reading this book, the longest chapters concern our Champions League campaigns in 1998/99 and 2007/08. The heart-stopping finale in Moscow is still sending ripples through me as I write, yet I can state without fear of contraception that this life has nothing left to offer me that in any way, shape or form that can come close to the highs I experienced on that barmy Catalan evening.

However, I was not to know that when in my tender teens, eighteen to be precise, United were drawn against the mighty Real Madrid in the semi final of the European Cup. As I've written elsewhere, I actually saw the last league game played by the original Busby Babes, the incredible 5-4 victory over Arsenal at Highbury. Only at an even tenderer seven and a half years of age, the enormity and significance of that match would only dawn on me as I grew older.

The terrible tragedy that was Munich will forever be inscribed in the make-up of United fans past, present and future. For the players, management and fans that had to live through those dark, incredible days, one man came to symbolize everything that Manchester United stood for. Matt Busby.

All our hopes, fears and dreams were channeled through this remarkable, fearsome and lovely man.

Even in those days, being a United fan was as much a roller coaster ride as it is today. It took eight long, hard years for Matt Busby to once again fashion a team capable of competing with Europe's best. The original 'Phoenix from the Flames'. When in the 1965/66 campaign we overcame the brilliant and, up to then, unbeaten at home Benfica in the quarter finals, we felt that at long last United would make our dreams come true.

After an absorbing but narrow 3-2 victory at home, not many people, me included, gave us much of a chance in the Stadium of Light. But of course, as history recalls, Manchester United came of age that night and a certain George Best, empowered by the Gods, wove his magic that transported him and the team onto the world stage. Defying Busby's defensive instructions he tore Benfica apart as though his feet were on fire. When the draw was made for the semi-final, Partizan Belgrade seemed a bit of a come down after the glory of Lisdon. A hardworking but basically functional team, the press and ourselves considered them below us in terms of skill and imagination. European Cup Final, here we come.

As far as the papers and ourselves were concerned we were unbeatable. The long sought after European Cup would finally be ours. I fear the players had read and believed the papers as well. All they had to do was turn up because they played the away leg as though qualification for the final was a formality. When we suddenly went 2-0 down, the realisation that Partizan Belgrade hadn't read the script became apparent. The biggest party poopers in history scored a deserved victory to set up a pulsating second leg at Old Trafford.

We huffed and we puffed but we couldn't blow the house down. As was "de rigeur" at the time, the British team would win by a single goal but go out over the two legs.

The disappointment was painful in the extreme. Our best chance of ever getting to the final and winning the European Cup seemed to have disappeared that Spring evening in April. I was distraught. Seventeen years old and the pinnacle of club football achievement was wrenched from my grasp. I never expected such a good chance to present itself again.

I've since read that Matt Busby secretly felt the same way.

In the morgue like dressing room afterwards. Paddy Crerand put his arm round the Manager and promised to make amends in two years time. Nobody, and I suspect even Paddy himself believed what he had said. But it was the right thing to say in the circumstances. Someone had to say it and with hindsight it seems right that Paddy was the man. And almost forty years on he's still as biased and blinkered as any hard core Red. What a man.

Of course I was not aware of this as I went back to work the following morning to be greeted by a mixture of condolences and piss take. How times have changed. Today it would be piss take only, even from those armchair fans who don't deserve to lace my boots let alone borrow my stapler.

Two years on and, as Paddy had predicted, United won the League Championship and once again qualified for the European Cup. Playing disappointingly sterile football we drew 0-0 on a terrible pitch under a boiling sun in front of our adoring fans in Malta against Hibernians. An unremarkable 4-0 victory at home brought us to the second round tie against the hard and extremely dirty and ruthless Yugoslavs of Sarajevo.

0-0 away and a narrow 2-1 at home brought us through to the quarter finals against the equally hard but marginally less dirty Gornick Zabrze from Poland. We won 2-0 at home and lost a very tense away leg 1-0. We hung on in the freezing snow by a thread, my one overriding memory was of Alex Stepney looking so unsexy in long legged black tights.

Now we were drawn in the semi-finals against Real Madrid, imperious in reputation but slightly less so in recent performances. The Streford End was heaving that night as the two teams took to the field. Real in their famous all white strip and United glorious in Red. United did all the attacking but chances were few and far between as Real had sacrificed attacking flair for masterly defense. And the bastards were bloody good at it too.

Come the half hour come the man. John Aston, so average in the league but majestic in Europe, pulled the ball back from the byline and Best's left foot shot thundered into the net. We went ballistc. The roar which had been ever present since before kick-off rose to new heights.

"We're on our way to Wembley, we shall not be moved" sang the Stretford End as we waited for Real to crumble against the awesome Red onslaught. However the Spaniards were the masters of two legged ties and as hard as we tried we hardly created another opening. It was high powered and nerve tingling but the match ended 1-0 to the Reds.

I was hoarse as we made our way back to our coach for the drive back to London. It was the policy of the Manchester United (London & District) Supporters Club not to arrive back in London before 05.30 the following morning as this tied in with the start-up of the tube. This gave us a lot of time to reflect on matches we had just seen and predict the future. We didn't need David fucking Mellor in those days.

Experience had also taught us, the hard way, that to arrive any earlier was the signal for gangs of Millwall, West Ham, Chelsea et al to hang about and welcome us back in their own inimitable style. I had perfected the art of descending the escalators with the speed and grace of Eddie the Eagle in order to escape those evil morons. Scenes like that don't get broadcast on programs like Match of the Day or Soccer AM.

Opinion on the coach was divided. All the usual clichés.

"They'd have to come forward more leaving gaps in the back."

"Yeah, but they could tear us apart if they attacked."

"This is our year. Our name's on the cup."

"Bollocks. Two years ago was OUR year and look what happened."

"Yeah. But we've leant from that." Blah, blah, blah.

By 03.30 we pulled into Watford Gap services. As we queued up for stewed tea we heard Spanish voices.

"What the...?"

Instead of the youthful supporters we expected we turned round to see a table full of rich, middle aged, middle class Spanish businessmen and their wives. As we sat down they called out to us in worryingly good English, taunting us with claims that Madrid was going to destroy United again, just like they had done in the past.

We were too flabbergasted to respond. If they had been teenage hoolies it would have been the excuse for a ruck, and motorway service station food can make pretty lethal weapons. But we were caught in the headlights of bourgeois Spanish bravado and we weren't programmed to respond. We settled for good old-fashioned swearing and "V" signs but it was unsatisfactory. A missed opportunity to illustrate superior British intellect in the face of disturbances in the Colonies.

However it did make us all the more determined to stuff their smug rhetoric down their fat, turkey necked throats.

I hatched my plan that very night.

The Manchester United (London & District) Supporters Club were organising a two day trip to Madrid for twenty two pounds fifteen shillings, which included return flights, coach transfers, hotel, match ticket and insurance cover.

Milestone time. Growing up in London I had first seen United 'live' when I was eight years old. My first trip to Old Trafford was in 1967 at the age of sixteen and a half. Now, at seventeen and a half I was to embark on my first Euro away. Rights of passage, or what? I sent off my five pounds deposit.

Today we take these trips in our stride. Even before the Ferguson era as United fans we travelled in our thousands for Inter-Cties Fairs Cup or European Cup Winners Cup ties.

But for me, in my blossoming teenage years, living at home in suburbia with lower/middle class parents and commencing a career in Advertising, the thought, let alone the action. of taking two/three days off work in the middle of the week to watch a...a...football match was unheard of.

My parents were already unhappy that their eldest son was spending almost every Saturday ploughing the motorways of England for... for... football.

Now I was really going to go over the edge into the abyss.

For the past year, and for many years to come, I had developed an intricate web of mates who would take turns to phone up and invite me to come over on a Wednesday. I claimed that their parents would be willing to drive me back so my parents could go to bed early, safe in the knowledge that their precious offspring would come to no harm. This would placate my parents and allow me to go to Manchester and back without detection. Will the British army arrive before the Indians? Many a time I would arrive home around six thirty in the morning, creep ever so softly upstairs and change into my work clothes. When my mother woke me up literally minutes later I would wait until she was out of the room then spring out of bed without having the hassle of getting tired limbs into news clothes.

I would fake brightness at breakfast before collapsing on the tube to work. My performance at work that day would directly correlate to United's performance the previous evening.

But this was different. I was planning my first trip to Europe in support of Manchester United. This is what I had been put on this planet to do. This was my mission. This was my quest. Lord of the Rings had nothing on me.

Getting the occasional Wednesday afternoon off work hadn't exactly endeared me to my respective bosses and possibly reduced my promotional prospects but at least I had stayed one step ahead of the sack. But two whole days.

Hmmmm.

I needed a two pronged attack. One for my parents and one for my work. At this time I was a Production Assistant at Rex Publicity Ltd, an advertising agency in Chesterfield Gardens in Mayfair. I worked on the ABC Films account, which meant that space on my bedroom walls competed with United programs selotaped in chronological order together with giant posters of 2001-A Space Oddessy on the ceiling (cool), Jane Fonda as Barberella (those giant metal enclosed breasts. Brrr) and many more whose titles I have long since forgotten.

Got it!

For my parents I devised an imaginary two day training course in Oxford. I was very friendly with the receptionists at the I.P.A. (Institute of Practioners in Advertising) at the time so one lunchtime I went down to their offices in Belgrave Square and requested some obscure information.

When the hapless girl left the reception unattended for a few minutes I went round the back of her desk and nicked a few blank sheets of I.P.A. letterheading. Once back at work I got one of the secretaries to type out this imaginary two day training course. Looking good, Houston. Looking good.

Work was a little trickier. I didn't want to jeapodise my job, though if push came to shove I would have done. I needed a watertight excuse. So many people seemed to be able to get fake doctor's sick notes, but I didn't know any fake doctors. (Boom boom). I asked all my work colleagues and eventually I came across a sympathetic ear and the promise of a sick note. Don't ask me how he did it, but a sick note in my name duly arrived. Sorted.

I counted down the days. I was really nervous. I had never executed a blag on this scale before and I wasn't sure I was up to it. My United mates were. We talked endlessly on the phone but as the day drew nearer I withdrew into myself.

What if I'm found out?

On the evening prior to the trip I bottled it. I came home from work and told my parents that the training course had been cancelled as not enough people had enrolled. All I had to do was go to work in the morning and say I had been miraculously cured. I felt relief but overwhelming shame that I had not held my nerve. My United mates didn't give me the stick I had expected. They realised I was making an enormous sacrifice by not coming on what was at the time the most important match in our match going history and offered sympathy and the promise to sing their hearts out for the lads and me as well.

How I got through the following day at work I'll never know. At every moment I imagined what I should have been doing in Madrid. Eventually it was time to leave work.

I made my way to Green Park tube wrapped in my own thoughts. Standing all the way home, as usual, I prepared myself for the evening. I had a tiny 'Aero' transistor radio which I hid under the bed. I would normally listen to Radio Luxembourg under the covers until I fell asleep, then wake up the following morning with another flat battery.

On the way home I bought a fresh pair of batteries.

I couldn't afford any slip ups tonight of all nights.

I had my tea and counted the minutes until kick-off.

I mumbled "Night, night." to my younger brother and my stunned parents who usually have to force me to go to bed and went to my room.

Radio. Check. Batteries. Check. Scarf. Check.

The match began. Real seemed to be dominating pocession. Then on the half hour the worst happened.

Real scored. 1-0. Shit.

"Come on lads." I shouted. Transistor radios can be so damm impersonal. You can't see what's happening and the desire to shake them has a negative effect on proceedings. Ten minutes later I heard the name Gento and then we were 2-0 down.

"No, no, no. What's going on?" I cried. I heard shouts from the lounge.

"Fuck 'em." I thought.

As half-time approached, a lifeline. Zoco, under pressure from Kiddo, turned the ball into his own net.

"GOOOAAAL!" I jumped up and down on the bed.

Immediately my Dad came in.

"How many times have I told you not to jump on the bed?"

I thought for a moment. Forty two? Seventy three? What a time to ask such a meaningless question. He gave me a look that could curl custard then left the room. Normally I wouldn't have the bravado to answer him back but under the influence of United I was seven feet tall. Or I was if I stood on the bed.

I went back to my "Aero". What? What? Oh no. We were 3-1 down now. How did that happen? Shit. Shit and thrice shit. Bastards.

Half-time. Fuck it. It's not fair. But hang on a minute.

We're only a goal down over the two legs, and if we score another we'd be level. Yep. I had given myself one hell of a half-time talking to. Roll on the second half.

This time all I could hear were the names of the United players on the radio, as we swept onto the attack. Then after only seven minutes I heard the commentator say the words 'David Sadler' and 'Goal' in the same sentence. Were we really only 3-2 behind? Yes, we were.

"GOOOOAAAAL!" "GOOOOAAAAL!"

This time my Dad did not come into my room as I celebrated in style, the bed creaking under a different rhythm from normal. I came breathlessly down to Earth and flattened my left ear once again to the radio. I was so exited but the infuriating commentators were so deadpan.

Seven minutes later, what should have been the greatest moment of my life up till then almost passed me by.

I heard them say that George Best had run down the left wing and crossed into the middle but there was no mention of a shot. I heard the words "Bill Foulkes", "Was it or wasn't it?" but it was all so monotone that it was a full minute later when they said that Real were kicking off that I realised we had actually scored, and that at 3-3 we were actually in the lead.

What should have been my loudest roar to date turned out to be an unsatisfying, churning in the throat, "Yeah!".

Returning to the radio I thought perhaps the match was over. Impossible. There was almost half an hour to go. Why were there no crowd noises? The Spanish fans, just like their team, were in shock. Where were those smug Spanish bastards I'd met at Watford Gap two weeks previously? Oh, what I wouldn't have given to see their faces now.

The rest of the match appeared to be a formality as the Reds hung on without too much of a problem for the greatest win in their history.

I had trouble sleeping that night. In two weeks time United would be in their first European Cup final at Wembley.

And so would I.

6

WEMBLEY, MAY 29TH 1968

WEDNESDAY MORNING, the 29th of May, 1968 dawned bright and sunny. As I got ready for work I laid out two sets of clothing. Dark suit, shirt and tie for work. Red jacket with white emulsion paint exclaiming MAN UTD on the back, white trousers, United top and my six foot long scarf for the evening. I took out my large nylon United holdall and put my red and white ensemble inside.

Standing on the tube going to work I looked normal to anyone observing one of life's regular scenarios. I nodded briefly to faces I recognized but never spoke to. I looked around for one or more women to squash against for the forty five minute standing Olympics to Holborn. My face was a mask but inside I was quivering like jelly. In twelve hours time I would be inside Wembley Stadium squashed along with thousands of fellow, i.e. male, Reds and enjoying myself a whole lot more.

The last time United had been to Wembley was May 1963. But I was only fourteen at the time and so had watched the match on our black and white TV at home.

The following year West Ham reached the finals and a number of my local mates got tickets. I was asked if I wanted one but I declined. Not only had they knocked out my beloved United on a quagmire of a pitch at Hillsborough that year, but to set foot inside Wembley Stadium other than for a United or England match. No, I couldn't do that. I wouldn't do that.

An FA Cup Final without Manchester United. Thanks, but no thanks lads. I'd rather watch it at home on the box. In fact, right up to 1976 I'd always turned down opportunities of FA Cup Final tickets. Why should I go to the game just because I'd got connections when thousands of genuine supporters of the respective teams, who had followed their heroes through thick and thin, would be denied their chance of glory by some suit or hanger-on. Sorry.

Some principals are worth fighting for. I'll do anything, and I mean ANYTHING, to get a ticket for a United game, but as Meatloaf once sang, "I'll do anything for love but I won't do that."

Now, for the first time in my almost nineteen long years on this planet, me, myself and I was going to see Manchester United at Wembley.

Needless to say, my concentrating at work that day was sorely lacking. Working in the production department of an advertising agency meant, amongst other things, attention to detail. One fraction of an inch out on measurements meant that thousands of pounds worth of ad space was wasted as the blocks or plates I was ordering would not fit the respective publications. My body was at work but the internal elements required to calculate size, shape and screen were being submerged by images a few miles up the Metropolitan Line.

I was also debating whether or not to ask my boss if I could leave early. Previous European nights at Old Trafford had been wangled by various ploys, none of which gave the 'game' away as to my real destination. But today was different. I had been unable to conceal my growing excitement since the weekend so even non-football fans in the office knew exactly what my intentions were, including my non footballing boss.

If I asked him and he said "Yes" I would be in the clear.

If I asked him and he said "No" I would be fucked because he'd keep a sharp eye out for me not to escape early. If I didn't ask him and just slipped away unnoticed during the afternoon I would certainly get to Wembley in time for all the build up but I would possibly endanger my position.

Decisions, decisions, decisions.

I opted for the cowards way out by just slipping away when he wasn't looking. At around half past three I went to the loo with my United holdall and performed a quick Clark Kent. In a hand shaking two minutes I was transformed from office creep to...well, United creep.

I was admiring my reflection in the mirror, as you do, when my boss came into the toilets. Worse case scenario.

"Come into my office, David."

Whoops.

Dressed like Coco the red & white clown, I followed him sheepishly to his office where he gave me the mother and father of all talkings to, but after a few moments I sensed that although I was in hot water I wasn't going to drown. I wasn't going to get the sack. I may have ruined any chances of promotion at Rex Publicity Ltd but there were a lot more agencies in the sea.

And anyway, at almost nineteen years of age I was indestructible. In those days London advertising agencies were a bit like London buses, they'd always be another one along in a minute.

I kept my "Oh I'm so sorry, it won't happen again (well, not until next year anyway) lapdog" expression going for as long as I could, hoping he would soften his assault. In the end he gave me a written warning about my behaviour and attitude, which under the circumstances I considered a score draw. In fact I believe I won on penalties because he reluctantly gave me permission to leave early.

1-0 to the workers.

At four o' clock I exited the building, turned right into Curzon Street and then right onto Park Lane, looking like a prize twat but I didn't care. It was boiling hot in my polyester United shirt and red jacket as I strolled up Park Lane towards Marble Arch. Disappointingly, there weren't many people on the street but taxi cabs hooted at me and wished me luck. I felt like royalty. Oh, how I crave for the innocent sixties. No one questioned my parenthood or attempted a second Jewish operation. All was sweetness and light.

When I arrived at Marble Arch underground station I encountered my first fellow Reds.

Fists were raised in unison as we descended the escalators and onto the platform. Hollow sounding chants filled the air.

We were royalty and we were on our way to Wembley to annoint our King, Matt Busby.

At Baker Street the fun really began as hundreds of Reds filled the platform. The singing and chanting took on an urgency of its own. Twenty minutes later we spewed out of Wembley Park station into more bright sunlight.

Reds were here, Reds were there, Reds were...yes, you've guessed it...everywhere.

Not a Benfica fan in sight.

At eighteen years and eleven months I was finally going to walk up Wembley Way to see Matt Busby's Aces. It was a dream come true.

Many players have commented over the years that the day they played at Wembley passed in a flash, and what they wouldn't give to relive the experience and this time take it all in.

I haven't got many saving graces but I have got the ability to be wise before the event. To know that I am on the threshold of something special and not to take things for granted. I don't need to lose my senses or languish in prison to appreciate the beauty all around me. To see the sea, sun, sand and Angelina Jolie. To feel female flesh or the wind in my face. The sound of the Stretford End, babies laughter, power chords or a woman's soft moans. The aroma of baked potatoes. "These are a few of my favourite things."

From the top of Wembley Way by the station I ever so slowly made my pilgrimage towards the twin towers. I took in every tatty souvenir stall, every odious dogburger stand, everything. This was my day and it was going to be a day I was damn sure I would never forget. Boy, how right I was.

I arrived at the top just in front of the twin towers.

I looked back and took in the sea of Reds. I felt like Moses as thousands of fans divided themselves before me. Then I checked my ticket and made my way to the correct entrance.

I mounted the steps to the gates above and peered once more down upon the mass of humanity below. Then I was in.

Darkness enveloped me until I grew accustomed to the lack of direct sunlight. A massive concrete corridor curved away out of sight in both directions.

I had plenty of time so I slowly made a complete circuit until I found my next entrance number. Leaving the toilets and the disgustingly over-priced carbonized beverages and processed carcasses behind, I took the final few steps up to the opening to my section of the lower tier standing.

My vision was saturated with a light so brilliant and a pitch so intensely green that it looked like a painting from the gods. Which of course it was. Although barely a quarter full the Stretford End on Tour was already in fine voice.

Remember, these were the days when the Stretford was packed and swaying by half past one prior to a three o'clock kick-off. I made my way down to the front. I was just to the left of the players' tunnel. I spotted Hairy and a couple of others in the next enclosure so I jumped over the fence. Singing and joking, interspersed by nervous silences, before we knew it Wembley Stadium was full and both teams were walking out side by side to a deafening roar. For some reason we were in royal blue which I thought was a bit odd.

Handshakes, national anthems, presentations and then...game on.

The first half was very tense. Very few clear cut chances.

The good news was that John Aston, so anonymous in the league was taking the Benfica right full back Adolfo to the cleaners. The bad news was that George Best wasn't, how shall I put it... George Best.

He was being shackled very well (i.e. filthily) by Cruz which significantly reduced the number of chances we created. Eusabio, that wonderful talent, performed a horrendous tackle on Paddy Crerand and faked a number of dives which set the tone for the first half and left a sour taste in the mouth. Why do such great players have to resort to such tactics? Evidently the fear of losing was paramount and harsh tackles dominated.

We continued to take the game to Benfica in the second half but with greater urgency and flow. And this time United were attacking our end. Then in the fifty third minute David Sadler sent over a cross and right in front of our eyes Bobby Charlton soared into the air reminiscent of the sorely missed Denis Law and glanced the ball in to the far corner of the net.

"GOOOOOOOOOOOAAAAAAAAAAAAL!"

The entire ground took off as one. The release of tension was exquisite. As play restarted the whole crowd was rocking. "We Shall Not Be Moved." The noise swirled around the stadium like Hi Fi speakers slightly out of sync.

But then Benfica came out of their shell. They began creating chances of their own and our songs stuck in our throats. Not for the first time, and, as everyone of you will concur, not for the last time either, United unnecessarily conceded the initiative. It was also, I remember now, unusually and unbearably hot in the stadium.

Without a breath of air it must have been stifling for our players.

The Portuguese were more in their element and with nine minutes to go the inevitable equaliser happened.

I saw that skyscraper Torres nod the ball down to Eusebio who passed the ball out to the right and from a narrow angle Graca hit a thunderbolt in our net and our hearts.

"NOOOOOOO!"

This was not meant to happen. This time United were rocking, but for the wrong reasons. Benfica were on top and twice Eusebio broke through on his own. The second time the Black Panther broke through he was one on one with Alex Stepney. Even though it was at the other end of the ground I could see it only too clearly. He was bearing down on our goal and our defense was conspicuous by its absence. Eusebio seemed so large and Stepney seemed so small, and from where we were standing behind the opposing goal we could see what Eusebio could see. A giant set of goalposts and a tiny goalkeeper. Any moment and our dreams would be shattered. A goal was inevitable. Time stood still. We froze.

"Alex!. Do something! Anything! ALEEEEEX!"

And you know what? He did do something. HE FUCKING SAVED IT!

To this day I don't know how Eusebio missed. I've read since that he always liked going for the spectacular instead of a safe side-foot. But this was his undoing and perhaps why he's not mentioned in the same breath as Pele or Marodona.

In full flight he hit a powerful shot straight at Stepney.

Anywhere else and the record books would have to have been re-written. We escaped, and somehow we made it to ninety minutes.

Thirty minutes of extra time beckoned. We sang our hearts out for the lads. We prayed that Matt Busby was doing the same on the pitch. Now was the time to think positive and win it, not fear losing it. The best form of defense is attack.

It's United to the core, and coupled with the British Bulldog spirit we could triumph.

The first fifteen minutes of extra time began and it was, literally, a whole new ball game. We were all over them and this time we were beating them to the ball, getting in crosses, beating defenders. Within a couple of minutes the ball broke to George who raced for goal. This was the real George Best. Arrogant, weaving his magic, leaving players for dead. We roared in anticipation as he beat a full back and advanced on Henrique in the Benfica goal. He rounded him as though he wasn't there and hit a shot with his left foot. Agonisingly, time stood still as the ball seemed covered in sticky syrup. It rolled ever so slowly towards the white line. He hadn't hit it hard enough. Surely someone would scramble it away. Look. There's Henrique. He's going to stop it.

No he wasn't.

"GOOOOOOOOOOOOAAAAAAAAAAL!"

Unbelievable roar. Unbelievable noise. Believable score.

2-1 to United. The elation and relief was overwhelming.

Instead of playing in lead boots United were flying.

A minute later and we were in the stratosphere. Aston won us another corner. Charlton crossed and Brian Kidd headed goalwards. It came straight out to him and this time his second header went straight into the net.

On his nineteenth birthday Kiddo had scored our third and killer goal. Pandemonium.

We were there. We knew it. The players knew it. Even birds in the trees knew it. We were finally going to win the European Cup and lay to rest the ghosts of United's past. The noise was deafening. You had to be there to really feel it.

Wembley Stadium was like a giant space ship, ready to take off with 80,000 roaring engines. We were rampant.

Benfica were out of it. As United fans we were in a world of our own. When I replayed the video of the match years later I heard Kenneth Wolstenholme tell the TV viewers, "Undoubtedly the Manchester United fans are outshouting and outsinging the England fans in the World Cup Final."

Now, when I recall our fourth and final goal or see it on TV my mind always drifts back to the twelve inch LP I bought soon afterwards which had the entire BBC Radio commentary.

"And there's Kidd, dragging Cruz over. This looks dangerous. Charlton. WHAT A GOAL BY CHARLTON".

His shot, on the turn, was everything Bobby Charlton stood for. It was the perfect end to an imperfect match.

Bobby raced to the far corner flag and was surrounded by a million flashing photographers (now there's an image for you). I went to heaven and stayed there. The noise really was unbelievable and I was a part of it.

I stood on my mates' shoulders and took a flag off someone and sung and swayed like the French revolutionaries out of Les Miserables. Extra time half-time came and went without the Red Army taking a breath.

"Goodbye Benfica Goodbye. We'll see you again but we don't know when. Goodbye Benfica goodbye."

"John-ny. John-ny. John-ny."

"Busby. Busby. Busby."

The deed was done. We roared the lads home in the final fifteen minutes. Walls of noise came tumbling down. From the throat and from the heart. We were majestic. At the final whistle I cried uncontrollably. (A recurring theme I'm afraid to say). All the anguish and heartache over the past twelve years was exhumed. I was floating on air. The relief. The sheer and utter relief.

The players and Busby embraced. Doctor Johnson would have been proud of the numbers of people I embraced. I kissed and hugged any and every orifice on offer.

After what seemed an age, Bobby wearily lead the players up the steps to collect the pot of gold at the end of the rainbow. It really did exist.

"ROOOAAAAR!"

By this time I had no voice left but defied medical opinion by extracting a roar that felt like razor blades shaving my larynx. Pleasure and pain. As a United fan wasn't it ever thus?

The players descended the steps and then came the moment we were all waiting for. They were running round Wembley with the cup. Our cup. The European Cup.

"BUSBY. BUSBY. BUSBY. BUSBY. BUSBY. BUSBY..."

The players finally left the field with the never-ending "BUSBY" chant filling the air. Now, I've read top shelf books and magazines in which women actually feint from excessive sexual pleasure. The feelings and emotions being so intense that the body cannot cope with the overload and the recipricant just loses it.

At fifty eight years of age I'm still waiting to climb up that carnal ladder of pleasure, but on May 29th 1968 I entered the pearly gates of football heaven. To this day I cannot remember anything from the moment I walked up to the back of the terrace and down the steps on the other side leading to the exit of Wembley stadium. The next image I can recall is Trafalgar Square just before midnight. My theory is that at nineteen years of age I was at my sexual peak (more like a molehill). Without the equivalent of a randy thirty something woman at her sexual peak to quell my burning thighs I did what any red (in both senses of the word) blooded male would have done. I took it out on my football team. Manchester United was "the other woman" and at that precise moment we orgasmed together. My body couldn't take any more pleasure so my mind just cut out.

But at Trafalgar Square the fun was only just beginning.

The shock of the cold water brought me back to my (limited) senses. I was in one of the fountains. Fully clothed I was a jumping and a frolicking with the best of them.

Singing, flag and banner waving. Conga lines round the square. This was the greatest night of my life and I never wanted it to end. But with work beckoning in the morning, at a quarter to four I found a mini-cab office and booked a car to take me all the way back to Gants Hill.

My luck. I had to pick the only driver who wasn't into football. All I wanted to do on the hour long journey through the East End between four and five in the morning was to talk United. All he wanted to do was to get that sopping wet urchin out of his cab as quickly as possible.

I was ruining his car. I should act my age (I thought I was).

If he had known the state I was in he would never have accepted the fare.

He took me to the cleaners in both senses of the word. He overcharged me, even allowing for 'night rates', to compensate for the state of his car, so he said.

But try as he might, he couldn't put a damp squid on my night. Oh no, siree!

We are the Champions. Champions of Europe.
Europe, Europe.
We are the Champions. Champions of Europe.
Europe, Europe.
We are the Champions. Champions of Europe.
Europe, Europe.

7

BUSBY OUT?

ACT 1

"FERGIE OUT", "Atkinson Out", "Sexton Out", "Kenyon Out", "Glazers Out", "Lights Out", "Way Out", "Far Out", "Out Demons Out", "Get Your Tits Out For The Lads".

"Busby Out". No, I don't think so.

No, it's true. I don't think I ever heard the said chant. As you know I first saw the Reds, as an eight year old living in South Woodford, one night at Highbury in a long, never to be forgotten 5-4 victory. (Yes, that one.) I would subsequently see them whenever they came to London until that fateful day aged fourteen when I discovered the one of the three United Supporters' Clubs in London. My geography class at school saw an immediate improvement as I brought the road atlas to life.

One Saturday during the 1966-67 season saw the Red Army descend on Ipswich. For a home game, the ritual would start with rising at 05.30 without waking up my younger brother Andrew, or I'd be for it – whatever "IT" was, and without the aid of an alarm clock. Now I don't know about you, but getting up for work is as natural as a salmon swimming against the current in its desire to spawn, but getting up to see the Reds – piece of cake!

My system? All I would think about when I went to bed was Manchester United. I fell asleep thinking about Manchester United and, guess what, I woke up (just like that) thinking about Manchester United. I was an Ad man's dream.

I woke up with a glint in my eye (well, both of them actually) and a matinee idol whiter than white smile on my lips.

Ipswich away was a bonus for a Cockney Red. I could stay in bed an extra two hours as the train didn't depart until around 10.00am from Liverpool Street station. Needless to say I got there miles too early yet there still seemed to be hundreds of United fans milling around. And then I realised why. Without any prior warning THE TEAM was spotted walking through the concourse on the way to the train.

ROOAAR!

We all steamed over to them. The players, to a man, looked at us with utter disdain as they fought to eradicate themselves from the masses and seek refuge in the arms of the first class compartments.

"Working class, moi?" each expression exclaimed, as they disentangled themselves from our hero worshipping mauling.

Except one. The Manager, Matt Busby.

Sandwiched between two luggage trolleys he proceeded to have a word and shake the hand of every single one of us, or so it seemed to me at the time. Eventually I pressed my soft, clammy hand into his whereupon he said unto me.

"Hello. What's your name, son?"

"David" (Sir, Your Honour, God. I mean, how do you address THE man)

"And where are you from David?"

"London, sir...but...but...(quick, quick, think of something to say before the moment is lost for ever.).........I go every week!"

"Wonderful David. We need more supporters like you. Good luck."

And so it came to pass that the man and his right hand were gone.

Time stood still. In my world there was only silence.

I looked at my hand. HE had touched my hand.

No, he had actually SHOOK my hand.

"I will never wash this hand again", I thought as the outside world began to infiltrate my senses.

A moment later I was back to normal as I joined the crush to board the train. We spent the entire journey running up and down the corridors of the train, singing and chanting, banging each and every window through which we caught the glimpse of a player and wondering why they never acknowledged our presence.

ACT 2

Three weeks later, after a game at Old Trafford, the Manchester United London & District Supporters Club held its Annual Dinner & Dance at Belle View. Rumour had it that one or two of the players had promised to attend.

If the truth be told, the "do" was a bit boring. But then at around 9pm the mood changed as a couple of players were spotted nervously entering the room. As a member of one of the official supporters clubs I was a bit more reverential in my behavior than I had been three weeks previously.

OK. I agree, I was a bit wet.

But then I realized that the great Matt Busby was also with them. My heartbeat quickened as I crossed the dance floor to take it upon myself to welcome them to our humble "do".

Before I could say a word, Matt Busby smiled and said:

"Hello David. Nice to see you again."

INSTANT GOLDFISH

My mouth opened and shut but nothing came out. My eyes welled up with stinging tears. I was so embarrassed, awestruck, overcome, immobilised, in love and incomprehensible that I was unable to speak.

GOD had remembered my name. From three weeks beforehand when I was just one little "oink" amongst thousands of Reds (Sorry. Did I say hundreds before? Well, passage of time, artistic license and all that) pressing our flesh against him.

Over the next thirty years of licking and groveling I must have had over a dozen conversations with the man. And he always remembered my name. Extraordinary.

It got to the stage that when, as a shareholder, I regularly attended the United AGM. Sir Matt would enter the room yet I would resist the temptation to join the throng which descended on him like a swarm of locusts. I would pretend to continue to converse with whoever I was speaking to at that moment until, with the start of proceedings imminent, fellow shareholders would begin to make their way to their seats leaving Sir Matt room to breathe. He would then catch my eye, and HE would come over to ME and we would have a little chat, whilst all around I was aware of expressions which translated into......

"How the hell does HE know HIM?"

Along with Nelson Mandella, Mother Teresa and Spike Millighan, Sir Matt Busby was one of the greatest human beings of the twentieth century. I'm almost inclined to say Sir Matt Busby was perfect, but human beings are not perfect.

But if perfection were possible, the term used by scientists, biologists and Tomorrow's World to explain this phenomenon would be "Busby".

"Busby Out." I don't think so.

8

BETWEEN A ROCK AND A HARD CAFE

BY THE TIME I started looking for work football, and Manchester United in particular, had taken over my life. Learning early to prioritise in order of importance, my number one aim was to embark on a career that kept my Saturdays free. That meant "retail" was out for a start. I plumped for Advertising as I figured one could be further down the ladder yet still have an effect on proceedings. In seven years I rose to the giddy heights of Progress Controller with the advertising agency Lintas before I became disillusioned with the superficiality of it all.

What to do? Well, my dad wasn't going to let me mope around the house "finding" myself (man) so he forced me to do minicabbing like himself. Well, he figured it would keep me off the streets (boom, boom!). Now, I'm not saying I was bad, but boy, was I bad. All that I knew at that age was how to get from Gants Hill on the central line (the red one, significant that) to the West End and back for work and occasionally (and I do mean, "occasionally") from Gants Hill to a girlfriend's house and back. I'll always remember my first fare, from the Meridian Hotel in Piccadilly to St John's Wood, the base area of my mini-cab company.

"St John's Wood. Hmmmm. That's on the brown line, isn't it? Help!"

So, more by error and error, as opposed to trial and error I learnt my way around. At this time, one of our regular clients was an abortion clinic with offices in Ordnance Hill which treated French women and girls who had done what all French women and girls are famous for in France without considering the consequences. Subsequently they would come over to dear old Blighty where they could be legally be relieved of their little burdens.

With perfect French and imperfect English, Helene was working there as a receptionist, welcoming French females, putting them at ease and arranging all their travel requirements. As a mini-cab driver, as well as collecting and delivering them, we would pick-up and take home the staff. And so this is how I "picked-up" Hélène.

I always noticed her because she wore really tight jeans with matching jean jacket and waistcoat which showed off all her best assets. Then there was her smile and laugh. As an imperfect Englishman this worked to my advantage.

"Make 'em laugh, make 'em laugh."

Jokes and chat-up lines that left local girls cold actually made her laugh. We got on like a house on fire on off-peak central heating. I would often drive her to her bedsit in Tufnell Park. When she confided in me that she had been there for almost six months yet spent most of her nights home alone in her studio apartment I was upset on her behalf. With so much activity and entertainment on her doorstep, not to mention the glory of Hampstead Heath, I felt it was my duty to do my Blatto Tours impersonations and show her the delights of London town...and me.

Being the shy, retiring type I arranged an evening out with some of my friends so she wouldn't think she "had" to go out with me. It would also act as a cushion for me if she decided to repel my advances. However, Eric was to take a hand as, one by one, all my friends fell by the wayside. So, on Valentine's Day 1973 Helene and I went out for the very first time. I took her to see Sparks (Chris Spedding's new super group) and Wizard at the Imperial College behind the Royal Albert Hall. Then, to REALLY impress her with my "cool", we went to the Hard Rock Cafe (Remember, this was well over thirty years ago when the Hard Rock cafe really WAS cool)

Things were progressing nicely as I drove her home and invited myself in "fuckcoffee". I hadn't allowed for her inane Yorkshire Terrier, Cheeky. We made awkward conversation around the bed which dominated the room, and Cheeky, who dominated the conversation.

"Get down!"

"Down!"

"Sit!"

"No, not you. The ******* dog!"

In the end we went to bed as a threesome, fully clothed, with that pesky dog in the middle.

Sunday was always Sunday in the Blatt household, so Hélène looked at me rather quizzically when I announced I had to go home as Mum had cooked Sunday lunch. My yet to manifest itself British bulldog lover reputation took a nosedive as I drove back round the North Circular. I was pretty pleased with myself for a first date but what Helene thought of the situation I would only find out in the weeks and months to come when my sheltered, suburban upbringing would be well and truly shattered.

However, our first real date, and by that her accompanying me to a match, was to be her rights of passage. If only I knew then what I know now. Where's men's intuition when you need it? If only I'd read the signs.

I thought, what could be better for stoking up the fires of passion than a derby match. United verses city at Old Trafford. Even writing this it gets me going and I've been to dozens. I tried to imagine what effect it would have on Helene. Surely she would be overcome with desire and emotion? Well, yes. But not the desire and emotion I envisaged.

It was a cold, cloudy day and the match was crap. In the early seventies both sides were on the way down, and it showed. At half-time Helene made an announcement that made my blood run cold, and even today I shiver at its implication.

"This is soooo boring. I want to go shopping. How can I leave?"

Surely my ears were deceiving me. How could a girlfriend of mine come out with a statement like that? Oh, the shame of it all. I tried to explain that it would be nigh on impossible to get out as there were about ten thousand outside without tickets who would kill to get in.

Unperturbed, she left my side, not to be seen again until gone five o'clock next to my car. She told me that the jobsworth on the gate thought she was from planet Zog, so incomprehensible was her request to leave a derby game at half-time, and that he had no training for this eventuality. In the end she got her way and out she went.

The game ended 0-0. It was a poor, bad-tempered game played in freezing conditions. But so fucking what? I'd only "cum" to see United.

Women? Fuck 'em.

9

BELGIAN WAFFLING

IMAGINE MY JOY one summer on holiday in Brittany in the mid 70s when I learnt that United were playing a pre-season friendly just down the road in...eerrr...Ostend." Look luv. Look at the map. It's only...well...about nine inches from here."

We were young and in-love, and Hélène was blind enough not to yet realise the extent of my 'other' passion. My younger brother, Andrew, was staying with us, and although a non-football fan (yes, every family's got one), the drive across rural France and into Belgium appealed to him. (And to think, he went to university!).

I called my Red mates back home and we all agreed to meet up at a designated campsite. Scouring the British press, it soon became clear that United fans' reputation as the Attila the Hun of English football fans had alerted the Belgian authorities who were preparing another Dunkirk, but in the opposite direction. It seemed every avenue open to Reds, by land, sea or air across the Channel was being watched?

But...

They hadn't made allowance for the Trojan Horse in the form of my dark blue Hillman Hunter with United stickers front and back and scarves out of all the windows coming up from behind, i.e. inland. Ostend's suburb population hid their daughters from view as raping and pillaging Brits drove into town.

As France turned to Belgium so sun turned to clouds and by the time we located the campsite we had to pitch the tent in the pitch-black rain.

I'm not saying it was crowded but it seemed to contain Bob, Ted, Carol and Alice, Beaky, Squeaky, Mick and Titch. Oh yes, and my younger brother.

Now considering he had studied geology in the wind and rain on Fort William up in the Hebrides, Andrew didn't half bleet when we acted out the children's' song "Roll Over" as he rolled out of the tent on numerous occasions throughout the night and into freezing cold and wet muddy puddles. I don't know, the yoof of today (well, 1970 something actually)

Everybody except my brother was in high spirits the following morning as we threw everything and the kitchen sink into the Camping Gaz stove for breakfast. Surrounded by Red fanatics, Andrew saw the true error of his misjudgment as, still shivering and soaking wet, he contemplated the oncoming 24/48 hours in the company of people from Planet United about which he didn't have one iota of interest or affinity. (That'll teach him to tear up my dirty books when we were younger)

The police presence was everywhere as we wandered around the town and the harbour area during the day. Nobody had heard of Ostend in the context of world football, which just went to show how far United had sunk in the few short years since we had won the European Cup back at Wembley in '68. In fact, they had just been promoted from the Belgium second division and were looking forward to welcoming a famous team on their way down. Then it was off to the game, singing and chanting along the grey beach by the grey sea with a group of 50-60 Reds. Soon we were tucked in behind the goal and a riot of singing and colour ensued. Except for the sound of that annoying base drum in the stand along one side of the pitch. Belgium's equivalent of QPR had to be silenced. It was only a matter of time. As if on queue a Red raiding party invited themselves to the Ostend "end" and the drum was silenced.

I think we won the match 2-1. I remember we were head and shoulders above them in class and our players took their foot off the pedal almost as soon as the match began, knowing that there was no way they would be beaten. Therefore you'll understand why there's very little comment on the match itself.

Grey drizzle was falling as we made our way back along the grey beach by the grey sea towards the town centre. I could almost envisage the Marie Celeste coming out of the mist towards us. However, our stupor was shattered as we hit the town and the pouring rain and the police hit us. It was going off in pockets everywhere. 70s type discos with multi-coloured glass windows were either barring all Reds or evicting the ones that had got in.

I forget where we ate but, boy, I was miserable Now.

As Morrissey once sang, "There's a place in hell for me and my friends". Yeah, I found it. It's called Belgium.

10

PICTURES IN THE SECOND DIVISION

SUPPORTING MANCHESTER United is a bit like sex – Even when it's bad, it's good!

The trauma and resignation of relegation had been creeping steadily through Red veins throughout the preceding season, as the Doc steadfastly refused to acknowledge the uselessnessnessness... of his "defense is best" policy until it was too late. Too late being that glorious Good Friday 3-0 victory over Everton at OT. False dawn. On bad Easter Monday we were beaten 1-0 at Goodison Park and back to square zero again. But at least we went down with all guns blazing and it gave us hope that we could bounce back in one season. If not...no, the thought was too horrendous to even contemplate.

By the time August 1974 arrived I was ready and raring to go. I wondered what it would be like travelling to those cute little away grounds without ever driving on the motorway. Names like Bristol Rovers, Hull City, Oldham Athletic, York City, Notts County and Leyton Orient I had only ever heard pronounced by James Alexander Gordon when reading the football results towards the end of Grandstand on a Saturday afternoon. Or Millwall, as mentioned regularly by Shaw Taylor on Police 5.

Did they really exist?

Just as every aspiring band ploughing the circuit since the 1960s knows the roadsign "Hatfield and the North", so every travelling English football supporter knows the sign,"A5 Brownhills". Of course, as you know, Brownhills does not exist, but every football fan from the Premiership to the Conference and below has travelled its n oble path at least a million times. Brownhills is known to supporters from Plymouth to Darlington who otherwise would only be aware of local geography within their own personal compass.

But at least the Second Division had one saving grace. It brought my wife and I closer together. With the promise of minor roads and quainter towns, Hélène agreed to accompany me. Not to the matches, thank Eric, but to re-inact the age old proverb..."When the going gets tough, the tough go shopping." Or in my wife's case, browse the antique shops. That was fine by me. I got to go to the matches and I escaped the depressingly dark, dank hovels inhabited by old men with smelly, poorly fitting clothes.

Now, the hype, hurt and happiness surrounding each game deserves its own dedicated chapter, so as the temperature drops, the light fades and the nurses envelop me one last time I'll spew forth a few 'Parkinsonesque' memories. Now, where's me washboard, mother.

LOCK UP YOUR DAUGHTERS

If the press were to be believed (sic), Hitler's intention to invade our sceptered isle, the Darleks bid to colonize planet Earth or Russian attempts to free 750 theatre-goers or a submarine full of sailors were nothing compared to the hell and damnation, rape and pillage that was to befall the Eastenders of Leyton in dear old London town for the opening game of the season on a bright, sunny day in August.

Walking along Leyton High Street from the underground station towards Brisbane Road was like a scene out of 28 Weeks, Mad Max or High Noon. (There, that reference should satisfy all age groups) Shops and houses were boarded up and all the locals dressed the same. Oh sorry, I've just remembered – they were the rows of police.

Inside the antiquated stadium, three quarters of the ground were Reds in fine voice. The adventure had begun. The ITV commentator, Brian Moore, was given particular vocal encouragement as he climbed up the rickety metal ladder to the TV gantry. And so to the game itself. You have to remember a free-flowing Leyton Orient had only narrowly missed out on promotion to the First Division the previous season and we were expecting a really tough game. Competitive it certainly was but we were head and shoulders above them in sheer class. A wonder strike by a George Best free Willy Morgan and a second by Stuart Houston put the first two points in the bag.

"We're only two points behind the leaders", said George Petchey, the O's manager after the game. "Football – marvelous, isn't it!" as Ron Manager would say. Who says there's no humour in football?

Our first home game of the season was against those perennial cockney rebels, Millwall. Old Trafford was heaving in the sunshine and at half-time how we chuckled as the loudspeakers read out the second division scores FIRST.

Gery Daly was on fire that afternoon and scored a hat-trick with a fourth added by one of my all-time favourites, "Pancho" Pearson.

THE BEST DE"FENCE"

The next game of note was Cardiff away. Cardiff's reputation was (and sadly still is) second only to Millwall and Leeds. From the moment we parked our car we ran a torrent of abuse right up to the stadium itself. United fans were all along one side with the Cardiff "faithful" behind one goal. Separating the two sets of supporters was the highest wire fence I'd ever seen.

I soon realised why. Just like some primitive David Attenborough observed ritual, fans on both sides of the fence would take running jumps at it, informing their opponents on the other side, with gestures that would not have been out of place from the opening sequences in Stanley Krubrick's "2001 – A Space Odessy" that if it wasn't for this fence, they would all get their fucking heads kicked in.

The 64 dollar question is, of course, if the safety fence hadn't been there, just how many would have actually gone for it? Answers on a postcard please.

Another striking memory from the day was buying the most extreme steak & kidney pie in the world. I could hardly hold the bloody thing the wrapping was so hot, yet when I managed to unwrap it the pie was literally frozen inside. Tomorrows World over to you.

The match itself was a tough, passionate affair with the Reds coming out on top 1-0 thanks to that man Gery Daly again.

SOME MOTHERS DO LUV 'EM

Millions of newspaper, police and psychologist column inches have been written trying to explain the phenomenon that is Millwall. Although this is not the time and place, I can tell you that as a committee member and one time chairman of the London branch of the FSA (Football Supporters Association now FSF – Football Supporters Federation) I have witnessed the club itself go to great lengths over the past 25 years to improve its image by introducing dynamic initiatives to improve the lot of the local community.

For example I believe they were the first professional club to offer crèche facilities to parents throughout the week.

Unfortunately all this has been like water off a ducks back because the majority, not minority, of Millwall followers (I can't call them supporters) are simply nasty, white racist thugs. And so to the eagerly (not) awaited midweek clash with the BNP in blue. Dressed incognito, three of us stood along the side. I tried without success to locate our "end" but a combination of Millwall and midweek kept Red attendance down to pockets. Midway through the first half we were awarded a penalty and Gery Daly did the business again. My celebration followed the lines of the famous Jesper Carrot, "Yup". Those poor Reds behind one of the goals who celebrated publicly were soon silenced and not heard of again. Nasty place, nasty people, nasty taste in the mouth.

ROMPY POMPY

Portsmouth are pretend Millwall. They think they're hard because they're harder than Southampton, but that's not hard, is it?

A car load of us drove down to Fratton Park for the evening, midweek fixture. More Reds this time, with plenty of good time banter and bad time kicking. The match was not one of our best. Pompy dominated pocession but were woeful in front of goal. Result 0-0.

BLACKPOOL – THE BITCH OF MANCHESTER

Reds even older than me had waited years for this one. A weekend away was called for and three of us plus Hélène made our merry way to Blackpool. Once installed in our B&B we went on the town. Brilliant. Reds are here, Reds are there, Reds are every fuckin' where. Prior to Barcelona, this was the ultimate town take-over. Inside the ground, 2/3 were United fans. The noise and carnival atmosphere had to be experienced to be believed.

Now, not for the first time, and sadly I'm sure, not for the last time, I've had to choose between women and football. Or to be more precise, Hélène and Manchester United. Except for match days I can give a convincing impression of a responsible, well adjusted adult to the outside world, but come the day of the game and my true allegiances come to the fore. Many a relationship has dissolved and many not even taken off because of Manchester United. It's an old saying but true. How can a man be in love with one woman when he is in love with eleven men?

And so it came to pass that from the moment I entered the ground I was singing, jumping, pushing and acting the fool.

Which is totally acceptable in the circumstances except for one thing. Hélène was five months pregnant.

Perhaps it was the shock of seeing Jim McCalliog playing well for the entire 90 minutes, or perhaps it was just the sea air but each time we scored we all went even more mental than normal. As our massive support behind the goal surged forward Hélène and her stomach were crushed against a barrier. The match and the atmosphere had been brilliant, but as we were streaming out of the ground I looked at her and her expression assured me that a second Jewish operation was on the cards.

The next hour or so of our relationship has been censored so as not to offend the squeamish as my parenthood was continually brought into question. Suffice to say she did not accompany us on our night on the town which turned out to be a right damp squid as all the pubs and bars were banning United fans.

MR PLOD DOES IT AGAIN

There are some games you know you aren't going to win. As fans we would pay our clubs for the privilage of putting on the shirt and representing our team on the pitch. We'd run through brick walls for that moment of glory. Getting paid thousands of pounds a week comes way down the pecking order. So it's always pretty galling when, for one reason or another, our heroes can't seemed to be arsed.

From the moment we kicked off against Bristol City at Ashton gate we knew it was going to be " one of those days ". With the realisation came the opportunity for singing and chanting with gallows humour. A brilliant atmosphere ensued until half-time when the Bristol Plod decided to have a ruck. They charged into our end behind the goal and in an instant all the bonhomie turned to anger and resentment. The second half atmosphere degenerated and it was all the fault of the boys in blue. Aren't British policemen wonderful? We lost 1-0.

THE SECOND BEST TEAM CAME FOURTH

During the 80's this was Merseydive's jibe against us. This particular season it was ours against Sunderland.

They played some brilliant football that year but someone up there just didn't like them and they failed to get promoted. Our away match at Roker Park was one of the most intimmidating I ever encountered. Their fans' noise was awesome and how we got away with a 0-0 draw that day I'll never know.

The return match at Old Trafford was voted 'Match of the Season' on BBC's " Match of the Day " A titanic sea- saw struggle. Our opening goal will always live in the memory. In the 11th minute 'Pancho' Pearson, one of my all-time faves, pilloeted on a sixpence and hit such a sweet volley into the net to put us one up.

I was still celebrating this wonder goal five minutes later when we were 2-1 down!

For sheer excitement this match had it all. We pulled it back to 2-2 and then the move of the match saw Ron Davies, who we should have bought ten years earlier, cross in the dying minutes for McIlroy to crash in the winner. Phew, what a scorcher! What a game! What a season!

11

CLOSE ENCOUNTERS OF THE TURD KIND

THROUGH A COMBINATION of bush telegraph, good fortune and cowardice I have survived fifty years of following the Reds at home, away and in Europe with surprisingly few life threatening incidents. But I have had a few close encounters.

By the law of below averages, it has been a sad but inevitable fact that I have encountered the underclass of football fans from time to time. I am as passionate as it's possible to be, but I don't feel the compulsion to kill or maim an opposing supporter just because he hasn't got the intelligence to recognise the futility of following a second class football club. However, despite reports to the contrary I am normal, and from time to time the pure racist aggression of some team's followers fills me with untold anger. I've been known to crush a grape with my little finger. However, my philosophy when attending football matches in general is, "If I learn to run away, I'll live to fight another day." Occasionally however, my luck ran out when I didn't.

Two of our oldest friends, Katy and Eddie, used to live in Malpass in Cheshire. We would sometimes stay a weekend at their place and I would go off to Old Trafford or close away trips. During the seventies Stoke City fell into this second category. I would drive down to meet my mates and we'd go off to the match together. During the seventies huge numbers of United fans used to take over most away towns and a riot of carnival atmosphere and, err, riots would ensue. Even though the trouble was exaggerated by the media for their own ends, outbreaks of violence certainly took place. Opposing fans would flex their muscles when the famous Manc gunslingers came to town.

After one particular game in Stoke, about half a dozen of us walked back into town as one of our party knew a safe and friendly cafe to consume the obligatory dogburger before going our separate ways. We watched the football results on the TV as we spent quality time consuming and conversing. Eventually it was time to leave. We strolled along together until my mates turned left towards the railway station. I waved them a fond farewell with a loud and hearty, "U-NI-Ted", and made my way back to my car. Coming towards me were a bunch of Reds. "U-NI-TED." I cried. They immediately surrounded me and two stepped forward. "Hey, guys. I'm United. It's OK." It wasn't OK. They were Stoke City fans looking for stray Reds and they had just encountered a prize walley.

Me.

I had lost all track of time. It was now a full ninety minutes since the game had ended and United had left town. Our sojourn to the cafe had completely thrown me. I was on my own in hostile territory.

Whoops.

As often happens in stress situations like these, adrenaline pumps through the veins and you feel razor sharp. The time for shitting oneself comes later. One of them then took a swing and caught me on the cheek. Lightening certainly struck twice, as just like my experience on the Embankment with those City fans back in 1968 the punch was poor. This time though I fell back and my head hit the lampost behind me. I hadn't seen it before and it provided me with the prop I needed for a truely Oscar winning performance. I suddenly fell writhing and screaming to the ground, crying......

"My eyes! My eyes! I can't see! I can't see!"

I heard a voice above me exclaim, "Shit. He's really hurt."

And before I knew it they ran off. I continued my theatricals until I judged the coast to be clear, then calmly got up and walked back to my car. Only once I was driving through the country lanes did my underwear change colour. Over to you, Desmond Morris.

Another experience concerned a visit to White Hart Lane in the early eighties. Tottenham had a decent football playing team at the time, with Garth Crooks, Ardilles, Villa and Archibald. Their success had attracted a particularly nasty section at the time, who delighted in causing havoc wherever they went By the time I got to the White Hart Lane the United 'End' was full and the police directed us to the first gate along the side. I would say there were about five hundred of us in this section with the rest of the stand Tottenham baying for our blood. One of my eyes watched the game whilst the other looked out for coins and bottles the generous Spurs fans were projecting our way.

In the end we lost a tight game and I hoped this would put the Spurs fans in a better mood. Some hope. The loudspeakers informed us that we would be kept in for our own good. I've always queried this police strategy. By the time we are let out, the vast majority of "ordinary" supporters have drifted away, leaving us exposed with no hope of "disappearing into the crowd". On this particular occasion we were being kept in for what seemed like an eternity. We sang and chanted to keep spirits up but sound and vision coming through gaps in the huge, locked wrought iron doors at the base of the stand revealed thousands of Tottenham waiting for us and not a policeman or woman in sight. So that's what we pay our taxes for. You can never find a policeman when you want one certainly rings true at certain football matches. What to do? We were making a hell of a racket inside the stadium but reality check had revealed we would be heavily outnumbered when the gates were finally opened and we were let out. Despite my outer bravado I was shitting myself. But I kept my wits about me. I had a sudden thought. They had locked the gates in front of us so we couldn't get out of the stadium the way we came in, but surely there was no way to lock us in from behind. I reasoned that if I did a reverse and went back up the stairs and into the seats, it might be possible to walk along the side of the stand and out by exits further along. And so I made my way back up the stairs, which I have to say confused a lot of United fans waiting to be lead like Christians into the lions den. Once back at the top of the stand I did my crab impersonation and walked sideways for about one hundred yards and down another set of stairs. Lo and behold the gates were open and I simply walked out into the street and disappeared into the night. That night I was lucky, but stories crept back that a lot of Reds weren't.

12

ALL THINGS BRIGHTON BEAUTIFUL

I DON'T KNOW ABOUT YOU, but the thought of a weekend away makes me horney. Unusual location, strange bedroom, clean sheets, room service, somebody else to make the bed afterwards. It all contributes to helping me rise to the occasion. Unfortunately Hélène doesn't share the same hormonal imbalance as me and often rejects my over-enthusiastic, unsubtle advances out of hand. (Pity, in her hand would be nicer).

Out of season, many four and five star hotels which cater principally to business and conference clientele offer amazing packages for the weekend, with a room for two, for two nights, at a fraction of the normal rack rates. Living in London, one of our favourite destinations had always been Brighton. It's only a ninety minute drive, it's by the sea, it has elegant architecture, the long and winding Lanes, a pier that catches fire every couple of years or so, in fact all the elements that add up to what the brochures call "A Romantic Break".

Throughout the eighties and most of the nineties I was involved in the Premiums and Incentives industry. For many years one of the leading trade exhibitions took place every April at the Hotel Metropole in Brighton. A large, opulent 4 star hotel on the sea front, at £80 per person per night in the 80's it was far too expensive for the likes of us at exhibition time, so we would decamp to The Regency Hotel, a small B & B round the corner in Regency Square. To be fair, this was a delightful establishment. It was owned and run by two gay Spanish brothers, who, when the standard rate for a double room in a B&B was £15 a night, would charge £25 but it was worth it. Every room was individually decorated and their service was a cut above the "take it or leave it" attitude that prevailed at the time. We actually found this place by accident.

For our first year exhibiting in Brighton, we had booked into one of the nondescript B&B's within walking distance of the Metropole.

Twenty four hours later we fled kicking and screaming after a night and following morning of hideous smells, horrendous noise from a broken boiler above our heads, limp food and sour landlady. Modern English tourism at its best! Just what we need to keep tourists and their wallets from our shores.

At exhibition time it's almost impossible to find a hotel room, let alone a room that's not at a rip-off rate. Fortunately for us, two doors down the Regency Hotel had had a cancellation and a room was ours.

Meanwhile, back at the Metropole, around this time they offered weekend breaks from November to March, excluding exhibitions, at approximately £40 per room per night including full English Breakfast. Sorted. It became a regular getaway for us. Living the life of Riley for 48 hours, even if Tea was one orange juice and two straws, please.

The pleasure barometer went up a further notch or three during the eighties when Brighton & Hove Albion were in the (then) first division. With lines like... "the match only lasts ninety minutes and we have the rest of the weekend to ourselves", I was able to have my cake and eat it. However, one March weekend stands out in the memory as I truly gorged myself.

I had convinced my Red mate, Joe, and his lovely girlfriend, Kim, to join Hélène, Melanie (now my eldest but then my only, three year old daughter) for the weekend. Kim, who almost, but not quite, hates football with the same intensity as my wife, agreed to come as long as we didn't talk football all weekend. I repeated my mantra..."only 90 minutes, only 90 minutes, etc. etc..."

We met up after work and drove through the treacle that is South London traffic late on a Friday afternoon. Some of the "bonhomie" had worn off by the time we arrived in Brighton some two and a half hours later. Brighton's crooked parking Gestapo are on a par with London's traffic wardens and finding a parking space in the final half hour had been a test of everyone's patience. Joe and I eventually huffed and puffed our way up to the steps of the Metropole Hotel and into the lobby. We looked at each other and let out a cry.

"Oh shit", we exclaimed.

When Hélène and Kim glided up the steps of the Metropole Hotel and into the lobby they too looked at each other and let out a cry.

"Oh shit", they exclaimed.

There in the reception, before our very eyes, were the entire Manchester United football team and management. McQueen, Jordan, Macari, Wilkins, Robson, et al, plus Sexton, Cavannah...you name them, they were there. All thoughts of a romantic weekend went out of the window. Promises, what promises? Someone had moved the goal posts. Rules and priorities had changed. If a player took the lift Joe and I went in the lift with him. We were male United groupies of the worst kind.

When the players had finally divested themselves of our unwanted attention, the four and a half of us went out for a meal. Trying to re-kindle romance under these circumstances proved a pier too far, so I consoled myself with the thought that carnal service would be resumed once the players had checked out the following morning. Best laid plans of mice and men, eh? How was I to know that fate would take a hand and that the goalposts would be moved once again.

TAKE BREAKFAST AS RED

Normally, on a Blatt "have it away weekend", breakfast in bed is 'de rigeur'; However, as we were accompanied by Joe and Kim, we thought it would be more sociable to meet up and go down together to the restaurant around 09.00 am. Entering the said edible 4 star establishment, our senses were exposed to an array of delights, namely – the players and management. Stereo daggers from Hélène and Kim put us firmly in our places. We chose a table next to Ray Wilkins and his family.

I just HAD to strike up a conversation. Only how? Between kippers (yum, yum) and grapefruit segments, I noticed he had a kid, a similar age to Melanie.

"Melanie, darling. Wouldn't you like to play with that little boy at the next table?"

"Don't want to."

"Aw. Go-wan. I'm sure he'd like to play."

"No."

"Melanie. Look at him. Maybe he's shy. Go and say 'Hello'." "No." "Melanie," I said through gritted teeth. "Go, and, play, with, that, little, boy".

With that I used my right foot to literally push my daughter into Ray's son. Whatever he was playing with got knocked over (C'mon. It's over twenty years ago. You can't expect me to remember everything.) Ray looked up and I smiled sheepishly and said.

"Kids, eh?"

I can't remember what he said but we struck up a decent conversation. So much so that by the time we had all finished our collective breakfasts Ray and I went out into the hotel reception and continued rabbiting for over an hour. He was aware that he hadn't been performing to the level he had at Chelsea. I sympathised and offered encouragement and he turned out to be a really nice, intelligent bloke as our respective offspring played under the table. We parted as firm friends, confident in the knowledge that our paths would never cross again.

And we were right.

By this time Joe had come downstairs, forewarning me that two women we both knew quite well were planning revenge on our wallets in the shops of Brighton.

So many players. So little time. His words fell on deaf ears as row upon row of suit covers partially, but not completely, obscured our Red heroes. Confusion and male United groupies reigned supreme until the last player disappeared through the revolving doors.

Silence. I looked at my watch.

"Where are the girls?" I said.

"They've gone." He said.

"Gone where?" I said

"Shopping". He said

"Shit". I said

Double anti-whammy. Not only was I heavily in "La Maison du Chein", I would also be considerably lighter of wallet by the end of the day. However I put this to the back of my mind as thoughts of a higher nature took over.

"U-NI-TED! U-NI-TED!"

"Hi Ho. Hi Ho. It's to the game we go. La la la la, la la la la, Hi Ho, Hi Ho Hi Ho Hi Ho, etc..etc..."

EXTRA TEA TIME

OK. Can we not talk about the game? I know you found this book in the Sports section and expect me to talk football, but like going to a dentist and enduring an extraction without anesthetic, I'm trying to save you from the pain I endured. Surffice to say there are 0 -0 draws and there are 0 – 0 draws, but believe me when I tell you, this really was a 0 – 0 draw. I'm gonna have to explain to United fans under twenty years old that during the Sexton years this was the rule, not the exception. For those of you living the dream of 1991 onwards, we paid your dues. The occasional FA Cup sprint could not disguise the fact that we were also-runs in the true long distance League.

The only yard stick that really counted.

Did I hear you mention the European Cup? That was in another solar system. Runs in the Inter-City Fairs Cup and European Cup Winners Cup were the heights of our ambition. Not that this diminished the pleasure. Oh, my word no. Much binding in the marsh, drinking in the bars and singing in far flung squares filled our travelling lives with joy.

At the final whistle. Yes, you heard me, the Final Whistle.

I'm sorry but no matter how good/bad the experience, I refuse to EVER leave a match before the end. Fuck the traffic, fuck the tea, fuck the wife (did I just write that? Note – must make appointment with shrink), the game lasts 90+ minutes and anything can happen. And with United this is the rule, not the exception. Cloughie famously once said, "It only takes a second to score a goal", and, "A goal in the last moment is worth a goal anytime" and, unlike Sting, I do subscribe to this point of view. Obviously the world's greatest ever sporting comeback, Barcelona '99, remains No. 1 in the hearts, minds, blood, nervous system and underwear of Reds worldwide, but there have been others. Fans of other clubs all have their own moments. Against us, notably Arsenal at Wembley in 1979 when our amazing two goal comeback in the last four minutes was eclipsed by Alan Sutheland's "it could go anywhere but it just had to end up in the back of our net" winner.

I shouldn't continue on this tangent 'cos I'll lose my thread, but I have to comment on another victory for "I was there" over the lounge lizard, in front of the tele species. I've seen those last five minutes replayed many times on TV and the sofa supporter has absolutely no idea of the intensity of emotion regular match going fans go through. Unlike the majority of opinion about this game, I don't subscribe to the point of view that Arsenal were the better team on the day. Biased, moi? But I will concede that we didn't flow like we could do. With five minutes left Jordan crosses from the left and McQueen sidefoots in our consolation goal Or so we thought.

However, straight from the kick off, everything changed. You could just sense it. Arsenal imploded as though embarrassed to have been leading 2-0 for so long. The noise levels in the United end were deafening as we went for their jugular. Then Sammy McIlroy picks up the ball on the right, beats one, beats two, beats three (beats me how he did it) and shoots.

GOOOAAAAAL!

Absolute bedlam. You had to be there to believe the scenes I witnessed. On the tele, all you hear is the roar from the crowd celebrating a goal. Being in the middle of it was akin to the top being kicked away from a massive ant hill and thousands of ants cascading about in 25,000 different directions.

And the noise.

Television never conveys the awesome power of noise and how it effects you physically. Its intensity vibrating though every core of your being. My blood was pumping dangerously fast through my veins as Arsenal kicked off as though their entire team had been given instant Jewish operations. They had nothing left. I was vaguely aware of their half-hearted attempts to kick the ball upfield, as far away from their goal as possible. This was the pitiful sight of man at his lowest ebb, where survival meant existing purely on instinct. Prehistoric, pre-brain cell, pre-final whistle. The referee was about to blow for extra time and United's inevitable onslaught to victory when the ball was somehow crossed into our penalty area and Alan Sutherland and THAT Brillo pad haircut vainly attempted to squeeze between our two Greek Gods in defense.

"Pathetic", I thought. "No chance".

GOAL.

"You're fucking joking. Oh God...Oh God Noooooooooooooo!!!!!!!!!"

This wasn't happening. This wasn't in the script. My heart and stomach reacted as though run over by a steamroller. I couldn't catch my breath. We kicked off. Final whistle. Lost 3-2.

No, no, no. It's not true. It's not happening. Why is the other end of Wembly Stadium celebrating? It should be us. They can't even celebrate properly. Only United fans know how to truly celebrate. We are the champion celebrators.

I looked around me. I couldn't believe my eyes. Total devastation. It was like the final scene out of Mad Max 47. The end of the world. There were now gaps in the terraces. Some people were standing. Staring. At nothing. Some people were crouched on the ground, head in hands. There were dead bodies everywhere, lying motionless. Tears had taken over from beer as the principal liquid on offer. Our life force had been extracted. The future's dull. The future's Arsenal.

Meanwhile "grey" was certainly the most apt word to describe United's away 0-0 draw with Brighton. Grey day. Grey football. The future's grey. The future's Sexton. We made our way back along the beach towards the centre of Brighton. If the truth be told I actually quite enjoyed the eeriness of hundreds of subdued Reds trudging along the sand, with the backdrop of a calm, grey sea. I could imagine the Marie Celeste rising out of the gloom, it's ghost like appearance whispering to us, "Sexton. Four more years. Four more years." It was hypnotic. Beautiful. Deadly.

The dark red brickwork of the Metropole Hotel came into view. About ten of us broke away , crossed the main road and entered the lobby. A look of consternation descended on the 4 star hotel staff as they were confronted by a group of disheveled United fans. However, our "murderous" look won, and we headed unopposed for the huge, ornate Tea Room. Slumped in our chairs, we dissected the afternoon's events. Some of us got quite agitated whilst others, seeing no light at the end of the player's tunnel, concentrated on slumping. The vast Tea Room remained empty. The odd head popped round, took one look at us and hastily bid a retreat. Very wise.

The door opened again and I heard what I thought was a Scottish accent.

"Excuse me lads. Have any of yoooose got the scores?"

We looked up with a collective "We're United fans. We're pissed off.

Don't mess with us." expression when, lo and behold, we realised that the voice, and the face it emanated from belonged to our Lou. Lou Macari.

"Hey. Lou. Over here, mate."

Wow. I could have sworn all the players had checked out around midday. What was Lou doing back here?

He came and sat down. It was obvious he was also pissed off and was just dying to talk to some United fans who would understand where he was coming from. Somehow we all sensed this, so instead of all talking at once in gushing tones we let him dictate the conversation. Lou was brilliant. He was funny. He was angry. He was everything you would expect a non politically correct football hero to be. And no, he didn't try to sell us any watches. His main point was that the dressing room was divided at this time between Sexton's buys and the players he had inherited. Coming off the pitch that afternoon, the Manager had commiserated with those players he had bought and bollocked those he had inherited. And Lou fell into the second category. Pissed off by the injustice of it all, he just wanted to talk.

We covered all the usual suspects. Respect to Lou who confided to us in confidence. There's no way, despite the D-notices rule, that I will betray this trust, so the points made and revelations revealed will remain within those very large four walls.

Everybody contributed. From opinionated bastards like me to the more shy, retiring types who preferred to let their fists do the talking. One of my mates at this time was Tony Bumstead.

A true blinkered Red, he's now emmigrated to Brisbane in Australia, having left Maggie's bleak Britain in the mid 80's to seek employment in pastures new. We still keep in touch although he would agree he's not the best communicator in the world. Even during this enlightened encounter his principal remark was, irrespective of the subject matter in hand...

"I fuckin' 'ate Leeds."

A truly remarkable and laudable statement I grant you.

Yet somehow its power was diminished when debating the benefits, or otherwise, of Sexton's deployment of Pearson in a midfield role which, in my opinion, diminished his unique finishing prowess coming from so deep. "I fuckin' 'ate Leeds" was perhaps a little more relevant when discussing the roles and effectiveness of Jordan and McQueen, who had yet to reproduce their best sheep shagging form for the Reds. However, this incisive comment failed to bring the debate forward or to reach any positive, long term conclusions. Still, his heart was in the right place. And still is.

Eventually we broke up. I had hoped Lou would invite us all out for a meal but he had to go back to Manchester, so we bid him a fond farewell. We settled back in our chairs to go over everything Lou had told us. A magic meeting with a great player with a mind of his own. How refreshing in these PR times to talk to a real person with real opinions instead of the "Hello Brian. I'm opening a boutique." variety. I know that dates me but you get the idea. By this time it was dark. We looked at our watches. Almost 9pm. Joe and I made our way up to our rooms. Empty. Shit. We weren't just in "Rue de la Merde", we were up to our necks in it. Another nail in the marriage coffin. And for what? Just one of those great evenings that only come along once in a Red moon. That's what.

13

EUROPE, EUROPE, HERE WE COME...

GOING ABROAD ON holiday is one thing. Going abroad on business is another. But going abroad to support your football club is completely OTT.

As a United fan, the reason I have been put on this planet is to follow United in Europe. It's our Holy Grail. Our quest. Our destiny.

Work, study, debt, girlfriends. All responsibilities pale into insignificance as another Euro jaunt looms on the horizon. Rape, pillage and boozing are the order of the day, and night, with the small matter of a footy match in-between to take the mind off rape, pillage and booze. A few years ago Glasgow Celtic fans deservedly won a UEFA prize for the behaviour of their fans at the UEFA Cup final against Porto in Seville. On that basis Manchester United fans deserve a life-long achievement award for our outstanding contribution to football supporting and world peace in the face of constant provocation by European clubs, their fans and their national riot police.

There's no other way of putting this. United are the best behaved supporters in the land. And considering the unique size of our support at home and away, for the past forty or so the percentage of our fans found guilty of causing trouble has been miniscule. As the Spanish press reported after our historic last gasp Champions League Final victory in Barcelona, "Manchester fans. Ugly but beautiful." I couldn't have put it better myself.

And, lest anyone forgets, there was not one arrest amongst both sets of English fans at this year's Champions League Final in Moscow. More surprising, perhaps, was the fact that almost half of these supporters were Chelsea fans. Of course, the natural law of relativity was restored when it was reported that hundreds of Rent Boys watching the match in the Kings Road/ Fulham Road area were a trifle miffed that their boys took "one hell of a beating" and took out their frustrations on any passing crustation that got in their way. True blue.

The incredible lightness of being I experience when another Euro jaunt approaches is exquisite. The Red Army on Tour is a sight to behold. Rape and pillage competing with drinkadrinkadrink to Eric the Kingthekingtheking. Looking back I don't know how I got away with all that time off. Since I moved to France in 2000 I've fallen seriously by the wayside. Just keeping financially head above water is a struggle in itself so I have nothing but 100% admiration for those Reds who have hardly missed a game in decades.

Outsiders have no concept of the sacrifices, ear bashing, joy and despair. Feelings so intense they defy classification. All I can say for myself is, "Je ne regrette rien." To give you a flavour of what it's all about you could go straight to the "1999" chapter, but it hasn't always been so glamorous or successful but all have been unforgettable. The craic, the sunshine, (no, just sunshine, no double meaning) the girls that (always) got away, the booze, and finally, the booze. And here comes a confession. I don't drink. Alcohol that is.

There, I've said it. Of course, I could have mentioned it in the beginning of the book but, be honest, how many of you who have now bonded with me may have been alienated by this bizarre revelation? Would you have been able to relate to my strange behaviour if you had known I was stone, cold sober throughout? Or, more importantly, if I had revealed I was whiter than white and not just redder than red, would you still have bought my book? I couldn't risk it. I need the money. You see Manchester United may arguably be richest club in the world, but United fans are just a cross section of society like the fans of any other club. (I hear ABU's sniggering. You're thinking, hang on a minute. United have wiped the floor with us, cornered nearly all the trophies, why should we feel an ounce of sympathy for them?)

Well, think about it. Our success, especially in Europe, has meant a black hole in most Red fanatics' bank accounts. Wives and girlfriends' presents have to come second to the Red cause, with the resultant negative financial and sexual liquidity. And ABU lot have a lot to answer for as well. You may hate us but it's funny how the visit of Eric's Disciples on Earth results in a category "A" match with Sky high ticket prices to match. You only have to pay this once a year. We have to cough up throughout the season. So in the end I have enough material to make a case for "Support a Red, you know it makes cents."

I may as well get it all out in the open now I've started. I don't drink, smoke, go out with men or play around (No, not golf you idiot). So what ARE my vices? Well, as a teenager and beyond I built up my record collection. I was one of the lucky ones. In 1960 I was eleven and by 1970 I was twenty one. Now I'm even sure City fans don't need any help with the maths, but the point is that I officially became a teenager in 1962 (Elvis, Cliff and the Shadows, Billy Fury, Adam Faith, etc...). The following year exploded with the Beatles, Rolling Stones, The Kinks et al) and by the time the decade drew to a close I had soared onto another plain with the likes of Led Zeppelin, Captain Beefheart , Frank Zappa, Bob Dylan, Cream, Joni Mitchell, Jethro Tull, Taste (Rory Gallagher) Yes, the Allman Brothers Band and Pink Floyd.

So while my mates drank and smoke and their teams won trophies, I OD'd on sounds. Hunting down promotional copies was my anorak activity. But the important thing was, second only to following the Reds around the globe, going to live concerts at that time was an experience never to be forgotten. And dare I say it...never to be repeated again.

Not only was I young, ungifted and white during (in my opinion) "pop" music's greatest era, the musicianship was of the highest order and the atmosphere at gigs was just out o' sight. As Nick Lowe once sang, "What's so funny about peace, love and understanding?" The free-flow exchange of revelations, possessions and bodily fluids. The breaking down of traditions, barriers real and imaginary, the rejection of convention. Eric, wish they'd asked me to come out to play. But, hey, the music was special and although my collection takes up too many wardrobes for my wife's liking it's staying with me forever. No matter how dire our finances, and we've done our fair share of boot sales and 'vide greniers' in France, some things are not up for grabs.

Of course, the other benefit of not abusing my body with both legal and illegal chemicals is that I just had enough money to follow the Reds from an early age. After the heartache of missing out on Real Madrid away in 1968 (see Real Madrid Got Away) I vowed to catch as many United matches in Europe that I could. And don't forget, in the seventies and eighties, United's jaunts in Europe normally only lasted one or two rounds so every match was to be savoured as though it would be our last. Then and now, though, one unsavoury aspect of following the Reds in Europe exists today (Lille & Rome) as it existed then. The (mis)treatment of English fans abroad and the (mis)reporting of English fans behaviour abroad. I'd double the number of pages of this book if I were to recount the number of times we have been ripped off for ticket prices, abused by away fans, stadiums and their staff, their country's police and UEFA. Why let the truth get in the way of preconceived opinions about all English football supporters? Undoubtedly a minority of so-called English fans have tarnished us all with the same brush. We've all had to live with the legacy of incidents such as Leeds fans rioting at the Parc de Prince in Paris when their side came second to Bayern Munich in the European Cup final, and I know the vast majority of decent fanatics wish to see the back of those racist thugs that pollute our national game. But the European football authorities have just been lazy cowards and vindictive in administering punishment to English clubs and their fans over the past half century. Now we have arrived in the 21st century, 'hooliganism' is far worse in a number of European and South American countries than it is in England, yet still English clubs and their fans are targeted whilst foreign clubs literally 'get away with murder'.

I'm proud to have been a member of the FSA, Football Supporters Association (now FSF – Football Supporters Federation) since 1986, and proud of our tireless work in informing and persuading the powers that be to re-examine their policy towards British football both at home and abroad. The FSF represents all English fans, whether travelling to support their club or country. I urge supporters of clubs throughout the land to join the FSF. Details can be found at www.fsf.org.uk Having got that off my chest I'd like you to kick off your shoes, lay back and think of Manchester as I recount a selection of tales from my road to Mandalay.

WE CLEANED THE KOP FROM BOTTOM TO TOP WITH AJAX FROM AMSTERDAM

I've waited a long time to incorporate the words of one of my favourite songs from the swinging sixties. Although only the "Ajax from Amsterdam" bit is relevant, I'm sure all United fans will appreciate this blast from the past. It refers to a European game at Anfield a few years before where the glorious Ajax had murdered Liverpool 5-1 on their own patch. Memories like that are worth finding an excuse to re-live.

It had been six years and four months since THAT referee standing on the halfway line had disallowed Denis's equaliser against the theatrically diving AC Milan in the return leg of the semi-final of the 1969 European Cup at Old Trafford. The ball had clearly gone over the line. In the Stretford End I saw it. Millions on BBC TV saw it on Sportsnight with Coleman. The only person on planet Earth not to see it was the referee. On moments like these history is made. In our case, thirty one years.

By the time we drew Ajax in the first round of the UEFA Cup in 1976 they were no longer the force that had dominated Europe in the early seventies, winning the European Cup in three successive years from 1971 to 1973.

But they were still formidable for our young, exciting but inexperienced side which had bounced back from a year in the second division with such aplomb, playing fast and furious football that was a delight to watch. And after my cop out in 1968 when I bottled my trip to Madrid there was no way I was going to miss out on our new European adventures. My first chapter of "The Reds on Tour" was about to be written. Six long, long years of hibernation were finally thawing out. The flowers of Manchester were about to blossom once again. A trip to Amsterdam whetted all our appetites.

Half of Manchester thought so too. Euro aways for us in those days to our near neighbours such as France, Belgium and Holland were our recipe for Mini Bus mayhem. Twelve seater rust bucket Transits with scarves and full moons out of the window. I had a full payload for this excursion to the sex capital of Europe. It would be a chance for some of the snottier, anorak types amongst us to get a close up of naked women with marble veined breasts in the famous red light district. We chose the Dover – Ostend route and we were greeted with a bright sunny day. Scarves, beer guts and

bottoms dangling out of the window, Europe was our preferred play-
ground.

Arriving in Amsterdam was a revelation. It was Manchester at play.
There were Reds of all ages and sexes everywhere. The six year cold turkey
had had the same effect on everyone. Ok, it wasn't the European Cup but
we were back in Europe where we belonged and we were going to extract
every last ounce of pleasure. We would never take Europe for granted again,
and to this day I never have.

Finding a parking place was no easy task but at last we could get out
of the car and join fellow Reds at play. We saw all the old crowd. Mrs
Stewart, Vena, Pat the Twat , Oldham and Danny Swanson from the
coach, assorted Cockney Reds from Dobbin's trains and a supporting
cast of thousands. After the obligatory tour of the red light district drinks
were in order but everywhere was packed with Reds and the chances of
being served before making our way to the new Olympic stadium seemed
remote. Then one of our party remembered a student bar on the first
floor in one of the university buildings, right in the middle of town. As
he had his student card with him, a bit of banter at the door and we were
in.

Guzzling thirstily, we found ourselves on a row of stools by the
window overlooking a street full of Reds below. They were in full voice, as
only Reds on Tour can be. Opposite I noticed a couple of girls in the
window of the departmental store. They were window dressers and they
wore very short skirts. We waved, vainly trying to attract their attention. A
few moments later and the Reds below discovered the pair of beauties as
us. Only they had a different view. From street level looking up, they
believed they could see up right their skirts. Queue an enthusiastic
rendering of United ditties, interspersed with reference to the female
anatomy and requests to get "their lips out for the lads". Yes. United were
back. United were back – on form.

All good things must come to an end as another takes its place, and we
departed this fine establishment and made our way out to the stadium.
Surprisingly for such a successful team, Ajax had for many years played in
a relatively small ground, reserving the Olympic Stadium for major
European nights. The United fans were all amassed behind one goal with
the obligatory cycle track separating us from the action and the atmosphere.

The rest of the stadium and the game seemed to be across the road. A strange out of stadium experience.

Throughout the first half we all sat down and reflected passively at events on the pitch somewhere over there. Ruud Krol had put Ajax 1-0 up and the night was passing us by. Then as the players came out for the second half one demented Red raged at us for not singing our hearts out for the lads. That did it. We rose as one and the second half was a kaleidoscope of sound and colour. Stewart Houston was denied a perfectly good equaliser but both team and fans had given a good account of themselves and, all in all, we felt our first Euro away had been a resounding success.

We were looking forward to the drive back to Belgium but we reckoned without the Dutch motorway signage. All over Europe, the UK and America, the general rule is to put the name of the major city, followed by, as you drive along, the names of the smaller towns as they come near. From Manchester city centre it's not long before you can spy signs for Birmingham M6. It's logical. However, the Dutch motorway system is, how shall we say, eccentric. Maybe it's the effect of those funny cigarettes but at no point leaving Amsterdam was there a sign for the second largest Dutch town, Rotterdam.

We zigged. We zagged. We zagged and we zigged. We doubled back so many times I didn't know if I was zigging or zagging. And so thus ended our first live Euro away.

A great learning curve that left us yearning for more.

ALLEZ LES (PER)VERTS

In 1974 we were drawn against another mighty but ever so slightly over the top team if the truth be told in St Etienne in the UEFA Cup.

To illustrate the power of Manchester United to melt even the coldest heart and to create world peace, my mate Joe Lewis had been trying for ages to go out with this lovely girl named Kim. Whatever tactics he had tried up till then had obviously failed in their strategic objective so he brought out his secret weapon (stop it) "Would you like to come with me and the lads in our rust bucket Transit for a two day mid-week jaunt overland to the south of France?" "OK." No. You really will enjoy yourself, There's ... sorry, what did you say?" "Yes, I'll come." "Fuck me."

Her next response has long been lost in the mists of time but surffice it to say that she had her first date with Joe and ten other Red fanatics on the back bench of the Transit.. No, we didn't all sit on the back bench...we...oh, you know what I mean. The epitaph to this little anecdote is that Joe and Kim have been together now for almost thirty years and have four kids, two girls and two boys, and one of the boys is called Matthew. What else? Conclusion. What's red hot and full of passion? "U-NI-TED! " (What else?)

Meeting up in Central London early on the morning of the game we made our way down to Dover for the ferry to Calais. We then bombed our way along the autoroute to Paris, round the Peripherique and onto the Autoroute de Soleil towards Lyon. By the time we had passed Macon, Les Verts were out in force, filling each motorway service station to overflowing.

My friendly wave was greeted by the single finger. Eric, they can't even count properly, let alone drive on the right side of the road. Well, they do actually drive on the right side of the road, but we drive on the left side of the road which is right. Right? Oh, you know what I mean. So I made a decision. Approaching the last service station before Lyon, and without informing anyone on board, I veered off onto the slip road and, almost without taking my foot off the accelerator, drove through the green hordes like a Red hot rust bucket through butter. They scattered like green flies. Pale weak piss masquerading as lager cascading in all directions. 1-0 to Les Diables Rouges. Cheshire and Lancashire grins were the order of the day.

The final forty kilometres from Lyon to St Etienne were a nightmare. Rush hour + football traffic = standstill. Why do they call the rush hour the rush hour? You don't rush. In fact, you hardly move at all. They should re-name it, "the hardly moves at all hour." Tempers and throats fraying, we were parched. Even weak French piss lager took on the mantle of "elixir of life". Eventually we parked and trudged along to the nearest bar that contained singing Reds. However, the locals were not that friendly and small skirmishes were witnessed, although these would have been a lot worse but fortunately most of the Reds couldn't understand French.

"Hi Ya."

"Encula!" "Pauvre con!"

"Ta mate. Mine's a pint"

To make matters worse, football matches in France are policed by the CRS, the Neanderthal undead Riot Police, and unfortunately, as Lille so vividly illustrated this year, nothing has changed in the thirty or so years since this game. "Guilty till proven innocent." seems to be their motto towards English fans. European clubs, whether they are first time minnows to European competition which have taken a crash course in hysterical British tabloid journalism, or seasoned campaigners who have staged countless European ties and who really, really should know better, "Bash the British" is the order of the day. Prior to this match the French press were having an "off the field" day, whipping up a frenzy of anti-English sentiment regarding "Les hooligans." The CRS and their ferocious barking dogs of war gathered all the United fans together and made us take off our shoes which they then confiscated. That autumn, friends and families of the local 'flics' wore the coolest British footwear. We were then frog marched us (offense intended) right into the midst of the St Etienne "end", irrespective of what was written on our tickets.

I don't know. Maybe the CRS were running a sweepstake on exactly how many heads they could crack open once the aggro they had instigated by the provocative act of placing all the United fans in the home end erupted. Certainly the logic of their actions defy intelligent analysis. Within a few minutes stale baguettes and bottle of piss came flying over. No, not French lager. The real thing, French piss. Our lovable Gallic hosts had literally pissed in empty water bottles and flung them in our direction. Next they charged, armed with knives and blades. Cue for the Riot police to join in and bash anything wearing red, whether scarf, shirt or blood whilst the provocateurs, the St Etienne fans, escaped unpunished (sound familiar?)

Eventually a kind of simmering peace was established as the players came out onto the pitch, although our lot had been scattered in the mayhem. In all the excitement of staying alive I've omitted to mention that we had a tasty side at the time. Admittedly not able to sustain a conserted challenge for the league but capable of playing some breathtaking football when the mood took them. With Gordon Hill and Steve Coppell on the wings, the majestic Martin Buchan at his best in the middle and Stuart 'Pancho' Pearson leading the line, tonight they played football from the

Gods. We tore them apart and won 5-1. Except that the referee kept disallowing our goals in the most blatant attempt at match rigging I have had the personal misfortune to attend.

When St Etienne went ahead early in the second half I couldn't believe it. If Gordon Hill hadn't equalised a few minutes later there might have been no stadium left at the end of the match, such was the feeling of overwhelming disgust at the treatment of the United fans and the players. Later UEFA blamed the English fans and fined United. They only took our pre-match red top press into account and the reputation of English fans called the "English Disease." and not the facts submitted by hundreds of United fans including middle aged men and women, couples of all ages and professional people as well as our hard core travelling support. These people and organisations run the beautiful game. What hope is there? "Gis a job. I could do that." First time I've agreed with a scouser for ages.

Meeting up after the final whistle we decided that going out in St Etienne was no longer an option so we squelched, some of us footless and fancy free back to the mini van.

We discussed our options as we headed out of town and it was agreed to stop at the first hotel/motel we passed. Soon a suitable one came into view. Imagining French TV repeating their version of the Battle of Trafalgar, the sight of a dozen English football fans descending on a suspecting hotel might work against us, so Joe and I hatched a plan. Joe and Kim were now an item whilst I had known Diane, one of our party for a good few years now. Originally there had been four of them. Diane, Christine, Val and Linda. Then and now Manchester United have three Supporters clubs in London. Diane and Christine had started to follow United from London with Dobbin's lot on the train from Euston whilst Val and Linda succumbed to the charms of the back seat of the coach. Eventually all four girls came with us. This was vitally important for sensitive souls like us at such an impressionable age. For the first time since I had been following the Reds we had good looking girls accompanied us. "The times they were 'a changing." We parked our van at the far end of a dark motel car park, then Joe and Kim, me and Diane posed as two couples and requested two rooms. It worked. We walked back to the others with two sets of keys. Joe and Kim disappeared into one room whilst the remaining ten of us filed into the other, reminiscent of that scene from The

Marx Brothers film aboad the cruise ship where they were all holed up in the broom cupboard and came tumbling out when a maid opened the door at the end of the scene.

Now, during my confession at the beginning of this piece, I proclaimed that I don't play around (I'm not doing that joke again). I may have bent the rules a little there because this night I went to bed with Diane...and Mick and Andy and blond Tony and......It was that sort of night. Meanwhile Joe converted Kim to the Red cause in the other bedroom.

Eventually some of the others went to kip on the mini bus. It was a great night and we had a laugh the following morning as some of us fought over the tiny shower room. Significantly some didn't join in. Dirty bastards.

VALENCIA – DON'T MENTION THE WAR

The Iron Lady, the Blue Rinse Bitch from Hell had recently taken Britain to war over the Falkland Islands, and won, which was difficult for a left wing pacifist like me to accept. Even though, as both a person and a politician she stood for everything I didn't, our victory gave us additional ammunition to direct at Valencia supporters in the up and coming first round tie in September 1982. I'm nothing if not shallow.

The first leg at Old Trafford had ended 0-0, but the overriding memory was the vicious and illegal takling of the Spanish players. Revenge would be ours in Spain. Mick Shenton and I chose the club's official one day flight and match ticket organised by the respected and sorely missed head of all the United supporters clubs, Dave Smith. The flight was uneventful and we landed at Valencia Airport around 3 o'clock. A coach transferred us to the stadium. Everything, cars, buildings, people, seemed to be covered in a yellow dust. Valencia is not a tourist town. It's an industrious, hard working town where working class families from Madrid took their seaside holidays. It was also very pro Franco and had been pro Los Malvines.

Alighting from the coach we were handed our match tickets and warned about straying too far in colours. Also, in order not to antagonise our Spanish hosts, Dave Smith had traveled to Valencia the previous week and spoken to club representatives and the Spanish police to arrange parking for our coaches away from the stadium. It had been agreed a fleet of coaches right outside might have acted as a Red rag to a Spanish bull so instructions were given where to find the coaches after the game.

The majority of Reds settled themselves in time honoured fashion inside and outside the nearest watering holes but Mick and I wanted a little bit more. All our friends and colleagues were at work and here we were, a thousand miles away in the hot sun with the Mediterranean Sea beckoning. I flagged down a taxi. Our first problem. As I've already mentioned, Valencia was not a tourist town so why should taxi drivers learn to speak English? Words like "Beach, "Sea" and "Swim" meant nothing to them. Well, we British are nothing if not inventive. I started to do Marcel Marceau impersonations of someone swimming, brandishing my arms like a hyperactive Lee Evans. Eventually the taxi driver cottoned on, but not before we had become the butt of piss-take songs by the tanked up Red hordes all around us.

Ahh. The beach. Magic. Wide and empty and all for us.

Stripping down to the min. we plunged into the Med. This was the life. Mates and other halves working back home, Reds splashing about in the sea. By the time we got out a massive all Red, hundred a side beach soccer match was in full flow. A short kickabout later we made our way up to the line of restaurants at the back of the beach. Now the summer season was over, all had closed except one. By this time we were starving so we went inside and the owner suggested a home-made paella cooked over a charcoal grill. Magic. Whilst we stuffed ourselves he told us he used to live and work in England but had settled back in Valencia and worked with his son. The meal was wonderful and we bid him farewell with hope in our hearts and paella in our stomachs.

Defying orders we walked back through the tough dockland area in our United tops and didn't encounter any trouble. Local street urchins grinned at us as they rode by on their bikes or kicked a ball about in the hot, narrow streets. Forty five minutes later we turned a corner and stared at a scene out of Apocolypse Now.

There were pockets of fighting everywhere. Then I spied a large convoy of motorcycle police to our left. They revved up and drove, Dr Zivargo like, into the middle of the United fans. It was horrendous. Provocative and totally over the top. Mick and I decided to cut short our afternoon delights and make our way into the stadium. The United fans were put in the bottom corner of a two tier section by the corner flag. As the ground filled with Spanish fans it became apparent that once again UEFA's rules had been flouted by the European club. The top tier was home to the Valencia 'end' and by kick off time they had kicked off against the small number of Reds in the upper tier. The Spanish riot police who could clearly see what was happening from their position surrounding our section of the pitch did nothing. They simply let the fighting continue. Now it was our turn to feel the force of Valencian venom. Chairs began to rain down on us from above. Now with the best will in the world, throwing chairs back up in the air towards the upper tier is nowhere near as affective as hurling them down on us. We were powerless. And still the police did nothing. The Valencia 'Boot Boys' now freely entered the bottom tier and made their way to our section, throwing chairs in their primitive attempts at greetings. And still the police did nothing. Twenty plus years have since passed but the following is crystal clear. United in the lower tier had been magnificent in their restraint but then one of the chairs thrown by the advancing Spanish fans hit the nearest United fan on the head. He picked up the chair and threw it back. That was the signal the Spanish riot police had been waiting for. They surged towards us, battoning anybody wearing red.

It was St Etienne all over again. One came right up to me and I looked into his eyes. He was mad. All I could see was white. It was like something out of "Children of the Damned". We jumped over seats in an attempt to evade their indiscriminate battering. With nowhere else to go the police formed a line between us and them.

Meanwhile, on the pitch United were dominating proceedings in the first half, despite Valencia continuing where they left off at Old Trafford two weeks earlier by scything down any player in red. We knew then that we would have to beat the referee as well as the opposition. Robson had a perfectly good goal disallowed by the referee for a challenge by Whiteside on their goalkeeper. Then, just before half-time, justice. Wilkins crossed and the ever-brave Captain Marvel headed home. We went bananas. After all the aggro, the release was incredible. All through the break Reds did conga lines along the rows of seats. "We won the Falklands" was sang with gusto (whoever he is). Despite my previously stated opposition to the war, I joined in with a passion.

Words were obviously spoken at half-time as the referee came out dressed head to foot in Valencia's colours. No, of course he didn't, but decision-wise he might just as well have handed the whistle over to them.

Early in the second half substitute Ribes dived so dramatically that in that one moment he re-wrote the book on gamesmanship. The penalty was converted and the score was now 1-1. We were still in the driving seat as away goals count for double but we hadn't counted on a fresh breakout of Spanish violence all around us, aided by the non-intervention of the Spanish riot police to protect us. Scandalous.

Four minutes later and Valencia scored again The rioting on the terraces had clearly affected our players and their concentration went. The game was played out with safety uppermost in our minds.

Exiting the stadium and thankful just to be alive, what did we see but our fleet of coaches right in front of us, and by definition in full view of all the Valencia supporters as well. We nervously got on the coaches when all hell broke loose. Our windows were being attacked by bricks and stones. I looked out of the window (I have non-existent survival skills). These were not just teenagers and twenty year olds. There were old men with pot bellies. In fact, the whole world seemed to be throwing anything they could get their hands on.

Our driver tried to run away but a couple of lads in the front held him fast in his seat. Some more wanted to get off and give them some of their own medicine, but were persuaded against it, although by this time emotions were running dangerously high and even I was having trouble hanging onto reason in the face of such hostility. Sitting next to the window I pulled the curtain across and wedged my United sports bag between my seat and the back of the seat in front. I figured this would reduce the force of the impact of any brick or stone that would come my way.

After what seemed like ages our coach finally set off, though only at about 10mph. Valencia fans were running alongside the coach and throwing missiles and, guess what, there were no police to be seen. We slowly turned a corner when the inevitable happened.

I heard a crash and the glass of my window shattered into thousands of very pretty particles. If in slow motion my holdall fell onto the road below.

Now, you know it's often been said that at certain moments some people can see their whole lives flash before their eyes. Well, I had a similar moment and it wasn't fucking Condor. A voice called out, "Dave, do you want the coach to stop so you can get your bag?"

In an instant all the issues raised by that question came to the surface:

1) If I got off the coach in order to retrieve my bag, the welcoming committee outside may not let me back on.
2) If the coach stopped to let me off it would put the lives of the rest of the coach in danger.
3) In my bag was, amongst other things, all my clothing except what I was wearing, which was my (now) bloodstained United top, a pair of bloodstained jeans and my trainers. This included my wife's very expensive £300 leather jacket which I had borrowed and thought made me look cool, and my passport.
4) Would I be allowed out of the country without a passport?

An instant later, having weighed up all the pros and cons, I said, "Drive on."

A voice behind me then said, "Dave, have you seen your elbow?"

To tell the truth, my elbow, together with Mozart's fifth symphony, the highway code, the Common Market's agricultural policy and a million other things were way down on my list of priorities at that moment. I was concentrating on my right hand which was steadfastly refusing to let go of the curtain in case another missile came my way, therefore my right elbow was out of my line of vision.

Not wanting to lose my grip on said curtain, I sent my left hand to investigate. Now, do you remember that old trick from school where somebody told you to close your eyes and then asked you to touch the end of your nose with your left hand? It wasn't as easy as you thought, was it? You didn't automatically go to the right place straight away.

It was like that with my right elbow. I couldn't see it but I thought I knew where it was.

It wasn't there! Where I thought it should have been was just air.

Still gripping the curtain as hard as I could, I brought my left hand closer to my body.

"What's that?" I thought, as I felt something soft flapping. Then I felt something hard.

I couldn't work it out so I turned round. Where my elbow should have been were two flaps of floppy white skin. What I had touched was the bare bone of my elbow. The strange thing was, I hadn't felt a thing. And still didn't.

"Shouldn't I be feeling pain?" I thought, though secretly grateful that I couldn't. And with that I went back to holding onto my curtain.

We arrived at the airport to utter chaos.

Ahh! There are the police. Thousands of them. At the airport where no Valencia supporter would bother to come. Good thinking.

We trudged into the departure lounge and I made my way straight to the toilets. The police started to stop me but I just showed them my elbow. They backed away.

"Good weapons, elbows," I thought.

I ran cold water over my elbow and wrapped toilet tissue around it. Back out into the departure lounge and Spanish mayhem. I made for an airline member of staff. I pointed to my elbow and tried to tell him about my lost bag and passport. He didn't speak English. He started waving frantically and this beautiful blond woman came floating over.

"Wow! She's gorgeous. I wonder who she is?"

It turned out she was a representative from the British Embassy. She spoke calmly to a myriad of angry, shouting, gesticulating Spanish police and airline staff. One by one my fellow United fans were processed and sent out on the tarmac to board the plane for Luton Airport and civilisation. After an hour I was the only one left in the airport. Well, that is apart from thousands of animated Spanish police and this vision from the British Embassy.

I tried to catch her eye and give her a knowing wink but she just looked at me with disdain and continued to communicate in Spanish to everybody. Eventually some sort of agreement was reached and she came over to me. It was the first time she was going to speak directly to me.

"You can go."

"What?" I thought. "Is that all? What about... oh, I don't know. How about...Come back to my place and I'll take care of your elbow. That would be good for starters."

It was not to be. I had just been a thorn in her side, as opposed to a body at her side. I packed my fantasy away and was ushered onto the tarmac. In the blackness the plane seemed an awful long way away. I walked briskly across the tarmac. There wasn't a soul about. I felt like an extra from the film "Airline". As I approached the steps of the plane an almighty cheer went up. I had beaten the system.

I looked for Mick, who had saved a seat for me.

"Wotcha gonna do at Gatwick?"

Yeah, of course. No passport, and British immigration amongst the strictest in the world. Well, there was nothing I could do about it now. I got up and spoke to Dave Smith and told him what had happened. He tried to get some help for me on the plane but there was none. I'm sure it was illegal but there were no medical facilities or equipment of any description on the plane, not even plaster or bandages.

We finally arrived back at Gatwick. I washed my elbow again and rejoined the queue. Gradually the customs officers were getting closer. I couldn't see any handcuffs but I was sure somebody had radioed ahead and "they" were waiting for me.

My turn. "I'm sorry. I haven't got my passport." And I recounted the events of the last few hours.

"Could you fill in this form then please sir?"

"Certainly."

Five minutes later I handed it in and he just waived me through. "Fucking hell. I could have been a terrorist masquerading as a football fan and I'm through with practically no questions asked. What sort of a system is that?"

Political debate was for another time and place. It was now 4 o'clock on Thursday morning and I was due into work in a few hours. Mick and I made our way to the entrance to Gatwick train station. I noticed that the newsagents had just opened.

I bought a copy of one of the red tops:

"United fans riot in Spain"

Fucking brilliant. Investigative journalism at its best. "Spanish fans riot in Spain". I expect that doesn't sell newspapers, does it? Well done the Daily Scums. What planet were you on when we were being battered by all and sundry a few hours beforehand in Valencia? Sipping fucking G&Ts in the players' lounge, no doubt. As that character from Monty Python often said, you know, the idiot with the handkerchief on his head and the clenched fists:

"It makes me sooooo mad!"

By now I realised I was freezing cold. All I had to wear was my half-sleeve United shirt and jeans with dried blood. The train to London seemed to take ages. Then another hurdle presented itself.

Hélène.

Oh, shit. Having survived the Spanish inquisition I now had the prospect of facing Mademoiselle le Guillotine. Would this night ever St Etienned?

On the train back to Victoria Station I tried to make a list of excuses for the state I was in. Nothing sounded plausible. I decided to wing it.

We arrived back at my garden flat off the Finchley Road at 6 o'clock in the morning. Mick and I had concluded that we'd enter as quietly as possible and go to bed without waking Hélène up and work out what to say later.

I thought we had done a good impersonation of burglars. Mick accompanied me to the bathroom as I began to undo my bandage and re-wash my elbow.

Worst case scenario time. At the other end of the hallway Hélène had woken up.

"David? Is that you? Is everything all right?"

"YES!" replied Mick, much too loudly and a split second too fast.

Women's intuition is a wondrous but terrible thing. Hélène instantly picked up on the faint hysteria in Mick's voice and was at our side like a special effect out of The Matrix.

Melanie remained asleep and totally oblivious to the soap opera being played out in the bathroom.

"What are you doing?"

"Just washing before coming to bed, my love."

"What's wrong with your elbow?"

"Nuffink."

Every picture tells a story, don't it? The look on Hélène's face when she saw the remains of my flapping elbow will forever be indelibly imprinted in my brain. A melange of disgust, horror and smug "I told you so".

"You're going straight to the hospital."

"Aw. Do we have to?"

"Yes. Now, get your clothes back on. Mick, you can stay here." You can tell who wears the trousers in our relationship. From Stretford Ender to mouse in one easy lesson. Be warned. Learn from my experience. It could happen to you.

We drove to the Royal Free Hospital in Hampstead and made for the Accident & Emergency department. We waited a surprisingly short time before I was seen by a nurse.

"What happened to you?" she inquired, her look a melange of disgust and "I told you so", as if I had just come from a fight outside a pub at closing time.

"I was attacked by Spanish football fans in Valencia."

"Oh, really" was her disinterested retort. I'm sure she didn't believe me. Being a coward I prepared myself for the worst.

"You'll need about ten stitches. Hold still now."

Ah. Good news and bad news. Bad news first? Would it hurt? Good news. I had a United war wound to wear with pride.

The fact that the flapping skin around my elbow was still white meant there was no more blood, so there was no pain. In my mind I impressed her with my silent bravery, cracking jokes and trying to chat her up. I think she'd heard every line I used a million times but it kept me off the matter at hand, or should I say, elbow.

Fully bandaged I went home and simply changed for work. I was in my office with the radio on, as per normal, when the eleven o'clock news came on Capital Radio. Surprisingly, I thought, the lead item was United's adventures in Spain, only this time they emphasised the terrible treatment handed out to United fans by both the police and the home supporters.

Who should then come on the radio but our very own Dave Smith from the Manchester United Supporters Club. He gave a blow by blow account of what really happened both inside and outside the stadium and invited the club to respond on behalf of all the United fans that had travelled to support their team and had been the victims of sustained attacks by Spanish hooligans and the Spanish police.

The response the following day by Martin Edwards was to refuse to take United fans to away matches in Europe for the foreseeable future. Although an understandable knee-jerk reaction, it didn't confront the issues of the fans that had literally given blood for the Red cause.

When I approached Martin Edwards a few weeks later at the United AGM and asked him why the club hadn't sought some kind of redress and justice, he replied that "English clubs are not flavour of the month at the moment within UEFA and we thought a softly-softly approach was appropriate."

In other words, the board's policy of "the best form of attack is defence" sold the fans down the river. Only Dave Smith had had the guts to stand up and speak out on behalf of the travelling supporters. If the roles had been reversed and the match had been played on English soil you can be certain UEFA would have fined United and kicked us out of the competition.

Boards of directors, the FA, UEFA, FIFA. Guardians of the beautiful game? Don't make me laugh.

14

BARCA/JUVE 1984

YOU WIN YOU LOSE YOU AGE

UNITED HAVE A REPUTATION (in my book anyway) for handling transfers like a Sean Goater in a china shop. Plodding, predictable and telegraphing their every move to all and sundry well in advance. In my lifetime the anti-Tesco philosophy of buy high and sell low seems to have been the sum total of the Boards business acumen in this sector. From the ones that got away, (Mike England, Alan Clarke, Peter Beardsley, Paul Gasgoine, Alan Shearer, Ronaldihno) to ones that were virtually given away, (Johnny Giles, Paul McGrath, Norman Whiteside, Andy Cole, Seba Veron, David Beckham) to ones where we had to pay and pay (Gary Birtles, Ted McDougal, Gary Pallister, Rio Ferdinand, Michael Carrick)

Let me say straight away that some of our purchases have or will prove to be diamonds. And some of the sales at low prices or "frees" have been a reward for loyalty. Yet the underlying trend in our transfer graph is that more skilful negotiations would have secured us better deals and, from time to time, even better players. Running a tight ship is one thing, running a tight fisted ship is another. When doing their checks and balances the board keep omitting one very important element. An element that sets Manchester United apart from any other football club on the planet. The incredible loyalty of its fans. And this is not just a recent phenominum that ABU's would have you believe. For over forty years Manchester United have had the highest average home attendances in Britain in all but a handful of occasions. And one or two of those were only due to a reduced capacity whilst Old Trafford was being renovated, although to their everlasting shame, when we went all seater in the 80s the money men on the Board considered one seat equaled something like 2.4 standing and reduced the capacity to 43,500. The spreadsheet might have looked OK but outside the ramifications were horrendous. Lifelong supporters were excluded, the ticket distribution system was a joke and good will went out the window.

The words "brewery" and "piss up" come to mind.

The point being, even the most conservative analysis cannot ignore the rock solid certainty that our stadium will be full to capacity for 98% of all Premiership and Champions League fixtures. That's a guaranteed income, irrespective of the performance of the team on the pitch. Arsenal, Chelsea, Newcastle. All have attracted a number of less than 20,000 gates in their recent history, reflecting respective lack of success. United fans passion and loyalty are unique in world football. In 2002/2003 Manchester United attracted the highest average home attendance of any football club on the planet, all the more amazing when you consider there are a number of stadiums with far greater capacities than even the increased capacity Old Trafford.

If only the club would take this on board, we wouldn't have to compromise on purchases which belies our claim to be the "biggest" club in the world.

Two "on-off" transfers stick out in the 1980s. An entire season of Mark Hughes / Bryan Robson "will they, won't they" which affected their form and the team as a whole. If you cast your mind back to our mid 80s team, with "Butch" Wilkins finally coming good and Captain Marvel forming an attacking "Dolly and Daisy" in midfield, we were actually more formidable away from home than at Old Trafford.

Throughout my forty odd years following the Reds, although each team had a number of players that walked on water, there always seemed to be one that, if he wasn't playing, your heart sank and you knew that the team just wouldn't be the same. I'm sure fans of other teams have felt the same about some of theirs.

For us, Bryan Robson was such a player.

For years he represented the "never say die" attitude that epitomized the spirit of every true United fan. I would run through a brick wall and sell my wife into slavery for Manchester United. I just knew that Robbo felt the same way, although to the best of my knowledge he has never met my wife.

Every fan was Robbo and Robbo was every fan rolled into one.

The very idea that the club could even THINK of selling him seemed so alien to our way of thinking. He was our engine room, our heart, our life support system.

In 1984 we were drawn against Maradona's Barcelona in the quarter finals of the European Cup Winners Cup.

In the previous season's tournament Barcelona had literally kicked their way through Tottenham Hotspur and their reputation for gamesmanship was up there with the worst of the Italians and Leeds of the early seventies.

I wasn't able to make the away leg so I listened to the commentary on the radio. One rule I used to employ in these situations was gauge which teams players were being mentioned more often and thereby determine which team were dominating proceedings.

United were dominating proceedings.

Although trailing 1-0 with five minutes to go, and that was only due to a Graham Hogg own goal, I remember the commentator stating quite clearly just how well United had played and in the context of a two legged tie this would be a satisfactory result as long as the score remained only 1-0. Right on cue a mighty roar went up and my heart sank as I was informed that Rojo had scored a wonder goal on the volley for Barcelona and now we were up against it.

When the match finished I was in a really black mood for over an hour until I forced myself to watch the recorded highlights on TV. As the match unfolded in front of me I realised just how well United really had performed and my spirits rose. But the telling moment came when I saw the wonder volley. It was so out of keeping with the rest of the game that in that moment of time I knew, I just knew, that we would overcome the two goal deficit and progress through to the semi finals. When interviewed after the game, Bryan Robson stated quite categorically that we would get through, so who was I to argue?

It's cast your mind back time. Ever since the start of European club tournaments the script went something like this. The British club would lose valiantly, and often unfairly (Derby and Liverpool come to mind), by two or more goals in the away leg. The British club would then win the home leg by a single goal in a pulsating but ultimately glorious failure.

Up until I witnessed that wonder volley on TV I had accepted the inevitable as it is written. Now all that changed. History, as Peter O'Toole as Lawrence of Arabia once exclaimed, was about to be rewritten.

Like thousands of Reds I spent the following two weeks selling my arse for a ticket but to no avail. But like the same thousands of Reds I knew, I just knew, that I had to be at Old Trafford to witness history in the making. Without the ability to articulate my feelings at the time, I now recall that my head was attempting to comes to terms with the "glorious failure" scenario whereas my heart was pumping louder and forcing me to accept the possibility that...

By five o' clock on the afternoon of the game the Warwick Road was chocker block with thousands of ticketless Reds drawn by that age old magnet, "I WAS THERE." A strange thing at this time was that a number of the regular touts we all saw outside Old Trafford would also be found outside the Empire Pool Wembley or the Albert Hall or Earls Court in London, flogging concert tickets for the biggest and baddest bands in town. Politically correct, I agree they are all piranhas but one thing I will say for the regular touts is that, whether for matches or concerts, when all other avenues have failed they have never sold me a fake. Credit where credit's due.

My bulk purchases over the years counted for nowt as I bagatelled from one tout to the next, hoping against hope to find a ticket in my stratosphere. In the end, with kick-off perilously close my £4.40 ticket for K Stand, Stair 15, Row 31, Seat 53 cost me £35 and a bollocking from 'er left indoors the following day. But boy, was it worth it. It was to be the best £35 I ever spent in my life.

Once inside the ground one thing immediately became apparent. 360° of Old Trafford was singing. Not just The Stretford End and The Scoreboard but all the boring old farts along both sides. My skin tingled and my breath came shorter and faster. By the time the match started my voice was already hoarse.

The game itself was everything I had come to expect. United attacking in waves and a classy Barcelona repelling and scaring us with the odd breakaway. Then in the twenty second minute, right in front of us, Robbo

came running in and threw himself forward in a stooping run to force the ball home with his forehead. We went bananas. When I came back to normal (?) my brain sent me a message. "OK. That's our obligatory goal. Enjoy it while you can. You won't get another. We'll win 1-0 on the night but lose unfairly 2-1 on aggregate. Read the script."
However my heart was pumping.

"Wrong. Wrong. Wrong. This is just the beginning. Sing louder. Sing longer. Sing you bastard, sing..."

Half time. 1-0. Time to catch our breath. No chance. The chanting for United and for Robbo continues throughout the break. All 360° of us. I'd never seen or heard anything like it before at Old Trafford, or since it has to be said.

Second half. United continued to dominate. And then, cometh the fiftieth minute cometh the man. And so it came to pass, my prophecy came true. Robbo scored number two. 2-0 on the night. 22 on aggregate. Forty minutes to go.

Bedlam.

Heart, head and voice working independently from the rest of my body. Then just two minutes later, the moment that thousands of Reds, and Robbo, had instinctively predicted two weeks earlier. Whiteside crossed the goal in front of the Stretford End and there was Frank Stapleton to wack the ball into the net.

"AAAAAAAAAAAHHHHHHHHHHHhhhhhhhhhhhhhhh"

The noise. My God, the noise. It was incredible. In most games you have moments of excitement and periods of mediocrity and this is reflected in the crowd. At Old Trafford, before it became an all seater stadium we used to defy the odds. The Stretford End put the Kop in the shade. Our collective voices, and sometimes it has to be said, other parts of our anatomies spread fear and awe in away supporters throughout the land. In the good old days when kick-offs were 3 o' clock on a Saturday afternoon the Stretford used to be full and rocking by 1.30.

And our support for The Reds was legendary. Many a lost cause wasn't, due to the famous 12th man – us! But even by our standards this was a night apart. Why was this night different from all other nights? Not just The Stretford End but the whole stadium started at the top of their voices then rose steadily throughout the match.

We defied logic and medical science.

Personally, I was on automatic pilot. I had no control of my bodily functions. I couldn't feel anything but an almighty burning in my throat. It was on fire. I couldn't stop jumping up and down. I literally couldn't stop.

Then began the longest thirty minutes I have ever experienced at a football match.

I feared the worse as Barcelona had a side full of the most incredible talent. Maradona at the height of his powers, Schuster et al, and a team with a nasty, spiteful reputation carried over from the previous season.

However, to their credit they played brilliantly but vainly in their attempt to pull back the deficit. Don't ask me how we held out but hold out we did.

When the final whistle went I soared into orbit. Whilst circulating above the Republic of Mancunia I looked down to see wave after wave of United fans, from all corners of the ground, surge onto the pitch and make for one man. Robbo was hoisted into the air in a spontaneous display that said more than words ever could.

We knew. He knew. The Board knew. He stayed. We won.

The excitement, joy and disbelief outside the ground afterwards was palpable. The looks on everyone's faces said it all.

"Did I really see what I just saw?"

"Did you see what I saw? Tell me you did. Tell me it wasn't only me and that I'll wake-up and find we've been unjustly knocked out."

We hopped, skipped and jumped back to the car. On the way out along the A56 we made our ritual stop at the Chariot Wheel American hamburger bar in Hale, before wending our extremely merry way back to London.

Now, you have to understand that the only other passion that comes anywhere near Manchester United for me is my love of music. From progressive, underground in the late 60's and early 70's to the present day I have somewhat "off the wall" and "left of centre" musical tastes. (Whatever that means)

Not content to purchase, when funds permitted, obscure heavy metal or spaced out West Coast sounds that were never played on the radio, I would compile, in true "High Fidelity" fashion, compilation cassettes of my own. (I know. I know. I should have gone out more)

Every time we drove to a game I would bring with me my plastic attaché case with 36 of the best music cassettes the planet had ever heard. When you consider that every home game for us was a 400 mile round trip, you'll understand just how important music, as well as booze and funny cigarettes was to the buzz of the whole day. And with an additional amplifier and four speakers we didn't just drive, we flew. (remember, back in 1984 this was pretty cutting edge) We would lose ourselves inside the car's cabin full of head banging, no nonsense, mindless boogie, three bar riffs and power chords, with the volume turned up to a Spinal Tap ear splitting 11.

Hatfield and the North, the A5 through Brownhills, Watford Gap. How could girls compete with that?

Well, back to the dogburger in Hale. Picture the scene. At around 11.30pm the four of us were chomping away through the burgers with drinks precariously perched on various surfaces of the car's insides. As the driver I warned everybody to hold onto their own (drinks) as I drove off. Unfortunately, one of my mates who shall remain nameless (Michael Shenton, member of the Oxford Branch and now living in Southampton. Send a S.A.E and I'll forward his details to each and everyone of you.) had left his orange juice on the dashboard. Yeah. We were 'ard.

As I drove off the open carton of orange juice fell backwards and flooded the front of the car and my trousers. I slammed on the brakes, opened the driver's door and emptied everything that wasn't fixed to the car, including my prized and never able to be replaced plastic cassette case, in a vain attempt to de-orangeize the car.

Dripping and sticky (from orange juice) half an hour later we were on our way back to London down the M6 singing and chanting. Eventually, one by one our voices packed up and so I decided to put on a cassette.

Where's my cassettes?

"AAAAAAAAAAAAHHHHHHHHHHHHhhhhhhhhhhhhh"

On the pavement outside the dogburger in Hale.

By now I was passing Stafford, southbound on the M6. No problem. On a night like this I could drive forever, so I took the next turning off the motorway and drove all the way back to Hale, arriving outside a closed Chariot Wheel at 01.30 in the morning.

Surprise, surprise. No cassette case. Someone had won the lottery and won my life's work in recording.

No problem. I just started driving again and we arrived back in London at 05.30 in the morning. No point in going to bed. I was still too excited, Tommy. I wanted to get to work as early as possible and regale all the non-believers why Manchester United, once again, was better than sex.

JUVE v UNITED, RHODES 1984

What a difference two weeks make. We drove up to Manchester for the first leg of the semi-final of the European Cup Winners Cup against the giants of Turin. For some reason I couldn't put my finger on, the day felt flat. I don't know why. Against Barcelona our hearts had ruled our heads and we were so richly rewarded. This time our heads refused to let hearts get a look in. It didn't make sense. We'd just beaten the most feared team in Europe at the time. The power and the passion of Manchester United and their fans had swept Barca aside. They never knew what him 'em. We even surprised ourselves.

But Juventus were different. We knew that. The masters of defense with the ability to break and stop you in your tracks. In my water I didn't believe they would be as naive as the Catalans. They'd be cynical and dirty, and even worse, brilliant to boot.

The atmosphere outside was eerily calm. An accurate barometer of supporter expectations are the touts. Against Barcelona you needed a second mortgage to buy a ticket, if you were (un)lucky enough to find one on sale. "I'll buy any spares." Against Juventus the touts couldn't give them away. And this was the semi-final of a major European tournament! Strange indeed.

Inside the stadium we worked hard to re-create the barmy Barca atmosphere but to no avail. News that our midfield, including the irreplaceable Captain Marvel, had been wiped out through injury and suspension only added to our apprehension. It was an uphill struggle. In the opening minutes, as United launched a series of attacks, John Gidman, our full back suddenly pulled up to be replaced by our young Welshman, Alan Davies The dreaded United hamstring jinx had struck once again. Then after fifteen minutes the far sharper Juventus scored and we feared the worse. Lightening struck twice as once again the opposition's opening goal took a wicked deflection off the unfortunate Graham Hogg. Rossi, you lucky bastarda.

What a difference three weeks make. A stunned silence enveloped the ground. The feeling that the Gods were against us was overwhelming. United kicked-off again and took the game to the Italians. I don't know what "We was robbed" is in Italian but it certainly applied to us that night. Juventus were dirty, lucky, lucky and dirty. To make things worse they were also bloody brilliant, but not for the first time at Old Trafford they left us with a nasty taste in the mouth when we should have been drooling at their mastery of the beautiful game.

Seven years earlier United had drawn the giants of Turin in the second round of the UEFA Cup. They had played us off the park for half an hour and I remember thinking I was privileged to see for myself football that was literally in a different league when out of the blue (or should I say Red) Gordon Hill put us 1-0 up. Joy was mixed with fear as I expected Juve to step up another gear and wipe us out with football from another planet, but I wasn't expecting planet Cynical Filth. Instead of teaching us a footballing lesson they presented us with all the worst aspects of Football Italia and simply shut up shop and contented themselves with cutting us down illegally at every opportunity. We won the first leg 1-0 but lost in Turin 3-0.

However, after thirty five minutes of continuous pressure a shot by Whiteside was parried by their goalkeeper into the path of Alan Davies and his moment of glory arrived as he ran the ball into an empty Italian net. 1-1. And to think eight years later Alan Davies would tragically be dead. What a waste.

Juventus's spoiling tactics in the second half ensured the score remained 1-1 at full time.

I left the ground with the same empty feeling that had accompanied my arrival, yet something kept nagging away at me suggesting that this was just the lull before the storm and that, like the second leg against Barcelona in the previous round, all the drama and emotion was destined for the second leg. In the league we were still a better looking team away from home so I had plenty of straws to grab onto re-enforce my belief that all was not lost.

Around this time I was running a textile screen printing and embroidery company in London. Attention to detail was one of the overriding requirements of my job as clients, especially Advertising and Sales Promotion Agencies, tended to sit on things then demand a deadline of yesterday, whilst their accounts departments took up to ninety days plus to pay their bills.

Thought I'd get that one off my chest. Being one step ahead and anticipating any possible hurdles had given my company a competitive edge in a very demanding and ruthless sector against some of the bigger and longer established opposition. I would do half the work of my suppliers so as to appear reliable and efficient in the eyes of my clients. I was thus a major shareholder in Grecian 2000.

It's just a pity I could not transfer this attention to detail to my private life. Throughout the eighties, with my company doing "OK", my wife and I would take a week off in April prior to the hectic summer season and I would invite my mother to accompany us. We never had a summer holiday as that was our busiest period so the only time my wife, Hélène, Melanie and I took a holiday by ourselves was when we closed the company between Christmas Eve and the first week in January. Our Easter week invariably took in one of the Greek Islands. It was never warm enough to sunbathe but seven days was a nice break.

This spring I made an almighty error. I booked a nondescript two star, sixties high rise hotel in the centre of Rhodes Town. It was my intention to return on the 24th April and fly out with the Supporters Club on the 25th, the morning of the game. Well, that was my master plan. Only I cocked up the dates. With just one day to go before departure for our Greek week I was checking the dates when my blood ran cold and my underwear changed colour. I had booked the return flight for the 27th April, one day AFTER the second leg against Juventus in Turin.

A hearse, a hearse, my kingdom for a hearse. How could I have made such a mistake? I deserved to be shot. I was filled with self loathing. I couldn't blame anyone else but myself. As hard as I tried I couldn't find anyone to pass the buck to. My conscience would have been clearer if I could have blamed somebody else. "It's all your fault."

But it wasn't. It was mine. I set off on holiday with a heavy heart and a nice, lightweight Samsonite suitcase. I put on a brave face but my mask slipped a number of times as immaturity reared its ugly head. But the fickle finger of fate hadn't finished with me.

Rhodes was, and maybe still is, a duty free port. What this means is that goods such as booze, fags, jewelry, electronics, etc. are cheaper than back home. Which brings me to one of my pet hates.

Shopping.

Well, not shopping per say. Women's shopping to be more precise. And at the top of my list, shopping with my wife.

The proverb, "When the going gets tough, the tough go shopping." could have been written for Hélène. I've lost count the number of times I have wilted under the onslaught of her 'stop-start' attitude to shopping.

I like a nice walk. I'm a professional football supporter but no way could I be described as a professional sportsman. It's too much like hard work. Yes, I enjoy a kickabout, a game of tennis, a plunge into the pool or sea if it's not too cold and I like a nice walk if the scenery is pleasant and I can build up some sort of rhythm. But 'stop-start' strolling. It has to be the equivalent of Chinese water torture. It eats away at my thighs, the small of my back, my eyes, my patience, in fact, my very will to live.

When I was young I thought my mother was bad enough but even she fell by the kerbside when confronted by the shopper from hell.

Now, this all came to a head on the last day of our holiday. I'd forgotten that we had agreed that the last day meant "shop till you drop", literally. Soldier ant type scouting missions over the past week had pinned down all the best bargains and today was the day we would home in and mop up. This was also the day of the game and I had come to accept the inevitable, that I wouldn't be able to witness the drama that was to unfold in just a few hours time.

After breakfast we walked into town with me lagging a few yards behind, like a Basset Hound on prosaic. Hours passed like, well, hours actually. The sun overhead beat down with luke warm intensity, slowly draining the life from my body. I plodded around in a daze, sulking like a schoolkid who had to wear his uniform in public and fearing his 'cool' mates would see him.

It was mid afternoon when, passing the umpteenth jewelry shop I noticed a small black and white TV on the opposite wall. What's so special about that? Surely there are a lot of small black and white TV sets in Rhodes? I hear you ask. Well, I'll tell you what was so special. It was showing a football match.

I called out to Hélène.

"Hélène. Hang on a minute. I've just seen something you might like. I'm just going in to check. Stay there."

I entered and approached the counter. I came straight to the point.

"Excuse me, what game's that?"

"It's the European Cup semi-final between Roma and Dundee United."

"Oh really?" I replied, my voice betraying a little hesitancy. "What's the score?"

"2-0 to Roma."

"Shame." I retorted, feigning interest. Then I asked my sixty four dollar question.

"Eerm. Do you know if there are, eerr, any other games on TV this evening?"

"Yeah. Juventus and Man U."

"YES, YES, YES, YES, YES."

I instantly forgave him his ABU trespass. This little outpost of humanity was civilised after all. My heart started pumping again. Blood began to flow through my Red veins. I came out of my self induced coma. With a spring in my step I skipped up to the family.

"Nah. Nuffink special. Sorry."

The hands on my watch began to move. Every "tick, tick, tick." took me closer to the surface. I was no longer drowning in self pity. It would be alright on the night.

With bags full of goodies, my normal apprehension at the amount of non-existent cash languishing back home to cover the plastic dissolved in the heat of anticipation at the thought that in a few hours time I would be watching and kicking every ball.

We finally arrived back at the hotel around six o'clock. One and a half hours to go.

It's at this point I should inform you, dear reader, of another flaw in my character as it's directly relevant to what happens next. From the age of eleven to fifteen I went to Wanstead County High. It was a grammar school which made my mother very proud. Three of my cousins on my mother's side had gone to the same school and done very well. I had been average at junior school and it was touch or go if I would pass my eleven plus. I passed. Good news for my mum. Bad news for me. From being average and anonymous in junior school I was now constantly bottom and conspicuous in the grammar school. Fifty plus pupils in rows and in uniform filled every class. Kids with a memory like a sponge that simply absorbed facts did very well. Kids like me with the memory of a goldfish did not. Suddenly visits to the dentist were preferable to exams as they were less painful.

Wanstead County High was built in 1928. In 1965 a boy in a higher grade than me called Woodward and I set a new school record as the first pupils in the history of the school to fail all our "O" levels in one go. After the five worse years of my life I was resigned to the likely outcome so was not surprised. My parents were devastated. They thought I had been the epitome of false modesty. Now they knew the truth.

"I'm shit, and I know I am."

The days after the results became known were the worst days of my mother's life. The phone would ring constantly as one proud mother after another would politely ask after me, under the pretext of regaling the successes of their respective offspring. Of course, they offered condolences and encouragement to my mother but this was scant comfort for the shame I had brought to my family.

After the mother and father of all bollockings I fully expected to go to Loughton College of Further Education to retake my "O" levels. Imagine our surprise when I was informed by letter that Wanstead County High wanted me to begin 6th form in September. My first two days back were filled with all the magical choices denied to the younger pupils. This group, that group, travel options, theatre, music. Then on the third day I was shown the red card. The headmaster, Dr Gardener, called Woodward and I into his office. He towered above us, his veins throbbing and twitching in his blood red face. He bellowed, spat and dribbled with rage. The shame we had brought to the school and to him. He must have gone on for over a quarter of an hour and in all that time I don't think he mentioned myself or Woodward by name once. We were incidental to proceedings, so Woodward and I just looked at each other and mouthed, "Wanker."

And so I lasted two and a half days in the 6th form. It was nice while it lasted.

Why am I telling you all this? Because records show that, one year later at Loughton College of FE, despite dodging between the Debden Boys and the Mile End Boys who used to practice their gang warfare on us strays on route to Debden underground station, I actually passed two "O" levels, English grammar and mathematics. What the records don't show is my third "O" level.

Cowardice.

From the moment I learnt that there was a possibility that I wouldn't miss watching the second leg of the semi final of the UEFA cup I agonised over the best time to tell the wife, knowing that there wasn't really a "best" time. So being a coward I left it to the last moment. As we went upstairs to change for "the Last Supper" I mumbled something along the lines of watching the game and catching up with you guys later.

"YOU WHAT? NO WAY! You're coming out with us. We all agreed and you can't just change your mind at the last moment. It's so selfish!"

Mumble, mumble, mumble.

"You'll let down your mother. You'll let me down, and Melanie. Doesn't that mean anything to you?"

Yes, of course it did. But not as much as missing the match. Priorities and all that.

They continued to change into their best eveningwear, convinced I would buckle under their barrage of abuse and conform. But this night my yellow backbone turned red.

There would be other holidays but there's only one United. I figured I might as well be hung for a sheep as for a lamb so I changed into my United top, United shorts and scarf and left the room with a wicked parting shot straight out of "The Odd Couple" and "Terminators 1, 2 and 3".

"I'll be back...after the game!"

By now it was 7.15 and the game started in fifteen minutes. I rushed downstairs and straight to the hotel reception. The hotel only had one television set and it rested in a corner of the lounge. I'd never seen it working, assuming either Rhodes TV programs to be crap and/or holidaymakers had preferential forms of entertainment.

I asked the receptionist if she could possibly turn on the television.

"Sorry. It doesn't work."

"AAAAHHHHhhhhh! You're joking. It must work. It has to work. Can't you do something?"

"I'll get the manager."

This balding, sweating, middle aged, penguin dressed man came out of the back office. He gave me a pointed look and made his way over to the tele. I looked on with a knowledgeable look on my face as he twiddled with a few knobs. Within a few minutes I forgave him everything as he got a grainy colour picture going and we pushed the antiquated set into the middle of the lounge.

By this time quite a crowd had gathered to observe the commotion. I had been oblivious to the comments my United top had induced, but now the TV was working I was aware of a 50/50 split in the room. Half the people were wishing me and my team the best of luck whilst the other half were questioning my parenthood.

I didn't care. I had my TV. I had my game. I was sorted.

Now, picture the scene. The TV was in the middle of the lounge and I had parked my armchair slap bang in front of the tele. As the match began I was watching the match whilst the rest of the lounge was watching me.

Let battle commence.

I was worried that the old television was on its last legs as the screen seemed to dominated by a deep red hue, until I realised it was just the choking fumes set off by the Italian fireworks. I looked up as the picture began to clear and there was my wife and my mother on the stairs, dressed to kill with looks to match. Fearing they might summon the powers of the occult I dragged my eyes away from their terrifying gaze and back to the TV screen.

I was so wound up that I began to shout and scream at every United move. The armchair became irrelevant as I introduced a one-man unsafe standing campaign, as anyone unfortunate to be in my path ran the risk of being Blattened. In the eighth minute Hughes let fly but my premature celebrations were cut short as their goalkeeper parried the shot. As McGrath rushed in and I waited to exhale with glee one of their defenders booted the ball clear. We were dominating proceedings as I secretly hoped we would, and my animated antics were keeping the hotel lounge in hysterics.

Then a Bee Gee moment. Tragedy. Platini thread a beautiful pass through to the Pole, Boniek, who raced passed our defense as if we were standing still and cleverly beat an advancing Gary Bailey. I swore, I cursed. People came up to me and offered sympathy and patted me on the shoulder as though I had personally let the goal in. Which I had, of course. Any football fan worth his/her salt kicks every ball, feels every tackle, disputes every decision. And, boy, do I take it personally.

My performance had now brought the hotel lobby on my side. (Maybe that's the origin of the term "lobbying" for support?) Together we began to will United on.

Half time arrived and people returned to the bar and their loved ones. I looked around for Hélène and my mother. They were nowhere to be seen. I didn't know whether that was good or bad news and to be honest, I was so involved in the events unfolding in Turin that I didn't care a toss. No, that's not true. I did care a toss, as I was under no illusion that hell has no fury as a woman scorned when United score. I imagined them hatching a plot to extract their pound of flesh, in true Hannibal Lector style, with interest.

Still, no time to worry about that. More importantly the second half was about to start. The game continued in much the same vein except Juventus were posing a far greater threat in front of goal. They were no longer sitting back and letting us take the game to them. It was their ball and they wanted it back, and if it hadn't been for Gary Bailey we would have been on the plane home before the game had even finished. On the hour Stapleton, who had been struggling all night, came off and our Norman, Whiteside to you, entered the fray.

Within a few minutes Norman did the business. He rose majestically between two defenders to blast the ball home.

"AAAAAAAAHHHHHHHhhhhhhhhhh!"

I leapt in the air then charged round the lobby with half a dozen holiday makers hot on my trail, intent in joining in my celebrations. I felt as though I had scored the goal myself and the entire hotel lobby were my teamates.

"I TOLD YOU. I TOLD YOU. I TOLD YOU."

1-1. 2-2 on aggregate and, most importantly, we had cancelled out their away goal at Old Trafford. Oh, my boys, my boys. Oh, you disbelievers out there.

Juventus stepped up the anti. Wave upon wave of zebra attacks were repelled by Bailey playing a blinder. As the final whistle approaching I envisaged the Italians wilting in extra time as all their efforts came to nowt. Unfortunately they came to one more than nowt. In the final minute of normal time the ball acted like a bagatelle, ricocheting around our penalty area. Then in a moment that spoiled the taste of Southend's best ice-cream for years to come, Rossi latched onto a rebound and stroked the ball under a despairing Bailey.

I was stunned. After all I had been through. After all the ... I had had to endure. After all the superhuman efforts by Manchester's finest the roar emanating from TV told me it was all over. I was distraught. I had nothing left to give. In respectful tones reminiscent of a wake, the inhabitants of the hotel lobby filed past, offering their condolences.

It was alright for them. They were about to get on with their lives, going out for a drink and laugh about the crazy United fan back at the hotel. Like the ending of the bad guys in the film "Ghost", my wife and my mother were hovering with deathly intent. I had no earthly means of escape.

They re-appeared in my line of vision, with stares that would have turned Lot into a pillar of salt and salt into a lot worse. I knew my time was up. They had come for me. An invisible rope was cast round my neck and I was led outside. The mark of the beast was upon me.

We wandered round the darkened streets, my mother intent in relieving the locals of a sizeable percentage of their natural foliage, to be re-planted in her garden back home. Whether through guilt or innocence, they tried to make polite conversation to lift my spirits. But when one or both of them came out with dreaded line, "It's only a game." I knew that in this lifetime at least I would be a loner, travelling the Earth alone in my twilight world, waiting for a sign from the Govanor.

15

FIT FOR A KING

DURING THE 1980's my mate Graham Wyche (now living in Perth, Australia and running the official Western Australia Manchester United Supporters Club) had a company supplying financial publications to the trade. At this very moment in time (thank you David Frost) I was running a screen printing and embroidery company in London.

We'd actually met up in the early 80's when Graham drove past my showroom in Drury Lane and spotted a couple of United T-shirts and a golf umbrella in the window. This was because from Gidley (lovely man) through to Sandy Busby, my company was an official supplier to the Manchester United Souvenir Shop, that is until we got shafted by the Kumar Brothers and then Eddie 'Spice Girls' Freeman himself.

I have to put it on record that it was not good business. United never paid for designs, artwork, blocks, plates, delivery charges or any of the normal expenses incurred in servicing a client whilst running a business. On the other hand I got to visit Old Trafford in a suit on non-match days, making certain I arrived early enough so that I had time to watch the grass grow on the hallowed turf where my winged heroes plied their trade. In fact, it's amazing how many 'Jobsworths' you can get by just by wearing a whistle. Fact.

Meanwhile, back at the studio...I was doing a reasonable impression of working one afternoon when Graham phoned. Like many like-minded mates, we'd ring each other up to discuss the latest United topics, only this time the conversation took an unusual turn.

"Listen, Dave. I don't know if this is a wind-up but a rep from one of the print companies we use asked if he could pay me an unscheduled visit. He also happened to mention that he was being accompanied by, wait for it...Denis Law."

I also have to put on record that my mate Graham is as straight as they come. There was no way that passing him in the street you would imagine that he was almost as fanatical a Red as me. Nice suit, nice tie, nice ears – you know the type, whereas I was, and still am, OTT. Smart – United tie plus United pin badge. Casual – United T-shirt or Polo. Even United underwear. In the 70s and 80s perhaps this was cool, if not a little daring for someone living and working in London. Now my time has long since past but that hasn't stopped me.

But that's another story.

The point I'm making is that Graham kept his United affiliations to himself at work whilst I shouted it from the rooftops. So there is no way that this rep knew my mate was a Red. I just told him to keep me informed of any developments. Putting the phone down I told myself not to get worked up, but at times like this brain and bodily functions tend to travel on separate plains.

Forty five minutes later the phone rings.

Heavy breathing.

Great. I'd waited years for one of these. No, hang on...it's Graham's voice. Why's he whispering?

"Dave. He's here! In my office! What should I do?"

Taking command of the situation as any good management executive would, I blubbered incoherently for a few seconds, then was able to string an actual sentence or ten together.

"Whatever you do, don't let him out of your sight. I mean, lock him up in a cupboard if you have to until I arrive. No, seriously, don't let him go, or if you have to, make some arrangement for this evening. ANYTHING!!"

Half an hour later the phone rang.

"Right, it's on. We're meeting in half an hour in the lobby of the Royal Garden Hotel in Kensington High Street."

Queue for my Norris McQuirter, Guinness Book of Records attempt at the Clark Kent turns into Superman impersonation as I change, Norman

Wisdom like, from casual United wear to above mentioned suit and United tie and pin badge, which is always on a hanger in case I have an unexpected client meeting to go to.

In the middle of the rush hour I then skedaddle from my factory near Old Street, London EC1, through the underground system and arrive sweating buckets, Lee Evans like, at the hotel in west London in under half an hour. Another Guinness Book of Records record?

Needless to say I'm the first to arrive. I sit sweating and breathing in a 5-star luxuriously sort of way. Graham's the next to arrive. We converse quietly in a 5 star luxurious sort of way for a few minutes when two gentlemen approach us. One is the rep who turns out to be a complete pratt and a tall lump of liquorice from BBC Northern Ireland. We're informed that Denis will be a few minutes as he's changing in his room. (into what? I wondered)

A few minutes becomes 40 minutes as Roy the rep tries to dominate the conversation as only sales reps can when suddenly there is a flash of pure white light and there at the top of the stairs, his brilliant golden hair obliterating everything around him, is the King. Denis Law.

(Dear reader, you will just have to believe me when I say that journalistic license has not been called into play for the benefit of describing the following...)

Without warning, without premeditation, in fact without any form of pre-planning, ultra straight Graham and straight looking me simultaneously dropped from our chairs in the lobby of the Royal Kensington Hotel to a Wayne's World type pose and cried in unison...

"We're not worthy. We're not worthy."

You can imagine the look on Denis's face. I know I can 'cause I was there! Acute embarrassment does not begin to convey the look on his face. He tottered for a moment, battling the forces within to the tune of the Clash's, "Should I go or should I stay now". Good overpowered evil and he descended hesitantly yet majestically down the stairs.

After obligatory handshakes all round (this was a first date, after all) the five of us had a very pleasant conversation for almost an hour and a half. At one stage, someone even suggested if I had ever considered using Denis for my company. You know, advertising, PR, company brochure, that sort of thing. Thought about it? I'd wet myself in the past imagining famous

United players and managers, past and present, bestowing the virtues of me and my company. In fact almost as much as imagining a night with Raquel Welch, Jacqueline Bissett, Kelly Brooks, Angelina Jolie and...but, hey, you don't want to hear about that, do you?

Imagining his fee to be something in another dimension I nervously stuttered a reply and continued on another subject.

Much gushing and story telling later the subject of food came up. Here knowledge accrued over many years came to my aid as I impressed them by naming names of some of the more unusual eateries to be found in dear old London town. A Singaporean restaurant along the Holland Road was agreed upon. Denis and his subjects went back upstairs whilst Graham and I wet ourselves with anticipation at the thought of sitting at the King's table.

Half an hour later we were still humid, yet Denis and his entourage were nowhere to be seen. I asked the concierge to call his room.

No answer.

We'd been blown out.

Stinging tears filled my eyes. "Why?" I asked myself. (Well, I knew the bloody answer but I wasn't going to admit it to myself)

Graham and I then walked down Holland Road to the restaurant and, Yes, there they were, sitting and enjoying themselves in MY restaurant, but without ME.

Oh, the pain. To be so cruelly rejected on a first date. And we'd only shaken hands.

Graham and I agonised pitifully for a few minutes then decided to call it a day, or night to be more precise. I mean, Graham was the rep's client. In business terms he had more to lose than Graham by stitching us up. "He'll never get another order from me again", said Graham.

That told him.

The following day I went back to work. I tried to pretend that everything had gone according to plan so as to impress my staff. Professionalism and all that.

Then the phone rang.

"Hi David. Denis here. Sorry about last night. Bit of a misunderstanding. Roy (the rep) tells me that you're interested in using me for your company brochure?"

Taking command of the situation as any good management executive would, I blubbered incoherently for a few seconds, then was able to string an actual sentence or ten together.

"Last night? Oh, don't worry about it. Yeah, just one of those things. Brochure, er..er..Yeah, I was thinking about my next brochure and I had this idea see, gobble, gobble, gobble, gobble...bunny, bunny, rabbit, rabbit, yap, yap, etc...etc.."

I put the phone down.

"Fuck me."

I'd just had a telephonic audience with the King, and somehow I'd arranged to meet Denis at 12.30 the following week in (the much missed) Dave Smith's supporters club office at Old Trafford to discuss the matter in more detail.

Cometh the day cometh the man. I drove up there nice and early. No way were those dreaded road works on the M1/M6 going to slow me down today of all days.

Had a nice chat with Dave Smith. But then at 12.30 he said "Sorry Dave, I've got to close the office for lunch." I waited outside. 12.45. 13.00. I'd been stood up again! What had I done wrong this time?

13.15. This is getting beyond a joke. Hang on a minute. Is it a bird? Is it a plane? No, it's the King, walking down the Warwick Rooooooad...... "Sorry I'm late David. How are you? Got stuck at the BBC. Where shall we go?"

Taking command of the situation as any good management executive would, I blubbered incoherently for a few seconds but this time I was unable to string an actual sentence or ten together.

With Dave Smith's office closed I followed Denis through the maze and heart of Old Trafford, reaching parts other plebs couldn't reach. This was the most amazing journey of my (then) life. Better than Space Mountain. As the King swept past, minions came out of the woodwork to gaze in awe (well, talk actually). I'll never forget the look on their faces as first they saw Denis and then they spied me.

"How on Earth does Denis know HIM?"

You have to understand that for a good few years, as an official supplier to Manchester United, I had met quite a few of the staff. Most were pleasant and polite, some quite charming, but I always got the impression that if I had come from Manchester they would have warmed to me more. Accepted me for who I was, not where I came from.

This all changed in an instant. The look on their faces now read:

"Any friend of Denis's is a friend of ours."

My standing shot up. I felt 7 feet tall. I waved regally and Cheshire grinned at the same minions that spoke to Denis. In the end we settled ourselves in Sandy Busby's office at the back of the souvenir shop and talked for over an hour. It was wonderful.

In the end I had to cut short our meeting to go back to London, but not before he agreed to pose for the front cover of my company brochure.

Seriously, anyone who has met Denis since his playing days can vouch for the fact that the shy, retiring player has become one of the nicest, funniest, bubbliest and most genuine people in the game. Like Reds everywhere I was shocked when I learnt a few years later that he needed a heart operation, and, more recently, a scare over prostate cancer. He always seemed so fit and 'up for it'. Here's hoping the King many happy and healthy years.

"Oh, we'll drink a drink a drink to Denis the King, the King the King..

16

THE WIZARD OF OT

FOOTBALL MIRRORS life. You have to go through the bad to appreciate the good. Younger United fans who have only ever known the phenomenal success since the early 90s have no concept of the pain and anguish BOFS R US (boring old farts) had to endure for twenty years prior to the second coming.

Before I was old enough to appreciate what was happening the sixties ended and the seventies began. Metamorphosis set in. Music and fashion divided into mods and rockers, progressive and glam rock, hippies and skinheads, long hair and mullets.

I took a left turn, grew my hair and my flairs and declared Clapton was God long before le version francaise appeared on Planet United.

The Roundhouse, The Marquee, Bag o' Nails, Gangalf's Garden, Eel Pie Island and the ultimate high of Shepton Mallet '(Bath) '69. Musically and spiritually my world was growing and expanding. Unfortunately my football world was shrinking before my eyes. Glories and trophies receded over the horizon. From the town that grew rich on slavery, Liverpool, to the ominous black cloud that was to be called Leeds spread like the death of the first born over the land. Just like Monty Python's "Jehovah", in private or public, "CHAMPIONS" became a word you never uttered, let alone sang out loud. Like cancer and vindaloo curries it ate away at your insides. It acted as both a bond and a curse uniting Reds all over the world.

False dawns throughout the seventies and eighties were to be enjoyed, but deep down we knew we were as far away as ever from uttering the holy word, "CHAMPIONS", and even further away from the sixties Stretford

End splitting into "We Are The Left Side", "We Are The Right Side", and "Centre, Centre", then joyously exalting, "We Are The Champions, We Are The Champions", "Champions, Champions, Champions", "Champions of Europe, Champions of Europe", and finally, "Europe, Europe...Europe, Europe".

Oh, happy days.

And so it came to pass that Alex Ferguson was appointed Manager in 1986. For the first two or three years there was little sign of change on the surface, yet deep within the very bowels of the club, this man was laying the foundations for the most monumental decade in the history of Manchester United, and by definition...the World.

From the river that began to flow with the 1990 FA Cup final replay win over Crystal Palace the current grew and flooded the senses with Rotterdam '91, Mark Hughes 2 Barcelona 1. Now in full flow we entered the nineties proper. For someone who had lived every day of every week of every season of the previous twenty six years, who had had to go to work and suffer the slings and arrows of workmates and friends, what happened next was beyond my wildest dreams.

But I mustn't get carried away – just yet. Let me take you back to my first face to face with Sir Alex Ferguson.

Long before Fantasy Football, Soccer AM and internet fans forums we would argue over who we should buy, who we should sell, who was a diamond and who was a donkey. Why couldn't the management see what was so obvious to us from the terraces?

As a United fan, one step up for me was to become a Shareholder, so that once a year I could attend the AGM and tell the Board and the Manager, face to faces, exactly what they were doing wrong and what they should do to put it right. In fact, so succinct was my analysis of the issues that each time I expected to be offered a place on the Board with the mandate to "do the right thing" and we will follow.

I'm still waiting.

In the days before the PLC, one of the pleasures of attending the AGM was having a "one-to-one" with the manager once the press had departed. Holding court in front of an admiring throng, we would engage in a two way exchange that made us believe we were an integral part of the decision making process, whilst secrets were revealed that massaged our egos no end. For me this started with the Atkinson era and at AGMs and Euro aways us regulars built up quite a rapport. To be fair to Big Ron, before most Euro aways he would stroll over to wherever the United fans were being caged and exchange a few pleasantries with us.

At the 1986 United AGM I had my close encounter of the first kind with Alex Ferguson. The word was out that he didn't like long hair, so yours truly stood behind a pillar when I posed my first question, referring to my long hair and raising a laugh in the process. I remember his reply included the observation that there seemed to be more fans at this United AGM than Aberdeen fans at most home games. At the end of proceedings I followed my usual ritual of licking and groveling by asking each and every board member, including Bobby Charlton, if they would like to join fellow Reds, Michael Shenton, Graham Wyche and myself for lunch.

Wisely they all claimed to have made prior arrangements, except the new boy, Alex Ferguson.

"Hold on lads. I'll join you in a minute."

Trousers turning a collective brown, we followed the great man through the bowels of Old Trafford to one of the staff restaurants where we all ordered spaghetti. Once he opened up in our company we waxed lyrically for what seemed like hours. During the meal someone came over to our table to remind Alex that a Mr and Mrs Bosnich had flown in all the way from Australia and were waiting in his office, together with their son, Mark. Alex said he would be along in a few minutes, yet we continued to converse for well over an hour, discussing up and coming young players, especially Ryan Wilson, how the three of us had become United fans and what we hoped for the future.

In the end it was I, Davidius, that had to remind Alex of the Australian family in his office. And thus he shook each one of us by the hand and left. The three of us sat back in awe, rewinding the last two hours. Then reality struck as the waiter came over and we paid for Alex's meal.

17

LOST AND FOUND IN FRANCE

THE FIRST TIME I LIVED and worked in France was between January 1989 and July 1994.

My wife, Hélène, and two daughters, Melanie (then two months short of her 14th birthday) and Jasmine (aged 2) had moved to Brittany during the summer of '88. The reason was that Melanie had been diagnosed as suffering from a particularly severe form of scoliosis, whereby the spine develops a double curve and unless it is treated early the person affected can be permanently disabled by the time they are 25+.

To say this came as a shock to the family is the understatement of the decade. Although not sporty (in fact, Melanie hated sports) she was very fit due to the fact that for the past two years she had been attending the Sylvia Young Theatre School in Marylebone. For two days a week the emphasis was on the performing arts which involved lots of dancing and related exercises. Also her posture was very good. Whereas I am a slouch she used to sit and stand bolt upright, so we had no inkling of the impending torment that would literally split the family in two.

One day her dancing teacher asked Melanie to turn round and bend over (all right, stop tittering at the back). She had noticed that although Melanie was standing bolt upright, one shoulder was higher than the other. By bending over she had discovered Mel's curvature of the spine.

To cut a long story very short, the body brace didn't work so we arranged an appointment at the world renowned Royal National Ortho-paedic Hospital in Bolsover Street in Central London. They informed us that the only option was an operation that involved inserting a single metal rod in her back. She would have to lay flat on her back for six months and, if she was lucky, she'd be able to walk like Werzal Gummidge for the rest of her life.

My wife and I were horrified. We couldn't believe that this was the best the British medical profession could offer in 1988. Frantic searching and researching began, and, don't forget, this was long before the internet was available for the likes of you and me.

Then Hélène discovered this doctor in Nantes in France (Djemba Djemba country) who had pioneered a revolutionary procedure whereby three overlapping rods are inserted in the back. Melanie would stay on flat on her back for THREE DAYS as opposed to SIX MONTHS, then with the help of therapy she'd be able to walk, dance and play as before, with the exception of double back flips with pike.

When we went back to the hospital in London with our findings they dismissed them out of hand, claiming it was not proven technology, it was not approved by the BMA, plus a whole host of excuses just to mask the fact that they didn't have the funds or the will to invest in the future. And to think we think Britain rules the world in medicine.

So, we had no option but to decamp to France. Things were made a bit easier by the fact that Hélène came from Lomener in Brittany, twenty kilometres along the coast from the fishing port of Lorient (which is a bit like Leyton Orient but with abbreviations) and her elder sister, Mireille, actually lived in Nantes.

Why did I stay behind I hear you ask? Because my wife and I had been running a promotional clothing company in London for ten years and we couldn't just walk away. If you have a normal job you just hand in your notice, but if you run your own company it's not that easy. I put the company up for sale, but one of the conditions insisted upon by the new owners was that I stay on for one year as 'Consultant', whilst they got to grips with the business as they were new to textile screen printing and embroidery.

Another condition of the sale has similarities with modern day football transfers. They paid a 35% lump sum upon aquisition, with the remaining 65% to be paid after one year. Unfortunately they did a "Lazio" and defaulted on the balance, leaving me up the creek without a paddle. I could have sued them, but I would have had to pay my lawyers out of my own pocket, and if I had won, the sum awarded would have gone to my old company and not to me. What is known in marketing as a "lose – lose" situation. Plus I was consumed with worry over my daughter's medical condition which took precedent over fiscal matters. I was doubly upset because it was my intention at the time to return to the promotional gift industry once Melanie had recovered, but without the sale balance I couldn't fulfill my obligations to my suppliers who I would need upon returning to the UK. They would be questioning my parenthood without knowing the facts.

I was not a happy bunny.

I left England in January '89 wearing my United tie, twenty four hours after having witnessed our first victory at Upton Park since 1968/69, a 3-1 win helped in no small measure with a double by Mark Hughes.

I was a little happier. "Thanks lads. I needed that."

I settled back into family life in Hélène's parents house near the sea. Melanie had already started school in the area. When she arrived in France she could hardly parler a mot of frog so she put on a very brave face each day as she set off for school. Jasmine's initiation into the French education system wasn't anything near as traumatic as she was only two years old and didn't realise she was mixing English and French words in the same sentences.

Meanwhile, more by luck than ability I landed a position as joint Chef du Publicitie for the F.B.I. That is, Fishing Boat International, a recently launched international trade publication. My mission was to contact companies in all the English speaking countries around the world and try to convince them to advertise in our erstwhile revue whilst my French colleague would mirror my activities in France and the Dom Toms – French dependant territories.

I had been in two minds about accepting the job. First of all I knew less than nothing about commercial fishing. In fact, with my World Wildlife Fund allegiances, I considered commercial fishing bordering on blood sports and secondly, in the fifteen years or so I had run or been a partner in my own business I had grown cauliflower ears from having been bombarded by all those inane phone calls from cardboard cutouts reciting from the same script when desperately selling me the benefits of advertising in their purile publications.

Parodying Derek and Clive I had asked myself many times, "What's the worst job you could ever have?" and each time I made a promise to myself. I would never ever sell advertising space. Well, that just goes to show what a shallow character I am.

However the one major benefit was that I got to travel on the company's account. And that meant attending fishing and general marine exhibitions throughout Europe and North America. Now I'll let you into a secret. Apart from football, music and sex, I do get off on travel. Travel, like Manchester United, is like sex for me – even when it's bad, it's good.

As a new magazine, in order to establish "F.B.I." in the Premier League of fishery publications, I convinced the powers that be that taking a stand wherever possible in the most relevant trade shows was an essential ingredient of my marketing mix. Then if exhibiting was too expensive, just "being there", pressing the flesh, was just as important.

Commercial fishing does not take place in large urban conurbations. A rather obvious statement you may think. Well, yes and no. Yes, in Europe I would attend events in Paris, Copenhagen, Amsterdam and Glasgow, but also places not in the Michelin Guide top ten such as Aberdeen, Ancona, Trondheim and Reykjavik. To get the most out of each visit, imagining each one to be my last as my publication lived from issue to issue, I made sure I gave myself a couple of days before or after a show to see a bit of the region. My arguments to the company were so compelling I believed them myself.

1) As I knew the dates of each event months in advance I could take advantage of promotional airfares that
required booking twenty-one days/three months in advance.

2) If one of the conditions required an overnight stay on a Saturday night then this had the double advantage of enabling me to recharge my batteries, thereby returning a refreshed and revitalized employee

The two things I missed most about living in England were music and football.

Prioritizing as usual, I ignored Hélène's advice and, to partially negate the effects of withdrawal symptoms, I blew £900 of the family savings on the latest 82cm colour TV and a satellite television system. Not just your average fixed Astra model but a £1000+ fully motorized system, enabling us to pick up hundreds of channels from around the world in the 180°

heavens, plus all the British radio stations in stereo. This was something of a coup because in 1989 Virgin Radio had recently been launched in London and was playing a life enriching elixir of heavy metal and progressive rock, but only in mono! As Ian Drury once sang..."What a Waste."

Not for me though. I could receive MTV and all the football the BBC, ITV and Sky Sports could offer. All right. It was baked beans on toast as opposed to steak with all the trimmings, but at least it dulled the hunger.

MY WORLD WAS FLAT

They had taught me at school that the world was round. This, of course, is not true.

I know, because I lived near Lorient in Brittany, which is just on the edge of the world before you fall over the edge. "A" list bands rarely played in our area and the local football club, FC Lorient (Les Merlus) was then languishing in the second division.

However, once a year, around the first ten days of August, Lorient was on the map when the town hosted the Festivale Interceltic. Name artists and music fans from all Celtic nations, especially Ireland, descended and doubled the population. People would be playing and partying all over town, with sing songs and camaraderie the name of the game. In the five summers that I passed there, I saw such luminaries as Van Morrison, Planxsty, The Chieftans, Alain Stivell, Soldat Louis and one of my, and the world's, all-time favourite guitarists, Rory Gallagher.

But just like pissing in the dessert, no sooner had the music blossomed then it disappeared once again, leaving me to face another year in the wilderness.

Football was even worse. To say I was missing Manchester United was like breathing without lungs. I couldn't breathe in, I couldn't breathe out. The very air that I breathed was missing. I've always been a bit of a goer (ooh aah, missus). Whether through lack of tickets (chubbing), postponements or England internationals, from time to time I've kept my Red perspective intact and never taken things for granted by going to watch other teams, principally Leyton Orient or, when they were still alive, the Lions of Ley Street, Ilford.

The one connecting thread in all this is Passion. Whatever level of football you support, passion for your team is paramount. Without passion and self-deprevating humour, some of the mind numbing football witnessed at grounds up and down the country would be proclaimed by the Government as a health warning.

Despite reports to the contrary, France lacks passion in some of life's most important pursuits. Passion in France must manifest itself in other ways, because by and large it's conspicuous by its absence at football matches. Coming from an advertising background, two relevant aspects soon struck me about advertising on French television in 1989.

1) Every other advertisement contained the phrase "Le Passion" in its slogan, title or pay-off line. Beautiful young things with sleek, glistening bodies performed perfect sporting maneuvers whilst bestowing the virtues of biscuits, cars or soap flakes, watched by a myriad French versions of The Royal Family on their sofas. Performing sport or relaying passion was the alto ego for these people as they passively switched from reality to fantasy. Nothing could be further from reality than the images on the small screen. Lazy advertising.

2) Every other advertisement featured one or more beautiful women with bare breasts. At first I thought I had died and gone to heaven. On the basis that it's better to travel than to arrive, the thought of Twin Peaks always does it for me, as the likelihood that I would enter the Tunnel of Love was far more remote. However, as an advertising professional (stop tittering at the back) I soon began to question this approach. Any U.S.P (unique selling points – boom, boom), image or slogan should automatically trigger your recall of a particular product or service, hence the emphasis on the word "unique". It soon became clear that whenever I thought of bare breasts, no one particular product or service came to mind. I repeated this exercise over and over again in the name of research but the only images that filled my consciousness were naked breasts. Lazy advertising.

Hang on. I'm getting distracted. Where was I? Oh, yes, lack of passion. Football supporters in France are a pale shadow of ourselves, the Scots, the Spanish and even the Italians. Notwithstanding notable exceptions such as Marseilles whose home gates average 50,000 and Lens, whose stadium has a greater capacity than the population of the town, and fills it on a regular basis (I love that), numbers and noise levels are way below acceptable levels. Let me give you a couple of examples. During my first year in France, Les Merlus were due to play a league match away at

Quimper. At forty kilometres from Lorient, this was the nearest I could get to a local derby, so anticipating a cauldron of hate I drove by myself (OK, let's not be pedantic, I took the car with me) to Quimper's stadium. Parking was easy, so armed with an obligatory "merguez" sausage roll, I strolled ridiculously early towards the ground with my ears filled with the sound of... my own footsteps.

Once inside I identified the fifty or so Lorient supporters sitting in a single row along one side. I positioned myself alongside and tried to make conversation in my broken French. Barely an acknowledgement as the clique kept themselves to themselves, so I contented myself by watching the youth match already underway on the pitch.

"What a good idea", I thought. Two matches for the price of one, a chance for the youngsters to play in the first team stadium in front of their most loyal supporters, and for supporters to see into the future, right before their very eyes. An hour later and the real match got underway. By this time the ground was three quarters full and four thousand fans were merging into the background, reminiscent of the painting in front of the North Bank at Highbury a few years ago.

As far as I was concerned a match is a match is a match. I also thought this was an ideal opportunity to show the locals how real fans showed their support. When the Lorient supporters started singing I joined in louder than any of them, even though I was doing a strangled Franglais version of their lyrics.

Then after ten minutes something happened that none of us expected. Lorient scored. I went bananas. I leapt off the bench and into the air with the grace of a land-locked penguin and the outpourings of Chewbacca on ecstasy. On my way down I met up with the fifty or so Lorient supporters. They were clapping as though we'd just scored a four through the covers on an overcast afternoon in front of three men and a dog.

"What's wrong with these people?" I thought, as their damp squid of a celebration put me firmly in my place. I watched the rest of the match sitting firmly on the bench. I realised an outsider like me stood no chance of stopping rigamortis setting in so I passively accepted my lot.

Not convinced? OK. I'll give you another example. In England and Scotland football doesn't last just ninety minutes. It's the craic of travelling to and from the ground that can last a whole day. In fact it can last all week.

If your team has won at the weekend (you'll notice I didn't write Saturday. Significant, huh?), you can't wait to get to work and take the piss out of your colleagues. Conversely, if you've lost, Monday on the toilet or in the stationary cupboard has its advantages.

Throughout the seventies and eighties, and as far back as I can remember, France always beat England at Rugby (Union that is). And for the French, Rugby Union and not football is their national game. Yes, the French are strange. So near yet so far removed from the real world. Now, would you believe it, the moment I stepped onto French soil that all changed. If my memory serves me well (Judy Driscoll and the Brian Auger Trinity) from 1989 till 1994 England started to beat the living daylights out of the French.

One particular match comes to mind. Our first victory at the Parc de Prince for decades. A majestic 6 – 33 victory romp. Stuffed 'em in their own back yard. At the time I was Advertisement Manager for the F.B.I, Fishing Business International, an international trade publication and we had just been bought out by a publishing group based in Rennes. I couldn't wait for Monday.

The moment I arrived I went straight to my office, found a poster size sheet of art paper, a thick black magic marker and drew a giant "6 – 33". I then stuck the poster on the wall opposite my door which I kept open and waited for the response.

Nothing.

No abuse. No congratulations. Not even a raised eyebrow. I suspect the most animated reaction was out of ear/eye shot, just a Gallic shrug of the shoulders and an expression which spoke volumes.

"He's English."

"Oui. We know."

"Zat explains everysing."

Christ. They must be dead from the neck upwards and downwards. How can a nation put sex, wine and haute cuisine above football? They must be all in-seine. Je ne comprend pas.

MONTPELIER

Apart from Rubbish and Bollocks, for obvious reasons French is the only foreign language I have made any attempt to learn. One quirky offshoot of this is that I've always been on the lookout for United to draw a French team in European competitions. Throughout the seventies and eighties European Competitions plural meant the European Cup Winners Cup or Inter City Fairs Cup of course. The real European Cup was just a pipe dream. United fans are nothing if not pragmatic. Reality would have to do until our dreams came true.

I was working one morning in December 1990. (I know I should have worked more than one morning in the month but if you can get away with it, why not?) I was still in Lorient at the time and my trade mag was still a struggling independent publication. My colleague Michel came into my office.

"You've drawn Montpelier."

"Yeah!"

Great. I'm now living in France and we've drawn a French team. A just reward for beating Wrexham in the last round. I went straight to the map of France on the production office wall.

"We are here." I thought. "So, where's Montpelier? Shit, it's almost, let me see...two feet away. Bugger."

A quick dose of ruler and I realised that Lorient to Montpelier by road was almost a thousand very expensive autoroute kilometres.

"I'll need help." I thought and phoned my United mates back in Blighty. Everyone was enthusiastic. They would all come to me, either overland via Brittany Ferries from Portsmouth to St Malo or the more affluent by Brit Air from Gatwick to Quimper. Four or more sharing the petrol costs and we were all systems 'aller'.

The previous year Montpelier had won the Coupe de France for the first time in their history. As the weeks went by I discovered a bit more about Montpelier. The club in its present guise only came into being in 1989, as A.S. Montpellier Herault Sport Club. If Villa fans have had problems with egos the size of Gregory or Darlington fans with George Reynolds and previous generations of Burnley fans with Bob Lord, they have nothing on Montpellier's president, Louis Nicollin.

In girth and attitude he is Arthur Daley and Del Boy rolled into one. People either love him or hate him. Like poacher turned gamekeeper, his love for the club he adores knows no bounds. He sits on the bench with the manager and does most of the pre and post match interviews himself.

To say he rules the football club is an understatement. For example, if you go on the Internet as I did and discover their web site, "Montpellier-Hérault Sporting Club", one click does not bring you to the home page of the club but to www.nicollin.com and his group of companies.

The immanent arrival of Manchester United propelled him onto the international stage and he swallowed all the media attention like a glutton. He defied UEFA regulations and announced that United supporters would be awarded only five hundred tickets. Manchester United responded by similarly restricting tickets for their supporters at Old Trafford. However, with their ground's capacity set at fifteen thousand and rarely full, this was a hollow gesture.

The upturn of all this was that I was suddenly a very popular United fan indeed. I don't know whether it was due to my French aftershave or the fact that people believed that my French address automatically gave me a direct line to a bottomless pit of tickets. The fact was, that to keep me sane in the land of the frog, I had taken out subscriptions to all the United fanzines and so my details were on their respective databases.

It reminded me of the characature of the American who, when overhearing an English accent on his home soil, asked the said person, "Are you British?" When the reply was in the affirmative he asked, "Do you know Mrs Brown in Bristol?"

I received dozens and dozens of foreign phone calls, all offering undying love and tickets to any United game back in England, as long as I could get him/her/it a ticket or three for the Montpellier away leg.

I could have gone either way on this one, but my dominating motivation was to be involved once again with anything to do with United. The opportunity to live, breath and speak United was overwhelming. And the callers' beliefs were not without foundation.

I set my master plan into motion. I contacted all my wife's family and asked them all to apply for tickets. I also asked them to ask everybody they knew to apply for tickets. I then set about my work colleagues and French clients and suppliers. In the end I must have secured over fifty tickets.

And this is where my true character came out. I don't know whether I should be immensely proud or cringingly embarrassed by the following, but you should know that I didn't make a penny profit from these tickets. Again, the dominating emotion for me was that I belonged to the biggest and best family in the world, the global Red Army, and I felt compelled in my own Mother Teresa/Albert Schweitzer sort of way that I was helping the greater good and that I would be blessed in an afterlife.

Every ticket was sold at face value, many to those who offered lifelong friendship and never contacted me again. Naive or what? Moi?

Never mind. After a niggling 0-0 draw in Manchester where we under-achieved with aplomb, my blood began to race at the prospect of seeing my heroes on French soil for the first time since St Etienne fourteen years previously. (And what a trip and three quarters that was!)

However, fate was to turn against me at this point as, one by one, each of my mates rained off. All for very good reasons it has to be said, but the end result was that I was left with four tickets in my back pocket where they would have to stay.

I contacted French Railways. £140 pounds return! What a joke. I considered driving but the petrol there and back would have set me back almost as much.

Merde.

I had no choice but to stay at home and watch the game on my new satellite system. Not the end of the world I know but, as any regular match going fan will tell you, it wasn't far short.

By this time, dear reader, you should be aware that we had moved from Hélène's parents house into our own property in Lomener. At two hundred years old it had originally been a

farmhouse and later the first ever building in the village. One advantage was that the walls were even thicker than me. Eighteen inches to be precise, which meant that as I had wired my new satellite system through my Hi Fi, all my music and sports programs were broadcast at a Spinal Tap "11" whilst at the same time the neighbours heard......absolutely nothing.

All my ear splitting heavy metal rebounded off the stone walls like I was at the concert itself whilst crowd roars filled the giant through lounge. Brilliant.

I laid down the rules for the evening. My brother-in-law, Hervé, his girlfriend Karen and their newly born daughter, Emily were staying with us at the time. Together with Hélène, Melanie and Jasmine I made them all go upstairs and watch French TV in our bedroom whilst I set myself up in the middle of the lounge.

Why I had bothered to position the "comfy chair" I had no idea because once the match started I was totally absorbed, standing, jumping, shouting and gesturing at the TV. This time we were playing a lot better and I could hear The Red Army in full voice. Then just before half-time United were awarded a free-kick about thirty five yards out. Clayton Blackmore looked to be taking it.

"Oh no. Not Sunbed", I thought as he let fly with a scorcher that literally flew into the net.

"GOOOOOOOOOOOOAAAAAAAAAAAAAALL!!!!!!"

I ran round the room then flew up the stairs two at a time and into our bedroom without breaking scream. The scene that greeted my eyes will forever be imprinted in my mind.

Little weeks old Emily woke up with a jolt and started howling at the top of her voice. Jasmine, who had been asleep on the edge of the bed, fell on the floor. Melanie remained glued to the screen whilst Hervé wore a knowing smile. Karen and Hélène, however, wore expressions that would have won awards for Hammer Films, so black and evil that hell threatened to freeze over.

I knew my place. Without breaking scream I rushed downstairs and into the dark, deserted street. What the neighbours would have thought I had no idea, and to be honest, I didn't care.

I came back into the house as the referee blew for half-time. Catching my breath I made my way upstairs to apologize for my behaviour.

Bad move. As soon as I opened the door a catalogue of venom hit me square between the earlobes. Fortunately, as various offspring were being comforted, no-one could get up and give me a piece of their mind so I made my escape to victory.

Partially recovered, I settled down for the second half. Not five minutes had passed when another free kick was headed in by Steve Bruce and my lungs and larynx combined to produce another.........

"GOOOOOOOOOOOOAAAAAAAAAAAAAALL!!!!!!"

This time I had a better sense of direction as I ran screaming round the room then straight out into the street. I was halfway down to the little port before I stopped for breath. How considerate was that?

I ran back to the house and watched the rest of the match in a semi quiet happy hue, as Montpellier had had the stuffing knocked out of them and we coasted to an impressive victory on French soil. We had played with a style and belief I hadn't seen before. My insides told me that we were on the threshold of something but I daren't let myself believe. Not after all this time. No, let me just enjoy the moment, for the moment. The future? Well, that's for the future.

To engratiate myself back into my wife's good books I made tea and coffee for everyone and took it upstairs.

A subdued 'Thank You' was overshadowed by Helene's steely-eyed look as she gave me the cold shoulder and other parts of her anatomy. It was going to be a long night but at least I had my dreams to keep me warm.

18

I TOLD 'EM, OLDHAM

WHEN I EXITED Upton Park in May 1967 the sun was shining. United had just thrashed West Ham 6-1 to gloriously regain the Championship that we'd lent to Liverpool the previous year. Outside there were only Reds, no West Ham at all. And believe me they would have been conspicuous as they were covered in self raising flour. But that's another story for another time.

All was right with the world.

I was eighteen. I had discovered girls, even if most of them hadn't discovered me. But that was all right, because everyone knows that boys aren't at their most potent until they're nineteen, so I had time on my side. Time to look for those 39 year old women, that is, who would be gagging for a virile 19 year old.

United were champions again. Life, like girls, was on an unstoppable upward curve.

26 years later, as Aston Villa were about to kick-off at home to Oldham, needing just a draw to keep themselves in the hunt until the final day of the campaign, I was almost 1000 miles from Manchester, glued to my ghetto blaster in my daughters bedroom of our two bedroom apartment in Rennes, Brittany, wearing my United shirt, United shorts, scarf and cap. Yeah, I could make Robbie from Eastenders look cool.

How did I get HERE, when I should have been be over THERE?

My first trip and match at Old Trafford was in the Spring of '67, a glorious 5-2 victory over Leicester City (The King's double including a lob over the world's greatest goalkeeper, Gordon Banks, Herd's broken leg. Yes – an everyday story in the life of United fans.)

For the next couple of years I continued to travel by coach with one of the three United Supporters Clubs established in the London area until, bathed in testosterone, pig headiness, Brut, headbanging music and smelly socks, we outgrew the coach and on behalf of "The Backseat Boys" I began to hire 12 seater mini-buses for matches throughout our sceptered isle and Europe.

For the next 18 years I was the "Pied Piper". I'd hire the minivan, grovel for tickets, organise our euro excursions, everything. It was a real labour of love. My career suffered but, what the heck, priorities dear boy, What?

From 1967 to 1988 I must have seen the Reds between 30-35 times a season, with every home game a 400 mile round trip and every imaginable high and low this era was to inflict on loyal match going Reds. Thousands of miles and thousands of pounds. Do the suits really understand what we go through? I think not. Then as soon as I leave the country the giant wakes up from a 26 year slumber and begins to win everything in sight.

In January 1989, after witnessing our first victory at Upton Park for ages (a Mark Hughes inspired 3-1 win) I moved to Lomener near Lorient, Brittany in France for the first time and stayed there until 1994 (My eldest daughter, Melanie, needed a spinal operation that was unavailable on the National Health. Politics, eh? Don't get me started)

Unfortunately, during this time no-one took over my mantle, so when I finally returned to Blighty five years later most of my contacts had grown cold and, ever since, as far as tickets are concerned, it has been a case of "nose against the window pane time."

And so we arrive to Spring 1993. One weekend we had decided to drive down to Futuroscope near Poitier, a futuristic theme park. A good time was had by all. In a parallel universe back home we were neck and neck with Aston Villa for the Premiership title. The pain of the final cruel week of the previous season, when the FA had forced us to play four games in seven days, was receding as Villa and ourselves raced towards the finishing line. Both teams had played brilliant football that season and Villa had more than held their own in a 1-1 draw at Old Trafford.

By this particular weekend Aston Villa were one point ahead of us and the number of remaining weeks was reducing at an alarming rate. We were at home to Sheffield Wednesday and the Villa were at home to Coventry.

I did a passable impersonation of concentrating on the family whilst my thoughts turned to events a thousand miles north. Living in Brittany I would be able to get a weak come-and-go Radio 5 Live on medium wave in the car. Forget the Hi Fi at home. Now we were further south – forget it. On the drive back to Brittany I tried in vain to get a signal. I scanned the other stations without any success. It was now around 6 o'clock French time as I desperately searched for a reading of the English football scores. Hélène was starting to give me jip for endangering the family with my erratic driving. Eventually amid the whooshes and squeaks I heard an English voice. My pulse raced. I slowed down to reduce road noise. He was reading the news. Good start. Surely he would read the football results afterwards? Yes! Great!

I pulled over to the side of the road.

"What are you doing?" asked Hélène.

"I want to listen to the football results."

"You're mad."

She continued to bash my ear.

"Sshhh! I can't hear.'

She shut up, but I knew retribution was around the corner.

I went back to the radio.

" blah, blah, blah ....Aston Villa 0 Coventry 0

"YESSSSSS! They've dropped points at home. Come on you Reeeeeeds"

" blah, blah, blah......

Hang on. Hang on. What's happened to the United result. Oh Christ, what's going on? They're doing this on purpose. They know I'm driving in France and they're making me sweat. But it didn't make sense. Why wouldn't they announce the United result? OK, there could have been a few minutes of injury time but surely not enough to miss the 5 o'clock (English time) reading of the football results.

I was confused. Hélène was totally pissed off and Jasmine, my youngest at six and a half years, was picking up the bad vibes and began to cry.

Shit. This is all I need. It was fruitless trying to explain the importance of the scores within the context of my forty five years on this planet. The only result generated by attempting to justify my actions would be me digging my own grave.

I started the car and we continued on route for Lorient.

Conversation in the vehicle was minimal. Partly due to the frosty atmosphere down to Hélène accusing me of spoiling the family weekend with my ludicrous obsession, and me furiously trying to imagine what possible scenario of events had unfolded at Old Trafford that could possibly have resulted in the omission of our score. One of the most important scores in my United following life.

7 o'clock French time, 6 o'clock English time arrived and I tuned in to the same radio station, praying for a second reading of the football results.

YES! Here we go. I pulled over to the side of the road. Hélène's expression would have impressed a twisted Stephen King. No matter.

" blah, blah, blah ....Aston Villa 0 Coventry 0

"Yeah!"

"blah, blah, blah......Manchester United 2 Sheffield Wednesday 1"

"AAAAAAHHHHHHHHhhhhhhh!"

I jumped out of the car and dashed at full speed along the hard shoulder;

"AAAAAAHHHHHHHHhhhhhhh!"

I jumped up and down and continued to scream along the side of the main road. What the hell passing motorists made of my actions I had no idea, but I didn't care. We'd done it. We'd overtaken Villa with just a few short weeks to go. This was our defining moment. The ball was in our court and we weren't going to give it up.

My throat began to hurt so I made my way back to the car. Ye Erics. I didn't realise I had run that far. I got back in the driving seat. Hélène's expression of disgust mixed with pity is even now etched in my brain, but my heart was racing with joy that at last we would reach the promised land.

I tried to calm down. After twenty six years of being "nearly men", experience as a United fan had taught me not to take anything for granted until the fat lady blows the final whistle. Only the previous season we had fallen at the final hurdle, the final nail being Sheffield United losing at home to hand the title to Leeds. Then moments later entering Anfield to see and hear Liverpool fans creaming themselves at our demise.

"You lost the league on Merseyside." (untrue) and the banner,

"Have you ever seen United win the league?" were countered with "You never beat United" yet our hearts weren't in it and it was a day to forget. We've had our revenge many times over since then, including the constant showing on TV of our banner in the late 90s, "We won the league on Merseyside", but days like that described above shape and define your support and your commitment to the cause.

Hélène slowly thawed out as the miles (OK, kilometres) passed by. Once again the realisation that I was able to express more raw emotion for my football team than for the love of my life was a bitter pill for her to swallow. As a man I had once again failed the test. Even to this day her pained expression at the mention of Manchester United leads me to believe that I would be better off if I were to be caught in the arms of another woman. At least she could come to terms with the terrible betrayal. But to lose me to a football team? That was, and still is, beyond her powers of comprehension.

As for me, can you imagine my extreme conflict of emotions as the season reached its climax? As an unselfish lover I reveled in the joy and happiness that Manchester United was about to bestow on long suffering United fans everywhere, yet like Moses on Mount Sinai I was gutted that after all this time (26 years), after all I had been through, all the ear bashings, after all the sacrifices I had made in the name of United (girls, career, etc...) I was going to miss out on the (then) greatest moment of all.

On the final Wednesday of the season, Aston Villa were due to play lowly Oldham Athletic at Villa Park. An expected victory would take the settlement of the championship into the final weekend.

At this time I was Advertisement Manager for a bilingual (French-English) fisheries magazine. From our idyllic base on the Breton coast we had recently been bought out by a "group de presse" based in Rennes, and so we had to vacate our large, 150 year old farmhouse 100 metres from the sea and decamp in a small garden flat in the centre of Rennes. However this wasn't all bad. If you can picture a smaller version of the Barbican in London then you will appreciate how fortunate we were to find a garden flat in the midst of this concrete jungle.

If I stepped out into our little garden I would be surrounded, Pit and the Pendulum like, by four high rise monstrosities. At any one time hundreds of people could be looking down on what we were doing, which could be a turn-on or a turn-off depending on your point of view (and nocturnal habits)

Anyway, if my memory serves me right, it was still light this particular Wednesday evening. Of course Franceis one hour ahead of the UK so we always get an extra hour of sunshine in the evening.

Hélène, Jasmine, brother-in-law Hervé and his girlfriend were in the lounge whilst I retreated to my daughter's bedroom. My stomach was in knots and my hands were literally shaking as I sat down to listen to the commentary on Radio 5. I say "sat down". This was, of course, patently untrue. I was so nervous I couldn't sit still and paced round the room like a condemned prisoner on death row.

I don't know about you, but you can get a pretty good idea which team has taken the initiative in any match broadcast on the radio by the number of times the commentator mentions one teams players more than the other. Believe it or not, from the very kickoff, I could only hear the names of the mediocre Oldham players. It soon became apparent that the Villa had frozen on the night and were not playing their normal free-flowing football (Yeah, I know it sounds strange to see the words "Villa" and "free-flowing football" in the same sentence but, remember, this was fourteen years ago).

Then in the 17th minute the wonderful but not now totally unexpected happened. Oldham scored. Yeah, you heard me, Oldham scored.

I jumped, I roared, I banged the bedroom walls (Yeah, all of 'em). I ran into the lounge and then ran straight out again (not even Buffy would mess with my wife when she has THAT look on her face). I couldn't catch my breadth. I told myself to calm down. This was stupid. There was still almost 70 minutes to go. And, hey, I'm a United fan. There was bound to be another cruel twist of fate. Shit, there was almost another 70 minutes to go.

I don't know how I made it to half-time but I did. Then I had to talk to someone, anyone – even my wife! I went into the lounge;

"We're not interested" was the look slapped on the faces of my youngest daughter, brother-in-law and his girlfriend.

"You're sick and need help" was the look engrained on my wife's face.

No matter. I breathlessly gave my account of the first half to the room, then took myself back to my daughter's bedroom.

The second half. Now I know it's not recorded in the Guiness Book of Records but this has to have been the longest 45 minutes in football history. As wave after wave of spluttering Villa attacks rained on Oldham their desperation grew and even though they dominated play they had few clear cut chances.

I stood, I sat, I paced, I shit myself. I shouted at the radio then immediately told myself to "shut it" as I couldn't hear the commentary.

And then it happened. I remember quite clearly hearing the final whistle. Despite the poor reception of the medium wave signal and the background noise of the crowd I quite clearly heard the final whistle.

"AAAAAAAAAAAAAAAAAAAAAAAHHHHHHHHHHHH HHHHHHHHHHH!!!!!!!!!!!!!!!!!"

I ran and screamed round and round the room like a demented chimpanzee on speed. I then flung open the door leading out into our little garden and, dressed in my United shirt, United shorts, scarf and cap proceeded to run and scream round and round the garden in full view of the hundreds who could have been looking down on what I was doing.

Remember, by now I was 44 years old. What the fuck! Once a Red always a Red, and everything that goes with following the greatest team on Earth. Age doesn't come into the equation. Supporting United keeps me young and ages me a hundred years at the same time.

Round and round I went. My family and friends came outside to try to calm me down. 26 fucking years – no fucking chance!

"Stop it"

"Think of the neighbours"

"Stop it"

"David, for God's sake stop it"

"AAAAAAAAAAAAAAAAAAAAAAAAAAAAAAHHHHH HHHHHHHHH!!!!!!!!!!!!!!!!!"

I was on a roll. I was frothing at the mouth. I couldn't stop. Yeah,

I really couldn't stop! Round and round I went. Down and down I went. 26 years had to come out. A release. An exorcism. Leaving me pure, and on a higher plain.

That night my wife got her own back. Her own defenses were impregnable. But at least I comforted myself with the knowledge that I wouldn't have to wait twenty six years to score on that pitch.

19

SEMI-FINALS ANONYMOUS

HELLO. MY NAME IS David Blatt and I'm a semi-finalist. And I don't want to talk about it.

Oh, all right then. You see, it all began when I was a kid.

1956/57. I cried when I learned that my beloved team, Manchester United, had lost over two matches to Real Madrid in the semi-final of the European Cup. I was only 8 years old at the time but I still remember the stinging tears in my eyes.

1957/58. The following year, the stirring remains of the Busby Babes this time lost to AC Milan in the semi-final of the European Cup. 9 years old yet the pain was tempered by pride, although I was not totally aware of theenormity of the occasion and all that surrounded it.

1961/62. We lost 3-1 to Tottenham in the FA Cup semi-final at Hillsborough.

1963/64. We lost 3-1 to West Ham in the mud in the FA Cup semi-final atHillsborough.

1964/65. A brilliant year because we won the league, yet we lost to both Leeds United in the semi-final replay of the FA Cup 1-0 at the City Groundafter a 0-0 draw at Hillsborough, and Ferenvaros in the semi-final of the Intercity Fairs Cup. We beat them 3-2 at Old Trafford, lost 1-0 at the Nep Stadium in Hungary, and then lost the deciding tie 2-1, also in Hungary.

It should have been re-named the Intercity Unfair Cup!

1965/66. Two more losing semi-finals. First the one everybody thought we would win. (now this gets too close for comfort) After Georgie had defied Sir Matt's instructions and torn Benfica apart in Lisbon in the (still) memorable 5-1 victory, we lost to unfancied Partisan Belgrade in the semi-finals of the European Cup. 2-0 in Yugoslavia and then the obligatory 1-0 victory in Manchester. A week later we lost 1-0 to Everton in the FA Cup semi-final.

We now start with the "I WAS THERE" games.

1968/69. All eleven AC Milan players saw our second goal go over the line. All eleven Manchester United players saw our second goal go over the line. 63,103 people inside Old Trafford saw our second goal go over the line. Millions watching on TV saw our second goal go over the line. The only person who didn't see our second goal go over the line was the referee who was panting on the fucking half way line.

Was this the moment my life began to go astray? Who can tell? What I do remember was watching highlights in a pub in Central Manchester later that evening and the commentator replaying the "goal" whilst in conversation with Matt Busby and asking the first and greatest God of them all for his comments. What could the great man say? He was gracious in defeat, but you just knew.........

1969/70. This was a really bad year. The first of many. The famous 26 years was unknowingly spreading out before our eyes. Evidence? A mediocre league campaign where we finished a disappointing 8th and then two very bitter blows...First losing to City in the League Cup semi-finals. After an unlucky 2-1 defeat at Maine Road I drove with mates up from London for revenge. 2-2 was the final score and that drive back to London was one of my worst on record, almost my lowest point, because in my guts I knew that it was all over. Simple as that, and no amount of outer bravado coulddisguise the fact. And at 20 years of age this seemed like the end of the world.

Worse was to follow. Those three titanic FA Cup semi-final battles against that rising tide of evil – Leeds United. We should have won the first 0-0 match at Hillsborough. I listened to the first replay on my Aero transistor radio. Just how many open goals did the Lawman miss that night? We seemed to be all over them according to the commentator. So, on to Burden Park and my first glimpse of the famous railway track above one end which had been featured in an Arthur Askey film. Where's Georgie? was the cry from the massed ranks of Reds. It transpired later that Matt Busby had caught him 'on the job' just half an hour before kick-off. Truth or friction?

Meanwhile that bastard Bremner scored in the 9th minute, right in front of me, and no amount of Manc pressure was going to effect the outcome. The last ten minutes were the worse. To see the other Semi Finals Anonymous end celebrating was like a dagger in the gullet. You don't forget things like that.

Well, at least some form of compensation was in order because Tony Lee and myself had befriended exiled Mancess, the gorgeous Patricia Richards, who had begun to travel up to Manchester with us on the Manchester United London & District Supporters Club.

18 months of the most acne ridden, geek/nerd chat up had had its effect and Tony and I had been picked by her majesty to stay the weekend at her parents place in Manchester. Tony & I had come to an arrangement. Whoever got lucky on the first night would allow a substitute on the second night, etc., etc...

Twenty years old and still a virgin, I was desperate.

I lost this semi-final as well.

Tony scored the winner on the first night (26th March) whilst I failed to impregnate her defences on the second night. I sat on the edge of her bed. I looked at that body. I needed that body. I needed comfort sex. I needed someone to tell me that everything was going to be alright and that United would actually win a semi-final in my lifetime. It was never going to happen. Patricia's affection for me was not sexual. Far from it. She viewed me as her pet labrador. Tony 'romped' home to score each night after that until the final whistle 5 days later.

On the Saturday I saw the Bitters beat us once again, this time in the league, 2-1 at Old Trafford, then 2 days later I saw the Reds in a dismal 1-1 draw at home to lowly Coventry.

On the coach all the way back to London Tony & Patricia (my Patricia – for Eric's's sake. I had been the only one with the nerve to talk to her the first time I saw her standing there. It should have been me!!!) were kissing and cuddling in the back seat. Yuch!

The lowest points were getting lower all the time.

1970/71. Losing to a fucking third division Aston Villa over two legs, with that dirty, bald bastard, Andy Lockhead scoring the winner in front of "the faithful few" at Villa Park. Then travelling back to London with broken windows and no heating on the coach. Brilliant! Paying your dues never felt so bad.

1974/75. Norwich City. Ted McFucking Dougal. Say no more. 2-2 at Old Trafford in a game we should have won easily.

Defining moments.

On the train from Liverpool Street station on route to Norwich for the formality of strangling the Canaries in the second leg and taking our rightful place at Wembley I remember a gang of United youths, only between 12-14 years old at most, giving it large. Everyone was up for it. Everyone was talking about the final. Joe Lewis and myself just looked coolly (we hoped) and dispassionately at them and thought "Oh, the innocence of youth."

On the returning train, after a fucking Graham Leggett 1-0 defeat, these same youths looked like they had fallen into the abyss. They couldn't work out why Joe and I looked so..."normal". On the inside, Joe and I had died a little more that night, but 18 years and 11 (yes, ELEVEN losing semi-finals) does something to a man.

The sun came up the following morning. Birds still sang in the trees. Bills kept landing on the mat by the front door. As illogical as it seemed, life went on, as though there was a meaning to it all, even at its darkest moments.

1975/76. And so it came to pass. Saturday 3rd April 1976. Derby at that most treacherous of grounds, Hillsborough. Once Gordon Hill scored in the 11th minute I saw the rest of the match behind a vale of tears. I knew, I just knew, that this time it would be different. What a wonderful day. What a wonderful ground. What a wonderful world. (hang on a minute, I feel a song coming on.)

What a trip back to London in the (now) obligatory 12 seater minibus. One of my greatest days. Forget the final. After following the Reds for 18 years and travelling home and away for nine solid years, just to be able to walk up Wembley Way supporting Manchester United and not watching "other" teams and their supporters enjoying the "day of days". I'll never forget it.

And anyway, the Scummers goal WAS offside!

And you know what children? We went on to win   (yes, ++++++++ winning semi-finals). Leeds in 1976/77, Liverpool in 1978/79, Arsenal in 1982/83, Liverpool in 1984/85, Oldham in 1989/90, Leeds and Legia Warsaw in 1990/91, Middlesborough in 1991/92, Sheffield Wednesday in 1993/94, Chelsea in 1995/96, Arsenal and Juventus in 1998/99. The only blatts on the landscape were Juventus in 1983/84, Borussia Dortmund in 1996/97, Bayern Laverkusen in 2001/2003, Chelsea in 2003/2004 (League Cup) and Milan in 2006/2007 (ouch – still painful).

Eric, they hurt but now I am older, wiser and uglier (if that were possible) and have come to terms with my lot. Not that the pain is any less but at least I can "always look on the bright side of life". Sorry, I don't want to talk about it.

20

RUPERT MURDOCH
– MY PART IN HIS DOWNFALL

JUST LIKE certain other parts of my anatomy, very little.

Living one hundred and eighty miles from the Republic of Mancunia my contribution was peripheral, but in my own mind worthy of a footnote in the anaulds of history. For the truth, the whole truth and nothing but the truth you should all read, whatever club you support, "Not For Sale" by Andy Walsh and Adam Brown. It's an inspiration for every football fan in the country when your club is confronted by the big green eyed monster and everybody is telling you, "There's nothing you can do." I know as a united fan I shall be grateful, until the day I die or City win a trophy, to Andy, Adam and everybody else who sacrificed careers and relationships to keep United independent. (Obviously I wrote this prior to the Glazer takeover, but that should in no way detract one iota from their achievements.)

The morning the story broke that the Board of Directors at Manchester United had accepted a bid from Rupert Murdoch spoke volumes about the state of the British national press. My immediate response to the first headline was a blood curdling, deep throated, "NOOOOOOOOOOOOOOOO!!!!!!!!", reminiscent of the voice of a monster at the end of a horror movie as it's slain by the good guy, and girl, who save the world from a fate worse than Boris Johnson.

I then questioned my own reaction. Why had I rejected the notion of Murdoch and his millions so instinctively and violently, almost inducing nausea and diced carrots? Wasn't the idea of a man worth millions, nay billions, investing a significant slice of his fortune in our club just the solution we craved after years of chairman 'Fartin' Martin Edwards forcing Sir Alex to delve into the transfer market with one arm and wallet behind his back?

NO!

I instinctively recoiled at the thought of the man himself, his morals and the way he conducted his businesses. Now though was not the time for considered analysis. That would develop over the coming days,weeks and months. No. Now was the time to panic.

I scanned the papers for comfort, hoping that the headline was just a typical exaggeration and that the body copy would represent a more balanced view. No such luck. My blood ran cold as I read The Sun (sorry, I didn't mean to swear) and its headline, "GOLD TRAFFORD". It opened by quoting figures with a lot of noughts on the end and then it bestowed all the benefits that MUFC PLC would accrue. To make matters worse, it then quoted people with links both strong and tenuous with Old Trafford, claiming what a wonderful offer it was. People who I had respected, and in some cases, adored, were all blinded by the darkness. Quotes attributed amounted to mutiny. Most of the institutions or powers that be, if they were not quoted as in agreement, were saying, "well, let's give it a go and see what happens."

I was stunned. But then the first glimmer of hope. I started to read some of the other dailies and, would you Adam and Eve it. The very same people who were waxing lyrical in the Sun were urging caution or even outright opposition to the bid.

How could this be? How can a person be quoted as saying one thing in one newspaper and the very same person be quoted as saying something completely different in another? Don't we believe everything we read in the newspapers? They wouldn't print it if it wasn't true, would they? Surely there are laws, ethics, morals, that sort of thing?

Silly me. I must stop taking swigs of that gripe water.

Then my brain began to clear as I read more versions of the same story. It wasn't a done deal. Being a PLC there were procedures. It still had to be put to shareholders and, hang on a minute, I'm a shareholder. Aha! A glimmer of hope, a piece of straw, a needle in a haystack (*OK, we get the point, Ed.*)

What to do? No idea. I'm not not in top management for nothing. It's moments like this that separate the men from the boys, the leaders from the pack, the wheat from the shaff (I'm warning you, Ed) Then fate took a hand.

The phone rang.

"Hello. Is that David?"

"Yes." (I knew the answer to that one)

"It's Sky News here. We'd like you to do a piece on Sky's takeover of Manchester United. Can you come to the studio?"

You know that moment when your life flashes before your eyes? No, of course not. You're still alive, or you wouldn't have bought this book. Silly question. But we've all heard about it, i.e. all the important\events in your life flash before you in a split second. Well, it happened to me at that moment. All the options hit me at the same time.

He said "take-over" not "proposed take-over". Did he know something I didn't or was he just repeating the Sky mantra?

As chairperson of the London branch of the FSA, the Football Supporters Association, and as a London based heart on my sleeve Manchester United fan and member of IMUSA, I had often been asked to put over our respective organisations' views in the media on the issues of the day. Considered responses were normally the responsibility of the relevant National Committee and the elected spokesperson, but there were sometimes occasions where we had to strike when the topic was hot so as to gain maximum impact and exposure for our message. As we are all non-paid volunteers working for something we love and believe in, over and above our normal jobs, getting everyone together, as is written in our constitutions, in time to agree a response was not always possible. So I have to admit I became a bit of a maverick at times, when I judged the moment would be lost if we didn't contribute to the debate when, in the words of American students in Ohio, "The Whole World's Watching."

Also, IMUSA is based in Manchester (that's another myth exposed then) whilst the FSA, which represents football fans from all over the country and at all levels of the professional, semi professional and amateur game, has it's headquarters in Liverpool. It sometimes annoyed the FSA's National Committee that someone from London would represent their views, only the fact remains, whether we like it or not, that the majority of the national media are based in London. If they want someone to come to their studios in London then a London based representative was the best placed individual. In my book (no, not this one. I was talking figuratively.

Some people) the cause was more important than the individual. As long as we all read from the same program notes, where's the problem?

In this case, and at this time, I didn't know anyone personally from IMUSA to contact and ask permission, plus I was convinced they would have their throats full with all the media based in Eric's own country.

Did I have the time? I had to go to work. Fortunately at this time I was running my own small promotional gift company, so the only person I had to ask for permission to skive off work was me. And I always said "Yes." (Wouldn't you like to work for me? I know I would.)

What to say? This was the most important question. I may be a media groupie but only for the cause. There was no point in going on TV, radio or being quoted in the press if the arguments were not coherent and in line with our organisations' policies. It's so easy to be shot down in flames and be made to look a fool if you're not properly prepared. As some American sales evangelist once proclaimed..."If you fail to prepare, be prepared to fail."

Sound advice. But this time I ignored it. My instincts were that the story was so big and its impact on, not only Manchester United but on the whole of football in this country was so great that fans, especially United fans, had to be seen in the beginning as a key players. Manchester United was our club. Our religion. Our life. Owners, directors, they were just temporary custodians as long as there was money to be made. We were in it for life.

So I said, "Yes".

They would send a car for me in about thirty minutes and I would be on air soon after I arrived at their studios in Isleworth.

Panic. I switched on the TV and channel hopped. I picked up on a number of arguments and noted them down.

"Murdoch. Hardly kept a promise in his business life. Rode roughshod over many agreements or conditions laid down. Tick.

Sacked the editor of the Sunday Times after one year, even though he said he would never interfere with editorial policy. Tick.

United generate profits of approximately one million pounds from every home game whereas Murdoch's empire had (at that time) debts and liabilities of thirteen billion US dollars. What was to stop him asset stripping our profitable club in order to prop up some of his ailing businesses? Tick."

I scanned the papers as I was whisked along the A40. Not in one was there a direct quote from Murdoch or his cronies committing any funds whatsoever directly to the club. More ammunition. Then my mobile rang again.

"Hello David. BBC News 24 here. Can you come in and do an interview?"

"I'd love to, but Sky got me first. I'm actually in a mini-cab on the way to their studios as we speak."

"Dam. I mean sorry. Look, can you come to our studios when you've finished at Sky?"

Thinks. I had work to go to. Clients whose deadlines were yesterday. Suppliers who were not supplying. Clients who were not paying. Suppliers who wanted paying. On the other hand, in the words of John F. Kennedy:

"Ask not what Manchester United can do for you, but what can you do for Manchester United."

No contest.

"Certainly. I'll give you a ring when I've finished my interview. Meanwhile can you sort out with Sky who picks me up."

Wow. This was even bigger than my overdraft. I instinctually felt like Jack from Jack and the Beanstalk. I was at the foot of a ladder that stretched up beyond my vision and there was a monster over the horizon to be fought and defeated.

I composed myself. Went to make up. I feel sorry for these women. I mean, how can they improve on perfection? Must be a soul destroying job when someone like me walks into their windowless world.

At the right moment I was escorted to my seat and told not to utter a word as they were still on air. I shook hands with the two presenters and took deep breaths. Don't move, as this is exaggerated on TV. Keep smiling. Warn of hell and damnation but offer a haven of solutions. Remember, the fans way is the right way.

The interview went quite well. I got most of my points across. I felt pleased and relieved. The questions helped crystallize my thoughts. I'd learnt that no matter what angle the questions were presented, begin by agreeing (no-one likes an argumentative sod) but then suggest improvements or alternatives. Always look on the bright side of life.

When I'd finished I waited on the main journalist floor of Sky studios for my cab with everyone beavering away; One of the other presenters who I got on quite well with came over and said, "You know you've got no chance, don't you? What can you really do against an organisation such as ours. I'm not saying the bid is a good or bad thing, I'm just saying that it's inevitable."

For a moment I was taken aback. He's right. What was I doing here? I must have been stupid to think we had a chance against such a well oiled (well, oily) machine that takes no prisoners. I came up with a half-hearted attempt at bravado but looking around me at Dark Vader's throbbing empire my superficial confidence visibly shrunk.

On the way back to the BBC in White City I made some more notes. Re-reading them restored my belief. Surely Eric was on the side of good and not evil. Where was Gandolf when you needed him?

I was greeted at reception by one of the researchers and taken upstairs. I still had my original make-up on so I was taken straight to the studio. Five minutes later it was all over and I was waiting in the reception for my cab when who did I spot but BBC reporter and United statistician, Michael Crick.

Now Hélène has always complained that I am an anorak, but that's only because I know more about football than she does that it makes me in an anorak in her eyes. But then my daughter's dog, Holly, knows more about football than my wife. On the other hand, if you want to meet the king of the United anoraks, then may I introduce Michael Crick. And I mean that in the best possible taste (a la Kenny Everett). The depth of his United knowledge is awesome and he has published a number of books to prove it.

What was he doing here? He'd just done an interview on BBC 1, which is like playing at Old Trafford whilst my interview for BBC News 24 was like playing at Bury with the reserves. But that was only right and proper considering Michael's knowledge and connections.

We agreed to share a taxi to our next respective interviews. We swapped info and agreed priorities. The ball was beginning to roll and gain momentum, and it was still only half past ten in the morning on Day One.

I tried to keep calm and focussed but I had a premonition that I was getting involved in something bigger than any of us could envisage. We felt such anger and passion that something had to be done. But what?

In the days to come I read all the papers and the Internet, which was to prove a pivotal role in "Uniting", not just United fans but fans from clubs big and small across the land, in actions against the Dark Lord. We became Lords of the Webrings.

Independent United shareholders were invited to join a new organisation, SUAM, Shareholders United Against Murdoch. David was up and running against Goliath. As events were unfolding in Manchester of which I knew little I continued to do as many interviews as possible to spread the word. To keep occupied made me feel better. I was doing something for the cause, though if I was honest with myself, deep down I didn't give us much hope of somehow overcoming the menace from the depths of Mount Doom in the land of Sauron in Modor, i.e. Canary Wharf.

The media were indignant that at our first home game there weren't thousands of United fans with banners and funny costumes demonstrating inside and outside Old Trafford. When their battery of news cameras realised there was little for them to film they took their frustrations out on us. They claimed we were aquiescent . We had rolled over and died. The powers that be had nothing to fear from the silent majority.

Sorry guys. We weren't doing it for you. Fans were doing it for themselves. Championships are won and lost as a marathon not a sprint. We should know. The time to be at the top is at the end of a campaign, not the beginning. To quote The Carpenters (and I wish I didn't have to) "We'd Only Just Begun."

The next event I got involved in was a Fans Day at the Houses of Parliament. SUAM had entered an EDM, early day motion, on the Houses of Parliament web site and a record number of MP's had already signed. SUAM then booked a room and invited politicians from all parties to hear our case against the takeover. My heart soared as I entered the room. Representatives from clubs up and down the land were standing (OK, sitting if I must be pedantic) side by side. Even the most ABU was supporting us on this issue. Now I'm much happier to quote Sham '69,

"If the fans are United, they can never be divided." Phew. That's better.

Speaker after speaker echoed our sentiments. It was an inspiring event. Outside the media were snapping away. BBC Radio 5 Live came over and asked Mark Longden from IMUSA and me for interviews. Marc Longden, also a committee member of the Football Supporters Federation, is, along with Kevin Miles, Newcastle fan and another FSF committee member, one of the best public speakers there is. He knows when to be funny, when to be rude and when to be serious. He doesn't suffer fools gladly and unfortunately in football club and FA administration we have quite a few. His ability to hit home with the killer remark is legendary.

Only for the one and only time before and since, I matched him. On the green opposite the Houses of Parliament, in the pouring rain the interviewer went from one to the other, only I hadn't spoken at the Fans Day and all my facts and figures came tumbling out. Even if I say so myself I spoke with the perfect balance of passion, venom and humour to get our points across. I was on a roll. I waffled on yet just like that famous radio quiz game, "Just a Minute", there was no hesitation, repetition or farting. A perfect delivery.

I don't know how long I spoke for, and considering I've got a memory of a goldfish, it was a miracle I remembered all the facts and figures. I only came up for air once I stopped speaking, which gave the interviewer a chance to say "Thank you" and "Goodbye". Mark and I wished each other good luck and a job well done and went our separate ways. Him back to Manchester and me back to work.

On my way back home (I worked from home. George of both worlds) I began to come down from the high of socking it to 'em, big time. The interview we had just done was recorded, to be broadcast later that afternoon. Shit. That meant they would almost certainly cut down my ranting to a few soundbites, and who knows what bits they would choose. Yet when I got home Hélène said that she had heard me on the radio and I came over very well.

What's this? My wife complimenting me on something to do with football. Hold the front page. However it also meant that I'd missed it and didn't know what points they had broadcast. Asking Hélène was not an option, so I went upstairs to work and took BBC Radio 5 Live with me.

I must admit I didn't do much work that afternoon as I was on the hearout in case they repeated the interview. Then on the hour they did. And Lord have mercy on my red and white soul, they repeated the entire interview. It was like kareoke. I was able to mouth along to my own words, so well had I rehearsed the arguments. Sad or what?

David 1 Goliath 0

Soon it was time to prepare for the Manchester United AGM. Now, we can all "F and Blind" to our mates in the pub about who we'd buy, who we'd sack and what we'd do if we ran our football club. With egos suppressed for the greater good of the club we adore, I'm sure in lots of cases we'd actually do a better job. In fact, for any fan of a club listed on the stock exchange who hasn't already done so, I implore you to buy a share. That's all you need to go to the AGM and say what you feel directly to the people who run your club. They take our money then wish we'd run away. In the overwhelming number of clubs, money generated by the fans, either through the turnstiles or from other outlets is their largest single source of revenue and the very least they could do is listen to what we have to say. Is that too much too ask? Obviously for some big fish Chairmen in small ponds it is, as fans tend to ask pointed questions that they'd rather not answer. And more recently, May 2000 to be exact, in a rare case of Government insight, the Supporters Direct movement was created. A government initiative, funded by public money, with offices in London and Glasgow, its aim is to help people "who wish to play a responsible part in the life of the football club they support" and offers support, advice and information to groups of football supporters. All models used and recommended are democratic, mutual and not-for-profit principles. So that means every fan of every club can get involved. So don't just read this. Do it.

Meanwhile, as I was saying, the United AGM was soon to be upon us, and it was to provide a significant backdrop and fillip to our campaign. SUAM and IMUSA asked for volunteers on the day. A number of us agreed to distribute leaflets on the forecourt of Old

Trafford outside the entrance to the AGM. With an hour to go we took up our places, only there were more media outside than shareholders, although this gave us ample opportunities to put over our objectives for the meeting.

As the bewitching hour approached, club officials and security staff became more agitated, until finally Ned Kelly, the now disgraced ex-SAS Head of Security confronted the now sadly deceased and dearly missed Richard Brierly and myself and informed us that he had been asked to stop us distributing leaflets and to get off club premises. When Richard asked him politely who had given him these instructions he said it came from the top.

"Oh, so it was from Sir Roland Smith then.

"Errr...no."

"Oh, so you mean Martin Edwards?"

"Errr...no."

"So, was it Maurice Watkins?"

"Errr...no."

As Richard provided a roll call of the United Board of Directors the waiting media got a sniff that "something was up" and came rushing over, snapping and thrusting microphones up various orifices. Some welcome. Some not. But significantly it only helped double the embarrassment Ned Kelly found himself in as his "instructions" were shown to be bogus, and in front of the national media to boot.

He did an about turn and disappeared back inside, to leave Richard and myself with an Eric given opportunity to exploit the clubs ham-fisted attempt to suppress the legitimate and democratic right of "ordinary shareholders" to voice their opinions.

David 2 Goliath 0

Needless to say the AGM was packed to the rafters with shareholders and a hell of a lot more media than usual. Here we were about to face captains of industry, international power brokers extrodinaire, wheelers and dealers at the highest echelons of business and government. Oh, and Martin Edwards.

No contest.

We wiped the floor with them. I couldn't believe how unprepared the entire Board seemed to be for our onslaught. Instead of swatting our arguments like flies, they "hummed" and "harred" and lost the public relations battle by a landslide. It was exhilarating in the extreme. OK. It wasn't of Berlin Wall proportions and we knew in advance that they held an overwhelming number of shares, but we came to give them a bloody nose and to think long and hard about the risks and folly of going to bed with Murdoch and we succeeded far beyond our expectations.

The following day's newspapers further enhanced not only our arguments and our reputation but perhaps the first time the strength and power of our initiative dented Fleet Street almost 100% belief that it was a "done deal" and that we were powerless to stop it. We had sown the first seeds of doubt in the "Establishment" and from that little acorn in the months to follow we were to grow into an almighty, unstoppable tree.

Football fans of all persuasions came to our aid. Highly qualified individuals and organisations offered their invaluable expertise mostly free of charge. There are times when Anglo-Saxon terrace talk is the most effective weapon, but not for example when you present to the Mergers & Monopolies Commission.

Documents were prepared and arguments rehearsed that would stand up to the most intense cross-examination. I was not involved in any of this, I am just so proud and grateful to everyone involved who sacrificed so much that the club we all live and breathe for could remain independent. United for United.

A few weeks later I was working at home with the radio on in the background when there was a newsflash. There was to be an announcement from Stephen Byers, then Minister of Trade and Industry, now much maligned but at this moment in time a colossus of balance and reason.

"Blah, blah, blah, blah.........the Government has decided not to allow News International to proceed with their proposed take over of Manchester United."

"YEEEEEEEEEEEAAAAAAAAAAAAAAH!!!!!"

"We done it. We fucking well done it. I don't believe it. We done it. Fucking marvelous."

I switched on the TV and there was SUAM's Oliver Holt doing a monkey dance in front of OT. Everybody was ecstatic yet magnanimous in victory. Despite the mountain we'd had to climb this was the time to build bridges. Supporters had shown that we wouldn't be pushed around like a creative accountant's balance sheet. We had conducted ourselves with passion and constraint, anger and compassion. We proved that we were a force to be reckoned with. From this day forward the club would have to consult with us, liaise with us, involve us in their discussions.

OK, to begin with perhaps only on a superficial, PR level, but it was a start. Very soon afterwards the Board through Peter Kenyon agreed to meet with us three or four times a year to hear our concerns and suggestions and to communicate the Boards position. Words have been spoken louder than action but we continue to communicate and that is the name of the game.

POSTSCRIPT

Forward to 2007. Cuddly Peter Kenyon left his "dream job – I've been a United fan all my life" and decamped to the Rent Boys down the Kings Road, taking with him the hopes and future plans of Ferguson and the board and destabilizing the Ronaldinho transfer (and who knows what else in the process). He was forced to take a six month garden leave, but that doesn't effect weeds, does it?

United have now devalued the importance of the Fans Forum, whilst at the same time excluding members of IMUSA and the Manchester United Supporters Trust, the only non "yes men" on the forum.

The club has been taken over by the Glazer family, real estate, sports management and fish oily people based in Tampa, Florida. Prices were increased 12% in 2006 and by a whopping 14% in 2007 with no additional benefits, whilst the hated, compulsory automatic cup ticket scheme has been introduced. With the multi-million pound injection of cash from TV companies, almost every other club in the Premiership has frozen their prices, whilst some such as Blackburn and Wigan, who admittedly rarely sell out, have even reduced their prices.

Many observers have concluded that Premiership clubs could afford to let all their supporters in for free this year and still make the same amount of money as last year. So what do the Glazers do? Continue to make us pay for their increasing debts. Meanwhile, as Nick Towle, chairman of the Manchester United Supporters Trust wrote, "The money for transfers does not come from the Glazers. It comes from the club's own funds. The Glazers have not put a penny of their own money into the team and never will. All funds for the team and even the Glazers to acquire United has been borrowed by the club itself at vast cost to it (£62m paid out in interest alone, confirmed by the Glazers' own spokesperson).

So, who pays for these transfers? Why, the fans of course.

The official view is that United ticket prices "still represent good value for money" and this is true up to a point compared with Chelsea, Arsenal and Tottenham, yet the fact remains that thousands of life-long United supporters have simple been priced out

and denied access to their greatest love, only to be replaced by day trippers who sit on their hands and wait to be entertained. In my opinion this is tantamount to first-degree murder.

As Stuart Brennan wrote recently in the Manchester Evening News, "...and if, and when, the football boom starts to grind to a halt as the yuppies find a new craze, it is to the traditional support to whom United will turn, only to find that they have discovered the joys of F C United, bird-watching or DIY".

A response to recent events prompted a former United ticket office employee to write, "...Old Trafford no longer cares in the slightest about supporters, the only people they care about are their precious executive members." Every day, on United internet fans' message boards there are stories of terrible customer service, endless waiting in the ticket office, endless waiting on the phones, internet not working, cup scheme hasn't worked either, etc...etc...

One thing that is truly certain is that the Manchester United we all grew up with and loved is gone. Corporate culture now pervades every corridor and the quicker we come to terms with reality the better. "If you can't stand the heat, get out of the kitchen" I hear some of you say. True, there's no stopping progress, and "you've got to be in it to win it", but something inside me has died.

I'm lucky. I have my great memories, individual pictures in my mind, and there's nothing the Glazers can do about that!

21

TO THE RED DEVIL – A DAUGHTER

SOME OF YOU MAY have wondered, with a surname like "Blatt" and my Frank Spencer attempts to surmount life's little obstacles, if I could possibly be related to MELANIE BLATT, lead singer and soul songbird with the coolest all-girl band of the late '90s, "ALL SAINTS", and currently co-presenting "The Hot Desk" on ITV Mobile, together with her best friend, Nicole Appleton. Those of you who witnessed their memorable contribution as one set of Big Brothers on the Celebrity Highjack series will testify to the added value champagne made to their wonderful personalities. But don't think she's just limited to the benefits of the liquid lunch. Winning Gordon Ramsey's, The "F" Word, together with Nicole and my wife, Helene and Nic's mother, Mary, shows she knows the way to a man's stomach is through his stomach.

Certainly those of you who have heard me sing and chant will know that even when overwhelmed by thousands of Reds in full voice, my out of tune cats chorus still offends the most insensitive earlobes.

So it may come as a bit of a shock to you, dear reader, when I reveal my true status as... her Father! Don't worry. You are not alone. I am under no illusion as to the state of my voice. So much so that for the past thirty three years I have been trying to trace both the milkman and postman who regularly "serviced" the Blatt abode when I was out at work in June 1975.

Like many United fans I have reason to condemn and detest the distortions and downright lies printed in the tabloid press, especially the red tops. As close family to a "personality" it's a double whammy, as I have witnessed first hand the pain and distress they can inflict on innocent people, their friends and family. And unless you have the wealth and influence of an Elton John or a Sean Connery you are powerless to stop them.

But now revenge is mine. Forget the Daily Scums. If it's scandal you want, look no further. I will reveal all the sordid details that lead my eldest daughter announcing on both national TV and Smash Hits magazine that she is...... a United fan!

Why now you ask? After keeping a Cosa Nostra silence all these years, why should a father sell his own flesh and blood down the river? Not for a pot of gold, I can tell you. Not even a pot noodle. No, I want to get one over on the tabloid trash.

Remember you read it first here.

In the 1970s I was in lust with the American flower child, singer songwriter, Melanie. (Lay Down, Ruby Tuesday, Brand New Bicycle, etc... Before I lose all street cred, just listen to her early albums on Buddah Records before you pass judgement) Hence the name of my first daughter.

Don't forget, this was an era when being a BOF – Boring Old Fart, was cool. Et je ne regret rien. There was a time in the late 60s and early/mid 70s when no matter how great an album was on labels such as Vertigo, Chrysalis, Electra, Atlantic and Capricorn, when you saw a band live the extra dimension would blow you away. The power and musicianship had to be experienced to be believed. For example, many daughters from the "love generation" ended up with names like Melissa and Jessica thanks to beautiful, soaring instrumentals by the Allman Brothers Band.

Just to balance things out, and in order to (almost) re-gain the moral high ground, for years I had imagined having a boy and calling him Matthew. Named after one of the greatest human beings ever to walk on this planet, Sir Matt Busby, Matthew Blatt has a certain ring about it. Strong, modern yet traditional and not too common, I thought I'd cracked it – until it dawned on me that I would have created...wait for it...Matt Blatt.

Can you imagine the reaction of other children once they became old enough and discovered sarcasm, cynicism, piss taking, cruelty, etc...

"Fat Matt Blatt", "Fatty Matty Blatty", "What's the Matty Blatty?"

With crushing realism I realised I would never be able to call a son of mine, Matthew.

And you think you've got problems?

However, the Eric in the sky decreed that I would never have to face this dilemma, as my second child also turned out to be a girl.

I would like the world to know that my second daughter should have been called Rhiannon, as by now I was in lust with Stevie Nicks from Fleetwood Mac. However my wife, Hélène, and daughter Melanie both ganged up on me and Jasmine came into the world eleven years later, with Rhianna following as her middle name. Yes, girl power had been born years before those hideous Spice Girls.

Now, like all sensible Dads to be I bought Melanie United babygrows, United bobble hat, United bib, etc...even before she was born. Yes, I was 25 and she was minus zero. Boy or girl? Made no difference. He/she/ it would be a Red. From the moment she was born I would sing nursery rhymes with the words changed to accommodate the United song book.

"REDUCATION"

And then the golden moment came. December 1976. Melanie's first game at the Theatre of Dreams at the ripe old age of one year and one month. Dressed from head to squelchy bottom in the above mentioned Red attire, and with me feeling as proud as punch, my wife and I introduced our daughter to the next stage in her "Reducation". Not that it was all plain sailing. Oh no. Let's call it "bitter sweet". For a start this was my first home game in eleven years that I didn't stand on the Stretford End. Withdrawal symptoms were acute as I battled, Gandalf like with the forces of darkness, against the calm and safe haven of the Cantilever Stand. I made my way to the corner flag so as to be as close as possible to the "action". A policemen took pity on me and let me sit my daughter on one of the benches that surrounded the pitch. However he made it clear that once the match started we would have to hold her in our arms.

I remember welling up as I absorbed the look of wonder and pure joy on Melanie's baby face, her eyes bright with excitement, as she recognised her favourite nursery rhymes sung by 15,000 Stretford Enders. Fortunately, lyrics such as "You're gonna get your fuckin' heads kicked-in" and "You're going home in a body bag" sailed over her sweet head as 15,000 arms swung red & white striped scarves round and round in time to the rhythm.

CONFLICT OF INTEREST

Women have no idea, do they? As a single or married man with mates it's "de rigeur" to gesticulate in an over the top manner at every move by our team or their's, every decision by the referee and every ditty sang by the opposing teams' supporters. Some people prefer passive relief from everyday tensions, for example yoga, Buddhism or wanking. Whilst not dissing the benefits of one or indeed all of the above, for me Saturday afternoons at 3pm (older readers will remember those days) meant letting it all hang out before, during and after each match.

Obviously I preferred to win, but win, lose or draw I would come out of the stadium exorcised. All the frustration which had built up during the week, from suppliers letting me down to clients not paying their bills, from delays on the underground to girlfriends/wife refusing to give me my just desserts would explode in a frenzy of songs, chants, swearing and posturing. It was wonderful. And if we scored. Orgasm. I've said it before and I'll say it again. There isn't a feeling on Earth to match it. (Just ask any striker who retired too early and fell into a downward spiral of booze, drugs and failed businesses. Ask them what they missed the most and they all say "scoring".)

So there I was, by the corner of Cantilever and Stretford, holding onto my most precious possession, my new baby daughter, and holding in my most basic Red emotions that had been allowed to run riot for eleven years. They don't prepare you for this at antifucking natal clinic.

And you know what made it worse? We were torn apart that afternoon, 0-4, by a rampant Nottingham Forest, that picked us off like flies on their way to the league title. I couldn't swear, I couldn't jump up and down, I couldn't throw Melanie in the air or at the referee. All I could do was cry inside and smile on the outside, for the sake of my daughter and my marriage.

Talk about Rage Against The Machine. Driving all the way back home my inner torment was compounded by my wife telling me to "grow up", "slow down", "stop swearing", etc, etc...

Women. They have no idea, do they? They just give birth to babies. We have to walk the tightrope between team and toddler.

THE PIED PIPER

Melanie is now eight years old and attending Fitzjohn's Primary School in Hampstead. A lovely school in a lovely area. We are very lucky and so is

Melanie. She has a great set of school friends who often invade our apartment and an enthusiastic music teacher who builds on the foundations that I laid down from birth. You see, from the moment she was born there was always music in the house. Not just me singing United songs in the bath or shower, the hills were alive with the sound of music. Led Zeppelin, Pink Floyd, Bob Dylan, Rory Gallagher, Family, Status Quo, King Crimson, Fairport Convention, Yes, Allman Brothers, Black Sabbath, Eric Clapton, Jethro Tull, Stackridge, Bruce Springsteen, Focus, Derek & Clive...I could go on, believe me, I could go on.

However, there was a blatt on the landscape. Melanie's school mates, especially the boys, were into football but their parents were not. In the land of pre-Tony's cronies, football was not high on the agenda for the Hampstead set. So I extended my Reducational mission with true evangelical zeal.

Melanie was now a Red, even if she didn't realise it. If anyone asked her what her favourite football team was she would reply, "Manchester United" as if on automatic pilot. Subliminal brainwashing – works every time. Now to work on her chums.

This proved a more difficult task as most of them swore allegiance to Arsenal even though they had never seen them play live. I had to try and explain to them that there was no point in seeing Arsenal live because the Highbury Library would put them to sleep. They would listen with awe (well, that's my interpretation of theirexpressions) as

I regaled stories of the glories of watching Matt Busby's Aces play on our hallowed turf.

A constant bombardment of respective parents lead to these little cherubs being allowed to accompany Melanie and me to Old Trafford. However, I did tell their parents a little red & white lie. For most matches, home and away, I would book a 12 seater mini-bus and these parents assumed their precious cargo would be transported to the centre of the earth and back in this customary tranquil fashion.

However, the kids knew I owned a black VW Transporter that I used to collect and deliver T-Shirts, and they also knew that my wife Hélène, Melanie and assorted friends would travel to Glastonbury and other festivals in the back, protected from sore bottoms by the strategical placing of a mattress on the floor of the van.

They all preferred the freedom of this as opposed to the rigidity of fixed seats and seat belts. And so these kids threw off their parental straight jackets and for four glorious, carefree hours on the way up and four more hours on the way back (my mood depended on the result, so if we lost I had a ready made audience to take it all out on. He he he) they jumped and bounced off the walls and screamed at decibels only kids at that age and Jimmy Somerville can do.

They got so hot and sweaty that they all but stripped off. Being a pretty open minded family these kids then received additional biology lessons that their parents had somehow left out.

Kids talk, don't they? Let off the leash, they told their parents EVERYTHING. The end result was that individually and collectively the parents put all the pieces of their little darlings stories together and came to the conclusion that the Blatts were leading their innocent little urchins astray, as opposed to creating fuller, more rounded young people with less hang-ups than them.

The end result was that Melanie's acutely embarrassed female form teacher had to take these kids aside and give them the complete "Facts of Life" spiel a full two years before the school curriculum claimed they would be ready.

A result don't you think?

SAINTS AND SINNERS

Fast forward to Melanie reaching her twenties. As you can imagine I have a million stories from the before, middle and end and rise again of All Saints, but as most of them are not United related so you won't find them here. But a couple of incidents stand out that deserve a mention.

All Saints first official live gig, i.e. voices plus band not just singing live over a DAT, was headlining the dance tent at V98. Let me just put on record that the girls sang live from the very beginning because they had beautiful voices, both individually and together. When singing harmonies they sent a shiver down my spine, whether in the studio or selling out Wembley Arena. Even in the beginning most of their promotional appearances were live because they could cut it.

However, like many major acts they performed a warm-up gig the night before their first headlining gig at the festival. The powers that be chose the

"LA", an old converted cinema in Tottenham Court Road in the West End of London during Gay Pride week. I'd never been to a gay club before. Not that that bothered me, I just wasn't sure what was expected of me, or what to wear. In the end I decided that if it's worth doing it's worth over-doing.

I found my tightest pair of jeans and my very special twenty three year old air-brushed T-shirt. Please bear with me on this one while I explain. When Melanie was three months old in 1975 I fucked off to the States for six weeks. Now you're all against me I'll enlarge on that statement. Having gotten pissed off after leaving school and spending the next eight years working my way up in advertising agencies I decided to pack it all in. My Dad wouldn't let me laze around the house all day so he persuaded me to join him driving for this up-market mini cab company in St. Johns Wood.

The first few weeks were hell on wheels. My performance wasn't so much trial and error so much as error and error. As a cocooned youth from Gants Hill traveling to work on the tube, my sole knowledge of the streets of London was from my parents' house to the City and West End or if I occasionally got lucky, from my parents house to my girlfriend's and back. To give you an idea of my efficiency my first pick-up was in Piccadilly and the passenger told me to go to Swiss Cottage.

"I've heard of that. It's on the brown line, isn't it?"

Needless to say I got better as time went on. Well, I couldn't have got worse, could I?

From a pure and clean driving license since I had passed my driving test in '69, in the four years on the road as a mini cab driver I had numerous little prangs. My luck finally changed in the spring of '75 when I got paid out by the insurance company for an accident that wasn't my fault. For the first time in my life I had a three figure lump sum.

I had a heart to heart with Hélène. We had been living together for three years and she was just about to give birth to our first child. We'd struggled to keep head above water living near Hampstead on my mini cab income, especially in the last seven and a half months after she had announced to her bosses that she was pregnant and had got the sack on the spot. Like you I'd be up in arms like a shot at the injustice and insensitivity of it all if it hadn't been for the fact that she had been working as a receptionist welcoming French women at a private abortion clinic in St

Johns Wood, and becoming pregnant wasn't possibly the best advertisement for the company's services.

She agreed with me that I should spend the money on a six week trip to North America in July and August with my best Red mate, Joe. Are you still against me? OK, the case for the defense. Like most of us I'd been brought up during my formative years saturated by Americana, especially on the TV and in the cinema, and at the age of twenty six this was my first opportunity to see for myself what all the fuss was about. To separate myth from fact. I needed to get it out of my system. Also, I wanted to do it without having to take care of someone, to take the safe, easy option. I wanted to go through places like Harlem and the Deep South with my long hair and white skin and gauge the reaction for myself.

Hélène said she understood. I hope you do to. To redress the balance we have been back to the States a number of times, both as a couple and as a family, but the first time I didn't want to compromise. What was it like? Maybe if someone's nice to me they'll commission another book but if I have to sum up the States in one sentence then let me just say that the good bits were very good and the bad bits were very bad.

With Melanie a delightful four months old, Joe and I flew to New York on our £99 return tickets. Wandering around the Big Apple for a couple of days before our adventure really began I passed this cooler than cool T- Shirt shop on 66th Street called the "TEE HEE HEE" shop.

I was mesmerized. The most awesome collection of T-shirts I had ever seen. And right in the middle of the window display was this multi-coloured, fully bleeding off, airbrushed outer-space design that just blew my mind.

"I gotta have it. I just gotta have it!"

There were no prices in the window so I went inside. I came out an older and wiser man.

Twenty five dollars. Twenty five fucking dollars. Remember, we're talking 1975 here. Twenty five dollars in those days was worth, well, twenty five dollars I suppose, but the point was I only had $200 to last the full entire six weeks so to blow over ten percent before we'd even began was out of the question.

But I just had to have that T-shirt.

"One day, you will be mine. I'll be back."

Six weeks later and on the morning of our return flight back to Blighty my feet drew me once again to 66th Street. A triumph of self denial and stubbornness. I purchased the said T-shirt and twenty three years later once again put on the, by now, smooth and shrunken, skin tight garment from the Gods. For a reason I can't recall Hélène didn't accompany Mick and me to the gig. I think she was in France otherwise I know for a fact that she would never have let me out of the house looking like THAT.

We queued up, chattering nervously, then we were in.

You know how it is in a normal club. Couples or groups on the dancefloor, Pockets of unattached boys and girls like buffaloes around the outside eyeing each other up.

"Will she? Won't she?"

Not in this place.

They were hanging off the walls from the moment we entered. We hadn't even taken off our jackets and there were Lionel Ritchies everywhere, dancing on the ceiling, the walls, the tables and, yes, even the dancefloor.

It was mad. It was brilliant.

The word "wallflower" had been eradicated from the dictionary. Everybody, and I mean, everybody, was up for it. Personally I wasn't up for "it" but I certainly wanted to let most of it hang out.

As we got our bearings I realised it was all boys in the stalls and all girls in the circle, not that there were any seats. Mick and I did a circuit downstairs. Passing the bar I heard a voice announce, "There's a couple of aging queens in here tonight." Obviously my T-shirt hadn't impressed them. We then went upstairs where 'The Management' had segregated a VIP area and we settled down to enjoy the show, all around us.

Mick was still a bit nervous but I thought the atmosphere was electric. So much so that I got up and began to have a little boogie of my own. Dead or Alive, The Communards, Jimmy Summerville, Gloria Gayner, Kylie, all the young and old dudes were played, very, very loud.

Then I noticed this pretty little thing making her way towards me. She was petite, with short, straight silver hair, a skintight top and a lovely face. She came right up to me.

"You're that FSA guy off the Tele, aren't you?

"Yeah. I suppose so. Wow."

"I'm a Middlesborough supporter myself, and I find I agree with virtually everything you say."

Blimey. She's gorgeous. She's chatting ME up, and we're talking FOOTBALL!"

Was this my ultimate fantasy about to come true? Well, no. After a few minutes her partner came up to us, kissed her passionately on the lips, whereby my new 'friend' disappeared back into the crowd with her lady friend. Never mind, three out of four's not bad.

I settled back in my seat. I was actually feeling pretty pleased with myself. As I've always maintained, football is the international language. Black, white, young, old, straight, gay, no matter who or what you are, football unites us all.

Then the lights went down and there was my daughter, Melanie, up there on stage, together with Shaznay, Natelie and her best friend from school, Nicole. Moments like that are special for Dads so allow me a little Kleenex tissue as the memories come flooding back. Melanie was also six months pregnant at this time and Lilyella was minus three months.

All too quickly the show was over and the lights and DJ came back on. We hung around until the girls finally appeared. I rushed towards Melanie to offer my congratulations when she suddenly froze in her tracks and looked at me with a disbelieving look of horror on her face. It read..."How the hell could you have left the house dressed like that. You're not my father. I don't know you."

My wife was a thousand miles away yet her influence still permeated proceedings.

I never learn, do I?

On Sunday Mick and I drove up to Chelmsford for the last day of V98. All Saints were headlining in the Dance Tent so we had plenty of time to play the large field, so to speak. Being a veteran of festivals since the late sixties, I felt like an elder statesman wandering around. I had the luxury of alternating between the VIP enclosure and the outside world, depending on the acts on stage and the weather.

Port Vale's finest was on top form, with a wicked band behind him. Sharleen's a lovely woman but I have to admit Texas's music was a little too bland for my taste. Where's the good old fashioned head banging, no nonsense, mindless boogie when you need it?

Night and rain fell so we made our way to the Dance Tent which was heaving, in a good way you understand.

Faithless were up on stage and they were brilliant, as always. My only objection with them is that they claimed God was a DJ, when we all know he was a certain Frenchman who graced our lives and the terrain of Old Trafford.

They went off to a rousing cheer and to the moment I had all been waiting for. We swayed and sweated in the heat. The crowd's excitement was visibly rising as the coolest girl band on the planet was about to take the stage. After two years of working practically twelve hours a day, seven days a week promoting their records around the world, would they be able to win over a hard core dance audience? I was just beginning to think that perhaps I was getting just a little too old for this sort of thing when the lights went down, the curtains went up and All Saints came on to the loudest roar I had heard outside football.

Melanie and Shazney wore special red T-shirts in support of the striking firemen. Good girls, I'm proud of you.

Keeping it real, as always.

I frolicked with the best of them as the girls gave their all. The doubters were swept away. The girls' voices soared and I burst with pride. But enough of this gushing. Anyone would think I'm biased.

There was no way Mick and I could have made our way back stage to the inner sanctum so we made our way out of the tent and back into the pouring rain. In the blackness I had no idea where I had left the car so we spent a lot of squelching time wandering around the fields of Essex before finally locating our vehicle. My pace picked up as I spotted it. At that very same moment we heard a car horn right behind us and there were the girls and the band in their people carrier. We went over, waving and attempting to kiss all the right people. Unfortunately we were freezing cold and wet and they were hot and dry, so we were kept at arms length with waving and shouting incoherently at each other. I thought I made out "See you at home, Daddy" but I couldn't be sure.

Mick and I finally got into our car then stayed where we were for the next hour as not one car moved. Once we finally started moving, we crawled along the channels of mud towards what turned out to be a single exit for thousands of cars. Now I realised why these particular festivals are called 'V'this and 'V'that. All the cars in the car park have to drive to the apex, or 'V' of the field to get out. We were still in the field when my mobile rang.

It was Melanie.

"Hi, Dad. Where are you? We're at home. How long will you be?"

"We're still in the same field near Chelmsford in Essex."

Kids can be so cruel. All I could hear on the other end of the line was laughter.

Well, at least I had made her happy, so I was happy too.

22

NINETEEN NINETY NINE

MILAN AWAY – FAKING IT

I BET PRINCE NEVER realised the significance of "1999" when he wrote that song all those years ago.

Scoring twenty goals in the preliminary league section of the Champions League, United had secured their place once again in the knock-out stages.

When we drew Inter Milan in the quarter finals of the Champions League their players started giving it large.

"We know how United play. They're so predictable. Stop those crosses from Beckham and you stop United scoring".

So that's it then. No need for us to turn up.

Are you pasta a larf? You can recognize brilliance. You can acknowledge brilliance. But that doesn't necessarily mean you can do anything about it. We tore them apart in the first leg at Old Trafford, leading 2-0 at half-time and running out comfortable winners. You'll never guess how we scored our second goal. Yes, that's right. Cross from Becks and Yorkie's head did the rest. Belisimo.

For the away leg Jeff, an old friend of mine who runs a travel agency in the city of London, had reserved a number of seats on a flight to Milan for a reasonable £75 return. He also claimed my United mate Mick and I should be alright for tickets as one of his best clients, a city bigwig, Dave Van Small was a reliable supplier of tickets even in the most over subscribed of circumstances. As the days went by no ticket became forthcoming but I was constantly assured he wouldn't let us down.

On the morning of the game Mick and I took the train from Liverpool Street to Stanstead Airport. Once through the formalities of embarkation we met up with Jeff and what looked more like business clients than United fans, but I'm nothing if not flexible and so an intelligent discussion ensued as to what was in store for us that day/night and its possible outcome. Still no tickets but the plan was now to meet up in the hotel reception once we arrived in Milan and everyone would be taken care of.

Hmmm. By this time I had misgivings (but she didn't have me. Boom, boom.)

We were outnumbered in the departure lounge by over a hundred Chelsea fans on route to a UEFA tie in Norway. Time for some friendly banter I thought. I can't remember my exact words but they were something along the lines of...

"Hi. How you doing? Think you got a chance tonight?"

"Ugghhh." came the caveman response.

My friend Jeff attempted another greeting.

"I fuckin' hate United".

Hmmm. We looked around. Yup. Definitely full of pre-"Planet of the Apes" species here. More the pre-linguistic, opening sequence "2001 – A Space Oddity" variety.

A bit of rapid mental arithmetic was called for. Five of us, A hundred of them. We drink – no talk – catch flight.

I'm sorry. What a bunch of tossers. And I'm not talking about an isolated few. The majority of them were at the wrong end of the evolution chain. I know every club's got them but it still pisses me off that these guys feel the only way to show allegiance to their club and their white race is violent anti this and violent anti that. At least some of them with mothers love them.

Our plane seemed full of Irish Reds so the much sought after friendly banter previously mentioned was underway in earnest. In two hours Mick and I were all soul mates with them all but still no tickets. Once we landed Jeff blurted out the name of the hotel where we were all to meet up then disappeared puffing over the horizon after his clients before I could sufficiently take notes. Thanks 'mate'.

Being on a tight budget and not a company trinket, Mick and I worked out which bus to take to the centre. More by luck than judgement we found the said hotel about an hour later. Converging in the hotel lobby, Jeff explained that we were waiting for his contact to arrive but, wait for it......there may be a problem with tickets. Now there's a surprise – not.

"I can guarantee one spare but not two", he exclaimed.

We waited. We shuffled. We shuffled. We waited. We.........Oh, fuck it! It was now gone 5 'o clock and still nothing. Mick and I decided we stood a better chance outside the stadium so we made our excuses and left.

We walked to the nearest underground station and thus we arrived outside the magnificent San Siro spaceship.

Wow! Four giant silver circular cheese graters in each corner connecting the four outside walls. It looked just like the sandcastles I used to make on the beach, only bigger.

Reds at the top of the underground steps warned us to keep our heads down as there had been a lot of trouble an hour back. All the police had done was to aid the Inter fans in their attempts to eradicate United fans from Italian soil in as many pieces as possible.

"Nothings changes", I thought.

Hmmm. Time for a rant me thinks.

For almost fifty years United fans have been following their team in Europe. We are far and away the best behaved fans in England for supporting our team abroad but you'd never hear about this in the media. To us, European aways are like the Holy Grail. It's the reason United fans were put on this planet and 99.9% (f0.1% e.g. fat, pissed Yorkshire Red who threw that bottle in Lille town square, you know who you are) would do nothing, I repeat NOTHING, to jeopardize this privilege.

I'll always remember rushing home late from work one fateful evening in May 1975 to catch the European Cup Final between Liverpool v Juventus. I was still on a high from the previous Saturday when a Norman Whiteside special in extra time against the (then) all conquering Everton had secured the FA Cup for a 10 man United. I was dreaming of more Euro aways when I switched on the TV and began making my supper when it dawned on me that the images on the screen did not tally with what my body clock was expecting. By this time I should have been seeing fleeting glimpses of two teams coming out onto the pitch but instead there were just confused scenes of the crowd.

I sensed trouble and was overwhelmed by the premonition that my four day high would be taken away from me, and it wasn't my fault. After twenty years of a media campaign to convince the world that all English football supporters were 'hooligans', with only a handful of incidents to back-up this claim, this was to be the straw that finally broke UEFA's back.

I instinctively knew that I wasn't going to see United in Europe the following season, or the season after that, or perhaps even the season after that. I just knew that the knee jerk reaction of the authorities would be to ban English clubs from European competition.

I stopped cooking and concentrated on the events unfolding on the screen. Total bedlam and confusion. People were crying. Grown men were struggling against being crushed against a stone wall. The Belgian police looked like rabbits caught in car headlights.

I saw Juve fans wearing scarves over their faces, running onto the pitch at the other end of the ground. A camera showed a close-up of one of them brandishing a gun. A gun, for fuck's sake! What's going on?

The oh so predictable response of the authorities and the sheep masquerading as reporters for our glorious national press had been to immediately blame the Liverpool fans for the disaster. But this time the fans said, enough is enough. This was the second straw that broke the second camel's back.

Out of the ashes of this carnage the Football Supporters Association was born. Although not entirely blameless, Liverpool fans were outraged that they were portrayed as the sole villains of the piece, and so the FSA was formed as a vehicle for fans to express their views to the wider public and the relevant authorities.

For any politician, police spokesperson or commentator, blaming the fans has always been the easy option, and still is. So much for progress. The rumbles of the 70's had come home to roost. Now there wasn't even a need to establish the facts. Who needed the truth when everyone knew fans were to blame. The "something has to be done" brigade would be vindicated at last.

Of course in the late 60s and throughout the 70s, as well as dodgy haircuts and flairs, football in the UK had been infested with "hooliganism" and many "so called" fans have only themselves to blame for what followed. But to only blame fans is too simplistic and cowardly, as it absolved the authorities from looking in the mirror and reflecting on their own complicity.

Years later, as an member of the Football Supporters Association, we helped uncover what for the authorities was the unpalatable truth, that Liverpool fans played only a bit part in the horror that unfolded that day. The state of the dilapidated stadium that would never have been granted a safety certificate in the UK, the (dis) organisation of UEFA and their discredited ticket policy, the Belgian police – all contributed to "The Perfect Disaster".

Hooliganism will never be eradicated. It's in (some) young men's jeans, or combats, or chinos. Plus CCTV cameras and mobile phones have lead to changes. Let's be under no illusion. It will always be with us in some form or another, just as every wave of new music leaves some victims behind in a time warp of fashion the world forgot. However, hooliganism has been a lot worse on the Continent and South America than in the UK for over twenty years yet is still referred to as the "English disease". Almost thirty years later and English fans are still treated far worse than supporters from other countries by Europe's' police forces.

One fact is inescapable, and although it may dissuade some non-United fans from buying this book, I have to shout it from the rooftops so that the European powers-that-be take it on board and get their act together.

Manchester United are England's best behaved travelling fans. We travel in far greater numbers than supporters of any other team, despite attempts by UEFA and all European clubs, including Manchester United themselves (may they forever hold their heads in shame) to restrict us. In all this time we continue to be battered and bruised by the authorities, opposing clubs and the local police.

Flying in the face of UEFA's own rules, clubs abroad continue to rip us off by over charging United fans for tickets far in excess of prices paid by home supporters. The difference now is, we don't take it lying down, or more accurately – sitting down. To miss-quote Annie Lennox, fans are doing it for themselves. Now it's the fans who take the initiative. Using all the marketing and communication weapons at our disposal we're able to make the authorities abide by their own rules. In the case of Manchester United, IMUSA and Shareholders United/ Supporters Trust have been immensely successful in moving media mogul mountains.

OK. End of rant.

Back in Milan, our intrepid hero and chum (that's me and Mick by the way, in case you've lost the thread) did an exterior tour of the stadium. We asked stray Reds if they had any spares but we continued to draw blanks. The only people selling tickets outside were the Italian touts and they were asking 80,000 lira each (about £100)

Then I spied the Sky and Carlton television outside broadcast trucks and made my way over. Living in London I had given numerous interviews over the past few years on behalf of the FSA and IMUSA so had built up lots of contacts.

"Pay back time", I thought, as I sought out faces I knew. Requests for tickets fell on deaf ears. Thank you guys. However, the TV crews had it on good authority that thousands of forged tickets were in circulation.

When pressed, Inter Milan had promised any United fans who had unwittingly (?) purchased tickets that turned out to be fakes would be allowed into a special section of the ground. They figured this was a safer option than having hundreds, if not thousands of ticketless Reds marauding outside the stadium.

I then did two live interviews to the nation, pontificating on why I believed Inter would come out second in this particular encounter.

Comforted somewhat by the revelation that bad tickets were actually good tickets, Mick and I did another tour outside the stadium. With no Reds forthcoming we were welcomed into the arms of the touts. 80,000 lira each became 100,000 for two together. Not bad under the circumstances. The Irish Reds on the plane had shown me their genuine tickets and ours looked identical.

Upon closer inspection we realised the sequential numbers applied to the gates and not the seats. Those Italian rascals! Mick and I bid each other farewell as we began to line up in our respective queues. The knots in my stomach began to twist as I approached the turnstile. Someone flashed a special light onto my ticket and before I knew what was happening I was thrown out.

"Scorchio. Forgio. Fuck Offio"

Bastards. We'd been done. What about "Entante Cordial" (alright, that's French). What about "Hands Across the Water". What about "Bad Tickets are Good Tickets"?

What about...nothing. Suddenly the police who could speak perfectly good English were nowhere to be found.

"Me – bad ticket. Bad ticket = good ticket. Me go in ground, Si?"

Bastards. They wouldn't let me in. What to do? I made my way disconsolately back to the TV trucks where I found Mick recounting the same sad story.

Did another interview with Sky which I hoped would bring the police, Inter Milan and UEFA holding their collective heads in shame at the betrayal I had received at their hands. Well, at least I felt better telling the world how I questioned their collective parenthoods.

Now we were desperate. I begged. I pleaded. I pulled in all my favours.

"Ah. Come on guys. Surely you have a couple of press passes to spare? Guys. Guys."

"Sorry", they all said. We'd love to help but............"

Thanks guys.

Ah! Inspiration.

"Guys. Guys. Can we stay in one of your trucks with all those monitors in them. Please. Pretty please?"

I don't know if it was my lap dog eyes or the pitiful whimper in my voice but someone took pity on us and we were lead to this truck with hundreds of cables protruding from all angles.

"OK lads. You can stay in here, but...DON'T TOUCH ANY-THING!"

"Yes sir. Thank you sir. Three bags full sir."

And so we entered this full metal toilet with TV screens showing more than a dozen different angles of the pitch, plus the players' tunnel and other corridors in the stadium.

The only problem was...there was no sound. We tried touching everything but to no avail. Oh well, at least we'd see the match. All was not lost.

We found a couple of stools and then the match started and our surroundings were forgotten. Before the game Fergie had gone on about how Italian players tended to fall down in the penalty box if there was a strong wind so what this game needed was a strong referee. The whole of Italy seemed to be enraged by these outrageous comments but it did the trick. The French referee that night was brilliant and even booked one

Italian forward for diving when he was convinced he'd won a penalty. Half time arrived and I gingerly opened the door of the truck. Considering there were 80,000 people inside the stadium it was remarkably quiet outside in the car park. I spotted a couple of technicians who gave us a grin but didn't give us any tickets, so after a pee it was back inside for the second half.

I asked Mick if he'd like to chance our luck with another tour of the ground but he was of the opinion that a truck in the hand was better than two plonkers locked outside a turnstile and unable to get back. I looked at the monitors. How strange. When you're used to seeing a half-time analysis by a panel of experts in the studio, just to see a silent, static shot of the pitch was, well, strange. No Gary Newbold grabbing Sir Alex for a couple of pearls of wisdom. No adverts. Nothing. It was quite good actually.

So, 0-0 at half-time which meant that we were leading 2-0 on aggregate and just 45 minutes to go. Inter upped the tempo in the second half and the inevitable happened on the hour. Inter scored. Even in the sound proof truck we could hear the roar and my underwear changed colour. Still half an hour to go. Shit. That's thirty whole minutes, isn't it?

My cockiness had gone. I was hanging on by a thread. If Inter scored a second I reasoned, with 72,000 fans baying for our blood, they could easily score a third.

If the going gets tough, you need people like me in the trenches. I shit myself and fear the worse. It works as well. When the inevitable does happen you tell yourself:

"Told you so", and you don't feel so bad 'cos you'd prepared yourself mentally for this eventuality. On the other hand, if fate takes a hand and by miracles of all miracles the worse doesn't happen, the joy and relief is overwhelming.

In this case a certain ginger haired prince took fate by the hand, or more precisely, the foot. With just six minutes to go a cross comes over and there is Scholesy to volley into the net. 1-1 and no way back for Inter.

When I was too young living in Gants Hill I used to get the bus to the Essoldo in Ilford, the flea pit that showed sex films on a Sunday. For some reason I've always remembered this particular film set in Paris where the trailer was better than the film itself. The scene that sticks in my mind involves a 2CV rocking sideways in the middle of the Champs Elysee, indicating an amorous couple exchanging bodily fluids.

Keep that image in your mind as I transport you back to the full metal toilet in the car park of the San Siro stadium in Milan. Mick and I let out such a scream and jumped about in such a confined space that anyone passing at that moment would understandably have miss-interpreted the movements of the truck to be that of a couple releasing built-up tension and joy and bodily fluids. They would have been correct too. When I scream I have no control over the spit and dribble that emanates from my mouth and other orifices.

The final few minutes were spent in uncontrolled delight. Then the whistle blew and we were in the semi finals of the European Cup. We opened the door of the TV truck and rushed outside. A few minutes later the United hoards came singing by and we joined in the happy throng. Forty five minutes later we were back in the foyer of our hotel where some of the others had already gathered. Dignified grins and handshakes all round. It soon became apparent they were content to have a few quiet drinks in the hotel bar. That was no good for me. I wanted to let it all hang out. I wanted to celebrate with fellow Reds, so Mick and I went out in search fun and frolics.

Unfortunately Milan on a midweek evening is dead. For a city with a reputation of being a dedicated follower of fashion setting, this was a major disappointment. There were a few expensive clubs open down dodgy looking steps but sparsely occupied and with a handful of sorry looking characters. Even the restaurants were closed.

What sort of place was this?

Eventually we found a cafe open and had a quiet meal, which is not how I anticipated celebrating United's first home and away success against Italian opposition since the club had entered the European Cup over forty years previously. At least we got to see the goals again on the obligatory TV.

We walked back to the hotel and had a free kip on the floor of Jeff's room. We had agreed to split the cost, but after the ticket fiasco I felt this was my shilling of flesh.

JUVE AWAY -BREAKING IT

The greatest comeback I ever saw in Boxing was when Nigel Benn was almost battered to death in the first round of his title bout with Oliver McCall. Bent double over the ropes from his opponent's continual onslaught, Benn seemed to have no answer to McCall's superior power and dominance. How he survived that first round I'll never know. From the drowning depths most of us will never experience, Benn slowly and relentlessly clawed his way back into the fight. Degree by degree he chipped away at McCall who, bit by bit, lost his preening confidence in equal measure.

Their minds and bodies met at the halfway stage of the fight, with Benn on the way up and Mccall on the way down. As exhilarating as it was, the end was inevitable, yet the unbelievable courage and joy of Benn's victory has forever left a place in my heart.

Our tie in Turin against Juventus in the semi-final of the Champions League on 21st April 1999 left the same indelible mark.

Juve came to Old Trafford with a swagger, led by the maestro, Zidane at his majestic peak and Edgar Davids, whose strength and vision dominated our midfield in the first half. I knew Zidane was out of our price range but, Oh, how I wished Davids was one of us, not against us.

Half time arrived with us 0-1 down and not at the races and with another semi-final of "if onlys" on the horizon. But, lest you forget, dear reader, we are talking about Manchester United here. The spirit in the side is unmatched in modern football. Fergie must have given a speech of Bennian proportions to inspire the lads to stop admiring and start administering a bit of British bulldog. We started to "get at 'em" and slowly but surely Keano & Co wrestled the midfield from the posers from Turin who began to look like ordinary footballers.

Although not flowing like we were against Inter, the match was now more even. Teddy came on and with five minutes to go scored a typically Teddy goal, only for the linesman to rule offside.

"Drats", I thought.

Come on, lads. Just one goal. Give me something to believe in. Encouraged by this belated breakthrough, United played the last five minutes as they should have done the previous eighty five and the crowd's expectancy and noise levels grew. Then there was three minutes of extra time.

Brian Clough once said that a goal in the last minute was worth the same as a goal at any time. He must have had a premonition about United when he came out with that remark because no team in world football sums up that never say die spirit of lost causes better than Manchester United. How many times over the last ten years have United put their fans through hell only to reach the promised land in the last minute. And to think that the last minute of injury time in this home leg against Juventus was just a prelude, a mere bursting of a zit compared to the future volcanic eruption that was to be the last week in May.

Not that it felt like a bursting bubble at the time. When Giggsy caught the ball so sweetly to equalize we all went ballistic. Driving back to London on a night-time high, it seemed inexplicable that a 1-1 draw at home, with Juventus having scored a priceless away goal, should evoke such belief that this was to be "the" year. Karen Carpenter put it succinctly all those years ago when she sung, "We've only just begun." And Thunderclap Newman concurred with "There's something in the air".

The next day a strange series of events began to unfold, which was later picked up on by many ABU's and the media. On mass, United fans started to make arrangements for Barcelona. Why? You may ask, when we had only just scraped a draw in the last minute at home to Juventus, would United fans be making arrangements for the final in Barcelona. For a combination of reasons:

1) The illogical belief that this was "our" year.

2) The fact that the Spanish Grand Prix was at the end of the same week and all the cheap flights and hotels had already been snapped up.

It soon became clear that by far the cheapest option was to share the costs of travelling overland from London to Barcelona in my people carrier for those who could afford to take three days off work. But more of that later. I couldn't get to Turin so Red mate, Joe, and his three kids came over to my house. By this time Hélène had got the message. She made supper for all of us then disappeared for the evening. Much speculation, niblets and quavers later we settled down to watch the match. My stomach was in knots as this was the nearest we had been to a European Cup final for thirty one years. Although Juventus were favourites, away goal and all that, the way we had been playing of late, including that incredible extra-time 10 man win over Arsenal in the FA Cup semi final only a few days previously, had instilled in United fans the belief that "our name was on the trophy". Bollocks. Talk about tempting fate. Between 1964 (West Ham) and 1975 (Leeds) I had witnessed eight losing semi finals. Losing a final is bad enough, but losing a semi-final is worse. To know you are just 90+ minutes away from glory. To watch the other end go barmy as you trudge sadly home. To be aware of the build-up to the final that should have been yours. Walking up Wembley Way (or wherever). At least as a finalist you can enjoy the build-up and be part of the day.

They say nobody remembers losing finalist. Not true. As supporters of the losing team, we bloody well do. So we settled down on the sofa a mid an aura of conflicting emotions, confronted by the TV and individual plates of spaghetti bollocksnaise. We started off pretty well. Controlled passing, getting our game together. In fact I thought we were the better looking team for the first ten minutes when disaster struck, or should that read Inghazi. Against the run of play Juventus scored.

Bastards.

Still, we only needed one goal ourselves and the tie would be all square. Not so bad really when you consider it in a calm and rational manner.

But this was not the time for calm and rational thought.

Bastards.

We kicked off and it was encouraging to see that we continued to play controlled football. We were keeping our shape well and this bode well for the remaining 80 minutes.

Bastards. Bastards. So bad they named it twice.

Inzahgi again. I don't believe it. 2-0 down and we were the better team. What the fuck's going on? I don't believe in God but where is he when you need him? This has got to be a joke, right?

I thought I would touch the depths of despair, but I didn't. Because when we kicked off we still looked the better team. I know it sounds strange, and you can claim it's easy to write this with the value of hindsight, but I kid you not when I say that I still thought we could do it.

Juve were not ramming home their advantage. Admittedly Italian teams are not renowned for all out attack. Usually, given the opportunity, it's all out defence. But this time they were caught somewhere between the Red Devil and the deep Red Sea. They seemed unsure whether to attack and take advantage of the situation, or sit back and let us huff and puff to no avail. Their attacks were less inventive or incisive than they had been at Old Trafford the previous week. Edgar Davids, who had played with the wings of Zeus on his feet at Old Trafford in the first half just ran in to blind alleys in a Ray Wilkins with hair sort of way. Zidane was good but mortal. As Becks said to Gary at the time...

"They've gone."

An inspired Keano was now running the ship, dominating the midfield. We played like the home team. Then in the 24th minute a cross came over and, who else but Keane himself rose and guided a perfect header into the top right hand corner of the net.

"GOOOOAAAL!"

We all went leaping around the room along with an unexpected guest. Joe's plate of half eaten spaghetti. It went everywhere.

"Spaghetti's here. Spaghetti's there. Spaghetti's every fucking where, la la la la ..."

Shit.

"We'll clear it up at half-time." I gasped, secretly dreading the forthcoming race against time. Who'll get there first? The Indians or the British Army, i.e. will we be able to clean everything before 'er outdoors returns?

I put this disturbing thought to the back of my mind as play restarted. We continued where we left off, taking everything that Juve could throw at us and giving it back with compound interest. It only needed one more goal and we weren't just level – we were ahead. As half-time approached Moses appeared unto us and lead us up Mount Sinai and showed us a vision of truly religious significance.

Yorke equalised.

"GOOOOAAAAL!"

We leaped up once more in unison. This time Joe took the coffee table with him as extra insurance, which resulted in plates becoming deadly missiles. It also snowed Pringles and rained Coke.

Nice.

Against this warzone backdrop we danced, hugged and kissed. If only a slow motion CCTV camera could have captured the moment for posterity. Amid the ecstasy I was aware that my posterior was in for a kickin' if this new mess wasn't cleaned up in double quick time.

Half-time arrived. 2-2. Forty five minutes from the Promised Land. We tried to catch our breath and keep the emotions corked. It was too close, too near. It had been too long. We'd been here too many times.

Before we knew it the second half had started and we hadn't done a thing about the mess. We may have been only forty five minutes from heaven but I was in line for my second Jewish operation and this nagging menace stopped me from going over the edge.

The second half took on the same pattern as the first. We grew in confidence as the half wore on, yet Juventus were always dangerous. I made pathetic attempts at clearing up but my heart wasn't in it. Slowly but surely bottles, cups and crisps were reassembled on the coffee table as I kept both eyes on the match. Then another breakaway by United was thwarted when Yorke was brought down by the Juventus goalkeeper.

"PENALTY", we cried.

"GOOOAAAALLL!", we sceamed as Cole followed up and sidefooted the ball into the net at speed from a ridiculously tight angle. An orgy of celebration followed, as did the coffee table once more, with the remains of the saved edible and liquid refreshments. 31 years. 31 years. 31 years.

I was beside myself (split personality, you see). We danced, hugged and kissed, only this time we didn't stop as the match was over and we were off to Barcelona. If the neighbours' complained I didn't hear them. If Hélène knocked another nail in our relationship I didn't notice. After thirty one years I was going to the European Cup final.

Let me type that again...I was going to the European Cup final.

In a world of my own I went to bed, a very happy man.

BARCELONA – MAKING IT

Reality check. I woke up the following morning in a cold sweat.

"How do I get a ticket?"

You see, I'm not a season ticket holder. When occasionally season tickets became available in the sixties and early seventies I didn't have the money. When I did finally have the money season tickets were scarcer than a trophy in City's trophy cabinet (the obvious equation, I know, but enjoyable nonetheless.)

Plus, at the time, a season ticket meant sitting down, and that was the antithesis of everything I stood for (get it?). No, seriously, standing up, jumping, singing, chanting, gesturing were all part of the match day experience. All the constraints society places on you to conform, to compromise, to tow the line and to behave involve suppressing your basic emotions.

This is called responsibility, growing up, sophistication, acting your age, adult, conservative. It also leaves you dead inside.

Human beings are a complex and wonderful circuit board of emotions and feelings. As babies we respond and act on our feelings. As we get older, the brain plays a growing role in the decision making process. We compromise. We take other people's feelings into consideration to a lesser or greater degree, depending on our own judgement and morality/conscience. Society tells us to conform, not rock the boat, to be a good egg, dependable, reliable. Ordinary.

We look at leading sportsmen and women, show-business personalities, top business people, royalty, hooray henries and think...well, it's different for them. They don't have to play by the same rules as the rest of us.

Bollocks, of course.

Why shouldn't we have a bit of the cake – and eat it?

They say the best things in life are free. Obviously written by someone who hasn't got any money. On the other hand, pleasure allied to our circuit board of emotions is the same for all of us, whatever our status. You don't need money to enjoy sex, the sunrise/sunset, sex, beauty in creatures great and small, sex, music, sex, art, sex, and eerrr......well, you get the picture. It just makes it a hell of lot easier to obtain, that's all, but it's not essential.

If I had enough money to buy a Rolls Royce I would want to drive the bugger, not let someone else do it for me. I want to experience that excellence in engineering, to feel that steering wheel, to be in control of a hundred years of the best driving money can buy.

When I go to a football match I don't want to be cocooned from the intensity of combat by gin and tonics, wood panelling, ties and networking. I want to let it all hang out. I'm a human being. The outer shell you see houses the circuit board. It needs a release. Some human beings that cannot find an outlet for emotional release eventually take it out on their partners/children. They are the instigators of road rage. Intolerant of others at work or at home. They hang outside school gates. They watch daytime TV. They eat microwave meals for one. They think grey is an acceptable colour.

We all need a release. Society is becoming faster and more stressful, with lower salaries and higher commissions, targets, non football league tables, congestion charges, deteriorating public transport, divorce, Ian Beale, Anthea Turner, Jade Goody, Bobby Stokes offside winner for Southampton, spam, banks, estate agents, help lines that don't, small print and chubbing,

For some release can come from inner peace, in the form of yoga, religion, masturbation, a good book, etc.

While not dissing any of the above (except religion) I prefer animated outlets such as sex or head banging to Led Zeppelin, Pink Floyd, Black Sabbath, Rory Gallagher, Red Hot Chilli Peppers and last, but best of all, going to see United live.

Live football reaches parts other activities simply cannot reach and nothing, and I repeat, NOTHING, was going to keep me away from Barcelona on May 26 1999. And so, like a man pocessed, I began my concerted 30 day campaign to score a ticket for the final.

Just like those special effects in horror films or music videos, the background disappeared from view whilst I and my mission was thrust to the foreground.

Wife, family, job, clients, bills. You name it, it just went out of my consciousness.

To hell with the consequences. I could always re-marry.

I sat in the third bedroom of my house which, like many people, I had converted into an office. I made a list of all the contacts I had.

Route 'A'. I'll try my family first. "You never know", I thought, "Someone may have a contact I never knew existed." This line of enquiry drew a blank. Not even the distant wealthy side of my family on my Dad's side that I hadn't seen since the last funeral many years before.

Route 'B'. United mates were in the same boat as me. But we all agreed, with or without tickets we were going in my people carrier to Barcelona. After thirty one years there was NO WAY anyone or anything would keep us away. For those of us suffering from a liquidity bypass, I reckoned seven sharing the petrol and ferry would be the cheapest option, as long as everyone could allow a minimum of three days off work I also reasoned that there would be thousands of fellow Reds in Barcelona without tickets. We'd just take over a bar with a TV screen nearest the stadium, then join in the celebrations with the United fans exiting the ground.

Route 'C'. Non United but still football mates tried their best but fell by the wayside, just like the teams they supported.

Route 'D'. Non football mates in good jobs could not back up their words with deeds.

"Right", I thought. "Desperate times require desperate measures."

Route 'E'. I started to hit below the belt. I took out the equivalent of my little black book and looked up names and numbers I had stored since the world began. For a number of years I had been a mini-cab driver for some of the better collar & tie companies in London whilst I was resting between engagements (on the dole). I had taken down telephone numbers of various celebrities, from "B" list actors and actresses to singers and musicians, MP's, journalists, etc, etc...

Normally a sensitive soul, my skin grew substantially thicker as I waded through page after page of personalities, accepting rejection as par for the course and any conversation of more than ten seconds as a bonus to be enjoyed and maybe stored for the future.

Route 'F'. At the same time I sent a letter to Ken Merret, company secretary at Manchester United. As you know, for many years I have been a shareholder in MUFC PLC. In November 1998 I attended a rather heated AGM (no change there, then). As angry or upset as I may feel on certain issues, how I express myself to mates in the pub bears little resemblance to the David Blatt you see addressing the Board and fellow shareholders on the floor. They say sarcasm is the lowest form of wit. I think we go quite well together. I attempt to mix humour with passion in order to get my points across. My theory being that whilst they're laughing the serious points are seeping through the corporate consciousness. And I don't swear. This is important. No matter how strongly I wish to question their collective parenthoods, if I want to gain their respect and keep the lines of dialogue open...I shut it.

After this particular AGM at Old Trafford I asked where the nearest toilets were and I was directed upstairs to the Directors floor. Hmmm. Interesting. As I made my way along the corridor I was gripped by an overwhelming urge to open doors and slip inside. Imagine what gems I could discover, especially in Martin Edwards's desk. Details of impending transfers, salaries, bonuses, 'unofficial' payments, public toilets, telephone numbers of ladies of the night, or maybe best of all – free tickets.

With a sterling sense of character I resisted the temptation (OK, I bottled it). I did my business in the correct cubicle and emerged into the corridor. At the same time the United secretary, Ken Merret emerged from his office.

"Close call." I thought;

A pleasant fifteen minute conversation ensued. I forget what we talked about but I kept it going as long as possible before I noticed rigormortis setting in. Not wanting to out-stay my welcome I bid Mr Merret a fond farewell and disappeared back downstairs.

Now, five months later, it was payback time.

I sent him a fax, a copy of which I put in the post that very evening. On it I wrote words to the following effect...

"Dear Mr Merrek,

Who'd have thought when we spoke after the recent AGM at Old Trafford, that Manchester United would be on the threshold of a remarkable treble? Blah, blah, blah...

I know you must be inundated with requests at this moment in time, however I would like to point out that I have never ever made a direct request like this before. Blah, blah, blah...busy man...blah, blah, blah...once in a lifetime...blah, blah, blah...forever grateful...blah, blah, blah......"

Buried towards the end of this overlong and groveling correspondence was the killer line...

"I wonder if you could possibly see your way clear to offering me six (yes, 6) tickets for the Champions League Final in Barcelona."

Why six? You ask. I'll tell you. I figured, if I ask for two he'll simply turn me down. But, if I gave him a myriad of gut wrenching reasons why I needed everyone of the six, eight, ten (the figure wasn't important, it just had to be unreasonably large), he would feel he was doing his duty by refusing me my request outright, but he would feel a better all round human being if he contributed in some small way to my request.

Two, three, four days passed. Nothing. I phoned – constantly. The United switchboard was either continually engaged or, if by a miracle I got through, Mr Merret was unavailable. No surprise there, then.

I sent another fax. I wrote words along the lines of:

"Dear Mr Merret.

I know you must have been inundated requests similar to mine for six tickets for the Champions League Final but I'm getting rather concerned as I'm running out of underwear.

Yours sincerely, etc...etc...

I figured if everyone, like me, was jumping on the emotional bandwagon, I would try another angle. Short, sharp and (hopefully) humorous just to make mine stand out from the rest.

Hélène remarked around this period that if I gave as much time and energy to the business as I was currently giving to my Holy Grail pursuit of a ticket, we would all be millionaires by now. I pretended not to comprehend the significance of this remark, which I readily admit contained more than a grain of truth. Millionaires, shmillionaires, but certainly a lot better off. I couldn't deny it, so I did what any man would do when confronted by the undeniable truth – I pretended I hadn't heard it.

Route 'G'. Another line of enquiry involved expensive calls to Perth in Western Australia, where my old Red mate, Graham Wyche now lived and worked. (Remember him from the Denis Law Day involving Wayne's World impressions in the Royal Garden Hotel in Kensington? You do – good. You don't – cheat, you've skipped a few chapters. Don't take offence though, I do the same thing when I read a book. Who wants to wade through layers of shit when the headlines tell you where the good bits are?) Graham, his delightful wife Sue, and the rest of his family had emigrated there in the late eighties. He kept the Red fires burning by setting up the official Manchester United Western Australia Supporters Club. Members meet in Kings Park to talk United around the "barbie". They also watch recordings of games in selected pubs. Of course, a major benefit of being an "official" supporters club is that they have access to tickets. OK, for a supporters club ten thousand miles away I think I'm right in saying they only get about four tickets a game, but that's still four more than I get so it qualified as a major source of pleading.

Graham also hosts a British soccer program once a week on the local Channel 9 radio station. He told me it's amazing how many ex-players visit the area and even live there. Many of these visiting ex-pros appear on his program alongside his regular sidekick, Francis Burns, who also lives in Perth. So there you are, we've tracked down another ex-Red.

Bad news for me though. Of the four tickets available, he and Franny were taking two and the other two had been won as prizes in a members competition. He promised to keep a look out and let me know if anything came up. "Fair enough". I thought. Once I put the phone down I had a re-think. "Bastard. It should have been me. Bastard." Selfish? Moi? Fucking right!

The clock was ticking away and ticket(s) were conspicuous by their absence.

Route 'H'. Flesh and blood closer to home. I don't know why it didn't occur to me earlier that my daughter, Melanie, must have some contacts. All right, they were music not football, but surely at the top people know people who know people...get my drift?

I gave her a Bootie Call but unfortunately she didn't Know Where It's At, not even Under The Bridge. She was Rock Steady as she Never Ever had to ask for tickets so didn't know whom to ask. I had a Black Coffee and looked out of the window at the receding Pure Shores of opportunity.

Then I remembered. One important member of the All Saints management team was David Moores, son of the Liverpool chairman and a Liverpool fan himself. Talk about conflict of interest. David was, and still is, a lovely bloke. But he was Scouse.

Yet don't all clubs get tickets for major finals? I swallowed hard.

"Hello David. How are you?"

"Hello mate. How are you?"

"Fine".

A bit of football banter followed as I timed my run into the phonebox.

"Err. David, I was wondering if by any chance you could get me a ticket or three for the Champions league Final?

"You must be joking. Can you imagine the demand we get for our limited supply of tickets?

"Yeah. Of course I can. But you're all Liverpool. Surely you wouldn't want to watch US win?"

"It's not just about the match, David."

"Yeah. I know, I know."

"Look. I'll see what I can do."

"Yeah. Thanks."

Bastard. I thought of all the favours I had done for him and thought he owed me. Except, looking back, I hadn't done him any favours at all. Damm.

ERIC MOVES IN MYSTERIOUS WAYS

I don't believe in God. Certainly not the old deep voiced hippie with the long hair and flowing beard. In fact I don't believe in anybody's God. Conventional property owning religions/cults/ologies around the world are responsible for more wars, deaths, bigotry and unhappiness than anything I can think of. However, inside everyone of us there is a conscience. It's up to each of us whether or not we listen to and act upon our conscience. Often one's initial reaction to any given situation is the most honest and accurate reflection of our true feelings. We then compromise, think, consider, take account of other people's points of view, evaluate then conclude. Diplomatically, this is probably the wisest course of action in a complex and increasingly competitive world.

Now, whether you can call your conscience an acceptable alternative to God is a matter for debate. However, for the first time in my life I have no explanation for the events that followed, other than to quote from Fred Eyre's 1981 book, "Kicked Into Touch", in which he wrote..."You know, it's funny. The harder I worked, the luckier I got." Or maybe it was just man's intuition.

Route 'F'. With about one week to go I'm sitting in my office, which if you remember is the small box bedroom in my house. The clock was set precisely at 9 o' clock when the fax machine starts to whirl. Now, any mature individual would continue with whatever task they were performing and only acknowledge the presence of a fax upon completion. But it's me we're talking about. I've always been in awe of boys toys, most probably because I don't understand how the fuck they work. I was left behind the moment video recorders incorporated timers. Obviously invented by a superior race from outer space, it was not meant to be for the likes of someone like me. Not that a fax machine by any stretch of the imagination could be constituted as cutting edge technology in 1999, but in my world it still generated the "Wow" factor.

Any fax on or before nine in the morning could only mean one thing. Junk mail, the for-runner of spam for e-mails. Yet I immediately stopped what I was doing and looked at the paper that was slowly folding around itself, before the added weight of extra paper caused it to lower its angle of trajectory, and like one of those speeded up films of flowers in spring, blossom into a fully grown fax.

As (bad) luck would have it, Hélène decided to enter my office at the precise moment the machine stopped. She put out her hand to tear off the fax.

"DON'T TOUCH IT!" I screamed, at the top of my voice.

Hélène stared at me with a look that combined shock and disgust, coupled with a generous layer of condescending. But only for a mili-second. Then the eye of the storm broke and I suffered a close up torrent of abuse that included such well worn phrases such as "Grow up", "At your age", "Don't talk to me like that", "Pathetic", "Do some real work for a change" and the killer... "If it wasn't for me...".(always a good one that, whatever the argument/circumstances)

However, this time I was taking no prisoners and to hell with the consequences.

"Don't touch it." I repeated, a little less hysterically.

I stared at the fax which was upside down. By that I mean the message was on the other side of the paper. But, and this is the fucking big BUT, I use those thin rolls where the message disappears after a few months and I could make out the Manchester United logo at the top of the page.

My hand was shaking and my heart was beating so loud I thought the neighbours would complain. I could make out only three or four lines of type so I feared the worse. I tried to prepare myself for the gut wrenching disappointment as I anticipated the impersonal, automated reply.

I tore off the sheet, slapped it the right way up on my desk and covered the text with my hand, all in one movement. By this time Hélène's expression bordered on Angel on a bad night in Buffy. I slowly moved my hand down the page so that one line at a time came into view.

"Dear David"

Well, that was a better start than I could have hoped for.

"Blah, blah, overwhelming demand (Yeah. I expected that), blah, blah, unfortunately (Ahh! Bad word. Negative word. Heart contracts in cold terror. Must go on. Must go on.) blah, blah, only (Mmmm. Negative word, but with minority positive connotations), offer you two tickets, blah, blah, (WHOAH. Stop. Go back) offer you TWO TICKETS...

"AAAAAAAAAAAAAAAHHHHHHHHHHHHHHHHH HHH HHHHHHHH!!!!!!!!"

"I've done it. I've done it. I've done it. I've done it. I'VE DONE IIIIIIIIIIIIITT!!!."

I shouted. I screamed. I cried. (Yes, again.) The sheer and utter relief. I don't know when Hélène had left the room but there was just enough space for me to push my chair back and perform an outdated punk pogo dance on the spot. Emotionally I then made a twat of myself by phoning my best Red mate, Mick Shenton, in Southampton. (No, I hadn't made a twat of myself before this moment. All my preceding actions were that of any sane United fanatic out of control. Perfectly acceptable) I hadn't come down to Earth before I was put through to his extension.

"Mick!..................."

I couldn't get any more words out. They were stuck in my throat. I began to whimper. Once again, women's belief that they have cornered the market in intuition was exposed as a myth, as Mick started to mirror my grunts and groans. Without saying or hearing a word he instinctively knew what I was trying to say.

Grown men, eh?

Somehow, my voice breaking somewhere between Charlotte Church and that kid who sang 'The Snowman", (you know..."I'm walking in the air......etc...etc...) I was able to convey the fact that I had secured two tickets in the United end for the Champions League Final in Barcelona on May 26th 1999.

I was so happy. It's so much more satisfying to give than to receive, and I had made someone else's day, week, month, year, lifetime......

"I Feel Good, nu nu nu nu nu nu nu. Just like I knew that I would, nu nu nu nu nu nu nu,

I Feel Good, nu nu nu nu nu nu nu. Just like I knew that I would, nu nu nu nu nu nu nu.

So Good. Djoom Djoom. So Good. Djoom.

I Feel Good. Djoom Djoom Djoom Djoom DJOOM."

"I'm walking in the air.........I'm duh duh duh duh duh, duh duuuh".

I couldn't stop singing. That feeling of sheer and utter relief was overwhelming, overpowering. I'd sweated on tickets before but I never realised until that moment just how much United, Europe and all my previous fifty years on this planet were just a dress rehearsal, leading to the Greatest Show on Earth.

I had to tell the world. I phoned everyone I knew. All my United mates. I wanted them to share in my joy. And to a man, and woman, they did. Of course, we had all kept in constant communication ever since the Juventus semi, pooling and exhausting all our contacts, the UEFA website ballot, ticket agencies, etc... I just happened to be the first to score, and I hoped my good fortune would rub off on the others. It went unspoken, but I think they knew I wouldn't let up in my quest to obtain more tickets.

Route 'G'. An hour later the phone rang. Nothing out of the ordinary there then.

"Hello. Can I help you?

"Dave. It's Graham."

"Hiya Graham". I replied, over brightly. But before I could tell him of my good fortune he spoke again.

"Dave. I think I've got you a ticket."

"WHAT!"

"Yeah. You know I was coming over with Franny? Well, he's just told me he's been invited by the club, all expenses paid, to fly over as part of the 1968 European Cup Winners squad. So his ticket has become available and I thought I'd offer it to you if you're still looking."

Graham, I love you. And a little white lie won't go amiss, given the circumstances.

"Oh God, Graham. I was going out of my mind. You really think I've got one?"

"I've just got to confirm that Franny's trip includes a ticket. I'm sure it does, but the moment I can confirm one hundred percent I'll call you back. It's not too late is it?"

Remember, Graham was phoning from Perth in Australia which was, and still is, nine hours ahead of the UK.

"Graham. Given the chance of a ticket you can phone me any time day or night, whether I'm on the job or on the job."

"I'll call you back."

Later that morning he phones back.

"David. It's yours."

"Graham. I love you. That's brilliant. That's totally, fucking brilliant."

192

"I'll phone again, Dave, to make arrangements. Franny and I will be flying over together. We're going to the Cup Final at Wembley on Saturday and I've got to do a couple of interviews with the squad before they fly out to Barcelona. By the way, are you OK for the Cup Final?"

Amazingly I was. One of my clients was The Football Association. My company used to supply them with screen printed and embroidered clothing and accessories, and one of the joys of my job, by choosing clients from the right sectors such as sport and entertainment, was being able to mix business with pleasure.

With the FA I could talk football as well as business and I would find any excuse to 'press the flesh' and cement our relationship. At the same time I would further the fans' causes by bending the ears of the powers-that-be with FSA policy when their collective guard was down. I could also scrounge for tickets.

My principal contact was a Shrimper (Southend United fan) so obviously we had a lot in common, and he had got me two tickets in the 'neutral' section along the side. By way of a thank you, I gave him a lot of advice about Sri Lanka where he was going to take his bride-to-be on their honeymoon and where I had had two of my most enjoyable holidays ever. Meanwhile, back to my call with Graham.

"Why don't you both stay at our place? We haven't seen each other since you fucked off to Oz."

"You're on. Nice one. I'll phone you back, and thanks."

"No Graham. Thank you."

I felt like Father Christmas. A chance to make someone else's dream come true.

I phoned Valerie Jones. Val and I had known each other since she became a member of the London branch of the FSA a few years before. Originally from Manchester (another ABU illusion shattered), she was one of only two United allies on the committee in London. She had got me tickets to United games at Old Trafford on a number of occasions so I knew I owed her – big time.

"Val? Father Christmas here. Guess what I've got for you?"

"David, don't. If you're winding me up my heart couldn't take it."

Bad grammar, but that's what she said.

"I've got you a ticket"

I like it when grown women cry. It appeals to the chauvinistic side of my personality.

I left her a pale but ecstatic shadow of her former management self and burst into James Brown, part two.

The following day David Moores phoned.

"I know you asked me for eight tickets but four is the best I can do."

"AAAAAAAAAAAHHHHHHHHHHHHHHHHHH!!!!!!! David, you're wonderful. You're the man."

A gentle piss take of a conversation followed, and when he warned me that the tickets would have 'Liverpool Football Club' stamped on each one I just said that I would make sure we all wore protective clothing when handling them.

I felt like Eric. I had the power. I was the man. Lord have mercy!

I phoned Joe Lewis. Joe and I had been friends ever since we met at Liverpool Street station on the way to White Hart Lane for a United game in the late sixties. We'd traveled thousands of miles together for the Red cause over the years, shared the same taste in music including Taste, Rory Gallagher, Allman Brothers, Little Feat and Neil Young, and shared muddy fields and tents at Rock Festivals throughout the land. The last twenty years had seen Joe drift happily into marriage and fatherhood, beating me to it by naming his children after songs that had inspired us, and of course, United. For example his eldest son is called Mathew and one of his daughters is called Melissa.

Footballwise he'd wavered a bit in intensity, but whenever we spoke on the phone both British Telecom and France Telecom would send us Christmas cards, thanking us for keeping them out of debt with our interminable conversations about all things United.

Joe's Christmas came early.

I then phoned Geoff Petar who had (not) got me a ticket for Inter Milan but had at least arranged the flight. I beat all his high flying contacts in the City. I was on a roll. Being a travel agent he would make his own way to Barcelona but we'd try to meet up

From the London suburb that time forgot, Ilford, I didn't forget Jack Pikus. Jack had been an on and off mate for many growing up years in Gants Hill. His love of United, and in particular, Denis Law, had endeared him to me. In his teens he was manic and I admired his nerve and pranks that I never had the nerve to do myself. Married life and a successful career had smoothed the rough edges but beneath the suburban veneer beat a heart of pure Red. He deserved his place in the sun. Another two tickets found a very happy home. Pressure of work meant that he couldn't come out to play in our people carrier. He would have to go there and back in a day.

Colum was the eldest son of Hélène's best friend, Katie, who she had known since they worked together in St John's Wood back in the early seventies. Now based in Shropshire, Colum was a United supporter but not a regular match going nutter like us.

It would be the treat of his life if I could come up trumps and as my cup runneth over I made sure he received his trump card. He asked if we had a place in the minivan for a mate of his who had already secured a ticket. By my reckoning that was all seven places filled.

In all I secured nine, I repeat NINE (9) tickets at face value and sold them at face value for what was going to be the greatest day and night of our lives. Nice or naive? Looking back I realise I blew perhaps my only chance to wipe out our family debts in one go. Yet once again I had put my love of all things United first and everything and everybody else second. Story of my wife.

Tuesday 25th May

Sting has a reputation for bringing Tantric sex into everyday conversation. Recently on Friday Night with Jonathan Ross he admitted to a session many years before when he was a "young man", where he and Trudy had a session that lasted eight hours. To put the record straight he pointed out that penetration and full sex lasted minutes not hours, it was in fact the gradual build-up, i.e. foreplay, that makes tantric sex so intense and satisfying.

He should have come with us to Barcelona. Our trip lasted three days and three nights.

Everybody had spent the night at our house so waking up and 'getting it together' was a little less fraught than it could have been. Not that waking up was a problem. No siree. But getting up, washed and fed was a bit like the Marx Brothers on speed. The only one of our party not to party the previous evening was Val, who had an important meeting to attend this very morning and no amount of arm twisting could get her out of it. In the end we arranged to meet her at Toulouse airport at 11 o' clock later that night.

I was suffering from indigestion, having swallowed so many butterflies and they were swirling around in my stomach. To keep myself occupied at 5 o' clock in the morning

I adorned every window of my white VW Sharan with United posters, stickers and scarves. By six we were ready for the off. Clancarty Road in Fulham, SW6 was the scene of the Red exodus. I reminded Hélène for the umpteenth time not to forget to record the match, including all the build-up and the celebrations at the end. She doesn't normally swear but she surprised me with her command of ancient Anglo Saxon.

We hugged. Her's coupled with relief for getting me out of her hair, and me due to the relief of getting her out of my hair. I then immediately ignored her instructions and beep beeped the car horn as we pulled away for the trip to end all trips. I had waited thirty one years for this moment and I have to admit there were times when I thought I would leave this planet a pale, bitter and twisted human being (sounds familiar City?), so tears filled my eyes and other orifices as we turned onto the Embankment on route for Dover. Even as I type this it all comes flooding back as intense as if it was only yesterday, which in some ways it is as I watched THE video again last night to get me in the mood.

It was a bright, sunny morning. Eric was smiling at us and all was right in the world. As I drove through London I became aware of a strange phenominum. People were actually waving to us and wishing us "Good luck", "Hope you win" or words to that effect and quite specifically, "Fuck the Germans". Other drivers flashed us and/or sounded their horns. We felt like royalty. This was beyond my wildest dreams. Never in my non-sexual fantasies had I envisaged this particular scenerio. I started singing in a Julie Andrews/Barbara Striesand sort of way, which before 7 o' clock in the morning induced a torrent of abuse from the other occupants.

We arrived at Dover just before 8am. The customs guy told us that most Reds had gone through the previous day (Monday) and he didn't expect as many today. Once on board we spotted a few Reds but most were lulling before the storm and my advert like 'zing' smile was rubbing a few people up the wrong way. I had to try and cool it, yet I couldn't understand why everyone wasn't as excited as me. Then it hit me. Alcohol. This was the morning after the night before for most of them, and they were recharging their batteries prior to the main bout and the last thing they wanted was a non-smoking, non-drinking goody-goody geek like me in their midst.

So there you have it. Buried in the middle of the book. My secret is out. I don't drink.

I don't smoke and I don't go out with men. Am I too perfect/imperfect for my own good? Have I alienated or reached out to you? All I can say in my defense is that I've built up one hell of a record collection with the money I've saved AND seen United more times than a man on my salary has a right to. It also made me very popular when I was a teenager – that and the fact that I was the first one of us to get a car. It might have been a ten year old Mini but it was a real car. And here's how the equation worked. Boy + car – alcohol = invitation to parties, as everyone else could drink, safe in the knowledge that muggins here would drive everybody home. They were happy as they had transport and I was happy as I got invited to more parties than a 2nd Division nerd had a right to expect. A classic 'win-win' situation before those hideous marketing men stole the slogan.

But here's the rub. Very, very occasionally I'd win the battle but I nearly always lost the war. Let me explain. Being a Geek/Neek, i.e. a combination of both, a lack of confidence coupled with too much Brylcreem meant that I wasn't simply unattractive to women, I was invisible. Girls didn't know I existed. The few that did, either at school or at the youth club, thought I was nice. A boy they could talk to. I didn't want another girl friend. I wanted a girl fuck. I wanted my teenage kicks all through the night. Hand shandies were losing their allure. I wanted the real thing – and that was a poke, not a Coke.

For most blokes, especially when you're a teenager, there's a very simple rule to live by at parties. The more you can get a girl to drink, the more chance you have of getting your end away. Of course, in reality ninety nine percent of the time it's the girl who gets away with no "end" in sight. But just like the red, red robin that comes bob, bob, bobbing along, one percent of the time we can shoot the barmaid, shoot the barmaid, shoot, shoot, shoot.

With the Guinness Book of Records in my sights, my overloaded Mini would depart in the early hours, knee deep in male and female teenagers, testosterone and pheromone.

My devious plan was two fold: 1) Get a girl to sit squashed next to me so that I could get more than I bargained for when I kept unnecessarily changing gear. 2) Make sure the last person to be dropped off was a girl.

This way I hoped to benefit from all my pals' hard work, as the alcohol took effect and I would turn from Clark Kent to Superman in their eyes and knickers. Unsurprisingly, in 99 red balloons of the time I remained Clark not-fucking Kent and the girl in question would disappear into the night. But very, very occasionally nature and chemical imbalances would topple over in my favour. Eyes would start to flutter (hers, not mine) and signals would be exchanged informing me that fucking Father Christmas was about to ride his sleigh. (Yes, that's the right analogy. At this age, just like Father Christmas, coming once a year with somebody else was the best I could hope for.)

But just as I anticipated dropping down her chimney as Superman, I would encounter my Kryptonite moment, or to put it in more modern terms, my Marmite moment. Remember,

I didn't/don't drink and I didn't/don't smoke. Imagine, from my point of view, trying to kiss a girl whose breath and clothes smelt of stale beer and old fags. As I said before, in one per cent of the time I won the battle but lost the war. So dear reader, "whenever your down and troubled and you need a helping hand, and nothing, nothing is going right. Close your eyes and think of me" and you'll feel better because I've just proved the rule that there is always someone worse off than you...me. Now, where was I...

Ah, yes. On the Ferry across La Manche. Once on French soil the strange adulation surfaced once again, but this time in French. Everytime we stopped at some traffic lights, locals would smile, wish us good luck and "foutez une branlée aux Allemands."

Next came one of the more surreal images of the trip as we entered the rush hour traffic on Le Péréferique, Paris's superior version of our North and South Circular road. Spotting our red, white and black people carrier, vehicles of all shapes and sizes would change lanes like dodgem cars, just to come next to us, wind down their windows and hurl platitudes at us. We couldn't understand half the comments but the intent was clear and we were honked on like heroes.

The rest of the day passed singing and drinking with me as the loan driver. So as you can see, nothing much has changed in thirty years. The French autoroute system sped by at around 160 kilometres an hour and not "un flic" in sight. Wonderful. As we were aiming for Toulouse we didn't spot many United or Bayern fans on route so had to contend ourselves with make believe piss takes.

As darkness fell we neared Toulouse and attempted to make sense of inadequate French roadsigns to locate the Formule 1 hotel I had booked from England. At £13 a night for up to three people, France has a series of one star hotels that put the UK to shame. Sqeaky clean, with one double bed and a single bunk bed above, that worked out at £4.33 each plus breakfast. Incroyable!

Fortunately the hotel was near the airport so we quickly unloaded our bags into two rooms, then shot round to the arrivals terminal.

Then another surreal moment occurred, which was to be repeated throughout central and southern Europe w/c Sunday 26th May 1999. At Toulouse airport that Tuesday night there were only United fans. Was I dreaming? Was I back in Manchester? No. Just as I prophesied earlier, The Red Army was on the march like never before. Men, women and children, and those in between, were heeding the call to arms. From tiny hamlets to the great cities on Earth, United fans were being drawn to the Close Encounter of the Thirty First kind. Thirty one years of hurt was about to be exorcised. All other considerations counted for nowt. With or without tickets, Reds just had to be there. In years to come grandparents would sit their grandchildren on their knees and regale them with tales of wonder and heroism. And when asked, "Where were you on May 26 1999?" they would reply with pride and honour, the three most important words in the English dictionary...

"I WAS THERE."

Finally, at around 11pm the flight arrived and thirty minutes later another planeload of Reds cascaded into the arrivals lounge to the accompaniment of "U-NI-TED, U-NI-TED, U-NI-TED." The momentum was building and keeping a lid on it was becoming more and more difficult. I didn't want to peek too soon. My instincts told me that I would be called upon to perform vocals heroics above and beyond the call of duty in United's hour of need and I didn't want to be found wanting.

We met up with Val and returned to the hotel. The Magnificent Seven was now complete. Tomorrow was going to be the first day of the rest of our lives. Little did we know our lives would be changed forever.

I slept fitfully that night. Dreams and fears battled with glory and failure in Tolkein's "Lord of the Reds." The line between sleep and reality, truth and friction became blurred as even a crafty wank couldn't keep the demons at bay.

A PERFECT DAY

Wednesday morning broke bright and sunny, just like us. Rotten jokes and bonhomie masked our nervousness. Coffee and croissants, baguettes and jam were consumed at breakneck speed. In one orifice and out the other in record time.

We clambered into the good old people carrier, our cheeks and eyes shining like virginial schoolkids. An hour and a half later we were on the A8 autoroute which runs along the Mediterranean Coast from Italy, through France and into Spain. Now we joined the rest of the world as hordes of United and Bayern fans raced like chariots out of Ben Hur towards the Spanish border. United fans in vehicles of every description and Bayern fans predominately in motor homes (?) How bizarre.

There was good natured banter between both sets of fans. Bayern is to German football what United is to English football the most successful therefore the most despised team in the land. A dual affinity. Scores were predicted. Most United fans used two fingers whilst most Bayern fans used one, indicating to my way of thinking a universally accepted scoreline of 2-1 to Manchester United. (That's my theory anyway and I'm sticking to it)

As we approached the border the police presence intensified. Was that a truncheon I could see or were they just pleased to see us? (The old jokes are the best. Or maybe not). It became blatantly obvious they were solely targeting United fans. Vehicles were pulled over and searched. Everyone had to prove they had a valid ticket for the game just to be allowed to enter the country. Fucking cheek. Illegal as well I suspected but this was no time to raise a political debate on human rights. "Si senor, No senor, three bags full senor". Get through and get away was priority number one.

A little over an hour later and we were on the outskirts of Barcelona, bathed in shimmering heat. A rustle in my pocket produced a crumpled piece of paper with directions to Colum, a friend of a friend and his apartment in the centre of town. Good plan this. We would be able to park our people carrier in a private underground car park and leave our United embellishments in place, safe from break-ins and unwarranted design changes.

We relaxed over a few beers and nibbles, then gathered our loins before plunging into Red infested Barcelona.

Reds were here, Reds were there, Reds were every fucking where. Barcelona, not Blackpool was now the beach of Manchester. Everywhere we went there were pockets of Reds set-up outside bars, squares, traffic lights, singing and drinking, drinking and singing. Everything that getting to Wembley isn't, WAS in Barcelona. The best atmosphere, the best fans, the best reactions from locals (OK, Barcelona fans had just celebrated winning their own league championship the previous evening, so everybody save a few Espanyol fans was already on a high)

After an hour or so, hoarse throats screamed out for more liquid refreshments whilst stomachs waded in with requests for food, so we persuaded Colum to find us a cheap, and I mean cheap eatery. He succeeded and we descended on a backsteet cafe and devoured substantial amounts of local produce. Full marks to us. We ate local and not dogburger and chips.

We then went down to the beach. How cool was that? Actually it was bloody hot and the beach brought a slight respite from the searing heat. Then as we wandered back towards the centre I tried a little experiment. I strolled down a narrow alleyway by myself, with apartments and their ornate wrought iron balconies almost touching. I let out a yell.

"U-NI-TED."

Like the dogs chorus from 101 Dalmatians, the call was answered instantaneously by dozens of unseen Reds within ear shot.

"U-NI-TED. U-NI-TED."

I'd always wanted to do that. It felt soooooo good.

We stopped at various bars on route, singing and drinking, drinking and singing. In one little square a group of Bayern fans were drinking alone, so we joined them. A German radio crew then turned up and interviewed

US. I spoke to the German nation. I talked about the bond that existed between our two great clubs and both sets of fans, how good the atmosphere was, that Bayern fans' fashion sense brought back fond memories of the Glam Rock era in the 70s and how their team should be congratulated for coming second in this year's competition.

I felt quite smug with myself for thinking on the spot and cracking a couple of jokes in the process. Looking around it was quite obvious I was in a fan club of one. Back in the Ramblers the singing and chanting was gaining momentum. Outnumbered three to one, Bayern fans didn't stand a chance and United fans won the singing Battle of Barcelona hands down.

A prelude of things to come, I hoped.

At around six o'clock the bush telegraph called on everyone to make their way to the stadium. After waiting thirty one years, this was one occasion where being late was not an option. We agreed to guarantee arrival we'd share a couple of taxis. Unfortunately someone forgot to inform the taxi drivers as, to a man, they refused to stop for anyone who looked remotely like a football supporter.

After fifteen minutes a slight panic set in. Ok, the underground system it is then, except that the queue for the nearest station was not moving. Shit. A little more rising panic was called for. We set off in the opposite direction, hoping to find an underground station not on the direct line to the Nou Camp. Not the greatest plan in the world but the best we could come up with faced with being caught in the headlights of the match's approaching kick-off.

Fortunately this proved a successful strategy and we bolted down the steps and onto the platform. Although it was officially rush hour for home going locals, the platform was full of Reds and singing and temperatures were rising all the time. When the train arrived we all bundled in and within seconds we were sweating buckets. I've never been so squashed in my life. The train was overfull of Reds singing their heads off. All rational thought went out the window. I didn't care what I looked or sounded like. I sweated and sang like I've never sweated and sung before. The locals looked on in awe and wonder. Even my mates wondered what I was on.

This was what it was all about. This is what being a United fanatic on Planet Earth was all about. All those non-existent sing songs in Trafalgar Square due to London firms uniting against us, all those losing Euro semis, all the wife's verbals about not being able to afford to go, those scousers 4-1 & 18-13 taunts, all came together at this precise moment. A liberating explosion of joy, venom and frustration tore the words from my guts as my voice soared. They say it's better to travel than to arrive. For the first time in my life that made sense, as I actually hoped this journey would last forever.

However all too soon we arrived at ************** station and spewed out onto the platform. Our voices resonating in the hollow confines of the underground station, the noise and havoc we created was incredible.

Once outside in the late afternoon sunshine we worked out which direction United fans were meant to take, which involved walking three quarters round the stadium in the surrounding streets. At one point we spotted Dave Van Small, the guy who had promised but failed to get us tickets for Inter away .

"Are you alright for tickets lads? I have a couple of spares as two of our lot haven't made it."

I could have said a thousand things, but this time my cutting wit deserted me. Via Geoff Petar he had let us down. And for the final itself it was I, the perennial outsider who had secured Geoff Petar his ticket. There's a moral there somewhere, if only I could work it out. So I just waived and said, "No thanks. We're all sorted."

Round the final corner and there was the Nou Camp, Catalonia's cathedral of football. I was expecting to be blown away like I was with my first impression of the San Siro in Milan. But I wasn't. It only seemed two or three stories high. How first impressions can be deceptive. Though to tell the truth, this was really the second time I had been to the stadium. In November 1975, with Hélène five months pregnant with Melanie, we went on one of those winter-breaks, you know the sort of thing I mean, five days in Los Wankos with Costapacket Tours for 7s 6d. I had made it my mission to visit the stadium, and unlike those jobsworths who infect so many of our institutions in Britain, when I asked if

I could just look inside they said "Yes." And I was in. I went all over the stands. The views were magnificent. The view from the pitch was awesome. The stands seemed to go up forever. I then realised that the stadium had been built into the ground, with the majority of the stands and the pitch itself below ground level.

These images stayed with me as I encountered the first row of police, a good three hundred metres from the ground. Much chaos ensued as they pedantically demanded to see everybody's ticket. In the melee we all got separated as one by one we squeezed past the control. Within a few metres we came up against another row of boys in black. Talk about Gestapo tactics. In one fowl swoop the authorities had destroyed all the good will that had existed between themselves and the United fans throughout the day. Their bad attitude and aggressive behaviour was totally over the top and unnecessary.

I finally arrived at the perimeter of the ground. Pandemonium. Once again a "massive" club with an enormous capacity and decades of experience of putting on major European matches was demonstrating their anti-English credentials. With just four gates allocated to United fans (even this is generous compared to the likes of Real Madrid, Porto, the Milans and more recently, Stuttgart.) by 7pm we were getting nervous. We weren't moving forward at all but we were sure as hell unhealthily squeezed together.

Thoughts crossed the minds of many of us that we weren't going to get in in-time for the start of the most important match most of us would ever see in our lifetimes.

Some women and children started crying. People shouted that kids were getting hurt. The polices response was to mount a vicious Dr Zivargo style charge through the middle of the United fans on horseback, knocking many fans aside like pins in tenpin bowling.

Requests for help went unheeded as the police just battoned anyone who was unfortunate to be in their path, which bearing in mind none of us could move, we just had to stand there and take it.

What fun the police had that evening.

"How many did you hit, Juan?"

"Seventeen." Replied Juan proudly.

"That's nothing." Retorted Carlos. "I wacked twenty four, twelve from behind. They never saw what hit 'em. He He."

Bastards.

I saw grown men, some even older than me (now that IS unbelievable) shaking their heads and attempting to reverse, forgoing the match they had waited all their lives for, for the sake of saving their lives. I could have wept for each and everyone of them, as the enormity of their sacrifice hit me in an instance.

Access 4, Gate 96, Block 352, Row 28, Seat 11

But I wouldn't be joining them. This was the defining moment of my life and no two-bit, ramshakle army of parasite police was going to separate me from my destiny.

I summoned the powers of over forty years of Red watching, sharpened my elbows, took a deep breath and dived forward in a frenzy of pushing and shoving, diving between legs and general all round bad boy behaviour to achieve my goal – to arrive by Gate 96.

With just fifteen minutes to kick-off I was like the piper at the gates of dawn. I flashed my ticket, and I was in. Such joy and relief. There was no time to beg for forgiveness for my atrocious behaviour, I bounded up the stairs looking for Block 352. Found it. I raced to the top then just stood still, transfixed by the majesty of the sight before me. 98,000 people bathed in a perfect Catalan warm evening sunshine and blue skies. Giant multi-coloured inflatables on the pitch wavering in the non-existent breeze. Both teams were already on the pitch. All the Bayern fans were at the other end behind the goal, holding up red and white sheets, which meant that the rest of the ground was full of the Red Army.

We were here, we were there, we were literally every fucking where. What a sight. What an awesome sight. United fans, the biggest football family in the world. I felt the call of the Kleenex as I made my way to the middle tier, Row 28, Seat 11.

More joy. No-one was sitting. Everybody was standing, singing and chanting. The atmosphere was brilliant. I instantly launched myself into the middle of the madness. Whatever the evening had in store, my conscience would be clear. If I gave everything from this moment on I would have no regrets.

Then before I knew it the match started.

The opening few minutes were an untidy mess of missed passes and tackles amid a cacophony of noise. Neither team had settled into any type of pattern when after five minutes Bayern were awarded a fortunate free kick outside our penalty area, when Johnsen was adjudged to have fouled Janker by running into the back of him when the German slowed down. I was in mid chant when Basler ran up, scuffed his shot, and scored.

"Shit. That's not in the script." I thought. Then a moment later I mused. "Yes it is. We're Manchester United. We always do things the hard way." Sixty thousand United fans upped the anti even more, reaching a Spinal Tap "11", but just like the team on the pitch our chanting was disorganised. Pockets of Reds desperately started chant after chant, whilst a tier or two away a different chorus was underway. The team and the fans were as one. No lack of effort but we weren't flowing.

As fans we knew this was also our date with destiny. No-one wanted to leave the stadium after the game thinking, "If only I had sung louder. If only I hadn't stopped."

So nobody did. The players needed us. After such a momentous season of coming from behind and calling upon depths of character and courage normally reserved for the Gods, was this a game too far for our heroes? If that's what fate had in store for us then no-one would ever accuse The Red Army of desertion. We stood side by side with the players on the pitch, literally United in combat.

"Stand Up for the Champions" rang out with renewed vigor and meaning. Now they had the lead, the German's oh so predictable self punishingly cynical and negative tactics came as no real surprise to us, or to the players I imagine. Only unlike the Juventus semi-final our play lacked bite and conviction.

"Flow, flow, quick quick, flow;" I thought to myself. It's at times like these that non-sensickle phrases, puns and double entendres enter my head. I'm sure doctors can explain it but I can't. Luckily I didn't confide my retort to any of the hordes around me or they may well have questioned my parenthhood.

We made it to half-time without almost a shot on goal. In my opinion only Beckham had played to his potential. My voice was hoarse so I gave it a breather. I became aware that the back of my legs were aching. I looked down and realised that, like everybody else, I had been standing on my plastic chair and what with my constant rocking forward and backwards the stiff ridge along the top of the seat had been digging into my calves.

This was a hell of a time to give up standing on seats, so I didn't.

When the teams came out for the second half Gary Neville came towards us, gritted his teeth and raised both his fists in the air. Our Gary was us on the pitch. Always has been, always will be. Giggsy, Scholesy, Keaney, Ruudy, Becksy, Besty, Lawey, Charltony, Ericy, even Ronaldoey – we love them all but Gary Nevilley is the greatest of the lot.

Why?

Because he's one of us. In our dreams we swerve and run like Giggs, ghost-in and score like Scholes, battle and inspire like Keane, shoot cannonballs like Charlton, pounce arm raised like the Lawman, strut our stuff like Eric, etc..etc... But when we wake up we're mere mortals. Gary Neville is mortal. He is everyone of us. His ability is limited but he's won the fans lottery. With odds of fourteen million to one he's the one of us who every moment of every day thanks his lucky stars that he's living our fantasy. Never forgetting for one moment he is us on the pitch. By giving 150% every moment in every game, by practicing till it hurts he has made our mortal dreams come true. He plays like a United fan, savouring every victory, hurting every defeat.

He knew how we must have been feeling on the terraces because he felt it too. He knew that we knew that he knew (OK, that's enough. Ed.)

The second half began similar to the end of the first half, except United were kicking towards our end. We continued to take the game to Bayern but still failed to create any real openings. The only change I could discipher was the surprising spectacle of an occasional German attack. This made for a more open game, but this was no time to give grudging praise for Bayern. They were denying us our life's ambition and had to be crushed. Nice people come second and I was not prepared to be "nice". Fuck 'em. Fuck their smug superiority, Fuck their stifling tactics,

"Sing your hearts out for the lads".

Ten minutes into the second half, after a long spell of possession Giggs curled over a cross with his left foot from the right and found Blonqvist who, for the first time in the match, got the better of his marker but, right in front of us, stretched out but the ball went over the bar. A horrendous miss. We knew it. Blonqvist knew it too and held his head in his hands. We may not get another clear cut chance like this one.

As the game wore on we became more and more agitated by the German team's arrogance. They played as though they had already won it.

There was still about twenty minutes to go when they won a corner and Basler, their goalscorer, was milking the applause from the Bayern fans as he glided over to their end to take it. We read later the effect it had on our players such as Beckham and Giggs on the pitch and Sheringham on the bench. Therefore you can just imagine the effect it had on us. If ever we needed motivation to go where no vocal chords had ever gone before, this was it.

What before had been haltingly, unilateral pockets of vocal support was now a unified force of passion, voice, hate, despair, noise and yet somehow belief. Three quarters of the ground united as one against the enemy. Memories of Barcelona '84 came flooding back

The hard working but inefectual Blonqvist came off to be replaced by Sheringham who made an immediate impact. The team reverted back to 4-3-3 and slowly but surely little openings began to appear in the Bayern defence. In the cold light of day you could claim we were clutching at straws but that's all we needed, a tremor or two to act as a catalyst for the earthquake that was unknowingly about to erupt.

Inevitably the more we pushed forward the more we left openings at the back. Twice Eric was looking down on us as first Scholl's delicate chip over Schmeichel hit the inside of the right hand post and bounced back into Scmeik's hands. Then after Ollie, who makes me happy when skies are grey, Solskjaer had come on for Cole and Matthaus had been replaced by Fink, Jancker, with his back to the goal struck an overhead kick against the underside of the bar and clumsily missed the rebound.

Thanks Eric.

We could have been three goals down, but we weren't. And because we're United we held our belief, against all the odds, that we could still do it.

By this time I was all over the place. I was urging, shouting, bellowing, farting, singing, chanting. I was falling off my chair and getting up again. I was bumping into everybody but, hey, they were bumping into me so what the heck. The atmosphere was incredible. Despite the agony I was so glad I was there. Somehow I felt that from Access 4, Gate 96, Block 352, Row 28 and seats 11 to Eric know where I could somehow influence events.

Just like us the team exploded into action. Ollie, who had only been on the pitch for a Manchester minute, got in a header that forced a real save from Khan, I think only his second up to that point. Two or three luke warm shots kept Khan awake. Yes, we'd actually got shots in on goal. In the normal course of a United match this wouldn't be anything to write home about but within the context of how the match had gone for us over the previous eighty five minute this was worth a mass mailing.

Becks, his blond hair glistening under the floodlights, seemed to skip into overdrive in his Herculean attempts to push us on to even greater efforts. We could sense something was going to happen. The cocky Germans were not at their imperial defensive best any more. Matthaus's organising influence was missing. They were mortal once again, just as over the two legged games in the preliminary league section.

Our noise and tension rose further up the scale. Then suddenly I looked up and like a cow being branded by a red hot poker, the electric scoreboard opposite flashed the figure "45" and the searing yellow light pierced my brain.

"Oh, no. It's all over." I looked round, ready to wail out loud when a number of fans were pointing to the linesman, or more precisely, the fourth official next to him. The board above his head read "3". Three whole minutes. Phew. More than enough time. I resumed my relentless, mindless vocal onslaught. By this time I was incoherent and any noise was better than no noise at all.

A minute into injury time and we got another corner. I was the first of our lot to notice Schmeichel doing a Linford Christie into Bayern's penalty area. "Why not?" I thought. We've got nothing to lose, only the European Cup, but at this late hour I'd have come on if they'd asked me.

Obviously, having rewound my knob more in the last four years than I've ever rewound my 'other' knob in the whole of my life, I can tell you precisely what happened next. But at the time I just saw Beckham swinging in a corner which flew over everybody to land somewhere near Schmeichel who caused havoc and confusion in the German's defence. This was not in their script. The ball came out to Giggs who swung his right foot at it but mis-hit his shot and it ran tamely towards the goal. Sheringham, surprisingly unmarked about four yards out, swung unelegantly at the ball and managed to deftly change the flight of the ball – with his ankle.

Could two wrongs make a right? Your fucking right they could!

"GOOOOOOOOOOOAAAAAAAAAAAAAAAALLLLLL!!!!!!!!!""
AAAAAAAAAAAAAAAAAHHHHHHHHH!!!!!!!!!"

The earthquake had landed. I flew in the air. I screamed and screamed and screamed.

I landed badly on the concrete steps. I screamed with pain and joy. This was a hell of a time to discover sado-masocism. Hands helped me to my feet. How the hell did I get down here? Can't breathe. Don't care. Grown men were crying. Half grown men, i.e. kids were not. They were also screaming but they were not crying. They were cooler than us.

For some reason my eyes wandered to the Bayern players first not ours. One or two were still sitting or lying on the pitch. All that flash smugness had disintergrated. It was wonderful.

"They've gone. They've simply gone. The night is ours. C'mon lads. One more time."

No thoughts of hanging on for the final whistle then re-grouping for extra time. Our time was now. We all sensed it. The seething mass of United fans rose as one for another charge. This was incredible. The release of emotion. I'd never experienced anything like it before in my life. And there were still between two and three minutes left.

My brain split in two.

"Surely not. If you wrote a Hollywood script, no-one would believe you. Things like this don't happen in real life."

The other half of my brain was less coherent, it just sizzled with emotion.

"This is it. This is it. This is it."

I'd stopped singing by now. I was only screaming. Before I knew what was happening we'd won another corner. Beckham sent in an in-swinger. Sheringham came from nowhere and glanced a header across the goal. Solskjaer stuck out his right foot and that is how, from that moment onwards, the Guiness Book of Records longest, loudest, most intense orgasm ever recorded began.

"AAAAAAAAAAAAAAAAHHHHHHHHHHHHHHHHHH!!!!!!!!!
!!!!!!!!!!!!!!!!!!."

I simply exploded. My out of body experience returned with renewed intensity. I had sex with men, women and chairs together and separately for the first time. Two goals in two minutes of injury time in the most important match in our history. An orgy of excess. Bedlam. Screaming, dribbling, screaming, jumping, screaming, hugging, screaming, crying, screaming and more screaming.

Don't ask me how, but I still had the where-with-all to take a few pictures. Somehow I realised that I had to retain just a thread of discipline to record these moments for posterity. In later years I would never have forgiven myself if I'd missed the moment.

I instinctively knew that I was in the vortex of the greatest experience of my life. The reason I had been put on this planet. The reason I had endured all the shit that teachers, bullies, girls, suppliers, clients, bank managers, estate agents, taxmen, parking wardens, and help lines had thrown at me. It was to bring me to this place. This time.

This moment.

And it was good.

It wasn't just good. It was unber-fuckin'-lievable.

Four or five Bayern players were still lying on the pitch when the match re-started. And you know something? I actually felt sorry for Kuffour, their black defender. He hadn't been as overbearing as the others. He'd just brilliantly marked our forwards out of the game for ninety minutes then found himself on the losing side. He was punching the ground in frustration. He was inconsolable.

The final whistle. Ecstasy. Delirium. Hysteria. Incontinence. We'd arrived at the promised land. We'd overtaken Moses and left him standing on the mountain top. We were in heaven on Earth. I made love to everyone within touching distance. Stale beer stained sweat mixed with fag-end breath made for a heady aphrodisiac.

Nothing else mattered. We were immortal. We had won the treble. They said it couldn't be done. I had said it couldn't be done! What do I know? What the hell do I care? For I only know that there's gonna be a show and the Busby Babes will be there.

I kept flashing (the camera, that is). Our players darted from hugging one to another.

I didn't want to miss a single second of anything. I wanted to be filled to bursting point with everything that was happening around me. These moments were to be stored, so as to accompany me for the rest of my life and beyond.

Religion is the opium of the masses, which suggests it dulls the senses. Manchester United is the very antithesis. Every pore of my being opened to give and receive wave after wave of emotion. I felt I was hyperventilating.

Where did that podium come from? The players were waiting in line to go up and receive their medals and the cup. But the Germans went up first, heads bowed, shoulders hunched, beaten into submission by the boys from Manchester.

I applauded. I'm such a sporting winner, me. Throughout the seventies and eighties I had tried to be a sporting loser. I had had lots of practice. It's what we British do best; but this time the foot was in the other boot and I was putting it in, big time.

Now it was our turn, as one by one the United players kissed the cup then collected their medals. Then the moment I had waited thirty one long, long years for. Pandemonium on the podium as David May famously formed the apex of the triangle for Alex Ferguson and Peter Schmeichel to lift up the Champions League trophy against a background of thousands of flash bulbs. We erupted again.

Richard Attenborough has nothing on me when it comes to crying. I cornered the market that night. My whole body shook with uncontrollable sobs. My voice broke as I tried to cheer. The fuck the world bravado of battle had been replaced by the collapse of three decades of self-imposed veneers constructed to withstand crushing disappointment, as year after year the dream ebbed and flowed and disappeared over the horizon.

The players then broke away, did I don't know how many laps of honour then and ran towards our end, embarking on one of the most elaborate celebrations ever witnessed at a football match, in front of the whole world of United fans.

"My boys! My boys!"

The intricate details of the celebration have been put on record by a myriad of journalists and authors and witnessed on TV and videos/DVDs, so I won't repeat each and every nuance here. Surfice to say I never ever wanted it to end, and by the reaction of the players, neither did they. I remember Teddy doing a Marcel Marceau of his turn and shot for our equalizer. The "us and them" gulf between players and fans disappeared as we partied together for ages. The other end of the stadium was black but we were the centre of the world. Suddenly I was aware of

David May stepping towards us by himself but accompanied by the trophy. He stopped right in front of us, outstretched his arms and gestured for us to be quiet.

"Who the hell does he think he is?", I thought. "He didn't even play tonight."

It took some of us some time to comprehend what he was trying to do. Well, I was always a bit slow on the uptake. Eventually sixty thousand Reds fell silent. With better timing than Frank Sinatra or a Ferrari engine, David May, with an almighty flourish, lifted the cup above his head. The instantaneous roar was mindblowing, sending shivers down my spine and into my underwear. What a showman. Wish I'd thought of that.

Then each and every player took it in turn to quieten the crowd before lifting the cup in their own individual style. Roars of approval greeting each outlandish and gloriously childish display.

It was only after the last player had acted out his ritual that we realised that some players were missing. More than anyone, Roy Keane had been responsible for all this. Without his goal and ultimate sacrifice in the away leg in Turin we wouldn't be here now.

We started to chant. "Keano, there's only one Keano, there's only one Keano. Keano..." We hadn't realised he had walked off the pitch soon after the presentation. An immensely proud and private man, he couldn't face the celebrations. He believed he had no right to be there. How wrong can a man be. And we were going to prove it. This night of all nights wouldn't be complete if we weren't able to say thank you.

As our chants became more and more insistent, even the players joined in. No amount of officialdom was going to make any of us leave the stadium. The last piece of the jigsaw needed to be put in place.

Forty five minutes after the match had finished, Roy Keane, together with Paul Scholes and Henning Berg re-emerged onto the pitch to a tremendous reception. Even from the other end of the stadium Keano's body language spoke volumes. He didn't want to do this. For him it wasn't right. An stubborn man for all the right reasons, bullying and cajoling fellow pros to reach even greater heights, this time he had to take instructions from us. He had to be told just how great we felt he was, and we weren't going to leave until we had put him in his pedestal where he belonged.

The players, who by now were sitting wearily on the turf earning a breather, stood up and formed a guard of honour with arms around one another. Keane and Scholes passed through the middle of them and strolled towards us and where, who else but David May had placed the European Cup.

By now we had learned our parts and we again fell silent until the two raised the trophy together, then we let out such an almighty roar that even we were shaken to the core.

The exorcism was now complete. We had achieved what William Peter Blatty and William Friedkin had so spectacularly failed to do. The world could start turning again, but only after the biggest fucking party the world would ever know.

I found Graham and we slowly and oh, so reluctantly made our way up the steps. A last lingering look at the inside of the Nou Camp from the top of the second tier and then we were cascaded down the outer stairs with thousands of delirious fellow Reds of all shapes, sizes and sexes. Half way down a middle aged man in shorts and alcohol induced complexion called out to me.

"Oy! Aren't you that United fan from off the tele?"

I nodded, thinking back to all the anti-Murdoch campaigning I had done.

"You deserve the freedom of Salford."

Recognising that at moments of extreme excitement, such as approaching orgasm, we tend to exaggerate the superlatives, I was still taken aback by his comment. In an instant I was overwhelmed with gratitude. This one man, who I had never set eyes on in my life before (officer) and who disappeared from view almost immediately, had made my life complete. A southern softie glory hunter, living 180 miles from the centre of the world, who'd lived, breathed and died a thousand times, sacrificed career and women to fight on all fronts for Manchester United, had had his life vindicated, justified, ordained.

My efforts had been recognised by one of Manchester's own and there is no greater praise than that.

It had all been worthwhile.

We cavorted out into the street. Joy was unconfined. The thousands of Reds who hadn't been able to gain entrance into the stadium joined with us for our moment in the sun. Spontaneous celebrations erupted all around us followed closely by TV crews. We made our way to the agreed meeting point, a hotel sign at the corner of the street.

One by one we The Magnificent Seven reformed. Hugging, kissing, pogoing, we found re-newed strength in each other's company. We fed off each other. I then spotted Rob Bonnet standing next to one of those outside broadcasting trucks. He'd interviewed me on a number of occasions over the past year, principally on our anti-Murdoch campaign.

"I'm ready for my close-up now, Mr De Mille."

"Sorry David. We've finished filming now. We're just doing a re-run".

"Can I watch?'"

"Sorry. They're rather busy inside there."

Damm.

"What did you think of the game then?" I asked

"To be honest, it wasn't a very good game from our point of view. Thank God for those last three minutes."

Proof if ever we needed it. Somebody else saw it. God WAS on our side tonight.

I suppose having Sir Matt Busby as a neighbour must have its influences, and on what would have been on his 90th birthday too.

I can just imagine the conversation. In the morning God, holding Sir Matt in such high esteem, would have humbly knocked gently on the great man's door (I can only speculate here that angels have doors. Conversely I have no proof to the contrary)

"Err, excuse me Sir Matt, can I come in. (God was obviously being extra polite in the presence of such a great man, because as God himself and everyone else who believes in him knows, God is omnipresent. He is everywhere at all times, therefore he was already in as well as outside, if you see what I mean.) I'm aware it's your birthday today. In keeping with heavenly tradition I have come to grant you a wish."

"Aye lad. And as I'm sure you are also aware, it's my 90th birthday. Surely I'm allowed two wishes at the beginning of a new decade."

"You are right once again, Sir Matt. Forgive me. What two wishes can I grant you today?"

"Well, there will be two billion people on Earth watching a rather important football match tonight at the Nou Camp"

"Is that the same as the Old Camp?"

"God, please don't crack jokes, it's not worthy of you."

"Sorry."

"Now, for my two wishes I'd like two goals tonight, please."

"Certainly, Sir Matt. At what time exactly?"

Sir Matt thought for a moment. Compared with his life on Earth, heaven was a little, how could he put this...predictable.

"I want you to wait until the match is over. Then when they announce the injury time, that's when I want you to strike"

God thought for a moment. How come Sir Matt was allowed to crack the odd joke and not himself? Then he saw the twinkle in Sir Matt's eyes.

"Of course, Sir Matt. Enjoy the match tonight."

"Oh, I will, son. Believe me, I will."

Everybody in heaven believed him, because he was, Sir Matt Busby.

Back on Earth, we hugged, kissed and danced our way back to the underground station. The main topic of serious conversation was, what to do next? Instinct was to meet up back at my mate of a mate's flat, then make our way to The Ramblers for the party to end all parties. Yet the word on the street was that all the bars had been ordered to close, the thought of thousands of Reds drinking Barcelona dry was too much for the Catalans.

Some of our group had jobs to go back to on Friday and any delay would jeopardize their employment. They were already pushing their luck by taking three days off in the middle of the week, a sentiment I knew well from thirty one years before (Real Madrid away – don't you remember, or have you skipped that bit?)

In the end we agreed to celebrate in a bar near my mate of a mate's flat, then pick up the people carrier and drive over the Spanish border and onto Narbonne where I had pre-booked two rooms at the local Formule 1 Hotel.

We crammed into a small bar and creamed ourselves once again as the TV replayed the golden goals over and over again. It was strange to see them from a different angle, yet they were just as I had seen them. Only this time I could look at the players' faces and their celebrations. Ye Erics, I thought Ollie on his knees was going to burst with happiness. And look at Becks, running just as fast with his celebrations as he has all through the match itself.

It was around 1 o' clock in the morning when I suggested we'd better get back to the flat or we'd outstay our welcome. Fortunately my mate of a mate was still up so we bid him a tearful farewell, girded our loins into the van and eased our way out of town, scarves, and at times, buttocks, out of the windows.

I looked back, and unlike Lot I didn't turn into a pillar of salt.

Barcelona. "Say it loud and there's music playing,

Say it softly and it's almost like praying."

Coming down to Earth was having its effects and driving along the pitch black motorway in the early hours of the morning was hard work. As the only non drinker in our group I had happily accepted responsibility for the total drive. However, adrenaline and sleep were battling it out inside my head and I didn't know who was going to win.

After what seemed like hours, but was in fact only two, we arrived on the outskirts of Narbonne and I began to look for signs for the hotel. I had their brochure with me, but a combination of non-existent signs and matchstick eyes prolonged the search unnecessarily. Not that most of our party noticed. They were dreaming the dream that was in fact reality.

Eventually, in an industrial estate on the outskirts of town, we spied the magic yellow and black checkered flag that is the Formule 1 logo.

You know that feeling when you want a crap. You keep it in until you approach a toilet, then your bowels race ahead of your brain and your bottom muscles start to relax before you've opened the toilet door, let alone pull down your trousers.

Heavy waves of sleep dragged my eyelids down over my eyes, only we had a problem.

I couldn't open the automatic gates of the hotel. You see, one way these one star hotels keep their costs down is to only have live people available for breakfast and for selected times during the day. At all other times you enter and exit by entering a six-figure code into the keyboard by the entrance to the hotel and by the side of your hotel room.

Could I remember our code number? Could I fuck.

I'd actually written it down but a combination of sleep, poor handwriting and referee endowed vision had caused a breakdown of my senses. A few minutes later all seven of us were trying to decipher the code by the car's headlights. I was not the most popular boy in class.

At 5 o' clock in the morning we finally managed to do it. I drove into the car park which was full (of course), and parked badly. We trundled up the outside staircase to our two adjoining rooms and hastily agreed to meet at nine for breakfast, as any later and we'd seriously jeopardize our chances of making the last ferry from Calais which was around eleven at night.

Thursday 27th May

I could have danced all night.
I could have danced all night.
And then come back for more.
I could have spread my wings and done a thousand things As I told people what I saw.

I woke up three hours later lying on top of the world. I was ready to drive around the world and back. I'd never felt so good in my life.

The enormity of what we had witnessed the previous evening had hit me the moment I woke up and I felt like a man possessed.

I was on fire, only this time it was my heart and my head, not my arse that ruled proceedings. I woke everybody up and heralded everybody into showers and clothes. We made our way to breakfast in ones and twos. There were a number of Reds already there. Winks and grins abounded as we helped ourselves to tea, coffee, croissants and baguettes.

Everything tasted so good. Tales were exchanged. I bought as many different newspapers as possible as they all ran our victory on their front pages. By half past nine we were back in the VW and on our way.

Now I could really start to enjoy myself. I had imagined this victory drive a million times. Reality was a million times better. A day long tantric sex-drive.

I Felt Good, nu nu nu nu nu nu nu. Just like I knew that I would, nu nu
nu nu nu nu nu,
I Felt Good, nu nu nu nu nu nu nu. Just like I knew that I would, nu nu nu
nu nu nu nu.
So Good. Djoom Djoom. So Good. Djoom.
I Felt Good. Djoom Djoom Djoom Djoom DJOOM.

From James Brown I went to Roy Orbison/Cyndy Lauper.

"I drove all niiiiiiiiiiiiiiiii,iiiiiiiiiight." Only I changed the words to fit our situation.

My face set in an over-bright and disturbingly sinister grin a la Jack Nicholson in The Shining as I drove onto the Autoroute. Singing was the order of the day as we went through the entire United repertoire. When voices started to croak I put on the cassettes and we sang along with those.

All along the route drivers honked and waved. With fellow Reds we saluted each other. The Red Army was returning victorious to home shores and every mile of the journey was a celebration.

We turned off the autoroute for a break in Macon, a small town a little south of Clement Ferrand. Set in a valley surrounded by green hills, it looked like paradise as the sun blazed down. We settled in a cafe in the main square, ordered refreshments and surveyed our world. We were all in a state of afterglow. Locals detected a calmness about us that was misleading. We were just gathering our strength for the next onslaught on our vocal chords. By now we were seriously behind schedule so when we set off and returned to the autoroute I did my best impersonation of Alain Prost.

Without a cop car or radar in sight we zoomed along at 160 kph. Suitably re-enforced, our voices soared above the noise of the engine. As on the way down I parried a few calls from clients and suppliers on the mobile, letting only a trusted few into the secret of knowing where I really was. You never know, they could take it the wrong way. Them up against it with yesterday's deadlines and me swanning it on the Continent.

Just after midday Hélène phoned. She had watched the game last night on the sofa with Melanie and Jasmine. Will wonders never cease? After all the verbals the family had actually shared with me, in their own way, the greatest moment of my life. I was rather touched. She wanted to know how we were all feeling and what time she could expect us at home. She stopped me in mid flow as I geared up for a kick by kick account of the match, so I restricted myself to a sanitised version of the last 48 hours. And on the basis we caught the 11.00pm ferry we should be back at home around two in the morning.

I also told her that everyone would be staying at our place before dambustering off to their abodes.

"I'll go out and get a few beers and something to eat for everybody."

What a woman. Even in our hour of ecstasy she recognised that a way to a man's stomach is through his stomach. I told the others and a cheer went up.

Then I asked the sixty four dollar question.

"Did you record the match?"

"Yes."

"Yeah!" What a woman. Even in our hour of ecstasy she recognised that a way to a man's heart is through his football team.

Caught up in the euphoria of the moment my mate Mick, sitting next to me in the front, phoned his missus. Leslie is a lovely, gentle woman and like Hélène, has to put up with a lot of crap to keep the family going. Of course I could only hear one side of the conversation and everything seemed to be going suburbanly, domestically OK when Mick also asked the sixty four dollar question.

"Did you record the match?"

I couldn't hear the answer but I detected a reddening of Mick's face and neck and a raising of the voice.

"I'll take that as a no then." I thought.

"How could you?" pleaded Mick

"Surely "How couldn't you?" was better grammar?" I thought, then thought better than to rectify my mates English in his hour of agony.

It transpired that Leslie had taken their two kids over to the park for the evening and had been simply too occupied to set up the video.

Grounds for divorce, don't you think? I mean, we all go through a lot of shit. Bills, bosses, bankers, mother-in-laws, motorway cones, the list is endless. But to forget to record the greatest match of all time? Enough is enough.

Mick switched off the phone. He'd gone silent and was looking out of the window.

"Don't worry, mate. I'll just send you a copy mine."

His face brightened. The crisis passed. Phew.

Back to shiny, happy people.

Soon we came to the outskirts of Paris but by the time we had made it to the Peripherique it was rush hour. In the four and five lanes we crawled along at between 10-20 kph. Drivers wound down their windows and wanted to shake us by the hand. Anglo-French relations rea ched a new high as 'entente cordial' replaced 'up yours onion breath' and we all delighted in having beaten the Germans.

Finally signs for Aeroporte Roissy/Charles de Gaule and Porte de la Chapelle appeared and we were on the final autoroute hurdle from Paris to Calais. Picking up speed picked up the spirits as I vowed to break the land speed record.

Driving over the speed limit after winning an important game is like being let loose in a sweet shop. It's childish but exhilarating. Multiply by a factor of one thousand and I was no longer driving but

flying. I was on the back straight. I was on my second, third, fourth wind. I had already driven over two thousand miles and I could have driven forever. The thought of the White Cliffs of Dover greeting another glorious, victorious army was making me moist again.

But not before another gem of an encounter left its mark.

We stopped at one of the autoroute service stations for a pee when I noticed a Bayern car a few feet away with four of Aryan's finest young men inside. As I've stated before I'm one of life's great winners, magnanimous in victory, gracious in defeat. I strolled over to their vehicle to offer my condolences. The two in the front nodded sheepishly but the two in the back had a look of thunder.

What could I say?

"It's only a game."

Well, if you've read the previous forty odd pages you know that nothing could be further from the truth.

"There's always next time."

Well no. Why should I wish them a chance to win it next year? We'd want to retain it, surely?

Finding the right words was proving difficult. A life in the diplomatic corps was fading fast. Fortunately lady luck was at hand in the form a large, burly Dutch lorry driver, who waddled over and offered sweaty bear hugs to us all, pronouncing to all and sundry in his best Paul Whitehouse accent....

"Thanks guys for beating the Germans. We fucking hate them."

Ann Franks eat your heart out. Holland may only be a small country but they sure know how to express themselves. The backseat Bavarian bovver boys shrank back into their seats whilst Mick and I exchanged pleasantries. Would we have been so accommodating had the ball been on the other foot? Having experienced Wembley '79 I feel I'm fully qualified to say "Yes".

Back on the road again Rory Gallagher, Joy Division, New Order, Clash, Led Zeppelin, Status Quo and Bruce Springsteen anthems were belted out at the top of our out of tune voices. The final two hundred odd miles flew by as Calais rose out of the blackness with minutes to spare.

Another victory to The Red Army on tour.

I knew the route to the ferry port like the back of my hand. We screeched to a halt behind rows of Reds. Car horns were blasting all over the place. Another dream was coming true. How many times on TV had I witnessed scenes of streets full of cars in towns and cities all over the world with delirious supporters (and hangers on) travelling up and down in convoys.

Now it was our turn. Brilliant. I hooted with the best of them. Windows down, United anthems reverberated around the car par. Then we were ushered on board.

Christ. The sound of a hundred or more horns filled the hollow car decks. The noise was actually painful on the ears, it was that loud. Getting out of our cars we chanted with renewed vigour and the enclosed metal effect was awesome. It sent shivers down the spine.

Up on deck Reds were here, Reds were there, Reds were every fucking where. Cheshire/Lancashire grins were the order of the day. For many words did not have to be exchanged, just a knowing smile. Speech was redundant. For some communication was telepathic, others alcoholic. What a blissful hour and a half. Then the call to arms as all drivers and their passengers were requested to return to their vehicles.

Squeezed inside once again, the concophany of chants and horns rose to a cresendo.

We were finally about to set foot back on British soil, accompanied by the greatest trophy in world club football. I'm sorry. I broke down again. Great sobs shook my body as so many of the things I had dreamed of all my life continued to unfold before my very misty eyes.

History had been created and I was in the middle of it all. Everything about the trip had been a million times better than I could possibly have imagined and in a way I wished it would never end. I knew at that moment in time that life would never ever get any better. I was tingling and buzzing all over, with every fibre of my body. Yes, we may win the Eurpopean Cup again. Penelope Cruz, Jay Lo, Boyonce, Kylie and Elle Macpherson may all invite me up to their rooms for a nightcap but nothing, and I repeat, NOTHING will ever match the thirty one years of foreplay, the intensity of those three minutes and the lifelong everlasting orgasmic glow that has followed.

I was still so high. I was overloading on official, as opposed to artificial stimulation. My mates were giving me furtive glances as my reactions were getting a little OTT (little? Ed). They voiced concerns over my ability to complete the final leg of the journey. It was 1 o' clock in the morning. I had been driving almost continuously for two days and two thousand miles. Perhaps I needed a break? Perhaps somebody else could take the wheel for the final eighty miles?

"NO!!!"

I was a man pocessed. I wanted the glory of driving through capital ABU'sville. It was my town. My car. My ball. You can't play.

We approached the deserted Old Kent Road. In my mind thousands littered the route. "Hail Ceasar. Hail the mighty warriors. Hail the Red Devils. Long live the driver for he is one of us."

Over Westminster Bridge and round the Houses of Parliament.

"Fergie for Prime Minister."

Predictable I know but we had to sing it, didn't we?

Along the Embankment and right into Cheyne Walk. Left in Fulham Road. At Parsons Green it was left into Peterborough Road and, just like Cinderellas Castle in Disneyland, 2nd left into Clancarty Road and we were home at precisely 02.20am on Friday 28th May, 1999.

I didn't need to ring the doorbell. We were making enough racket to wake the whole steet but what the fuck. One or two of our party were trying to Shh us but "CAMPIONES" drowned everything else out.

Hélène came rushing out of the house. I'm sure a couple of minutes earlier she had been prepared to welcome us all with open arms but our grand entrance had transformed her features into thunder. She represented every postcard cartoon of the wife waiting on the doorstep with a rolling pin in her hand. Only Hélène didn't need a rolling pin. Oh no. Her tongue was a much more powerful weapon.

I bravely ignored the venom and attempted to cajole her back into the house. I put an arm round her shoulder and schmoozed my way into the lounge where a feast of beer cans and Pringles was laid out before us.

What a woman. I gushed our gratitude as we all took our places on the terraces, I mean sofa. I poured out the beers and put the kettle on for Hélène and me. Any thoughts of sleep had disappeared. All brewed up I went back into the lounge where everyone was talking at once, trying to put the last sixty eight hours into words.

Did it really happen? There was only one way to find out. Play the video. A debate went up. Just the winning goals or the whole match.

The whole match won hands down. Hélène couldn't believe it.

"Surely you're not going to watch the match again? Now? You've seen it already. Why do you need to see it again anyway?"

Women. They don't get it, do they? I gave her one of my most condescending looks that I've perfected over the years, which translated into English spelt out, "Surely it's obvious why we have to watch it all over again. And don't call me Surely."

It wasn't obvious to Hélène who gave me one of her own looks and disappeared up the stairs.

I went back to the lounge and checked out the video. It had already rewound itself back to the beginning. Great. So at around

03.00 the match began all over again. Only it didn't. No, don't worry, it had been recorded OK. Now that would have been a catastrophe. No, it's just that with the combined effects of all that travelling, so little sleep, emotional overload and now beer and Pringles, we just caved in.

After about twenty minutes of the match it was agreed to crash out and begin properly a few hours later. Which we did.

Oh what a beautiful morning
Oh what a beautiful day
Oh what a beautiful morning
Everything's going my way.

Epitaph

Hélène and I have been together now for well over thirty years and she's had to put up with a hell of a lot more than many women have a right to expect, but then she should have read the small print of our marriage contract more closely so she only has herself to blame. My two daughters, Melanie and Jasmine, continue to delight me with their take on life. Watching a child grow from the age of minus nine months and blossom into an individual and unique human being is something so special. I was actually in the operating theatre for the birth of my second daughter and those sights and sounds will remain deep within me forever.

Yet when people ask me what is the greatest day/night of my life my instinctive response is, and I know will always be, May 26th 1999. Friends and family are shocked. "You can't be serious!" they exclaim. Oh yes I can. Others think I'm just after a quick laugh. Oh no I'm not.

There are no words in the English dictionary that come close to articulating the intensity and depth of emotions that United fans experienced that night. To keep a sense of perspective in all this, and in an attempt to keep my marriage and remaining goolies intact, let me call my next witness, our greatest savior, Peter Schmeichel.

"It's difficult to explain the feeling that rushes through your body when you lift up the most important trophy in Europe in the direction of 45,000 ecstatic fans. In a way you can compare it with being handed your newborn child in the delivery room. And then you have to multiply that by a factor of two. There aren't many things that surpass the sensation of seeing your child for the first time, but that is the sort of experience most people have the opportunity to savour at least once in a lifetime. There are not many people who get the chance to hold aloft the European Cup to a roar of excitement. That is what makes it a little more special."

His words not mine. The defense rests.

23

IN THE MERRY MERRY MONTH OF MAY

THAT WAS SOME weekend that was. Well, I say weekend, but thanks to the proliferation of holidays on offer by our Gallic neighbours within whose bosom I then resided, it was a Wednesday night to Sunday night type weekend.

Life is made up of "if onlys" and "what ifs" and "so near but so far". However this weekend I hit all the bases. Everything I touched turned to gold, or should I say, Red. And believe me, as one of life's "nearly men", this was an extremely rare occurrence.

I had always earmarked Charlton at home as my last game of the 2002/2003 season. At the time it was just the last home game and, with all due disrespect, Charlton are not the biggest draw so I reasoned getting a ticket would be hard but not impossible. It also co-incided with the Shareholders United AGM, so I had an opportunity to help the "If you can't beat 'em, join 'em, then beat 'em" brigade.

A full six weeks before the match I booked my easyjet ticket for the Wednesday evening so I could spend a couple of days with Melanie, in London before making my way north to Eric's own country. Yet as the weeks past and the date drew nearer the significance of the fixture grew in importance, which had an equal and opposite effect in the availability of tickets. I licked and groveled. I posted umpteen messages on United forums but all to no avail. Every Red who was alive wanted to be at this game – and most of the 1400 dead ones as well. (Well, not all the dead ones, but more of that later.) I was in competition with some serious "I've been to every game since before I was born" match going Reds, so I was losing out on the sympathy vote.

Meanwhile, in a parallel universe not a million miles away, yours truly had been sweet-talked and convinced that my rambling prose was worth collating and putting out in book form. One being the esteemed editor of Red News and the other being my wife who hates football (yeah, I know), so there was no way their paths would have crossed to hatch this little pisstake plot together.

I decided to take the book by the horns and contact a number of publishers. I'd been warned by a mate that "Premier League" publishers would not be interested. You see, book publishing is a bit like the music industry. It's very conservative by definition. Better the devil you know than the Red Devil you don't know. For example, artists such as Elvis Presley, The Beatles and Oasis suffered multiple rejections because the business had not seen or heard anything like them before. So, when more by luck than judgement they became huge, the record companies fell over themselves to find or create copies. They then saturate the market which then eventually runs out of steam. Nick Hornby's (in my opinion) brilliant book, "Fever Pitch", opened the floodgates for what is now known in the trade as 'Fan Culture' publications. The last few years has witnessed a proliferation of such books by reformed nutters, anonraks, as well as some genuinely well researched and written masterpieces by fans themselves. Reds such as Richard Kurt, Jim White, Andy Walsh and Adam Brown, Michael Crick, Paul Windridge and Linda Harvey spring to mind.

So much so, in fact, that I was told this type of genre had past its sell by date, and my chances of kindling the interest of one of the September 11th/Irak cash strapped American owned corporations was neigh impossible below zero. With the chances of an advance to keep me in the sort of luxury I had always dreamed about dashed, I began courting specialised sports publishers in the "Nationwide League."

Lo and behold, two showed interest. And that's how I came to have two appointments, one in London and one in Manchester, on the Thursday and Friday prior to the Charlton game. (You're still with me I hope)

My luck now began to change. My first publishers appointment resulted in a written offer. Yipee! On Friday I was met at Piccadilly station by the Manchester based publisher who subsequently offered me a contract as well. Double yipee!

2-0 to me I think.

Plus, whilst negotiating (alright, drinking) with the Manchester publisher on Friday evening, who should phone me on my mobile other than the one and only Paul Windridge. I stepped outside into the pouring rain.

"Are you still looking for a ticket?"

"Are Siddy massive and bitter? 'course I'm still looking for a ticket".

"I think I may be able to help. I'll call you back later."

Later arrived.

"I've got you a ticket. Meet me under the plaque at High Noon".

"Paul?"

"Yes, Dave?"

"Will you marry me?"

Stupid question I know. We were both married, and to different wives.

But it's at emotional (or drunk) times like these that you say "things", don't you?

Fortunately he saved my blushes by laughing, so we left it at that.

I went back inside the pub happy and moist.

Saturday morning in Manchester dawned bathed in sunshine. (I told you the spirit of Eric was with me) I got up much too early and walked through deserted streets to Piccadilly for any bus to the ground. Stallholders were still setting up so I did a slow circuit of the ground and surrounding streets just breathing in the air around Old Trafford – the elixir of life.

For someone who lived through each and every one of those (in)famous 26/31 years, I intended breaking the habit of a lifetime by looking for a Champions T-shirt. Normally I would never entertain the thought. Words like "Luck", "Pushing", "Throat" and "Stuck" come instantly to mind. But living 1000 miles from Mecca dictated otherwise. If and when we achieved the ultimate goal, I would not be in a position to simply hop back. However, belief outweighed doubts and the said T-Shirt was duly purchased. In my defence I would like to record that I never touched the T-shirt. The seller put it in a paper bag and I put it straight in my holdall, vowing not to even look at it again until the dastardly deed was done.

My conscience was clear.

I know I'm risking the wrath of regular match going Reds here but I have another confession. I went into the Megastore. (Yeah, I know, but this was 2003 BG – before Glazer). But here's something. It may be vast but the choice is not. No United cover for my mobile. No car stickers. No small pennant for my interior car mirror.

No good.

Cometh the hour cometh the Shareholders AGM so I duly made my way to SamuelPlatts and upstairs for luke warm coffee and hot gossip. It was great to meet up with so many old faces (and bodies to match) but the meeting was kept to the basics as there was a more pressing engagement about to begin down the road. I agreed to distribute two bags full of "Join Shareholders United and have a say in YOUR club. United for United" leaflets after the game, then said my goodbyes and made my way to the memorial plaque to wait for the Golden Windridge.

High Noon. 12.05. 12.10. It's no good. Where's my mobile?

Ring, ring...

"Paul?"

"Yeah Dave. Sorry we're a bit late. Traffic you know."

What. On match days. Gerraway.

"Don't worry. I've left the others parking the car and I'm running towards you. Bye".

Good man, Paul Windridge. A few minutes later we met up.

"You're tall", I thought as we exchanged greetings and pretend relaxed conversation.

Richard, the good doctor, has your ticket. Ah, here he is".

I turned round.

Good Eric. You're fucking tall" I thought as I gazed into his neck. "Bet you never had a problem watching matches standing as a kid".

Paul and I exchanged CD's (We'd decided that somehow engagement rings would not be right). His was of a band he's producing called "SOSA" and mine was from mates of mine based in Paris, a funky 8 piece Afro-Blues band called "RAS SMAILA" whose album, "True Story", had just come out on Dixie Frog Records in France. (Yes, I know it's a blatant plug but, what the hell. And they are brilliant)

I then followed Mr Big into OT and to our position near the corner flag at the Scoreboard End, about half way up. I could clearly see the grey haired Pete Boyle giving it large below me, inspiring the massed ranks of Reds to..."Sing their hearts out for the lads".

There was an air of expectancy all around me. Somehow we just knew that Charlton were not going to be the banana skin that United have a habit of encountering at significant moments in any given season. The match started well but not brilliantly. We were dominating play but, after recent stuffings, Charlton were out to show that they were no pushovers. Their attacking intentions were limited by both intent and lack of talent in the required department.

After eighteen minutes United scored. Beckham cut in from the right and his deflected shot ended in the net.

1-0. I'm up. I'm away. We're on our way. At last, a match going along with the script. Then Carroll rolls a ball out to Keane who turns it back to Carroll who, not expecting this sequence of events, scuffs his shot to Charlton's Danish player who volleys it straight into our empty net.

Ah, yes. The United script. I should have known. 1-1.

Now, I've mentioned it before but I'll mention it again. I possess man's intuition, because somehow I just knew that this was but a mere blemish on an otherwise perfect day. For Charlton this resulted in a Ruud awakening as two devastating pieces of skill from the Dutchman meant, with a two goal cushion, we could relax at half-time.

United took the collective foot off the collective pedal for the second half, but not before Ruud got yet another hat-trick with a superbly balanced reaction and shot for our fourth. Charlton were a spent force and we were gearing up mentally and winding down physically for the final assault at Everton the following Sunday.

At the final whistle The Wizard came onto the pitch to thank us for our marvelous support and explained that as the team were chewing over the Toffees in eight days time he thought it would be inappropriate for the team to do a lap of honour. I was personally disappointed but I understood totally. They were a professional team and I was a professional supporter. We were as one for the cause, to get our trophy back.

As the players disappeared from view I rushed outside and set up my pitch to distribute the Shareholders United leaflets. The first fifteen minutes after the final whistle are the most important, didn't you know. I started waving them about and shouting, "Join Shareholders United. United for United. Kee United independent. "Just one share's enough to have your say".

Repeat, then repeat again.

You know something funny. Even though I'm a Cockney Red, when I shout like that outside Old Trafford I shout in a Manc accent. And when I sing and chant, I sing and chant in a Manc accent as well. Magic or sad. You decide.

My work done I take a last lingering 2002/2003 look at the stadium and slowly walk up Sir Matt Busby Way. A bus ride later I'm sitting in a new, slick overpriced cafe in the concourse of Piccadilly station waiting for my train back to London.

"The cheesecake's not bad", I thought, "but at this price it bloody well should be."

An uneventful trip back in the first class, upgrade for £15 type seat later, and I was back in my daughter's flat where Hélène and Lilyella, my beautiful granddaughter were also waiting. Happy families.

They talked to me about Mel's new record. I talked about Arsenal v Leeds. They talked to me about Lilyella's school. I talked about Arsenal v Leeds. They talked to me about life in France. I talked about Arsenal v Leeds. They talked to me about my flight back to Nice and how I didn't have the time to watch the Arsenal v Leeds match on Sunday or I'd miss my plane. I talked about Arsenal v Leeds.

They stopped talking to me.

I went through my family duties on Sunday morning on autopilot. I was giving Lilyella a cuddle when the match began.

Early on in the first half a through ball was met by Kewell who hit the best shot/volley of his career.

1-0 to Leeds.

At 53 years of age I fought for control of my emotions.

"Hélène? Could you take care of Lily for a second? Thank you."

Silent scream and much punching in the air. Pretty restrained I'd call that. Half-time. Still 1-0. Time for kettle boiling. Any excuse to keep occupied.

Second half. Arsenal equalise. Well, it was only a matter of time, wasn't it? But they still had to get a second to keep in the race. One thing struck me. The Arse weren't playing with their early season swagger and confidence. Things were not coming off that had seemed so effortless before.

Ian Harte free-kick. 2-1 to the sheep.

"Hélène? Could you take care of Lily for a second? Thank you."

Silent scream but, this time, a lot more punching in the air.\Significant that.

Bergkcamp equalises. 2-2. Bastards. Still, times running out and they have to win. By this time my breath is coming in short spurts. I gave Lily back to Hélène. It's at times like these that a man has to be alone with his thoughts, and I'm sure you were all thinking the same thoughts as me.

I paced around the living room. I wanted to say it but the word wouldn't come out. Too many campaigns. Too many disappointments. Too old.

With just minutes to go the ball goes out to Veruka who was, wait for it, TWO WHOLE BEAUTIFUL FUCKING YARDS OFFSIDE. He cuts in and lets fly. 3-2.

"THAT'S IT! THAT'S IT! WE'VE DONE IT! WE'VE DONE IT!"

I cry. I jump up and down like Woody in that scene from Toy Story 2, when his body stays in the same place – just his feet seem to be jumping. I rush over to my holdall and, shaking and sweating, do my Clark Kent impersonation by taking off my current T-shirt and putting on my brand new "CHAMPIONS" T-shirt.

It felt sooooooooooo gooooooooooooood!

The final whistle goes and so does the last of my self control. Even this keyboard is getting wet again as the memories come flooding back.

I kiss and hug my family goodbye (and to think they thought this emotion was directed towards them) then I run downstairs to get the taxi to the station.

I wait on West Hampstead station freezing my bollocks off, as I tried to catch the eye of fellow passengers and direct them to the wording on my "CHAMPIONS" T-shirt. There was no way any jacket was going to obscure the message I wanted the world to read. I arrive at Luton Airport only to find that my easyJet flight had been delayed for two hours. So, I needn't have rushed after all.

Brilliant.

As I wandered around the departure lounge trying out free samples of aftershave and reading extracts from those "Adult" books on the top shelf I spied the icing on the cake.

"It doesn't get any better than this", I thought as I put the book back and make my three legs back into the centre of the departure lounge.

Yes, there it was. Hang on, there's another one. This is getting even better. Blimey, there's loads of 'em. I'm in heaven.

Arsenal fans. Arsenal fans wearing Arsenal tops. Arsenal fans wearing Arsenal tops in Luton Airport departure lounge.

And me, wearing my United CHAMPIONS T-shirt.

Look at their faces. Boy, am I going to enjoy the next two hours. And my summer's wardrobe's sorted.

24

YORKSHIRE PUDDINGS

WORK, DEBT, GIRLFRIENDS. All responsibilities pale into insignificance as another Euro jaunt looms on the horizon. Rape, pillage and boozing are the order of the day, and night, with the small matter of a footy match in-between to take the mind off rape, pillage and booze.

By and large the locals look on in mild amusement as Reds take over town squares and bars and with missionary zeal attempt to convert the population to the Red cause. Instant life-long friendships are established that can sometimes last a whole evening.

Travelling United fans are almost unique in recognising and respecting local customs, even if they are of the overwhelmingly alcoholic variety, whilst at the same time imposing a Manc perspective on proceedings. This positive attitude extends to the UK as well. It's just a shame that opposing fans don't exhibit the same enlightenment.

When I was a kid I would watch many comedians or situation comedies on the box but rarely laugh. The characters or situations depicted seemed so far fetched that I couldn't believe in them, subsequently I couldn't relate to them and therefore I found nothing to laugh at.

Imagine my surprise then, that when I eventually went out in the world to seek my fortune (now there's a contradiction in terms if ever there was one) I began to encounter the very cardboard cutouts I'd seen on TV. It was a shock, and not a little disturbing to discover that stupid, sad, one dimensional, bigoted bastards actually existed.

Which brings me logically round to our sheep loving brethren across the Penines (thank Eric for the fuckin' Penines). What is it about Yorkshire that in-breeds such homophobia? For decades Yorkshire County Cricket Club was the only county only to field cricketers born and in-bred in Yorkshire. Now, as a United fan, I'm all for encouraging home grown talent, but I think we all recognise the contribution of non Mancs to our amazing success ever since Sir Matt took over after the war.

United are almost unique in displaying the right balance between locals, nationals and internationals. How can layers of limestone divide our healthy take on the world from that of the Yorkshire Yocals.

ACTION REACTION

Our hatred for all things Scouse is a thing of legends, born out of years of escaping with our lives after twin-pronged Zulu style attacks across Stanley Knife Park as we made our way back to our coaches. This, together with the totally obnoxious portrayal of Scousers as lovable rogues living in a twilight world between honest working class and villainy, surviving life's little catastrophes with a cutting wit, really jars.

However, a city that can produce the wondrous Jon Peel is surely only 99% evil.

No such saving grace brothers can be dug up in defense of Leeds. Their fans (now there's a contradiction in terms if ever there was one) are surely the vilest in England. The percentage of racists compared to their average attendance is on a par with Millwall. In the few short years they returned to the First Division/Premiership, collectively and individually they have fast-tracked to rival the granny stabbers as Manc public enemy No. 1. How sweet it is that relegation to the first division and administration for a debt only one sixth of ours should now envelope our sheep loving neighbours.

Let me give you a personal account of Yorkshirism. I recently came back from a funeral near Perpignan in the south of France of my brother-in-law, Hervé Guillaume. A renowned artist in his youth, a combination of excessive alcohol and old socks, sorry Gauloise cigarettes led to throat cancer. His partner of fifteen years was Karen, a not-so-bright spark Yorkshire stick insect from Halifax. (near enough to Leeds for the purpose of this story)

On the morning of the funeral I was making polite conversation with her father, Bob, who incidentally had fucked off when Karen was only five years old. Nice.

"Eee, ecky thump. I'll go t' foot of our stairs."

Within seconds I realised I was in the presence of a stupid, sad, one dimensional, bigoted bastard. Having lived in Cannes for the past three years I began by making polite conversation along the lines of...

"You know, one of the things I miss about dear old Blighty is good old fashioned English cuisine. Here in France local markets and supermarkets may stock better quality meat, fish, fruit and vegetables at lower prices but it's the little things that make all the difference, you know...... Cadburys Cream Eggs, Marmite, Ginger Biscuits, Trebor Mints, Real English Breakfast Tea and, of course, Indian Food."

"Wouldn't eat that shit."

I thought he was doing a Paul Kay piss-take so I persisted.

"No, seriously. I really miss a good curry. We have lots of Chinese/Vietnamese restaurants, and being near the Italian border we have a proliferation of superb Italian restaurants as well."

"Wouldn't touch any of that shit. Roast beef, Yorkshire pudding. Can't beat it. Wouldn't touch all that foreign shit."

He was for real. Not a hint of humour or exaggeration.

I asked him what he did for a living.

"Pub landlord. retired."

Images of him behind the bar with fellow Gentlemen in the same League came to mind.

"We'll have no trouble round here. Local pub for local people. You're not from these parts, are you?"

He wasn't just English. He was Yorkshire. Everybody else was a second class citizen.

I felt like holding up a mirror so that he could see his own reflection. But then I realised. creatures of the night that roam the land like the undead cannot generate a reflection.

The Halifax House of Horrors. Thank Eric for the fuckin' Pennines.

25

WHAT I DID ON MY HOLIDAYS

FOR ALMOST FOUR YEARS I had been living and working in Cannes in the south of France. Well, it's a tough job – but someone's got to do it! Three hundred sunny days a year. Sun, sea, sand and...satellite TV! United stickers on my car without fear of reprisal. Almost the perfect lifestyle EXCEPT I was 1500 miles from Manchester. So, what to do for my summer holidays? Got it! Two weeks in Manchester, what could be better? With the first edition of my book coming out on May 1st 2004 I had harassed the publisher to get me on Parkinson, Jonathan Ross, Soccer A.M. Coronation Street, even Channel 5. With me living in France he couldn't even get me on the bus, so I made the decision to sacrifice two weeks wages and decamp to Manchester for my UK tour.

The Young Ones had nothing on the student flat in Broughton that was to be my base. And bloody brilliant it was too. It took me back to my student days at University with one exception – I never went to university.

Earmarking Chelsea at home as the opening salvo in my marketing blitz, I easyJet-setted into Luton Airport late on a Friday night and arrived at Melanie's house around midnight. A quick tea and dunk then it was off to bed to prepare for my 05.00am alarm call. Borrowing Mel's car I hit the M1 at 06.00am and before I knew it I was parked in Samuel Platts car park in Salford Qyays at 08.30am. And it was pissing down. I was home.

The publisher had printed about 20,000 full colour postcards with the front cover of the book reproduced on one side and a Press Release on the other, and about eight of us were to distribute as many as possible before and after the game to match going Reds. By 10.00am we were all in place and the blitz began. With the rain dripping off every visible orifice we competed with all the fanzine sellers for the hearts, minds and outstretched hands of the Red hoards. I begged forgiveness when at 11.30am I made my way to the Shareholders United AGM. By the time it was all over there was no more time to give out any more cards so I went straight in the East Stand, 2nd tier.

Chelsea scored halfway through the first half. Good strike but where was our defence? Teams about equal I'd say although we seemed devoid of imagination and invention. Just before halftime we were awarded a penalty. I no longer celebrate automatically at times like these and I was proved right as Cudicini, the Chelsea keeper pulled off a phenomenal save to deny Ruud his just deserts. Fortunately Cudicini made amends with ten minutes to go by dropping a perfectly armless shot which let Ruud in for a stomach relieving equaliser.

However we weren't able to raise our game sufficiently to stop Chelsea securing second place. Maybe this is no bad thing. Last season we have put the blame on United's demise down to the Board's ultimately failed attempt to obtain Ronaldihno's signature, Fergie's battle over the Rock of Gibraltar, the possible take-over by both Stupid Cupid and that double Glazer salesman, the Rio debacle, injuries et al. But not enough blame was put on the millionaire, Ferrari driving players for not pulling their fingers out at crucial times.

I have one blinding memory from the Chelsea match which summed it all up for me. In the second half the ball was crossed over to the left and Giggsy started to run for it. then he seemed to say, "Oh, fuck it. I can't be bothered." It was so fucking obvious. I love Giggsy and all that he has done for us over the years. He's Red through and through but that (lack of) action said it all for me. If it now means that our pampered players have to cut short their luxury holidays and get back to training early, well, serves them bloody well right. They should look in the mirror if they want to apport blame. However, I got my camcorder out at the end and captured Ruud thumping his chest right in front of us during the lap of honour.

Back outside we continued to give out the cards until the last Red had disappeared over the horizon. Then we stared to attack the cars. This was pretty effective. They could either ignore us or tell us to run away in small jumps as a number of pedestrian Reds had, but these were a captive audience, their only line of defence was not to wind down their windows.

Surprisingly most of them did so lots of BMW's, Mercs and Range Rovers felt the full force of our onslaught. I even got Tony Banks whilst Colum got Roman Abromavitch. Who's Colum? you ask. On "Fergie & Son" he was the one seen on the United forecourt wearing a red T-shirt with "Manchester United Ruined My Wife" on the back. Media junkies the lot of us.

By now all was quiet except for a small crowd of sad, desperate hangers-on surrounding Fergie's car. Naturally I joined them. After what seemed like ages, but was in fact a hell of a long time, the great man finally came out and to my astonishment made straight for me. A few sycophantic phrases later and I had been invited to Carrington where I intended to present him with a personally signed copy of my book. Don't forget, guys and gals, he had written the Forward so this was indeed a defining moment for me.

I couldn't top that so it was back to Broughton and a quick Clark Kent later we were on our way to the Lowry Centre to see the wondrous John Martyn in concert. Boring Old fart music never sounded so good. Then to round off a perfect day it was off to Rusholme for a midnight curry. Pick the bones out of that.

Tuesday evening saw the final of the Manchester Senior Cup between United & City. I arrived early armed with another box of flyers to give out to the Red faithful. But first I made my way to the entrance to MUTV.

"Excuse me. Can I speak to Steve or Paddy please?" "Are they expecting you?" "Well......erm...erm...yes and no." I squirmed as I explained that I often phoned into their programme as Dave Blatt from Cannes and I felt sure we had bonded enough for them to want to meet me. A sceptical jobsworth went inside and came back with Steve's mobile number. "You can give him a ring." "Thanks mate." I'd actually met Steve Bowyer face to face outside White Hart Lane prior to the 5-3 (Oh, happy days) so hopefully he would remember me. He did.

"David, Paddy and I will meet you outside the players entrance at 6pm." For half an hour I waited, watching most of the young players arrive in impressively ordinary cars. Then I spied Paddy, or should I say Paddy spied me, broke into a grin and greeted me warmly, Steve following up close behind. I gave them each a copy of my book then made my pitch for an interview. Steve looked at Paddy then back at me. "Paddy, why don't we get David on Thursday's show? "Yeah, why not, Steve?" My thoughts exactly. "David", continued Steve.

"Come along on Thursday and we'll put you on for 10 minutes after our introductions." "Brilliant lads. You're on.

I'll look forward to it. Thanks a lot." A result.

I went back to my flyers with added gusto (whoever he was) then met up with the Broughton Brigade and three and a half thousand dads with their four year old sons on their knees for a tense but brittle match. The 3-1 scoreline flattered us. Kenny Copper took his two goals well, others played well in fits and starts but for me the only player who looked premier class to me was Roy Carroll in goal. Bit worrying that.

Wednesday morning broke bright and sunny as I poured over the A-Z. Carrington, Carrington, wherefore art thou Carrington? A-ha. There's Birch Road, but no mention of United's training ground. Never mind. At 09.00 I slipped unnoticed into my Bondmobil and made my way to United's headquarters. Half way down this narrow country lane I encountered an unmanned road block. Having spent more years than I care to remember practising on the McDrive assault course I surmounted this first challenge and soon found my way confronted by a second red and white bar blocking my progress.

With no impersonal intercom to communicate with I came mentally and physically to a grinding halt. However, the car behind me had calmly turned left prior to this second barrier. "What the...?" I thought. And then I realised...I was already in Carrington and the barrier would simply take me out the other side. "That's my street cred in tatters...again!" I mused as I backed up and meekly parked in the car park opposite the gleaming metallic silver building. I walked up to the crested double glass doors and then I was in. Up to the IKEA looking reception desk I strode.

"Excuse me. I have a 10 o' clock appointment with Sir Alex." "He's running a bit late, sir. (Sir? Moi? There's a first.) Would you mind waiting in reception?" "Mind?" I thought. I'd stay here all day if I could get away with it.

Just imagine – going down to the canteen to eat alongside Keaney, Giggsy, Scholsey, Ruudy, Butty, Silvestrey, Ronaldoey and, of course, Gary, the only sensibly named footballer amongst them.

"Yeah. No problem." I sat down next to a suave gentleman in a beige suit. He turned out to be the UK based journalist for France Football, waiting for his audience with the Wizard. Naturally I assaulted him with my book.

Then I convinced him to film me with my camcorder entering and exiting the main reception. (Grow up, moi?).

Next Sir Bobby appeared. I hastily scribbled a dedication on the inside front cover of my other copy and introduced myself. I was hoping he would remember me from the numerous AGM's and car parks where our paths had crossed and I had grovelled. He hid his recognition with ease yet a pleasant conversation ensued as he accepted my prize possession. Eventually Sir Alex came out wearing a dark blue Val Doonigan cardigan straight out of Dunn & Co. We spent what was for me an underwear changing 10 minutes chatting away. I gave him a photocopy of my last article from Red News, celebrating the 5th anniversary of Barca '99. I thought he would jus put it in his pocket and use it for toilet paper later but no, he actually sat down and read it in front of me AND laughed at my jokes! I tell you my friends, life doesn't get much better than that. Eventually he made it clear that my time was up so I handed over a signed copy of my book and had my picture taken with the both of us shaking hands. His parting shot as I left the building was to inform me that we will win back the league next year. He seemed pretty convinced about it too. I couldn't think of anything clever or intelligent to say so I just nodded knowingly, which either came over as clever and intelligent or as a nervous twitch. Floating back to my digs I prepared myself for my first book signing. That evening Borders in Stockport would be the scene of my next triumph. Unfortunately the evening turned out to be of truly Spinal Tap proportions as I was both author and crowd. That put me in my place.

The rest of the week found me in the offices of Parrs Wood Press, desperately phoning bookshops the length and breadth of the country, in a bid to get them to stock my book. It's a tough job but someone's got to do it.

Meanwhile I'd got back in touch with Graham Wyche. Some of you may remember Graham from my 'Fit For a King' story, when the two of us had met up with the Lawman back in the late 80's. Now installed in Oz, he runs the official Western Australia Supporters Club in Perth. He also hosts 'The British Soccer Show' on Access 31 TV and was over for interviews and the Cup Final. We hadn't met up since Barca '99 so a bulk purchase of Men' strength Kleenex tissues was on order. Finally Saturday arrived and Villa away. I love Old Trafford, it's my second home, but as an exiled Red the chances of obtaining a ticket for an away game are almost non- existant. Everybody knows the Red Army on Tour are a sigh and sound to behold and I'd been missing it with an unhealthy intensity. However, being on the ground I had obtained a ticket through the mysterious Ryan so five of us made our way down the M6.

Villa Park has been our lucky ground for ages, yet all good things must come to an end. Our recent indifferent form as players protected their expensive limbs so as to be available for FA Cup Final selection coupled with Villa's stirring march up the league table with a UEFA Cup place at stake led me to believe if ever we were going to end our winning streak this was it. (Shows what I know)

Another stadium, another flyer onslaught. By this time I was getting recognised. The seventeen people and two dogs who regularly watch MUTV came up and said 'Hello' which gave me quite a lift. Inside the Cap 'n Gown Reds were strangely subdued. I expected a good old sing-song but only spasmodic outbreaks occurred. Flyer distribution brought a mixed response, from backslapping congratulations to suspicious looks from the hardcore. In their eyes I was still an outsider trying to get a look-in.

Then my mobile rang and Graham had parked and needed directions. Five minutes later a lot of manly back- slapping and hugging ensued as Barca memories resurfaced. Ten minutes later he was gone, but not until I had done a quick interview on his camcorder to be broadcast later to the waiting hordes in Perth, and a promise to meet up after the game outside the said Cap 'n Gown. We had a lot to catch up on.

Once inside our end I observed that Reds had broken into two or three sections and were singing against each other. Before I knew it the players were on the pitch.

Funny game football, isn't it. There we were with nothing to play for and expecting the Villa to come at us with all guns blazing.

So what happened? Absolutely nothing. Villa seized up under the weight of expectation and we glided through the match unchallenged, restoring our confidence in the process. After only a few minutes Ronaldo cut in from the wing and let fly such a wicked shot that it was a full second before we realised he had scored. Then a few minutes later history repeated itself as Ruud unleashed a shot that seemed to us at the other end to have been cleared off the line when the ref pointed to the centre circle and Ruud went off on another of his runs. Ten minutes gone and 2-0 up without a Villa challenge in sight. The rest of the match was spent singing the full Red repetoir in preparation for the Cardiff capers. Villa couldn't get through our force field, and on the couple of occassions they did the referee ensurred they didn't count. Why couldn't we have had a ref like that at home to Porto? On the other hand he sent off both Fletcher and Ronaldo for two yellow cards.

Referees? Bastards, the lot of 'em.

We waited behind after the final whistle as Gary (who else?) led the players through two unnecessary thin blue lines on the pitch to acknowledge our support. It was too late now for any more flyers so we made our way back to the car. Sunny Sunday was another fifteen minutes of fame day as I had arranged to be interviewed by Alistair Mann from Granada TV, for the local sports programme to be broadcast on the eve of the Cup Final.

Bearing in mind the title of my book, he had wanted to interview me and 'the wife'. City have more chance of winning a trophy than him agreeing to an interview, so it was down to the substitute on the bench, my daughter Melanie, to accompany me on the sofa in the V & A hotel next to Granada studios.

Arriving early we indulged in a five star full English breakfast paid for by Granada. (Doesn't food taste better when somebody else pays?). Stomachs full and mouths ready to overflowing, Mel and I grinned and gobbled our way through the interview. Character assassination was never so painless. After it was over Mel and I went shopping before she made her way back to London. With time on my hands I went to the cinema to see 'The Football Factory'. I thought it my duty to see it even though I didn't agree with its message. I came out almost sick to my stomach. A truly nasty film almost devoid of umour, with ham acting and the worst possible ending.

Cliche upon fucking one dimensional cliche. You have been warned. Monday and Tuesday evenings were spent in readings together with David

McVay, who's superb book, "Steak, Diana Ross" was reviewed recently in Red News. Cue more Spinal Tap moments as we almost outnumbered the audience. Still, it was another opportunity to rabbit on about all things United and tell the same jokes.

The rest of the week was spent selling the book into the stores and desperately trying to score a ticket for Cardiff. Result? Book shops 1 Final ticket 0. On Friday I said goodbye to the Broughton Bunch, all good men and true, spent the morning in the publishers office for one last retail assault before girding my loins and setting off for Cardiff. Or should I say Caerphilly where I had booked a room in a local B&B.

Under no particular pressure I drove down in high spirits (or was it a Ford Fiesta, I can't remember) arriving around 6pm. I'd never seen so many speed cameras so close together in my life. Maybe they breed them down there. I was welcomed by a delightful landlady who had lots of curves, but unfortunately they went in and out in all the wrong places. Cowardice being the better part of valour, I dressed incognito (or was it in the bedroom, I can't remember) arriving in Cardiff city centre for a Friday night blowout. There were police and bouncers everywhere but it seemed pretty cool. However I didn't want a late night as I had been booked as a guest on Brian Alexander's breakfast programme on BBC Radio 5 LIve on the morning of the game, which was to be broadcast from The Angel Hotel just opposite the Millennium Stadium. I was told the Cup Final morning attracted their highest listening figures so it was an ideal opportunity to hit travelling Reds and lesser mortals.

Parking and driving in Cardiff on big match days is a nightmare, so I had arranged for the BBC to send a car for me at 6am. This meant getting up a 5.30am. It was a tough job but somehow I managed to do it. By 6.30am I had surmounted the jobsworth barriers outside the Angel Hotel which normally stop riff-raff like me from entering their refined portals, and was led to the temporary BBC studio. Brian greeted me warmly. We went back a long way. In fact it was Eric who unwittingly brought us together.

The morning after his famous Kung Fu kick at Selhurst Park the media were desperately trying to find someone, anyone, who could speak up in his defence. Everybody was coming to bury him not to praise him.

Due to my high profile at the time with the FSA they had my number.

I agreed to do an interview on the now defunct Channel One in London. Booked in the opposing corner was Brian Alexander, at the time Sports Editor of the Evening Standard, who like 99 percent of the seagulls was calling for our Eric to be hung, drawn, quartered, shot, killed, murdered and hung by the neck until he didn't feel very well. Initially I had problems finding coherent arguments on Eric's behalf, but the ferocity of the blind establishment attack on my hero inspired me to unknown heights of eloquence and reason. Result? A score draw. And after the programme Brian came over to me and congratulated me for basically bullshitting my way through based on emotion, heroworship and a few purist, anti-racism clich$%s of my own.

He called it defending the indefensible but he admired my front. (pity women never say that to me. I'd say it to them!) Since then I've appeared a few times on his late night phone-in programme on BBC Radio 2 and always been able to keep the Red Flag flying high. Even though the last four years I have disappeared off the media map since de-camping in France, he recognised me straight away and we hit the ground running.

Opposite me was a Millwall fan giving it large. "We've got Wisey and…" Oh, I can't remember their names. Who cares anyway? "Once Wisey gets stuck in they'll never know what's hit them." Brian looked at me, almost pleading with me not to blast this young upstart out of the water. Sorry, he started it. "Oh, that's original", I replied "Never heard that one before. Now let me get this straight. You say you're going to come at us from the kick-off and not let us settle. Once out of our stride you're going to hit us on the break and the cup is yours.

NURSE!" I enjoyed that. We kept up the banter but sheer class carried the day. An indication of events to unfold on the pitch in a few hours.

The next couple of hours was spent as a media junkie, crisscrossing the hotel reception area and sitting-in on various radio shows, pontificating to the nation. I even partnered Michael Crick on a couple. (When you're hot you're hot).

At 10 o' clock I then popped outside for a quick interview with Nick Collins from Sky Sports, who even though he is younger than me, looks like my Dad. It was at this moment that I realised the hotel was opposite the Millwall end and I was the only Red shirted hero in sight. I kept one eye on Nick, one eye on the camera and one eye on the blue hordes all around me. (Hang on minute, either my maths or my biology has gone astray)

I needn't have worried. The Millwall I met were OK. They just couldn't believe hey were actually there and were breathing in every aspect of the day. Once the media madness was over another 5 star English breakfast with all the trimmings beckoned paid for by the BBC (I could get used to this). Bloated of mouth and stomach my only disappointment was the failure to secure a ticket. I then set myself up outside the United end by the bridge and once again thrust myself and my flyers at United men, women and children. By now I was getting recognised and a number of people went by and said, "It's him, isn't it?" or came up to me directly and said, "It's you, isn't it?" Tom Cruise, Robin Williams, Dennis Skinner...eat your hearts out.

Down to zero flyers I joined fellow Reds kicking balls into the air and drinking, or was it the other way round? By five to three I admitted failure in the ticket stakes. For some reason even tout tickets were few and far between and I thought, "Shit. I could by a dishwasher for that sort of money." Not very Rock 'n Roll I admit but I was a bit Simply Red (Money's too tight to mention) so I retired to O'Neils which was full of ticketless Reds and joined in the fun.

I got myself in front of the big screen and squeezed myself between two pretty girls. (Get your pleasures where you can I say) An extremely enjoyable 9 minutes ensued with singing, chanting, and when we scored each of the three goals I made sure I celebrated with the two girls. (OK. Not the threesome you read about on the top shelf but enjoyable all the same) As I watched the teams' celebrations on the pitch I thought. "There aren't many teams that celebrate winning better than United. It must be all that practice I suppose."

Finally I reluctantly left the pub and the girls, to their relief I'm sure, and made my way back to the Angel Hotel where I luxuriated in 5 star opulence. I chatted to various celebrities including Arthur Albiston who'd I'd met for the first time at the World Travel Travel in London and then again a couple of years ago in Cannes where we both attended 'Football Expo', a trade exhibition and conference for which I sold stands. We swapped some cherished memories before I gave him the number of Grecian 2000.

At 7.00pm my BBC car arrived and took me back to my B&B in Caerphilly where he landlady with all the right bits sticking in and out in all the wrong places greeted me warmly. She asked me to sign her copy of my book (now, I'm not saying Caerphilly is a small town, but I'm sure she's going to dine out on the fact she met me for weeks to come, whereas my wife would happily dine out without me for much longer) And so my 2 week UK tour came to an end as I drove back to London and before you could say "City are a massive club" I was on the train back to Luton airport and all this bloody sunshine in the south of France. Well, as I said before. It's a tough job but someone's got to do it. So it might as well be me.

26

BARCELONA REVISITED

"THE CRYING GAME", directed by Neil Jordan, tells of an unlikely kind of friendship between Fergus, an Irish Republican Army volunteer, and Jody, a kidnapped British soldier lured into an IRA trap by Jude,another IRA member.

"The Crying Game" was a song recorded by Mike Berry that got to No. 4 in the charts in 1964.

The Crying Game is also a recurring theme that has begun to develop in response to some of my recollections so far. But, hey, United affects me that way and I make no apologies for it.

I believe I'm not alone when I say that May 26th 1999 remains the greatest day and night of my life. Yet when you consider I also have a wife and two daughters to support, you may appreciate the diplomatic tightrope I have to walk. What I whisper tenderly in my wife's ear differs somewhat with my exultations when United score.

1999, and the following year (2000 I think it was), many Reds took their summer holidays along the Costa Brava, Costa Blanca and Los Wankos, Costa Packet so as to be within striking distance of Barcelona. For reasons too boring to mention I had not been able to return, until the summer of 2004 that is.

Five years, five long years. Many a wet dream between the sheets re-living those three golden minutes (Yeah, I suppose that could apply to both activities. I understand your confusion dear reader). But with my youngest daughter, Jasmine, approaching her eighteenth birthday I thought a dose of the Balearic Beat in Ibiza as way of a rights of passage was due.

Campsite in Es Cana duly booked, Hélène, my ruined wife, Jasmine, her best mate Julie and myself left our apartment in Cannes in the second week of August by Renault Scenic for the six hour drive to Barcelona. "Say it loud and there's MUFC playing, saying it soft and it's almost like praying". Barcelona. I was going back to Barcelona.

Kleenex tissues in every compartment, we sped along the south coast of France, repeating the exact route I took half a decade earlier. I kept getting hot flushes as I relived those golden moments and imagined what tomorrow held in store.

We arrived at our hotel just off the Ramblas around 6.pm and just 'did the town'. What a buzz to be back. Tracked down a couple of watering holes where, outnumbering Bayern fans 3-1, we sang our hearts out for the Lads.

The following morning I put my master plan into action. Whilst the three girls set out to Goudy this and Goudy that, I set off for the metro station to continue the re-enactment. Alighting at Les Courts I needlessly walked three quarters round the stadium, just like they had made all Reds do that evening until I was outside Access 4, Gate 96. Kleenex moment, swiftly followed by "Bollox". It was closed. The only way into the stadium forecourt was round the other side. Bollox.

In by Gate 19, through their souvenir shop and out by the side of the stadium where the tours started. I was baking hot in my polyester "Treble 99 " United top but this was a special occasion and I wanted everyone to know where I was coming from. Disappointingly, there were no fellow Reds in the queue, cognito or incognito.

Eventually with ticket purchased and heart beating louder and legs and arms shaking more violently than I ever thought possible, I exchanged the sunlight outside for the gloom within. Surprisingly there was no guide, we were just told to follow the arrows. I didn't care, I just wanted to get back to Gate 96, Block 352, Row 28, Seat 11. I skipped various rooms, dressing rooms and television gantries until I got my first view out in the stadium.

Kleenex moment, swiftly followed by an awareness that people were looking at me. I was crying out loud and I couldn't stop. Hard core Red. Fuck me, this was embarrassing. Then I looked round. Bollox. I was at the other end of the ground. Bollox. Bollox.

I was up and down more times than Siddy fighting relegation and promotion. Each time I came up for air I was one step nearer nirvana. My block, my row, my seat.

Kleenex moments. If this was fucking foreplay put me on fast forward,\pleeeaaase!

At last. My spiritual home came into view. Blocks 353 and 352. I\stumbled along Row 28 in Block 353 until I came to ...Fuck! What's this? A bloody red & white temporary taped barrier. BASTARDS! At the last hurdle, after five long, long years there was masking tape between me and heaven on Earth.

I went down to a fluorescent, orange jobsworth and tried to explain my plight in non-existent Spanish. I don't think he grasped the significance of the occasion as he just shook his head. (or perhaps he did grasp the significance of the occasion and that's why he shook his head. Bastard!)

I made my way back up to the masking tape. I waited until Senior Jobsworth was at the far end of our section then asked a nearby couple to take my photo as I crouched under the tape and made my way to Seat 11. I got myself photoed standing, kissing and finally, sitting on it. Now, this was a cop-out, because five years ago I never sat down at all. I had just stood, jumped, swayed, sung, farted, chanted and bruised my legs something rotten, all in the Red cause.

Treble Kleenex moment. Gazing out onto the pitch it all came flooding back. James. "Oh sit down, Oh sit down, Oh, sit down. Sit down next to me." It had all happened at our end. Scmeikes running up, Giggs shoots, Oh, Teddy Teddy, he went to Manchester United and might win the lot yet. Another cross from Beckham, nodded on, SOLSKJAER. Bayern don't know what hit them. Manchester had hit them.

More fucking Kleenex. My whole Red life flashed before me. The 31 years of hurt between May 29th 1968 to May 26th 1999. I had lived every one. Thousands of miles, thousands of pounds, thousands of orgasms and thousands of premature ejaculations as United flattered to deceive.

A shout invaded my reverie as the jobsworth gesticulated for me to move.

No problem. Mission accomplished and misty eyed I made my way along Row 28 and back over the red and white tape. How appropriate, I thought. Exorcised, I re-joined the rest of the world. Outside I did a quick

Clark Kent and put my original T-shirt back on (I didn't want to look a plonker, now did I?)

By now I was running late but there was only one thing left to do before I met up with the rest of the family. Find a one hour development photo shop. Priorities, my friends. Priorities.

27

EUROPE, EUROPE, AFTER BARCA

MILAN – AUTOPISTA OFF

DRIVING FROM Cannes to Milan and back can be quicker than driving from London to Manchester and back, mainly due to the incessant roadworks that have blighted the journeys of traveling fans along the M1-M6 ever since the twin inventions of the wheel and various Departments of Transport.

At least that was the theory I intended to put to the test when United were drawn against AC Milan in the 1/8 final of the Champions League in the spring of 2005.

I checked my trusty Michelin. Along the A8 autoroute from Cannes to Ventimiglia on the Italian border, continue on the E80 towards Genoa but, and this is the trick, before you hit the city traffic to get onto the E62 to Milan, take the E26 to Alessandria, then a right on the E70 to Tortona and finally left and pick-up the E62 from Genoa to Milan.

Who needs TomTom when you've got DaveDave!

With tickets arranged through Manchester United's French supporters club, (we were to meet committee member Richard, who now studies in Manchester, outside the United end of the ground around 6.00pm) I met up with ex-Manc, ex-pat John Austin around 1.00pm. Together we had made The Tavern opposite the railway station in Cannes the centre of all things United on match days. But on this day we were coming out to play together. As an English teacher I had worked in the morning but taken the afternoon off. With the match finishing around half past ten, I reckoned I should be back in Cannes about three in the morning. Enough time to prepare my lessons for the morning and then grab two or three hours sleep.

We made good time and arrived on the outskirts of Milan around 5.00pm. We had agreed our strategy before departure. On the basis that cars go better with four wheels, not two or three, and heating and air-conditioning works more efficiently with a full complement of windows with the glass still intact, leaving the car near the stadium was considered a trifle foolhardy. So we parked in a suburb just off the motorway and next to a metro station.

However, John's demand for directions in broken Italian gleaned the fact that someone had just committed suicide by falling on the track, bringing the entire Milanese underground system to a halt. How selfish! Fortunately we found a bus route that went direct to the San Siro. Once we had done a tour of the stadium I phoned Richard to make precise arrangements for picking up the tickets. Unfortunately his mobile number was unattainable which gave us cause for concern.

We joined some pockets of Reds for a sing-song but without tickets in our hands my concentration wavered.

Finally I got through to Richard, only to hear he had also fallen victim to the invisible underground and was desperately trying to find a taxi to take him to the ground. Numerous stomach-churning deadlines were missed until a panting Richard turned up with just ten minutes to go to kick-off. And with genuine tickets unlike six years ago!

Once inside the stadium, typical Italian chaos as no-one could direct us to the right set of stairwells. In the end we just dodged past security and onto the terraces. Seat and row numbers were conspicuously ignored by the stewards, so we made our way down towards the front and just to the right of the goal which was less packed.

"I've Got The Devil In Me" read the banner which filled the entire opposite end of the ground. Impressive, I had to admit, although not at the time, naturally.

"You've Only Come To See United" we replied. And that was the truth, as it was the first time that season the San Siro had been full. However, our team wasn't. Having lost the home leg 1-0 Van Nistelroy was brought back in desperation and lacking match fitness. With only three shots on target the whole match, it wasn't a great game for either side. Yet

Milan always looked the most likely. After 61 minutes Herman Crespo was left unmarked to head past Tim Howard. Giggs hit the post for us but twice Ruud missed sitters that a fit Ruud would have buried, the second in the final minutes was right in front of me. You should have seen Ruud's face from where I was standing. On the other hand he would have seen mine if he'd only looked. We were that close.

Meanwhile bottles were raining down on us from above, and just like Valencia away twenty-one years previously, gravity was to prove our enemy as, with the best will in the world, throwing a bottle back upwards just doesn't have the same power.

The game petered out 1-0 to Milan, and so we waited patiently behind our goal for almost an hour and a half after the final whistle. To rub salt into our wounds, the giant scoreboard informed us that Chelsea had beaten Barcelona 4-2. Great. Finally, at around midnight we were lead out of the ground by the police and marched, who knows where, and then just left to our own devices.

To quote that age old joke, "Where the fuck are we?"

We had no idea where we were, no idea if we had missed the last bus, even no idea where the bus stop was. And I was due back to work in less than eight hours with a four hour night-time drive to look forward to. Glory, glory Man United. We joined groups of Reds walking back and forth. I tried to retrace my steps and eventually, more by luck than design we found our bus stop. And, would you adam 'n eve it, our bus just came into view.

Getting off the bus at the end of the line we found our car complete with doors, floors, windows and tyres. Halleluiah!

Too little too late, but at least it looked as though lady luck was finally shining on us.

Oh yeah? Hmm. Don't you adam 'n eve it. Ladies, luck or otherwise, have a way of getting their own back, just when you start to relax.

So, at 1.30am we start our return drive. Once on the ringroad we look for the motorway signs for Turin and Allessandria. Chatting to John the miles flew by. Only they shouldn't have. I slowed down and asked John to look for the next road sign.

"Ivrea. Aosta".

Fucking Ivrea! Fucking Aosta! What the fuck! Where the fuck are we?

I skidded to a halt by the side of the road and we checked the map. We were on the E64 direction Turin. The fucking wrong fucking motorway. Fuck! How come we had missed the sign for Allessandria?

We had no choice but to turn off at the next exit and drive back towards Milan, this time concentrating on the roadsigns and not on our weakened formation and Ruud's miss right in front of us. I don't know whether it was the late hour and lack of sleep, United's performance (or lack of), poor Italian roadsigns or maybe I just blinked too hard, but there was no mistake. There were the lights of Milan coming into view.

Four and a half hours after the final whistle and we were back in Milan. And I started work in France in five hours.

"AAAAhhhhhhhhh!!!!"

I parked the car on the hard shoulder, punched the steering wheel, turned off the CD player...and sat. A few deep breaths later I looked at the map again. Surely I had taken the right turning off the ringroad. It was clearly marked. As the Who once sang, "I Can't Explain".

John and I agreed we were in the right and the Italian roadsigns were in the wrong.

However, we'd try again, only slower this time and with the music turned down. I'd also play safe and take the more obvious "L" shaped route of simply the E62 to Genoa and the E80 (Italy) A7 (France) to Nice and onto Cannes.

We found the Genoa (Genova) sign and began to relax as the miles (OK, kilometers) flew by. I turned the stereo back on and I was boogying away when bad lady luck appeared in my headlights.

"DEVIATION"

Oh, fuck nooooo!!

Oh, fuck yes. Night roadworks had closed the autopista and a deviation was in place. We had no choice but for the next two hours follow gigantic articulated lorries along single lane "B" roads in the pitch-blackness of the Italian countryside with no chance of overtaking.

Happy days.

Matchstick eyes and heavy metal eardrums dominate proceedings as the horizon begins to lighten and at five thirty we approach Genoa and turn onto the coastal motorway direction France. John by this time was failing to appreciate the increasingly heavy sounds that emanated from my CD player, yet I needed my boring old fart music just to keep me awake.

I'm sure the sunrise and scenery was beautiful that morning. I mean, that's one of the reasons I had moved to the south of France in the first place. But I wasn't in the mood. I dropped John off at his home around eight in the morning and arrived home myself half an hour later.

I phoned my first student and apologized for being late. A quick Clark Kent later and I was back at work, minus sleep, and minus a quarter-final place.

That day, for the first time I could remember, I refused to talk football with my students. It was written exercises all the way. So there.

LILLE – WHAT A GAS

I make goldfish look good. Really. When it comes to memory I'm a bit like... like... Sorry, what was I saying?

I've lost count of the number of times I've gone into a room and wondered why the hell I came here in the first place!

Seriously, throughout my life my memory (or lack of) has had a significant effect on my decision making process. At school, in my day when there were fifty pupils in a class, emphasis was on passively memorizing facts like a sponge. Dates, chemical equations, etc. to be reproduced in exams, and less on understanding the subject at hand. Or so it appeared to me at the time.

You know when careers advisors at school ask you what you want to do for a living? Well, I'm sure 95% of us have no or very little idea. I know I didn't. In fact, it wasn't until I was fifty two years old that I fell into a job that I've been loving ever since. And when you consider that my five years at secondary school were the worst five years of my life, you may be a little surprised to "learn" that I am now a teacher (get it?). But not just any old teacher. I am a TEFL (teaching English as a foreign language) teacher. Thought you'd be impressed.

When I arrived in Cannes in September 2000 with Helene and my youngest daughter, Jasmine, then aged fourteen, we had no home, no job, no school for Jaja, nothing. Through a vague contact (parents of a friend of ours from London) we bullshitted a landlord into renting us an apartment just ten minutes from the sea. Not having satellite or cable, my priority was locating English/Irish bars and pubs that carried live Premiership football. Then for the first year I had a succession of jobs...two months selling stands for a trade exhibition called Football Expo, which folded one year later, (serves them right for sacking me, even after I sold more stands than anyone else during that time) one month on the English language help desk for Nortel Computers in Sophia Antipolis (the Milton Keynes of France) and three months as a tourist guide driving mini buses from St Tropez to Monaco.

Then after eight months I landed a job as an English Teacher in a language school in Cannes. Asked what experience I had I replied, "Well, I was a pupil once." They were obviously desperate because they hired me and the rest, as they say, is history. Well, English actually. Just like the first time I went to live and work in France in 1989, having abandoned a career in Advertising and Sales Promotion where every day I would get an ear bashing from one dimensional robots reading a script and trying to sell me advertising space, the one job I said I would never do was media sales. So what did I become? You got it...Advertisement Manager for a bi-lingual fisheries trade magazine.

This time round, considering how much I hated high school, teachers, bullying and the system as a whole, I surprised myself how much I enjoyed being a teacher. Yet the connection has been the same for both jobs. I had no idea what to do, but I sure as hell knew what not to do. And it's gone on from there ever since.

However, when I came back to England in September 2006, I found that any language school worth its salt is registered with The British Council, who insist that every teacher hold a recognized qualification. Despite forty years of experience in the world of work, only one language school was willing to give me a chance, and then only if I promised to study for the TEFL exam whilst in their employ.

Shit. Back to school, after forty years of running away. And with MY memory!

And so it came to pass that I took the whole of February 2007 off. With no income for one month I paid around £1000 for an intense full-time, four week course. With my memory handicap, I shall be forever grateful to Helene for taking care of everything in my life whilst I concentrated day and night attending lectures, researching, and writing reports up to 2.00am every morning. I knew that if I missed just one lecture I would drown and never come back up for air. I had to keep my head above water and prove to myself that, just perhaps, I wasn't as crap at studying as I thought I was.

But then we drew Lille away and all my good intentions went out of the window.

There was no-way I was going to miss this Euro awayday. I immediately booked a same-day return ticket for my car and four passengers at the cheapest Euro Tunnel fare, then posted pleas on both the Red News and Red Issue fans forums looking for fellow Reds to share the costs. Terra del Fiago and a fellow poor student accepted my offer, as did my mate Mick. Arrangements were made with fellow students on my Teacher Training course to get me copies of any paperwork I may miss, and then it was all systems Lille and a chance to show off my French.

With Lille's stadium not meeting UEFA's requirements, the match was taking place down the road at the sixty-five year old Stade Felix Bolleart in Lens which, in my opinion, doesn't meet UEFA's requirements either. Built in 1932, and with a capacity of 48,000 for a town whose population is only 36,000, one of the wonders of the world is that it is often full, even when the team is not doing well. And when you consider that another local team, Valencienne, attracts an average of under 10,000 a game, Lens is unique. However the town is as boring as shit, so after parking my car on the main road leading out of town and back on the motorway for "a quick getaway", we took the train to Lille itself for a "Lille" action. (where do I get it from?)

I had made arrangements to pick up our tickets in a bar in Lens from Christian, who together with his son James, run the recently formed official French Manchester United supporters club of which I am still a member. So once we arrived in Lille city centre, Mick and I and our two new best United buddies agreed to "do our own things" and meet back at the bar in Lens at around 6.00pm.

Food was by now uppermost in our minds and bottommost in our stomachs. Forcing ourselves to resist joining a large group of Reds singing inside and outside the bar opposite the station, we made our way to one of the enticing local eateries. Once culinary satisfied, our vocal chords demanded attention. The main square fitted the bill adequately, with

United flags and throats draped all around the main bar. A very merry, good natured and loud hour and a half was brought to a premature end when one fat and drunk Yorkshire Red threw a bottle at the passing traffic, then bolted bravely when the driver got out of his car.

There's always one, isn't there?

Returning to the railway station, we still had a few minutes to sing along with the first, and now larger group of Reds in the bar opposite. We pissed ourselves as a local demonstration passed in front; throwing the hordes of police and CRS into confusion as their worst fears were not realized and their batons remained reluctantly unblemished.

"Merde alors!"

I then spotted a small group of locals intent on confronting the United hordes. We just laughed as they came closer, then one of them threw a bottle, a signal for both plain clothed and uniformed police to descend on them and cart the ringleader away. It had been exactly thirty years since the horrors and injustice of St Etienne and, encouraged by this little vignette, hope sprung eternal that the neanderthal CRS had progressed up the chain of evolution and joined the human race.

False dawn, I'm afraid, as the evening's events were to reveal.

On the station forecourt we located the 16.50 train that was to take us back to Lens and took our seats. (no, we didn't "take them away", we just sat down. Some of you lot can be sooooooo fucking pedantic!) Half an hour later we were still in the station and a commotion could be heard at the other end of the platform. I descended and asked the nearest SNCF official, in French just to impress any Reds within earshot, what was happening.

"Ask the police." he replied in French.

I then asked the nearest policeman what was happening.

"Ask SNCF". (the French railway organization)

Yup. That age old French affliction reared its ugly head once again…"passé le buck!" Everybody in authority was blaming everyone else for the delay. I then confronted a woman on the train from the French Consulate. (Question. Why is it so much more difficult to have an argument when the person opposite is sexually attractive?) In my best worst French I discussed the situation with her up close and personal, accusing everyone of gross inefficiency. I then brought up the fact that SNCF had decided, in their wisdom, that the last train of the day would leave Lens for Lille at 22.30.

"Eh, alors?"

I informed her that the match was scheduled to end around 22.35, and with approximately 2000 of the 6000 traveling Reds committed to return to Lille and pre-booked hotel rooms, imagine their collective reaction if they arrive at Lens railway station and find there are no trains to take them back. They will not be happy bunnies.

With weeks to make all the necessary arrangements, I asked, how come F.C's Lille & Lens, the police and SNCF could all get it so wrong?

The implications of my assertions began to be reflected in additional lines appearing on her pretty face. She thanked me, took my mobile number and told me she would return in ten minutes.

She never returned. Note to myself...I must either improve my French or change my aftershave.

Meanwhile, local commuters on the train also confronted the authorities, as they could clearly see that us United fans, a mixture of silence and singing, were not a threat to anyone. Eventually we set off forty minutes late, which led to a flurry of expensive foreign mobile phone calls, in order to re-arrange the time for our tickets pick-up.

Back at Lens station we sang our way to the bar, located Christian and our tickets. As a member of manutd-france our tickets were for a special section at the front of the upper tier, above all the United fans below. Our two students wanted to be amongst the hard-core so told us they would attempt to infiltrate. No problem, I said, except I told them I had to leave straight after the match, as I needed at least a couple of hours sleep back in Blighty before I immersed myself back in my teacher training course. Fearing the "powers that be" would keep United fans back after the game, I told them the choice is yours guys, but I ain't waiting. Understood?

We could see the stadium from the bar but could we find our entrance? Could we +*%!. A mini Nou Camp '99 ensued, as we had to walk three quarters round the stadium to find our poorly signposted stand. Unnecessary police delays later we were finally in.

Down below I could see that the United fans were frighteningly squashed, pushed as they were against the barricades of the metal cage, especially to our right. Yet there were large areas of empty seats at the other end of the United section. Why weren't the stewards doing their jobs properly? I made out a few United fans signaling frantically for help. but the only reaction from "les flics" was to predictably over-react and baton any Red that attempted to scale the wire fence. Police re-enforcements arrived and in their collective wisdom began to tear gas indiscrimately at the United section.

One woman was dragged out by security stewards. Another fan ran on to the playing surface and signalled that the game should be stopped, and for five terrible minutes of confusion there were scenes that were worryingly reminiscent of the early stages of the Hillsborough disaster.

What is beyond doubt is that the police handled a significant safety issue atrociously. The firing of tear gas did at least succeed in moving the fans away from the cages but it was an absurdly heavy-handed gesture, the only possible explanation being that the police believed the supporters were trying to get on the pitch to cause trouble. Some supporters were also struck with batons.

Thanks to the wind the spray drifted up to our section and my eyes began to sting and my throat felt on fire. I could tell that Edwin in our goal was also affected. So, thirty years on from St Etienne and still the disgraceful French police and CRS remained in a time warp.

Meanwhile, it has to be said, we weren't playing all that well. Apart from a couple of scares, we contained them well but were not creating much ourselves. Then in the second half, Lille scored what I thought at first was a perfectly good goal. Fortunately the referee judged that Vidic was pushed as the Lille player jumped and headed the ball in, so yes, it was a foul. Initially I thought that we were extremely lucky and that the goal should have stood, but really, the ref got it right by the letter of the law. Thank Eric!

A few minutes later, with two Lille players continuing to man mark Ronaldo out of the game, his frustration go the better of him. He was substituted after seventy minutes and took out his anger by kicking something hard as he left the pitch, injuring himself in the process.

Doh!

Then with seven minutes to go United were awarded a free-kick right in front of us. Giggs seemed to take it before the Lille players were ready. I certainly never heard the referee's whistle and there was a full second of stunned silence before we erupted.

In the ensuing protests, Sylva their goalkeeper was booked and all 11 Lille players crowded around Dutch referee Braamhaar demanding the goal be disallowed. From the restart, Lille simply kicked the ball into touch and their coaches suddenly appeared on the touchline, beckoning for the players to leave the pitch. Grégory Tafforeau, the captain, was the first to walk off followed by several team-mates.

United's players, led by their captain Gary Neville, rushed over to confront their opponents and then came the extraordinary sight of Ferguson furiously signalling for them to return to the pitch. At one stage we saw Ferguson grab Neville and give him an angry shove. Neville responded with what I can only assume to be age-old Anglo Saxon. What a farce!

Meanwhile, I'm happy to report that although the Lille fans around us were incensed by events on the pitch, I felt in no danger. They were certainly behaving better than their team and the police.

A few minutes later it was all over. 1-0 to the Reds away from home. Yes! An announcement in English informed all United fans that a special train would be waiting for them once they were allowed to leave the stadium. A result, I thought, thinking back to my earlier conversation on the platform in Lille. As Mick and I made our way out of the stadium I phoned our two students and I reminded them I had to see them back by my car in no later than half an hour. Thirty minutes later...no students. Another phone call confirmed they were still in the ground.

"C'mon guys. You know the rules."

Another half an hour later...still no students.

"Where are you now?"

"We've been frogmarched (non PC but uncanningly accurate) to a coach park and they're hitting out indescrimately at any United fans they can get their batons on."

"Look guys. Sympathy and all that, but you chose to get in there. You've got to get yourselves out of it. Let me know what's happening."

By now it was approaching midnight and we were in danger of missing our pre-booked crossing. A flurry of calls ensued and at 00.45 our two students appeared on the horizon. It seems the CRS had taken exception to our friends' desire to extradite themselves from the illegal lock-in and had run a gauntlet of batons.

We were then threatened by the traffic police to get away as quickly as possible so we literally flew away, zooming through red lights and back towards civilization.

Whereas the journey down had been dominated by the likes of Faithless, Chemical Brothers and Fat Boy Slim, to accompany our high speed getaway a mélange of Muse, Kaisers, Arctics, Led Zep, and AC/DC seemed the perfect aural antedote.

Once on-board the train we settled down and chilled with the Floyd and Neil Young, hitting Kent and London with the best of Madness and Ian Dury and the Blockheads.

Maybe I should do a Boylie and bring out a CD of music to travel to and from football to. Then again...

28

WISE BEFORE THE EVENT

THE ONE THING WE learn from history is that we never learn from history. Conflicts, relationships, hangovers, you name it and Man has the ability to extract defeat from the joys of victory. Whether it's world peace or getting a piece we tend to piss it up.

At the end of the Great War people said there must never be another World War. So what happens? Twenty five years later we have World War 11. Well done lads. Come to think about it, why do people refer to it as the Great War? Sounded pretty terrible to me.

When it comes to relationships, why do so many women say they can't help being attracted to "bastards"?

They get abused, sometimes even beaten yet come back for more. When they have a choice between a "nice boy" and a "bastard" the majority choose the latter, which leaves a Forrest Gump geek like me out in the cold, literally. Nice guys come second? Not much of a consolation on those cold, lonely nights.

Hangovers. Ha! How many times have we said, "Never again." Nuff said.

THE UNTHINKABLES

Invigorated by 2006/07's sensational, brilliant and, I think we all agree, totally unexpected title success, Sir Alex committed himself to an on-going rolling contract. But when pressed, he claimed he wouldn't go on like Bobby Robson and still be in the job at the age of 70. The best news any sane United fan could have wished for. But what will happen when the unthinkable but inevitable moment comes and The Wizard decides to retire for good? Will we have learnt from history?

In 1969 the first unthinkable happened. Sir Matt Busby had topped Moses by reaching the promised land on Wednesday 29th May 1968. I know. I was there. Although comments were made at the time that this will just be a springboard to even greater things, it was in fact the beginning of the end. Apart from a sterling run in the following year's European Cup, when only a monumental cock-up by the referee in the second leg of our semi-final against AC Milan, (Yup, them again) when he refused our perfectly legitimate equaliser, stopped us reaching the final for a second consecutive year. What a difference a pair of glasses would have made that night.

A year later Sir Matt announced his retirement and, following Liverpool's successful policy of the time, promoted from within. The likeable and effervescent Wilf McGuiness was made Manager, or if I remember correctly (a rare commodity I must admit) Chief Coach with Sir Matt moving upstairs.

The Dream Team? Well, no. The senior players found it hard to accept Wilf, for so long their equal on the pitch and on the training ground, as their boss. Players who should have known better undermined his authority and although we reached two domestic semi-finals we could all see it wasn't happening. Players who had only ever known Sir Matt as Manager, no matter what they said publicly, could not bring themselves to accept changes and the team suffered as a result.

George Best made the point since that after winning the European Cup there was a feeling around Old Trafford that they had come to the end of a great journey. The end of an era. But instead of building on the success they let it slide. The famous youth policy was to become all headline but no body copy.

Eighteen months later Sir Matt reluctantly answered the call to arms and steered the team to mid-table safety in the league. But it was only a temporary respite for he retired for good in June 1971, only to find the place on the board that Louis Edwards had promised him many years before conspicuous by its absence. (The Edwards family. Don't you just luv 'em? And you thought the Glazers were the only 'bad guys' on the United horizon.)

A few years later the youth policy had all but dried up. One or two gems came through of course but United could no longer guarantee to produce the cream of England's finest. George began to get more and more disillusioned as the quality dropped. He felt the team relied too heavily on him to get them out of trouble and inevitably this got him down and the rest, as they say, is history.

THE INEVITABLES

Fast forward to the present. I get the impression, reading contributions to the various fans forums that too many United fans are loath to accept the fact that one day in the future Sir Alex Ferguson will no longer be Manager of Manchester United. Please read this sentence again. One day, Sir Alex Ferguson will no longer be Manager of Manchester United. It's so bad I wrote it twice.

Already a number of our current squad have come out publicly stating that they will find it hard to accept the day when Sir Alex is no longer there. For some of them he's been the only club manager they've known. He permiatates the very fabric of the place. I get the distinct impression that one or two players will feel like fish out of water, flapping on the deck, using up a lot of energy but achieving very little.

I hope this is just a wake-up call. A worst case scenario. Being wise before the event is what good management is all about, whether it's business or sports management. − It's what makes us rise above the competition.

Now, I have to admit, since writing the original piece three years ago I have been a rage of conflicting doubts and emotions. And as you know, emotions can speak louder than words. First the case for the defence:

Since the Premiership was formed we've won 10 of the sixteen titles on offer. Up to the end of last season we've played 582 games, winning 364, drawing 131 and losing 84. We've amassed 1232 points. We've averaged 82.13 games per season (first three seasons were 42 games). We've averaged 2.12 points per game in the fifteen Premiership seasons so far. We've won 63% of all games we've played in the Premiership. These stats are just unreal. Fucking phenomenal.

However, since we beat Bayern Munich at the Nou Camp in 1999, up to the end of last season the European on-the-road stats are: P49, W16,

D12, L21. Just two semi-final appearances in eight seasons and only three knock-out stage victories since 1999. And on a par with Nottingham Forest for the number of outright trophies.

United fans have been split over the continued employment of the greatest football manager Britain has ever produced. Since the title-winning season 2002/2003, even our domestic form has been patchy. Experimenting with the dreaded 4-5-1 in the Premiership had made us predictable. For two seasons Ruud van Nistelroy was the best striker in the world, then his head got in the way and his sad departure was inevitable. In the meantime the Manchester United we all love went missing in Europe.

At the beginning of August 2008, with a seemingly lack-lustre bench, and with one rule for Chelsea's billions and another for the rest of us, I shared Gary Neville's fear that another Premiership winning season seemed a long way off. When all the names were put in the hat as to who should take over from Sir Alex, one name was conspicuous by its absence. The greatest of them all. And, miracle of miracles, we got him. And he was right under our noses all the time.

The Sir Alex Ferguson of 10 years ago.

In 2006/7 the passionate, revitalized, robotic dancing in victory Alex Ferguson took over the helm once again.

From the 5-1 trouncing of Fulham on the opening day, United played with pace, style, fluency and passion. Blips aside, we were the good guys once more, fighting the negative stifling evil of Chelsea and ultimately winning our greatest Premiership title since the start of Alex's era in 1992/3.

England was a joyful place to be once more. My themed summer wardrobe complete with an assortment of leisurewear all containing the word "CHAMPIONS".

And now we arrive to the summer of 2008. Champions of England and Champions of Europe. Sir Alex Ferguson is now the complete manager. Any lingering doubts have been dispersed as he extinguishes his and our personal European demons. He's finally matured like the finest wines he so adores.

What will the future hold?

For 18-5 read 17-3. Will he stay on to overcome the greatest challenge of them all? If anyone had told me during the 70s and 80s that we would be where we are today I would have been the first to send them to the funny farm. As a United fan, not a day goes by without me realizing my life has been blessed and Sir Alex Ferguson is the overwhelming contributor.

But how long can it go on? The future's bright, but don't take it as Red.

29

LOVE UNITED, HATE... GLAZER, EDWARDS, MURDOCH, ACS, ABCs, JCLs...

LET ME STATE straight away that I don't believe the Ginger Parasite and his three younger Paracetamols (well, they give me a headache anyway) bought ManchesterUnited for the sole purpose of running it into the ground. That's a Marvel comics horror story and lacks credibility BUT, and here's the rub, for the first time in their business lives they're quite capable of doing just that.

Why?

Well, greater minds than mine (i.e. most of you) will have already worked out that their yearly interest charges alone are greater than the profits we currently generate. According to figures registered at Companies House, for the 2006 financial year Manchester United made a profit of £45.7 million. In that same period of time, the Glazers had to pay back interest charges of £62 million. Even allowing for the re-funding of debts, the carpetbaggers may end up paying more than £88 million a year to banks and hedge funds if they use all the loans. That's more than the club spent on Wayne Rooney, Ruud van Nistelrooy, Christiano Ronaldo, Alan Smith and Louis Saha put together! You do the maths before I do my head in. In fact I'll leave the myriad of financial statistics to others, but before I go on I'll throw a couple more at you.

According to Bloomberg, of the 187 seven year buy-out loans tracked since 1999, only 14 have margins higher than Glazer's 2.75 percentage points above benchmark lending rates. This will further limit their chances of making the kind of money they envisage and which our beloved Board of Directors, all of us and even my goldfish told them were "too aggressive and beyond reasonable expectations".

However, realism and not rhetoric should rule our heads, even if our hearts aren't beating the same anymore. The season following the takeover, if the figures released by the club are to be believed, then a record 42,500 people bought season tickets for the following season, an increase of 2500, despite a 10% increase in average ticket prices. Take away the 320 odd that didn't renew, and allowing for summer season slackness of around 200, that's only 120 who made the ultimate sacrifice. And don't the Glazers just know it.

Three years on and the average price of tickets at Old Trafford has now increased by around 50% with no additional benefits. To add insult to injury they've introduced the universally despised Automatic Cup Scheme whereby the club sucks the lifeblood of money out of your account for every cup game United play, whether you can or want to go or not. All this flies in the face of the highest amount ever paid by Sky and their partners for the rights to show live Premiership games. Some clubs, such as Blackburn and Wigan, have actually lowered prices, although admittedly it's easier for clubs that never sell-out to make the grand gesture. Analysts have even claimed that every club in the Premiership could let all their fans in for free, and still make the same amount of money as in the previous season.

The club's latest accounts released in June 2007 (brought forward so as not to interfere with activities surrounding the 50th anniversary of the Munich air disaster on February 6) forecasted record profits of £75 million on turnover of more than £200. But the Manchester United Supporters' Trust (MUST) say the retained profit may be as low as £5 million once you take EBITA (earnings before interest, taxes, depreciation and amortisation) into consideration. MUST estimates the £75m profit will be shrunk by £42m through debt interest payments on loans of £575m, £23m by amortisation and £5m by depreciation.

Increased ground capacity has added 8,000 seats at Old Trafford but much of the bottom line growth stems from the 50% increase in ticket prices, a four year shirt sponsorship deal with AIG is thought to have added £13.5m. The fear is that low levels of "retained" profit could force ticket prices still higher.

It's all very well us preaching to the converted (us again) but the silent majority are just sheep. But we shouldn't be surprised. If we widen the debate to other issues such as politics and economics then most people are silent. Very few get off their asses over a cause, no matter how noble or worthwhile. For every Live Aid / Live 8 there are hundreds of good causes that fall by the wayside.

Thanks to the silent majority we missed a golden opportunity. According to Brian Viner in The Independent, "the Glazers, terrified of a major boycott by fans after saddling the club with debts of over £650 million, knew that they had to keep Fergie onside." Viner's source, a fellow journalist with impeccable contacts at Old Trafford, revealed that "The Glazers are personally scared of him (Fergie), and he loves that. He's having a much better time than he did in the latter days of the plc".

On a personal note, when the Glazer's takeover became official I felt like I had been kicked in the stomach and the goolies and the nausea would last until the day the Gingerus Parasitus becomes extinct.

May 2005 will go down as the second worse month in United's history for me. You remember that scene in Lord of the Rings where Gandalf falls over the precipice dueling with the forces of evil, and disappears for half the book/film, only to rise triumphant but considerably older towards the end?

Well, that's how I feel about us and the Glazers. I'm mentally and physically prepared for the war ahead. It may another year or three, even a decade or more, but however long it takes I shall be there. At the time of the takeover, supporting Manchester United didn't feel the same anymore. I felt my one true love had been unfaithful. Now I've taken her back but the trust has gone. I no longer want to shout my love from the rooftops. I now feel embarrassed wearing United ties, pin badges, etc. at work – so I've stopped. Even my United underwear, and that gets pretty close to the heart of the matter. But I have a question for you. Cast your Red minds back to the sixties. Who was our chairman during the glory years of Best, Law and Charlton? Answer, "Champagne" Louis Edwards.

History, and a certain World In Action documentary in 1980, portrays Mr Edwards senior as a man who welched on a promise to offer Sir Matt Busby a place on the board. A man who packaged and sold sub-standard meat to schools in Manchester and beyond, and a man who, allegedly, conned/bullied various people in order to secure his majority shareholding in the club by illegal share trading. In other words, not a man with the highest set of morals in the land.

Yet how did we, as supporters react?

In fact, we didn't. It didn't affect our Red fanatism in the least. So, another question. Is it me or is it the media? If we had known then what we know now, would we have acted any different?

To be honest, I just don't know. Today we are more media savvy. With the introduction of the Internet into our lives we are saturated with information overload and can communicate and mobilize like-minded souls all over the world with a click of the mouse.

LOVE UNITED AGAIN – IT'S AS EASY AS ABC

Eric moves in mysterious ways. Just as I was feeling numb and number, along came Abromovitch and Muhrinio to generate emotions of hate, loathing, envy and all the other positive negative emotions that fans thrive on... to re-ignite the passion, light the fires, stir the cauldron (he's off on another one – Ed) For the first time in decades we were no longer the most hated team on the planet. Everything that Chelsea stood for...greed, arrogance, beautiful players playing ugly football, tapping-up Real Madrid style, bending the rules and last, and certainly least, Peter Kenyon, all acted as a call to arms. ABU became ABC (anything but Chelsea) In other words, after United winning, for lots of fans their greatest pleasure came in Chelsea losing.

Actually, that's not entirely accurate. Chelsea might have been our biggest rivals on the pitch for a couple of seasons, but history dictates that Liverpool, that city of culture built on the profits of slavery are our bitterest rivals. An excellent article entitled, "Two Tribes", commissioned by FourFourTwo magazine and written by Andy Mitten, editor of United We Stand, details the political and political history of the rivalry dating back to the industrial revolution.

Nobody else comes close. Not the bitter Blues or even Leeds, who've masterBated the insolvency laws to rise like a pheasant from the flames of bankruptcy.

However, I am also totally behind the concept and principals of F C United of Manchester. When some of the most dedicated and committed Reds on the planet, such as Andy Walsh and Adam Brown, made the ultimate personal sacrifice of turning their backs on their greatest love to set up F C United, it did bring into question my blind allegiance to the Red cause. As an antidote to the anti-Christ of rampant commercialism and anesthetizing of football, its naive idealism appeals to me, as it has done to thousands of FC United followers.

However, I have a problem.

When the Icelandic owners of Wimbledon FC ignored every rule of history, community and decency by transferring the club on mass to Milton Keynes, I can 100% ally myself with 95% of their fans who said they would never ever support the new enterprise. On the basis Wimbledon FC had disappeared forever, creating AFC Wimbledon was totally understandable and deserving of the highest plaudits.

Yet not withstanding the bastardizing of the club crest a few years ago, Manchester United Football Club still exists. And now F C United exists in a parallel universe. For many Reds it's been a case of one or the other. It's not as clearcut as that for me, I'm afraid. My first and true but tainted love is still here, and so am I. I couldn't give up my season ticket, even if I had one. Those that have have stronger principals than me. If I lived in Manchester I would follow FC United as much as funds and MUFC's fixture list would allow.

One may argue that the average home games are regularly watched by 76,000 so what's the problem?

How long have you got?

For a start, everyone of the finest vocal hard-core 5000 that has been lost have been replaced by silent, camera-clicking JCLs (Johnny Comes Lately). When Fergie complains about the atmosphere at the theatre of zzzzzzz, he should direct his comments at the powers that be, not us.

According to a recent study, in the sixties the average age of a Stretford Ender was 17. Today it's 42. The club has simply priced out thousands of normal, decent working class kids. The very kids that create the atmosphere so sadly lacking at many all-seater stadiums these days. Couple this with stewards that act like the Stasi and what do you expect?

Time is a great healer. The white hot hatred I felt when the Glazers took over has, well, not subsided as such, but transformed itself into a simmering, relentless, calculated quest for justice.

Now, I know two wrongs don't make a right, and bearing in mind nobody is born 100% evil, recent comments attributed to the Glazers with regards to the Ronaldo situation, that they would prefer to go along with SAF and stick him in the stands and/or the reserves rather than sell to the Spanish dictators, is just the hardball attitude needed to counter the cancer of Calderon, the Real Madrid president. Does this mean I'm softening in my attitude? No, but I take each case on its merits and react accordingly. Remember, Think not what Manchester United can do for you, but what can you do for Manchester United. Don't get mad, get even. Watch this space.

30

SONGS AT MY FUNERAL

IF YOU FAIL to prepare, prepare to fail.

So much for philosophy. But I have taken this little gem on board, as I've negotiated with the Museum department of the club to have my ashes scattered in the goal at the Stretford End. I can't trust anybody else to do it for me once I'm gone so I've done it myself.

As I've already stated, Manchester United is my religion, and long before it was cool to say so. In the conventional sense I'm a devout atheist. I may be many things but one thing I'm not is a hypocrite.

I can't think of a better send off, once all my good bits have gone to medical science (what good bits? – ed) than have generations of United players walking and running all over me. And if I can create a little divet to upset the opposition or get us a penalty, I'll know my death will not have been in vain.

Of course, I still have 18-5 as an incentive to keep going, but if it were all to end tomorrow, I'll rest happy in the knowledge that I'll be taken home to United Road, to the place I belong, to Old Trafford, to see United. Take me home, United Road.

Regrets? I've had a few, but then again, too few to mention.

Women? I've had a few, but then again, too few to mention

When it's time for us to move up to the Theatre of Eternal Dreams in the sky, most people, if they're honest, tend to regret what they didn't do, rather than what they did that went wrong. So, yes, I do regret not going to bed (or the bathroom, spin dryer, bicycle sheds, etc...) with more women.

But then again, my choice was the M1/M6 on a Saturday night so I can't blame anybody else but me, can I?.

Don't get me wrong. Sex is great. In fact, sex is fantastic. And the good thing is, just like football, it can be enjoyed by 99.9% of the world's population whether you play home or away......young

Songs At My Funeral and old, black and white, left, centre and right, religious and atheist, orgy and wanker, gay and straight, disabled and able bodied, democrat and dictator, republican and monarchist, employed and unemployed, skilled and unskilled, well endowed and...eerrr... "leaves a lot to be desired".

BUT, can it match Giggy's FA Cup semi-final winner against the Arse, Ronnie's recent free-kick against Pompy or those incredible 3 minutes of injury time at the Nou Camp?

No, of course not. So there you have it.

The defence rests. And so do I.

With a maximum of eight people allowed to accompany my ashes, much chubbing will ensue as people fight for my standing allowed ceremony. My other problem lies with the music. Have you ever thought what songs you would like at your funeral? I don't think I'll be able to keep everything I want in. Well, here's my choice. Wonder if I'll be able to hear it?

Comfortably Numb – Pink Floyd

Always Look On The Bright Side – Monty Python's Flying Circus

Slark – Stackridge

Gerundula – Status Quo

In The Hour – Melanie

Mano Negra – Mano Negra

Ding Dang Dong – Manu Chau

The Ying Tong Song – The Goons

Runnin' Down a Dream – Tom Petty and the Heartbreakers

Sit Down – James

Going to my Hometown – Rory Gallagher

Kings of Cydonia – Muse

I Can't Get No sleep – Faithless

Never Ever – All Saints

Take Me Home, United Road

31

"YOU LOVE UNITED MORE THAN ME!"

OF COURSE, THE correct answer is, "I love City more than you", but I haven't got the nerve to come out with put-downs like this except hiding behind the security of a keyboard. If I did I wouldn't be typing with a full compliment of fingers at my disposal. Short term laugh, long term wrath.

For a Cockney Red like me, midweek home league games are a bit difficult to attend, what with a wife, two kids and a full-time job in London to contend with. So for this season's home game against Portsmouth I settled down on the sofa, fully expecting 'er indoors to transfer to the bedroom and the other TV set. But no, inexplicably Helene remained on the right wing of the sofa, laptop on lap and e-bay on screen.

I, meanwhile, got into the match. After five minutes I reckoned United were settling into some pretty sublime football and I was privileged just to watch. Of course, at my age, I should have more control over my physical and vocal outpourings, but one of the benefits of immaturity is that I still possess the ability to "let it all hang out", much to my wife's chagrin.

After 10 minutes a beautiful move culminating in a decisive through ball by Anderson and Ronaldo homed in for our first goal. Cue a minimum of jumping and cheering from me and a maximum of wailing from her. However, a few minutes later United were awarded a free-kick and up steps Ronaldo. Until halfway through last season, his success ratio from dead-ball situations hadn't matched the proliferation of other parts of his game, but this season he's taken everything to another level. I sat with baited breath, in anticipation of something special.

"AAAAAHHHHhhhhh!!!" "DID YOU SEE THAT!!!!!." AAAAAHHHHhhhhh!!!"

Yes, Helene had just seen that, and she'd just seen me and she wasn't best pleased.

Once I sat down she turned to me, in an Exorcist sort of way, and said, "You love United more than me."

Fuck me. I'm still celebrating the greatest free-kick I have ever seen in my life and she comes out with the "L" word. (No, not Liverpool or Leeds) She's inviting me into a serious debate on the relative values of football over long-term relationships. I'm sorry, this isn't Loose Women or Jeremy Kyle, it's a fucking football match and it's on...NOW!

I mumbled something unconvincing like, "No I don't. It's just different, that's all. I love you too. (Whoops) I mean, I love you...more!"

Don't think I got out of jail.

32

WE'VE WON IT 10/17 TIMES

02.14
04.44
06.15

THIS IS A JOKE. Why can't I sleep? Of course, I know the answer immediately. In nine hours we play Wigan. I lie still. I don't want to wake Helene. More than my life's worth. My mind's racing and my stomach's in knots, just like it has been for days.

I consider my options. My wife's body is so near yet so far, if you get my drift. What about a wank? Groin central. A little hand relief (and I do mean 'little') might relieve the tension. I try to invite some sexy images into my brain. How about a lesbian kiss? OK, insert Madonna & Britney. Now add Madonna and one of her dancers from the Radio I Big weekend in Maidstone. Insert Angela Jolie with.....well, anyone will do. Shit, still 8 hours 50 minutes till Wigan. Lesbian kisses. The media blow it up out of all proportion, just for column inches. However, it's having no effect on my column inches.

Insert Angela Jolie and me, PLEEEAAASE! Wonder what it's like? Will Wigan's pitch be a quagmire and reduce us down to their level? Will we be able to flow or will we just crawl over the line. I'd love to crawl over Angela Jolie. Sorry. It's not working. I'm tossing and turning without tossing. Having "Wigan" and "sex" in the same sentence is not doing it for me. I carefully get out of bed and make my way to the kitchen. One cup of tea later and I'm in front of the laptop.

First stop, Red News and Red Issue fans forums. Blimey, there's never normally this number of people online this early on a Sunday morning.

Then I realize. Everyone is in the same boat as me. Can't sleep, won't sleep. I read some of the comments. I could have written them myself. Piss myself laughing. Contribute some cryptic gems of my own before I hear a sound behind me.

"What are you doing?"

"Couldn't sleep, darling. I'll make you a tea."

"Not football again."

"No. No. Of course not. It's just, you know, I get up early every morning for work and, well, you know, body clock and all that."

She wasn't convinced.

Fortunately it was a lovely sunny day, Helene and I spent a couple of hours together on the sun loungers in the garden. Any passing UFO would have observed a typical Sunday scene amongst so-called civilized human beings. Unless they had advanced equipment that could monitor human brainwaves from inside their spacecraft, all appeared normal. However inside my cranium war of the worlds was taking place.

By this time my granddaughter, Lilyella, was playing happily on my laptop so I didn't need to keep an eye open for her. Helene was still in the garden so I settled down in front of Sky Sports News, catching the drip, drip feed of news concerning the match. Trying to clutch at any straws that indicated an advantage, however minute, in our favour. Then I am aware that my labour pains have ceased and I have returned to normal (normal? Moi?) A strange calmness envelopes me and the voices assure me we will win. Mens' intuition is a strange and wondrous thing and who am I to argue with powers greater than my own.

Then Melanie calls and Helene has to go out.

"Will you take care of Lilyella?"

"Yes, of course. Leave her with me."

"I may not be back for some time. Can I trust you once the match starts?"

"Yes, of course. Leave her with me."

"That's what I'm worried about. Lily, don't get frightened if Grandpa shouts, it's only football. ....David......DON'T SHOUT!"

"Yes, of course. I mean, no dear."

Helene leaves, Lilyella taps, minutes pass, ever so slowly, and then the match starts.

First few minutes are tense but OK. The pitch is surprisingly good and Wigan play surprisingly well in front of their first full house of the season. Tension restricts the flow of our game and 0-0 is about right for the first half of the first half. In the meantime, during breaks in play, I switch from time to time to the Chelsea match.

Happily they seem to be going through the motions as if they don't believe it's possible.

On the half hour – penalty! Yes! Ronaldo – Goal! YES!

Considering the importance of the situation I thought my reaction quite restrained. Helene would have been proud.

Half time. Wigan 0 United 1. Chelsea 0 Bolton 0. "That'll do for me, Tom".

The second half is only a few minutes old when news comes that Chelsea have gone a goal up. Dam! We're still in charge but it's too close for comfort. Why can't we win anything easily? Just once. Please.

Heskey! Bastard. Phew, that was close. Oh, Giggs is coming on. Fresh legs. OK. I'll accept that. We now continue to press as Wigan begin to tire and our class tells. Rooney cuts in from the left and strings a delightful through ball to Giggsy who's sandwiched between two Wigan defenders. Turning on a sixpence (well, these days 6p just doesn't sound the same) and with instinctive speed of thought belying his advance years. Swivels and knocks the ball into the net.

"GOOOAAALLL!. THAT'S IT! THAT'S IT! THAT'S IT! That's the one that we want, oh, oh, oh."

Lilyella looks up.

"Oh, grandpa."

What a girl. Only nine years old but she'd seen enough of me not to get excited when I get excited. Secure in the knowledge she won't "tell" on me I continue to shriek. Overwhelming relief. The knowledge that the title is ours and for the second year running Abromovitch and his sqillions have come second.

I switch to the Chelsea match to see if I can catch a glimpse of unhappy Chelsea chavs. What's the point of victory if you can't enjoy the suffering of others?

Running down the clock is accompanied by the sight and sound of joyous United fans in the JJB stadium. I join in as best I could, a grown man with a nine year old granddaughter under his wing. It doesn't get better than this.

Yes it does. Bolton equalize at Stamford Bridge and the afternoon is complete. I lift up one of the cushions on the sofa and take out the brown paper bag I put there just before kick-off. Within seconds I'm resplendent in a "We've Won It Ten Times" T-shirt purchased the week before outside Old Trafford prior to the West Ham game. Heads shook in disapproval as I'd picked it up with my bare hands. "You're tempting fate" was the universal expression carved on Red faces as Moscow '08 shirts flew off the shelves.

"I have my reasons", I tried to explain, guiltily. "I'm a Cockney Red and it's unlikely I'll be able to get a ticket for Wigan. I promise not to wear it before next Sunday, in fact, I won't even look at it until then, honest". Images of 2002/3 came flooding back. I had bought a 'Champions" T-shirt prior to the 4-1 Charlton game, only I hadn't seen it or even touched it until Leeds, for once in their miserable lives, had done the decent thing and stuffed Arsenal at Highbury a week later.

The following half hour or so is torn, 75/25, between United celebrations and Chelsea misery.

Now I can relax. I tell myself that, whatever happens in Moscow, we are Premiership champions for the 10th time, seventeen titles in total and now just one behind the enemy. If anyone had told me during the 70s and 80s that I would live to experience days like these I would have committed them to the funny farm.

I now began to rationalize about Wednesday. We've got one. The big one. Winning your own league is the biggest and best prize of all. Europe is just the icing on the cake. The Premiership is where it's at. The hardest league in the world. If Chelsea win 'the other one' it can't take away the fact that we are the English champions. The majority of United fans on the various forums I contribute to prescribe to this point of view.

I don't.

History dictates that the European Cup/Champions League defines a European team's true greatness. Just as Manchester United defied Chelsea and the Football League's insular attitude on the 50s so I prescribe to Sir Matt Busby's view that there is a big wide world out there and we need to be in it, part of it, and.....on top of it.

Moscow, I mean Manchester, here I come.

33

MANCHESTER > MOSCOW

UEFA AWARDED the 2008 Champions League Final to Moscow in October 2006. Nineteen months later and five days AFTER the semi-finals, Michel Platini, brilliant footballer but inept anti-English administrator, instigated talks between UEFA and the Russian authorities trying to come some sort of agreement with regards to Visas.

Piss up and brewery come to mind.

Surely UEFA should have satisfied themselves that the Russian Embassy in the UK, the Russian Tourist Board, the Mayor of Moscow and the Russian Football Authorities and possibly the Russian mafia had everything in place BEFORE they decided on Moscow.

A logistical nightmare. What a joke! And once again it's the loyal, match-going fans that suffer the most. It tells us everything about how supporters are at the bottom of the food chain in the eyes of the powers that be.

The Lushniki Stadium in Moscow, with a capacity of 69,500, is the biggest in Russia. It hosted the 1999 UEFA Cup Final. Now, I admit I wasn't paying too much attention at the time, but I wonder what arrangements were in force for supporters for that match? Back in 1982, sixty six people died there during the UEFA cup tie between Spartak Moscow and FC Haarlem. Nice.

Today 50% of UEFA's 53 member associations are from eastern Europe so it's no surprise they would be looking to promote the game in that region. I've no problem with encouraging the beautiful game on a global basis, but if you subscribe to the "what comes first, the country or the stadium?" theory, surely there has to be minimum standards in place

BEFORE a country/stadium is awarded a lucrative match. For all the excesses of the Olympic committee, at least they satisfy themselves as to the merits and infrastructure of the competing candidates prior to awarding the contract.

They say that love always finds a way, but by the time United overcame Barcelona a Russian visa in 7 days cost £84 or a 24 hour visa £159 and the cheapest return ticket on a charter flight from Luton Airport was £799. With 45,000 English footy fans expected, and bearing in mind 70% of the 34,000 Moscow hotel rooms are regularly occupied, the result is that a £100 paint peeling, cockroach infested hotel room had gone up to an average of £263. In addition, face value match tickets, if you could get hold of them, were the most expensive ever, either £73 or £120.

UEFA and FIFA are notorious for distributing large blocks of tickets to VIPs and other clubs and their officials. On top of that, Russians themselves snapped up large quantities as it was the first time the event had been held in Moscow.

In my case, another nail in my wallet was the fact that as a self employed English language tutor to foreign students, every lesson I cancel costs me money, so I have to add around £125 for every day I take off work. So that's well over £1000 before we even begin to allow for spending money in the most expensive city on Earth. Thank you UEFA.

At this time I would also like to express my appreciation to our friends across the Atlantic. They say there is a special bond between the United States and Britain. Politically I believe this to be a myth, but financially it has recently been brought home to me as a result of the bonds taken out by US real estate agents and the banks. The losses accrued through negative equity transferred themselves in the form of the credit crunch to the UK property market, effectively reducing the sale price of my two bedroom garden flat in West Hampstead by £50,000 in six months. And still no takers. This meant I couldn't put my hand on a lump sum and divert it to more pressing matters. Eric bless America.

In conclusion, Moscow was a non-starter. As a blinkered United fan, having been at Wembley as a nineteen year old and Barcelona as a (cough, cough) year old, the idea of reality invading my decision making process was unpalatable in the extreme. However, with a wife, two daughters as well as a football team to support, I bowed to outside pressure and started on my Plan B. Watch the match in Manchester with thousands of fellow Reds.

Meanwhile, my old mate and Denis Law fanatic, Jack, originally from Gants Hill but now upwardly mobile in Chigwell, contacted me to inform me that some United fans who had bought their final tickets some time ago, either through the UEFA ballot or from the club, had begun to return them as the cost of travel to Moscow was just too ridiculously high. These tickets were now back on sale direct from the club. Was I interested?

Course I was fucking interested, only I explained, even if I could afford a ticket, there was no way I could afford the trip. End of.

On further investigation it turned out only season ticket holders could buy them anyway or those who had applied or been to a higher number of Euro aways than me.

No, forget it. Manchester > Moscow.

As a fully paid-up member of MUST I booked my ticket for Sam Platts. This way, I figured, I would be one of the first in front of Old Trafford to celebrate our glorious victory. I then phoned round my Cockney Red mates but nobody wanted to join me on my pilgrimage to Eric's own country. Without contributions towards petrol money I went on the internet to find the cheapest return rail fare. Normally mid-week travel by rail is ridiculously expensive but I was able to book two single tickets from Euston to Manchester Piccadilly and back to Euston for £13 each, or £27.50 return including booking fee and postage. Out on the 13.45 on the Wednesday and back on the 10.45 on the Thursday. Not bad, eh?

On the Friday, five days before the game, Jack phoned again to inform me that tickets were now on open sale. Damn!

"OK, Jack. Give me a few minutes."

I phoned Helene. I thought I remembered her telling me that Melanie had intimated that she might be able to help me out with regards to a flight.

Yeah, right!

Thirty minutes later I received a text from Melanie. "Don't worry about the flight, dad. Birthday present + father's day + thank you for everything........"

Daughters! Don't you just love 'em!

"Hi. Is that the ticket office? Could I have a ticket for the Champions League Final please? Yes, my One United membership number is ....

£73 please. My home address is .... My credit card number is ....
Thank you."

Sorted. Yes!

"Jack. It's sorted. Let's go!"

Jack preferred the Champions Sports Tours £899 two day and two nights in a two star hotel opposite the Luzhniki Stadium trip for just £100 per person more than the 24 hour trip minus hotel. He even offered to subsidize my trip to the tune of £100 as a single room supplement for him alone would be an additional £160. It was tempting but for two reasons:

The two day trip was only from Manchester which meant additional rail costs from London plus losing more money from more cancelled lessons. So after a flurry of phone calls and e-mails we booked the 24 hour, no sleep for two nights Luton – Moscow return.

Now, he may be poacher turned gamekeeper, but I have nothing but praise for Tony and his crew at Champion Sports Tours. You can just imagine the pressure he must have been under organizing flights to and from Russia, dealing with eastern block authorities, airlines, airports, etc... Unlike the vast majority of travel companies he was nearly always at the end of the line, 24/7. I received detailed e-mail updates on a regular basis and he rarely lost his cool, even when I overstayed my welcome on the phone by asking some typically nerdish questions.

With printed e-mail confirmation in my hand and the promise of ticket collection at Luton airport at 02.30 on the morning of the game, the remaining four days and nights passed in a flurry of incoherent activity.

Moscow> Manchester.

You better believe it.

34
MOSCOW > MANCHESTER

NOW THAT I was off to Moscow I only had five days to make arrangements. Roubles, schmoubles. Where do I find roubles? Everywhere as it turned out. Many banks had them in stock, even the Post Office, in anticipation of 45,000 English football fans invading Russia, the largest army since Napoleon.

All English conversation with my foreign students now focused on the match if they liked football, Russia if they liked geography, Ronaldo if they liked boys and, well, just plain rubbish.

I decided to cancel my last appointment on the day before the match so as to give me more time to get my act together at home and get a little shut-eye before setting off for Luton in the early hours of Wednesday morning. A quick bite to eat and I was in bed by 7.00pm.

Sleep? You must be joking!

Once again, pulling rank didn't help. Then at 11.00pm Colum and Finn phoned from Moscow. Sons of my wife's best friend, Katie, my influence at an early age in their "reducation" had paid off. Now decamped in that 2* hotel opposite the Luhnidi stadium, they thought a little friendly phone call was in order.

No it wasn't.

Fuck it. It's not going to happen, is it? I got up and dressed as I meant to carry on for the next 24-36 hours. Red, Red Star Sports Champions League Final T-shirt, blue jeans, black T-Shirts United Oli hooded top, and rucksack with United scarf, three box drinks, sandwiches, chocolates and crisps. The days of selling a pair of western jeans for wine, women and a song are long gone, and as one of the most expensive cities on Earth, I wasn't about to be ripped off. No siree.

A cup of tea and a dunk later (we're talking hardcore here) I got in the car with Helene at the wheel just after midnight. I wasn't taking any chances. Years of roadworks between Watford and Luton, with four lanes down to one, even at 1 o' clock in the morning it can seem to take ages. Coming back from Manchester after a mid-week game can be a killer, especially with work first thing in the morning.

She dropped me off around half past one, then with a quick peck on the cheek she was gone. Now the real fun could begin. I made my way into the main departure hall. Pockets of Reds and Blues spread themselves around. Surprisingly, or perhaps not surprisingly, there seemed to be more United than Chelsea. Queues of supporters waiting for their relevant flights, but no sign of the Champion Sports Tours rep. A quick call to Tony in Manchester at two in the morning assured me his Luton rep was sitting in the café area and, yes, there he was.

With no sign of Jack and no response from his mobile, I picked up both our tickets and joined the queue. I opened the envelope. Air Slovakia. OK. Not bad. At least it's not a manky charter airplane. Then what do you know, Jack had been in the queue all the time. Passing through customs a jobsworth identified my dangerous weapons and confiscated two of my three box drinks.

"Sorry lad. I could have allowed 100 ml box drinks but not these 200 ml boxes."

Fuck. He wouldn't even let me drink them. He threw them straight in a large bin. A glorious victory in the government's fight against terrorism. My arse.

Authorities 1 The people 0

Finally our flight was called and we took off around 05.00am, about half an hour late. I don't know about you, but sleeping sitting up – I can't do it. I tried, believe me I tried but to no avail. An hour into the flight and breakfast was served. A combination of eastern block processed meat and cheeses. A bit heavy but not bad. Being a tight-fisted bastard my first thought was, "Well, at least I've saved myself some money."

Then, 8 o' clock our time and 11 o' clock Moscow time we landed at Domodedovo Airport, the designated airport for United fans. The idea of different airports for fans of different clubs was novel and one which I approve of. However, we had to wait an age on the plane before we were allowed to disembark and then a further delay on the bus taking us to the arrivals terminal. Air Slowvakia more like.

With reports that a section of the 6000 policemen and servicemen of military force, in cars, on foot and on horseback would be our welcoming committee, we expected the worse. Therefore we were pleasantly surprised how comparatively quickly we passed through unsmiling customs and passport control. Out on the arrivals concourse, a Flight Options rep who worked with Champion Sports Tours directed us to our bus and a few minutes later we were on our way to Moscow, we shall not be moved.

An hour later, having witnessed a traffic jam to end all traffic jams going in the opposite direction, we passed by numerous characterless suburbs and arrived in Moscow proper. I saw a couple of impressively huge buildings that reminded me of an engorged Empire State Building but, apart from that, nothing of real interest.

At last. The bus parked by the side of the road and we were told it was just a short walk to the stadium. Brilliant. So the rumours had been just that – rumours all along. We were not automatically stuck in the non-alcoholic "fanzone" but free to do our own thing. Strung out like a chain gang, the whole busload of passengers walked for what seemed ages until we came to a decision. Stadium or city centre?

What's Russian for "downtown" or "city centre"? I don't know either, but that's what we did. Entering the metro station we reeled in horror when we realized that we had to communicate with a comrade behind the glass. Fortunately SuperMetro Robotman was at hand.

"Free for fans. Free for fans".

He gestured towards the ticket barriers and waved us through. There then followed one of my favourite aspects of traveling abroad following United. Chanting on the tube, re-enforced by the enclosed hollowness of it all, and observing the reactions of the locals.

Actually, chanting is great but singing is even better.

"Viva Ronaldo, Viva Ronaldo..........etc...."

Spine chillingly brilliant.

We got out at one of the stations near Red Square and tried to find one of the tourist companies that offered 3 hour city tours. Colum and

Finn phoned wanting to meet up but they had already done the tourist bit. Now, I can sing along with the best of them, and one of the wonders of the modern world is a Boyliesque sing-song with fellow Reds in far flung corners of Europe. The Red Army in Red Square has a special ring about it. However, this was my first time in Moscow, my first time in Russia, and despite my reservations about the country I wanted to scratch a little below the surface. Winston Churchill famously described Russia as a riddle wrapped in a mystery inside an enigma. However I'm no David Dimbleby. I only had a few hours and the unspoken stories of my Russian Jewish grandparents on my father's side to contend with.

Suspending my prejudice, Jack and I ran up and down the streets off Red Square until we finally found a group just about to start the tour. First of all the guide walked us around Red Square, the 4th largest square in the world, stopping in front of the Lenin Mausoleum and then onto a coach for the remaining tour of the city. As this is a footy book I'm not going into details. I get out my camcorder. Meanwhile I'll just leave you with my main impressions.

The engorged Empire State Building turned out to be one of seven called the Seven Sisters, arguably the most elegant buildings in Moscow, and now used as up-market apartments. However this was more than offset by the sterile grey monstrosities along the Moskva River and throughout the city commissioned by Stalin.

St Basil's Cathedral was built to commemorate the seizure of the Tartar stronghold of Kazan by the army of Ivan the Terrible in which he and his army killed millions of people. We were shown a black sailing boat on the river with a giant statue of Peter the Great who was also responsible for the mass destruction of entire populations. Peter the Terrible would be more accurate. I could also add Lenin the Terrible and Stalin the Terrible.

Pre-conceptions were re-enforced and I felt distinctly uncomfortable, with crimes against their own people and others such as Jews, gypsies and breakaway states continuing to the present day. The tour ended up the hill above the city, passing the mighty Moscow University housing fifty five thousand students. Only by this time it was pissing down and the top of the university building was obscured by clouds. I didn't even bother to get off the bus at the top of Sparrow Hills as we couldn't see anything. On the other hand I was getting excited as Moscow was looking more like

Manchester in the rain, and images of Rotterdam '91 came flashing by. Good times.

Back in Red Square Jack and I finally met up with Colum and Finn. I suggested we go for a genuine Russian meal together but they said they'd eaten already but agreed to watch us. Weird. Jack wanted an authentic Russian restaurant away from touristy Red Square whilst I wanted a sing-song. C & F took us to a bar in Red Square where they'd been outsinging the Chelse for the past two hours and the local media had been recording proceedings. At one stage, they told me, a posse of Rent Boys had got so incensed at coming off second best, again, they had stood up and belted out the National Anthem with venom and gusto (two of their foreign imports I believe). Said it all really.

Meanwhile we found a table amid the mayhem, highjacked the only ugly waitress in the bar and ordered drinks and a couple of Russian meals. All around us Reds caught a second wind and the verbalcuffs began again. I spent the following hour up and down like a yoyo, combining wine, wussian cuisine and song and risking indigestion in the process.

We outnumbered and outsung the Chelse, so left the bar an hour and a half later in good voice and good heart. Once again the metro system resounded to the songs and chants of the Red Army. Arriving back at Sportivna station, we spent the next couple of hours playing kick-about, drinking, and generally passing the time looking cool. Only by now I was aware of a distinct change in my stomach, in fact a direct reversal of my Wigan experience. If you recall, after a sleepness night prior to the JJB, a calm descended on your truly a few hours before the game as my male intuition kicked-in and I just knew we were going to win.

Now reverse osmosis was taking place. I had argued to all and sundry how close the Champions league final was going to be, with the match being decided by a split second of brilliance or a mistake. With Chelsea guaranteed to play like the death of the first born, the only question remaining from a United point of view was would we get an opportunity to impose our style and superior approach play or would we be swamped by the dark blue blanket of the anti-christ?

For the last few days I had felt sure we were going to win but now my stomach was lurching first one way and then another. A cold fear gripped me. Vague apparitions of demons whirled around me, like the final scene in the original Raiders of the Lost Ark. I couldn't explain it but I knew, I just knew, that tonight was not going to go according to plan. As United fans we know life is anything but predictable and that's why we love them, but, for the love of Eric, just once, just once, why can't we win comfortably, conventionally, conveniently, conducive to living just that little bit longer.

No chance.

Jack and I said goodbye to Colum and Finn who had tickets for another tribune and made our way up to the stadium. We got through the first barrier, but then at the second barrier a guard to one look at my rucksack and pointed to a portacabin and told me to leave it there and pick it up on the way out.

No chance.

I hovered around in no-man's land cultivating a master plan. I told Jack to go through whilst I plucked up the courage, put my head down and bluffed my way through the next barrier as though a rucksack on my back was the most natural thing in the world.

Authorities 1 The people 1

Next stop – the fanzone.

Fast food, soft drinks, a sound stage with dance music nobody was dancing to and a big screen showing repeated selections of United matches and interviews nobody could catch a word of. However, apart from relieving myself in one of the festival type piss boxes, we made a quick exit and soaked up the atmosphere around the stadium.

Once inside, Jack and I said our goodbyes as we were in different rows. I found my seat and surveyed my scene. For the only time inside the stadium I took out my mobile and snapped the vista in front and all around me. This is now the wallpaper I have you know.

Then I heard a shout.

"Dave!"

It was Paul, alias Red Tommo hot off the Red News fans forum, resplendent, if my memory serves me right, in his Humphrey Bogart mackintosh. If I'm wrong I'll apolojize in court.

Then I was alone again. And that's all right. Maybe I'm different from the majority of football fans. I love the banter traveling to and from matches, in the pub, in the service stations, etc... but during the match itself

I am so obsessed with Manchester United, so in love with the men in red that I don't want to share my affections with anyone.

I analyze every move, shout myself hoarse, make a complete tit of myself, but on my own terms. And when we score, well, it doesn't make any difference if I'm in an intense relationship or I've never met you in my life, you're mine. I'm all over you like a rash, with movements so uncoordinated it makes torette's Pete, the winner from last year's Big Brother look like Fred Astaire.

OK, I think you get the picture.

By now it was pissing down and I was loving it as I was bone dry. The atmosphere was building and Manchester in all its glory was out in force. Finally the players came out and the match began.

After the opening exchanges it became clear United were dominating play, dictating proceedings and I was pleasantly surprised. I've always advocated "attack is the best form of defense", so you can imagine how disappointed I had been with out tactics away to Barcelona in the semis and in the first half away to Chelsea in the league just a couple of weeks earlier.

Now I was a happier bunny. Yet one question remained to be answered. Could Ronaldo go one step further than King Eric and "do it" in Europe? In the 26th minute he rammed my doubts down my throat. Lampard's push failed to put off Wes Brown who sent over a perfect cross, and leaving Eissen standing, literally. Ronaldo rose like a Portuguese eagle and headed the ball into the net.

Cue bedlam.

Our end was rocking as everything was going according to (my) plan. I tried to dismiss my earlier fears as United continued to attack. We could easily have gone two or three up before the inevitable happened. How often, as United fans, have we seen the team dominate play, create chances, yet failing to put them away, live to regret it?

Queue demons.

A couple of minutes before half time, with United well worth their 1-0 lead, Essien tried a speculative shot that cannoned off both Vidic and Ferdinand before Lampard, running in, took full advantage and skimmed the ball over Van Der Sar.

For the first time in the stadium we heard the Chelsea fans.

Half time. Shit.

My fears began to take shape as Chelsea came out for the second half re-invigorated whilst we seemed deflated and hesitant. From where I was standing we still outsang the Blues but more out of desperation than belief. Ronaldo was less affective and Chelsea dictated the play. Drogba, who had been a petulant non-entity until now, released a superb shot on the turn and under pressure from our defense, hit our crossbar.

I comforted myself with thoughts of Barcelona '99 and similar escapes against Bayern, with an end result no United fan will ever forget, let alone get over.

By the end of 90+ minutes the score was 1-1 and extra time beckoned. I hoped we would get a second wind and regain the initiative. You've all seen the game so I don't need to go into detail, but I reckon 1-1 at the end of full time was about right. But by the time the referee blew the final whistle there had been a monumental shift in proceedings.

With four minutes to go of extra time Tevez knocked the ball out of play. From where I was standing that seemed pretty fair, but obviously the Rent Boys didn't. I couldn't see what was happening but an almighty, Chelsea induced melee ensued. After what seemed an age the referee pulled out a red card and we saw the mighty Drogba begin the long, lonely and, I have to say, hilarious walk off the pitch and possibly out of Chelsea.

Significantly, it seemed to us, the Chelsea fans were not universally applauding Drogba off the pitch. They also knew that the Incredible Sulk had gone a step too far and seriously dented their hopes

Of course, it was only when I got home would I find out what actually transpired, but at the time it immediately dawned on me, and a few thousand fellow Reds, that Chelsea had lost one of their main penalty takers. On the other hand, United don't win penalty shoot-outs, so it probably wouldn't make any difference if the entire Chelsea team walked off the pitch, we'd shoot ourselves in the foot, as opposed to the opponents net.

Now that it was penalties, I fiddled whilst all around me, Reds burned. Why couldn't they see what I could see. United don't win penalty shoot-outs. Period. OK, we'd won the Community Shield, but did anyone truly believe that would have any bearing on what was about to happen. If anything, Chelsea would have done their homework and nullified any weakness in their approach.

No. I'm sorry. That's it.

All around me Reds were in various states hyperactivity whilst I was a one man sea of false calm. I knew what was going to happen. They didn't. Fifty eight years on this planet and forty nine supporting United. I think that counts for something, don't you?

Tevez scores out first.

Yup.

Ballack scores their first.

Carrick scores our second.

Yup.

Beletti scores their second. Of course. No surprise there.

Ronaldo steps up, stops. The giant orange Czech fills the goal. Ronaldo shoots. Cech dives to his right and saves.

Yup.

Reds all around me recoil in horror. I just stand there.

"Told you so."

Hargreaves scores.

Nice.

Cole scores. Lucky bastard. VDS went the right way but the power of the shot beat him. Naturally.

Nani powers ours home.

Oh, well. And look, here comes the Ironing Man. Mr fucking Chelsea. John "I supported United as a kid but look at me now" Terry.

Must show these kids around me how to be a good loser. I'm older than them. I must show some dignity. I don't feel it but, I ask myself, what would Sir Alex do? What would Sir Bobby do? Age wise I'm catching them up. It's time I acted my age.

Terry comes up and shoots the winning penalty for Chelsea.

And slips.

And misses.

HE FUCKING MISSED! HE FUCKING MISSED!

What the fuck! This is not in the script.

What script? You know what? There is no fucking script. There never was no fucking script.

Game on.

I look at Terry. He's distraught. He's sitting on the pitch in front of us with his head in his hands. He can't move. My heart goes out to him. Honest. I know, I know. I've lost most of you but hear me out. I'm on £25,000 a year and have no right to be here. He's on £130,000 a week and acts like he earns £130,000 a week. Yet at that moment he's feeling the same intense pain any true supporter feels and I can relate to that.

Now Anderson comes up and scores our 5th.

YEESS!! Almighty roar.

Kalou come up, almighty boos, but they score their 5th.

Giggsy steps up and coolly scores out 6th.

YEEEESSSS!!! Another almighty roar.

Then we spy Anelka walking slowly towards the penalty spot. It's pouring down with rain and even from over 100 metres away you could sense he didn't want to be there. But it's Anelka. Ex-Liverpool, ex-City, ex-Bolton, with whom he had scored the winner against us this very season. The other half of the terribly moody twins.

At 01.34am on Thursday 22nd May he steps up and shoots. Van der Sar dives to his right and saves.

HE'S FUCKING SAVED IT! I DON'T BELIEVE IT! I DON'T BELIEVE IT! I DON'T BELIEVE IT!!!!

AAAAAAAHHHHHHHhhhhhhhh!!!!!!!!!!!

I jump up and down by myself in the isle whilst all around me the world has disintegrated. I scream and scream and scream and scream and scream. And then I run out of breath and have trouble breathing before I scream some more.

The players are running and hugging each other; I now begin hugging Reds in my immediate vicinity. I also start crying. I had been right all along, only I don't know how much longer my heart can take it. It's most mens' dreams to die on the job but this comes pretty close for me.

I have the wherewithal to check my mobile for the first time since the match began. There are a number of texts, creatively adapting Anglo-Saxon to fit in with the emotion of the moment. Even a few of my foreign students have text me. (Note, I'll correct these in the morning.)

I then remember I have my camcorder in my rucksack and begin to film the celebrations. I haven't forgotten the furor nine years back when ITV missed much of the David May inspired cup-lifting shenanigans and I was going to make sure I didn't miss a thing.

I capture everything including both sets of players going up to get their medals. The rain is falling harder than ever. I shoot a close-up of the puddles. Soon we'll be out in all that. What the hell!

"I'm singing in the rain, just singing in the rain, what a glorious feeling United's winning again."

With the help of my zoom I spy Peter Kenyon leading up the Chelsea. What the.....?

"Peter Kenyon. You're a wanker, you're a wanker. Peter Kenyon. You're a wanker. You're a wanker."

What a cock. Leading up their team and accepting a medal round his neck. The man's got no class.

Then Sir Bobby Charlton leads our boys up the steps. I alternate my camera between real time and zooming onto the big screen at the other end of the now half empty side of the stadium.

By the time the players have left the pitch the Chelsea end is almost empty. We make our way down the centre isle. Jack finds me and we embrace. Then we stop. Nobody's moving. Why not? It's 02.00 in the morning. It's an hour and a half's drive to the airport and our flight's at 04.55. This is not good.

The authorities had assured us before the game that fans wouldn't be kept in the stadium for hours after the game. We would be allowed to catch our flights or head back to the city.

What's Russian for bollocks?

We wait. We sing. We wait. We sing. It continues to rain Russian buckets but what the hell do we care. "Cos we only know that we're gonna see a show, and the Busby Babes will be there."

Yup, we were "raining" champions.

Sorry.

An announcement comes over the loudspeakers informing us that directions out of the stadium to our respective destinations would be forthcoming in the fanzone. Bearing in mind I had no idea where our bus had dropped us the previous day, I needed all the help I could get.

The euphoria was gradually evaporating as there seemed no logical reason for keeping us in for so long. Eventually, just before 02.30am they let us out. The one saving grace was that it had stopped raining. Arriving at the fanzone there was no information whatsoever.

Surprise, surprise.

We made our way out and back to the main road. There was absolutely no-one official to give us directions. We needed the buses that took us back to Domodedovo airport. The police couldn't speak English and didn't know anything and we couldn't find anybody from either Champion Sports Tours or Flight Options. Jack suggested one way and I suggested another.

Another won and we began our walkabout back up the road we believed we walked down the day before. Eric, that seemed so long ago now. We came upon a line of coaches but they looked too nice to be ours. We were right. It was MU travel taking clients back to the 5 star hotels. Ah, how the other half lives.

As the first flickering darts of half light punctured the glorious night sky's solid blackness (yes, it was a fucking long walk) we finally spied (a good analogy that, considering where we were) our buses. Jack and I clambered on-board and slumped in our seats. However, fate was to take a hand, as Jack received a call from Mother Nature. Leaving his bag with me, he hopped off the bus and disappeared into one of the rows of portacabins lining the pavement. (Note. Selling portacabins in Russia must be lucrative) This was the signal the driver had been waiting for, as he pulled away with undue haste.

"Oy!" I shouted. It wasn't Russian but I hoped the inference in my voice would be universally understood.

I ran to the driver.

"Excuse me. My mate's in the toilet"

The driver waved his hand at me, grimaced and accelerated away.

"Bastard." I thought. But there was nothing I could do. I gave Jack a ring on his mobile but there was no answer. His hands and ears must still have been preoccupied with more pressing/pissing matters. I closed my eyes and attempted anything between 1-40 winks (I said "winks". Can't you read?)

I must have drifted off because we seemed to arrive at the airport a lot quicker than the outward journey. Descending from the bus we made our way into the departure lounge and, halleluiah, there was a Flight Options rep directing us to the escalators. However, once we got upstairs, it all went downhill.

There was an almighty queue, and it wasn't moving. Then I spied Jack. He had caught the following bus so I gave him his bag back. By now it was gone 04.00am and our flight was due to depart in under an hour. No chance. The monitor never changed. The Manchester flight was displaying "Last call" but nobody could move. The police holding us didn't say a word. They were used to queues.

Luckily we'd won, I wondered how the Chelsea fans were reacting. They'd come second, don't you know.

We waited together but standing on the terraces had not been Jack's forte so he went to sit down. That was the last I was to see of him this trip.

I met up with Barney and the Red News massive. A problem shared is......well, still a problem. We all complained together about the ridiculous situation but reveled in the afterglow of victory.

Finally we were allowed to move. Passing though customs and disrobing in the process, I was still talking to Barney when he politely informed me that I was standing in the wrong queue.

"Do you want to come back to Manchester with us, Dave?"

Whoops. The Luton line had already shrunk so with a quick, awkward wave I also disappeared. The Luton plane was already full and nobody was respecting seat numbers so I squashed myself between two fellow Reds. Lack of sleep had caught up with everyone and the 04.30 now 06.30 flight passed uneventfully with just a break for the exact same breakfast we had on the way out.

We landed around 07.30 GMT in Luton. The advantage of traveling without suitcases is that you can pass immediately through customs so by 08.20 I was on the train back to West Hampstead. Then before I knew it I was home as a European Champion in my own home.

My wife suggested I get some sleep. I suggested I switch on Sky Sports and get the latest. My wife suggested I get my lessons ready for the two sets of students I had in the afternoon. I suggested I turnover to MUTV to get the latest. My wife suggested I act responsibly. I did. I rewound ITV and started to watch the match all over again. Well, you would, wouldn't you? I must admit my heavy eyelids became my editor, so I forwarded most of the build-up and found Ronaldo's goal. I watched it over and over again, but then I had to witness Lampard's equalizer. Lucky bastard. Lucky fucking bastard.

I then forwarded to Drogba's sending off. I was dying to see what really happened.

What a dickhead. What an almighty, selfish, self-induced dickhead. I must remember to thank his mother, if he's got one of course. Then it was on to the penalties. No need to fast forward this. This was to be savoured in full, with a close-up of every goal, every expression, every nuance. The agony and the ecstacy.

Oh, well. Time to go to work. Now, where's my United tie? And my Champions lapel badge from last year? Nobody will notice: there's no date on it. Wonder what I'll talk to the students about this afternoon? And tomorrow? And the day after that...?

35

THE RON DECISION

WITH CHELSEA FIGHTING Inter to keep their star players outer the clutches of the Special One, Arsenal maintaining their morally correct but commercially naive policy of not being held to ransom over extortionate high wages and Liverpool being, well.......Liverpool, this promised to be my summer of content.

Two months of reveling in the afterglow while the rest burned, compensating for the withdrawal symptoms of Unitedless months. But then the Clash monologue, "Ronaldo, will he stay or will he go now" grew, from an annoying verse to a crescendo chorus of headlines and poisonous body copy.

With so few direct quotes, I put 95% of it down to unheathen hacks and evil editors out to sell papers by any unscrupulous means at their disposal. In other words, a normal day at the office. Originally I wasn't going to write anything about the situation in this book, as I didn't want egg on my face if it all came to nothing and we had all been duped by the media's interpretation of non-events.

Yet the outstanding 5% ate away at my insides, refusing to accept my intellectual analysis of the situation. It also dominated all the United fans' forums I contributed to and demonstrated once again how some players live on a different planet from the rest of us.

Let's start by looking at it objectively.

If you had been working for a company for five years and a headhunter contacted you with a proposal to double or even triple your salary, would you seriously consider it? You'd be a fool not to. In fact, it would take exceptional circumstances to refuse such an offer.

Then again, as extortionately high as some Premiership players' wages are, they pale into insignificance compared to some golfers, formula 1 racing drivers, NFL footballers and NBL basketball players. It's simply a case of supply and demand. When a sportsman or woman retires, history judges them by medals and titles not money and trinkets, and by the pleasure their special talents have evoked.

Public affection is also affected by loyalty. We are responsive to brand loyalty, but pricing, quality, availability, etc.. can all make us change to a competitor. Unless your name is David Mellor or Peter Kenyon, no football fan will EVER change football clubs. So whilst we recognize players will never experience the same intensity as us, one-club players hold a special place in the heart of supporters. Players such as Harry Cripps at Millwall and Billy Bonds at West Ham, or in the modern era where the Bosman rule has made it almost impossible for either player or club to demonstrate loyalty, Paolo Maldini at AC Milan and our very own Ryan Giggs deserve all the plaudits.

However, the dividing line between genius and madness, murder and self-defense, love and hate is a brittle one. One moment we love Ronaldo, the next moment we hate him. If he stays, we'll welcome him back with open arms, if he goes he'll receive the mother of all hostile receptions on his return. Is that a right way to react? Can it ever be justified?

Well, let's have a look. Who are the villains of the piece? Ronaldo himself, Jorge Mendes Ronaldo's agent, Real Madrid, Luiz Felipe Scolari, the board at MUFC, the media? All of them in my opinion, I'll leave the swingometre up to you.

Real Madrid's tactics are like a cancer, eating away at the resolve of players and their selling clubs, all with the approval of UEFA. Last year they went after Kaka, but both AC Milan and Kaka told them where to go. Crucially, this time, Ronaldo did not, which brings us to his involvement in this conspiracy.

Having lived for six years with sea, sun and satellite TV on the French Riviera, I can understand the pull of a more glamorous location. Ronaldo himself has stated he would relish the prospect of playing in Spain. I've no problem with that. Just look at Tevez. He's expressed his desire to play in

Argentina before his career ends and if we sell him after five years he will still be young enough to make an impact in his home country. The difference is the way he's handled the situation that separates Tevez from Ronaldo. It's called class.

Yet recent reports of United stalling over completing the conversion of Tevez's loan deal into a permanent transfer brings our board's attitude and policy into question. If Tevez grows in frustration at the board's delay, the blame will lie firmly at the board's door....and not for the first time.

United themselves have been accused of doing a "Real" over the years, pursuing the likes of, amongst others, Hargreaves, Carrick and Davide Petrucci the new Italian wonder kid we secured from under Roma's noses for just £200,000.

Ronaldo's agent, Jorge Mendes, would be £10m better off if his client moves to Real, but with a history of other deals such as Anderson and Nani with him as the middleman and United, I don't believe he is a protagonist in the affair (what do I know?)

Big Phil Scolari has been reported as advising Ronaldo to join Real. Nothing to do with reducing the effectiveness of the competition when you take over at Chelsea, eh Phil? No, of course not. Silly me. However, the supposed quote, "The train only passes once" is complete bollocks. If Ronaldo continues to play at the peak we witnessed in the 2007/08 season, they will keep coming back, just like a train that stops at all the stations. On the other hand, what if last season was his absolute peak? With two or three defenders on him at every game would he be as effective? I saw how successful Lille's tactics were in Lens and I wouldn't say he set Euro 2008 alight, would you?

On the basis that no news is good news and good news doesn't sell papers, it's in the media's interest, and especially the written press, to create havoc and unrest. With no England team competing in Euro 2008, they've had a field day filling their back pages with their bile, innuendoes and falsehoods. Having a daughter in the public eye, I think I'm qualified to comment on the unscrupulous lengths they will go to, just for a story. And just as UEFA are totally ineffective in bringing Real Madrid to task, so the Press Council has no affect on the lies or dammed lies perpetuated by their members.

As football fans, emotions speak louder than words. That's why we're football fans in the first place. The joy, the pain, the highs, the lows, no other activity on the planet can generate such emotions.

United fans, more than any other I know, welcome back ex-players with a heroes welcome. In my lifetime, only Paul Ince has been on the receiving end of abuse, and he brought it on himself. If ever Heinze returns, he'll also be booed, but not to the same extent as Ince, as he never (though perhaps he should have) realised the history of animosity between United and Liverpool.

Ronaldo, though, will bring vitriol to a whole new level because, as in the words of the song...

"It's not what you do but the way that you do it."

He has played us like fools, totally disregarding our adoration and kicking our affection where it hurts most. Our love for United is unconditional, total, without compromise. As with any intense relationship, the greater the physical and mental commitment the greater the pain of rejection. And with that, the force of United fans' reactions will be in equal and opposite measure to the adulation he has received over the last five years.

Which makes one 'sensible' compromise a virtual non-starter, that of convincing Ronaldo to play on for United for one or two more seasons, then with his current contract still in place, the club can still fleece Real Madrid for £80-100m and he can slink off to play for his white shirted heroes. Being the petulant spoilt brat that he is, what guarantee would we have that he would show the 100% commitment to the Red cause on the pitch, and how do you think he would handle the combined hostility of both away AND home fans?

Now, nobody can deny that without Ronaldo's 42 goals last season we would never have won the Premiership and for that I/we should ever be grateful. He was also a significant but not overwhelming contributor to our Champions League success. Yet it has been United that has made him the player he is today and for that he should forever be grateful.

If he were to leave, I believe it could turn out to be a Henry type situation. Without one dominating character, Anderson and Nani would excel and blossom, Rooney could be returned to a more effective central role, although a lot would depend on any possible additions to our squad.

The Glazers have, allegedly, come out with a statement saying they'd rather keep Ronaldo in the stands or playing in the reserves. For once their hardboiled, unsavoury approach is welcomed. I know two wrongs don't make a right, but with the Glazers reputation as bad as Calderon and Real Madrid, and if they're serious about giving Sir Alex the money to strengthen the squad instead of paying off our horrendous debts, then maybe it's not all bad.

Manchester United may have ruined my wife, but Cristiano Ronaldo has ruined my summer. I suspect he has also ruined Sir Alex Ferguson's summer and for both of us that is totally unacceptable and totally unnecessary.

36

UNITED IS BETTER THAN SEX

YOU KNOW THAT feeling when you see a beautiful girl for the very first time and you really fancy her? Immediately you imagine her hot, voluptuous body naked and the two of you wrapped in a passionate embrace.

Just thinking about it your heart begins to beat faster and there's a knot in the base of your stomach. Walking on three legs, fear of rejection grips you as you approach her, the hesitancy apparent in your faltering steps.

Finally summoning up that long lost courage you mumble one of these magic phrases:

"Can I carry your books?"

"Would you like a cup of coffee?"

"Do you want to dance?"

"Do you fancy a shag?"

WOW! She says Yes! Disbelief and elation are overwhelming. You want to say a million things. Your mouth opens and closes like a goldfish but nothing comes out. Then brain and body are back in unison and you go to the next stage.

Over the coming minutes, hours, days, weeks or months (depending upon how slow you are) you progress to the ultimate physical expression of your passion and desire. Clothes become disrobed and your original fantasy becomes reality as you view her naked body and touch her soft, warm flesh for the very first time. Touching turns to caressing and finally you are making love.

All that pent-up emotion you kept locked-up inside over the preceding minutes, hours, days, weeks or months explodes in sexual joy. And when you are finally spent, the delightful weight and warmth of her naked body as she collapses on top of you, your senses heightened by the knowledge that you are the source of her pleasure.

Reveling in the afterglow you ask yourself the question that has perplexed man ever since Adam discovered Eve.

"Can life ever get better than this? Is this the meaning of life?"

For Monty Python the answer was 42. For me it's..."Of course it can. I'm a United fan."

Supporting and following Manchester United has taken me to higher highs and lower lows than anything else on this planet, including sex. (Just like the old American Express advert, this says more about me than psychiatrists ever can). Football is a bit like sex, even when it's bad, it's good. And Manchester United is like tantric sex. After thirty-one years of foreplay, no-one who was in Barcelona on May 26th 1999 will ever experience an orgasm to match the intensity of those last three minutes. In fact I still get repeated orgasms whenever I playback the video or even just think about it.

Needless to say, the new 2007/08 Double DVD currently takes pride of place, with the resultant and predictable effect on my bodily juices.

Now, don't get me wrong. I love my wife and I love my two daughters but I am "IN LOVE" with Manchester United. From head to toe, from January to December, from cock to cunt, from John O' Shea to Lands End and from here to eternity I am in love with Manchester United.

I remember the moment quite clearly. It was the summer of 1994. I was forty five years old when I realised that the pendulum had finally swung and that I had begun to think more about sex than Manchester United. I'd finally arrived at the healthy state of a "dirty old man", or should I say "dirty middle aged man". I don't want to be accused of exaggeration, now do I? They say (who are "they", by the way?) that men think about sex every seven seconds. I'm not counting but I know that for most of my life I fantasized more about United matches I'd been to or pulling on the red shirt and scoring wonderful winning goals for Manchester United than scoring in the other net. Am I a sad fuck, or what? I don't know whether it's the male menopause or the fact that United have exceeded my wildest dreams that my only unobtainable fantasies lay with women.

Put it this way. What are the three most important words you can ever say to anybody on this planet? In fact, the deeper your feelings are about a person the more these three words grow in significance.

Coming in a close second is that perennial favourite..."I Love You", but the clear winner just has to be..."I WAS THERE!" Home or away, when I orgasm along with thousands of fellow Reds there is no feeling on Earth to match it. What other activity can instill such intense emotion? Football, music, sex, even cookery and travel programs on TV. No matter how entertaining, nothing beats being there. The government should ban armchairs so that everyone has to experience life in the raw. Passive football, it's got its good points but doesn't hold a candle to the real thing. And what about music?

OK. As you asked, here comes my "High Fidelity" moment. I was at the Odeon Hammersmith in the 1979 to see Bruce Springsteen's first live performance in the UK. It was reverential. He was brilliant. Only people who were there felt the true force of his talent and power. I was at Shepton Mallet (Bath) in 1969 to see Led Zeppelin in their overcoats play a blinder, even though they blighted their copybook by reminding us how grateful we should be as they'd sacrificed a lot of American dollars "to be with us today".

At the same festival, as I rested outside my tent up in the hills, one of my all-time faves, Pink Floyd, performed Atom Hearted Mother against a backdrop of awesome pyrotechnics. I was also at the Rainbow Theatre when Little Feat blew everybody away with the perfect set.

The summer before I met Hélène I was at the Lincoln Festival in 1972, setting up our tent with Red mate Joe on a cold and rainy Friday night, when over the loudspeaker system it was announced that top of the bill Helen Reddy would be unable to play that evening. In her place, at the eleventh hour (literally) would be Saturday's headline act, the Rory Gallagher Band.

Brilliant. My all time favourite axe man fronting the best live band in the business. The people's friend. What a man. Only Rory would do something like that. We left everything in a mess, put on our temporary Pacamacs (cool or what? Yeah – what) and headed back out into the night accompanied by the cold and rain off the North Sea.. We got right to the front and let it all hang out.

"Did you ever? Boom. Did you ever? Boom. Did you ever ever ever ever ever? ... Did you ever wake up with those bullfrogs on your mind?"

Wonderful. And we were there. We went back to our tent deliriously happy, grinning like goons.

The following morning we got out of our warm, dry sleeping bags and put our warm, dry legs into freezing cold, soaking wet, mud encrusted jeans. Who said 250,000 people can't be wrong?

Put it another way. Imagine you've been parted from your "loved one" for between two to seven days, roughly the same time span as United matches, what with Euorpean and League Cup games. When you see her again, do you:

a) Give her a peck on the cheek?

b) Give her a hug and a kiss?

c) Jump up and down and go utterly mental in the company of complete strangers?

Only football can do this, because football reaches parts other activities cannot reach.

OK. I'll put it yet another way. As you go through life there are many things you think are permanent but are not.

If you grew up with a mother and a father you think the family will stay at home together forever, yet statistics in the UK show that people move approximately every seven years.

When you're young and find a good job you think about promotion and a logical career path. However, in this day and age a "job for life' has all but disappeared. We all have to consider changes of direction and learning new skills, not just in the job itself but perhaps moving to another town or, as some of the most loyal Reds on the many United Fans Forum can testify, another country or even another continent.

And for all those traditionalists who were shocked when "I Love You" only managed second place, let me put it THIS way. Part of the marriage ceremony contains the words "Till death do us part" yet statistics prove that, today, almost 40% of marriages end in divorce.

BUT, and this is the crunch, when you choose your football team, or it chooses you, it is not just for Christmas – it's for life. Period. You can change your job, your career, you can change your town, even your country, you can even change your life soul-mate but a true football fan will NEVER EVER change his/her football team.

Am I right or am I right?

Priorities.

READ A UNITED LEGEND'S BOOK

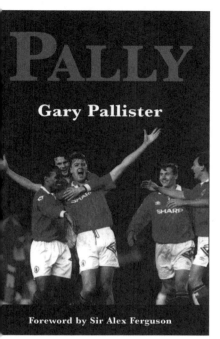

Gary Pallister

Foreword by Sir Alex Ferguson

When Gary Pallister was in his 1990s pomp there was no finer central defender in the British game. In this book he relives his early days at Middlesbrough, the glory years under Sir Alex Ferguson at Old Trafford, including 4 Premiership titles, 3 FA Cups, a League Cup and a European trophy, his England career under Graham Taylor and Terry Venables and a host of dressing room stories.

Pally relives tales of Robbo, Bruce & Keane, Schmeichel & Giggs, Ince & Kanchelskis, Sharpe & Cantona plus some fierce rivalries and hair-raising clashes, including one with a knight of the realm.

"The best footballing centre-half in the country, bar nobody." Alex Ferguson

RELIVE UNITED HISTORY

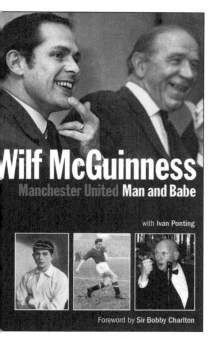

The rich history of Manchester United has never thrown up a more colourful character than Wilf McGuinness. As one of the Busby Babes he won silverware and plaudits before the hell of Munich, shortly followed by the ending of his own playing career by injury. As a coach he helped United win the 1968 European Cup and England win the '66 World Cup. He then succeeded Matt Busby as United manager, but was sacked - a topic he has rarely openly discussed until now.

Man and Babe is the moving and sometimes hilarious tale of Wilf's life with United and England, including triumph, tragedy and hair loss!

With a Foreword by Sir Bobby Charlton & includes over 100 photos

RELIVE UNITED HISTORY

Bill Foulkes
United In Triumph and Tragedy

The story of a
Manchester United legend

Bill Foulkes with
Ivan Ponting

Foreword by Sir Alex Ferguson

Only Ryan Giggs and Sir Bobby Charlton have played more games for Manchester United than Bill Foulkes, the granite rock of United's rearguard for 15 years from the Busby Babes to the 1968 European Cup-winning side.

At the heart of his story is, of course, Munich. Bill emerged almost unscathed from the stricken aircraft which took the lives of so many of his colleagues and he recalls the days around the tragedy with candour and poignancy.

United In Triumph and Tragedy is a harrowing, incredible and ultimately joyous celebration of one of United's truly great legends, who roses from the ashes to win silverware and play in two of the club's greatest teams. Featuring tales of Best, Law & Charlton, Edwards, Taylor and Byrne, and Sir Matt Busby, this book is a must for any United supporter.

ORDER NOW FOR JUST £17.99 (plus £2 P&P in the UK)

Why not add a copy of United legend Paul Parker's autobiography
Tackles Like A Ferret to your order for a very special price?
Simply tick this box and add £7 to your payment. ☐

KNOW!
THE SCORE